THE BUDGET AND THE POOR

The Budget and the Poor

A study commissioned by
IDPAA, PROSHIKA and
conducted by Shamunnay

The University Press Limited

The University Press Limited
Red Crescent Building
14 Motijheel C/A
P.O. Box 2611
Dhaka 1000
Bangladesh
Fax: 8802 956 5443
E-mail: upl@bttb.net.bd
Website: www.uplbooks.com

First published 2000
Second impression 2002

The Budget and the Poor is the first in the series of a longitudinal studies on the national budget from the perspective of poverty eradication.

Cover design by Ashraful Hassan Arif

ISBN 984 05 1496 2

Published by Mohiuddin Ahmed, The University Press Limited, Dhaka. This book has been set in Book Antiqua by Computer in Development Programme (CDP), PROSHIKA, Mirpur, Dhaka. Printed at Elora Art Publicity, 635 North Shahjahanpur, Dhaka, Bangladesh.

Dedicated to the Poor of Bangladesh

Study Team

Dr. Atiur Rahman (Team Leader)
Senior Research Fellow
Bangladesh Institute of Development Studies
and
Executive Chairman
Shamunnay

Dr. Pk. Md. Motiur Rahman
Professor
Institute of Statistical Research
and Training
Dhaka University

Mirza M. Shafiqur Rahman
Research Fellow
Shamunnay

Nigar Nargis
Research Associate
Bangladesh Institute of Development Studies

Contents

List of Boxes, Figures and Tables

Boxes

Figures

Tables

Glossary of Abbreviations, Acronyms and Local Terms

ADB	Asian Development Bank
ADP	Annual Development Programme
ATAP	Annual Technical Assistance Programme
BBS	Bangladesh Bureau of Statistics
BIDS	Bangladesh Institute of Development Studies
BRAC	Bangladesh Rural Advancement Committee
BRDB	Bangladesh Rural Development Board
CBR	Crude Birth Rate
CDR	Crude Death Rate
CPEWC	Compulsory Primary Education Ward Committee
D.W.	Durbin Watson
DE	Development Expenditure
DRR	Directorate of Relief and Rehabilitation
DSS	Directorate of Social Services
DT	Direct Taxes
DWA	Directorate of Women Affairs
DYD	Department of Youth Development
ER	Essential Rationing
ERD	Economic Relations Division
ES	Economic Services
FFE	Food For Education
FFW	Food For Works
FM	Flour Mills
FPMU	Food Planning and Monitoring Unit
FS	Free Sales
FWA	Family Welfare Assistant
FY	Fiscal Year

GDP	Gross Domestic Product
GLEW	Group Leader Extension Work
GNP	Gross National Product
GO	Government Organization
GOB	Government of Bangladesh
GR	Gratuitous Relief
HA	Health Assistant
HDI	Human Development Index
HYV	High-Yielding Variety
IDA	International Development Association
IDPAA	Institute for Development Policy Analysis and Advocacy
IDS	Infrastructure Development Sector
IFDP	Institutional Feeding Development Project
IMED	Implementation, Monitoring and Evaluation Division
IMF	International Monetary Fund
IRD	Internal Resources Division
IRDP	Integrated Rural Development Programme
KAP	Knowledge, Attitude and Perception
Kaviraj	Herbalist
Kcal	Kilo calorie
KSS	Krishak Samabaya Samity
Kutcha home	Thatched house
Kutcha road	Unmetalled road
LE	Large Employers
LGED	Local Government and Engineering Department
LSD	Local Supply Depot
MO	Marketing Operation
MR	Modified Rationing
MT	Metric Tonne
MWA	Ministry of Women Affairs
NBR	National Board of Revenue
NEC	National Economic Council
NEMAP	National Environmental Management Action Plan
NGO	Non-Governmental Organization
NPO	Non-Productive Overhead

ODA	Official Development Assistance
ODA	Overseas Development Administration, now it is DFID (Department For International Development)
OM	Operation and Maintenance
OMS	Open Market Sales
OP	Other Priorities
PAR	Participatory Action Research
PFDS	Public Foodgrains Distribution System
PFW	Project For Women
PKSF	Palli Karma Shahayak Foundation
PL	Poverty Line
PRA	Participatory Rural Appraisal
PRRA	Participatory Rapid Rural Appraisal
PSI	Infrastructure Support for Productive Activities
RD	Rural Development
RDP	Rural Development Programme
RE	Revenue Expenditure
RIBEC	Reforms in Budgeting and Expenditure Control
RMP	Rural Maintenance Programme
RPC	Rural Poor Cooperative
SA	Structural Adjustment
SAARC	South Asian Association for Regional Co-operation
SIFAD	Strengthening Institutions for Food-Aided Development
SMC	School Management Committee
SR	Statutory Rationing

Acknowledgement

We gratefully acknowledge the various important roles played in the course of the study by different sections of society such as intellectuals, researchers, NGO activists, grassroots people's organizations and other stakeholders. We are particularly thankful to Dr. Qazi Faruque Ahmed, President, PROSHIKA, for placing his confidence on us in accomplishing this challenging task. We would like to thank the former Head of IDPAA and now Senior Vice-President of PROSHIKA, Mr. Mahbubul Karim under whose able leadership IDPAA conceived the original advocacy campaign and initiated this study.

We are grateful to all our experts and field officers involved in this study. We are also grateful to Dr. Zahid Hossain, Dr. Chowdhury Saleh Ahmed, Dr. Bazlul Haque Khondker, Mr. Khondker Golam Moazzem Rana and many others for their early inputs in this study. We must record our gratitude to Professor Rehman Sobhan, Professor Anisur Rahman, Mr. Sayed Ali Kabir, Dr. Abdul Moyeen Khan, MP, Minister for Environment and Forest Syeda Sajeda Chowdhury, Ms. Panna Kaiser, MP, Dr. Borhanuddin Khan Jahangir, Mr. Mahfuz Anam, Dr. Binayak Sen and a number of representatives of the poor belonging to different grassroots organizations for participating in the panel discussion organized by IDPAA. Honourable Prime Minister Sheikh Hasina inaugurated the panel discussion as Chief Guest and Minister for Local Government and Rural Development Zillur Rahman participated in it as the special guest. We are grateful to both of them for their valuable policy observations on this study. Also, we are grateful to the participants of the workshop organized by the European Union on some of the preliminary findings of the study.

We are particularly indebted to Professor Anisur Rahman for meticulously going through the report and making critical comments on various aspects of it. His in-depth comments led to substantial revising and reorganizing of the report. The quality of the study also improved substantially in the process. The comments of our colleagues at IDPAA and Shamunnay helped significantly in improving the final version of the report. Particularly the contributions of all the study team members are highly appreciated: Mr. Pk. Md. Motiur Rahman and Ms. Nigar Nargis took care of the quantitative part, and Mr. Mirza M. Shafiqur Rahman conducted the qualitative investigation using PRA tools. Mr. Shanti Ranjan Dey, Ms. Kaniz Rashid Lubana Mamun, Ms. Sunzida Sultana, Ms. Sadeka Fatema, Mr. Molla Anisur Rahman deserve thanks for assisting the study team in various ways. Mr. Md. Mazharul Huq, Mr. Lutfur Rahman Patwary, Mr. Md. Ruhul Amin, Mr. Ashraful Islam Babul, Mr. Md. Ashabul Hoque, Mr. Md. Shamsul Hoque Mandal, Ms. Ayesha Hoque of Shamunnay for their excellent management and computer support. We thank Mr. Farooque Chowdhury of Shamunnay for co-ordinating the study.

We are thankful to Dr. Jyoti P. Dutta, Director, PROSHIKA, Mr. Golam Faruque Khan, Managing Editor of *Discourse,* a Journal of Policy Studies of IDPAA, Mr. Omar Tarek Chowdhury, Mr. Bayezid Dawla, Mr. Anowarul Haq and Mr. Badrul Hassan of IDPAA for their editing and overall co-ordinating support for the publication. We thank Mr. Ziauddin, Mr. Shahadat Hossain, Mr. Bishutosh Das and Mr. Akramul Haque of Computer in Development Programme (CDP), PROSHIKA, who took the pains of text composition.

We thankfully acknowledge the support and co-operation extended by Mr. Mohiuddin Ahmed, Managing Director, The University Press Limited, for publishing this book.

And finally, we are indebted to the people who were consulted at different stages by the study team and without whose participation this study could have never been completed.

The limitations, if any, are all ours. We will welcome any comment or criticism on this book at any time.

Md. Shahabuddin
Head of IDPAA
and
Director, PROSHIKA

Atiur Rahman, PhD
Team Leader
Study Team

Introduction

The Budget and the Poor is a timely contribution to the literature on the outcome of public interventions targeted to the poor. Its attempt to use the participatory approach to generate qualitative information through focus group discussions with the poor provides a useful perspective to quantitative research which is normally used in poverty studies. Such Poverty Line (PL) studies have a long history in Bangladesh through work mostly originating from the Bangladesh Institute of Development Studies (BIDS) but also drawing on other well-known researchers. The data published by the Bangladesh Bureau of Statistics (BBS) drawing on the periodic *Household Income and Expenditure Surveys (HIES)* is usually the source material of most poverty studies in Bangladesh though BIDS has also been generating its own primary information on poverty which draws on panel data from its poverty surveys which go back to 1979.

The present stage of quantitatively derived poverty studies in Bangladesh reflects an improvement in the quality of the data and in the refinement of analysis. However, such research still leaves Bangladesh in search of a definitive conclusion on the extent to which poverty levels have been reduced over the last two decades. Obviously the methodology as well as the conceptual foundations of poverty research in Bangladesh need to be further refined if we are not to remain locked in the academic debate on whether poverty has gone up or down. There is a desperate need for putting such controversies to rest by developing an academic concensus on the measures needed to make estimates of the number of households living in poverty and to ensure that the data collected is consistent as to its measures as well as collection. Such a definitive estimate should ideally derive from the Government of Bangladesh (GOB) who should publish annual estimates of poverty in the same way that they present GDP estimates. Such generally acceptable measures of poverty should be used to gauge the performance of the economy in the same way that GDP growth is used as a yardstick for economic performance.

However, quantitative measures of poverty alleviation will always need to be supported by qualitative measures of poverty originating in the self-perception of the poor as to whether their conditions of life have improved or not. Such self-defined perceptions of poverty may correctly move beyond PL measures of poverty to address broader conceptions of well-being such as the health, living conditions, sense of personal security and measures of the opportunities available to particular households. Whilst such concerns do lend themselves to quantitative observation it is useful to give a human face to such estimations by encouraging the poor to speak for themselves. Such participatory research (PR) based on self-perceptions of the poor has established its own niché in the academic work on poverty where the work of Robert Chambers at the Institute of Development Studies, Sussex, Anisur Rahman at Internationl Labour Organization (ILO) and Mahar Mangahas, through his Social Weather Stations Project in the Philippines have drawn attention to the value of encouraging the poor to define their own circumstances. Participatory research does, however, need to establish its representative credentials so that its findings, however articulate, are not seen as anecdotal information which provides good copies for journalists but is of limited value to policy makers.

The present volume, prepared under the leadership of Atiur Rahman of BIDS and Shamunnay and Pk Md. Matiur Rahman of Institute of Statistical Research and Training (ISRT), Dhaka University, for IDPAA, PROSHIKA is a laudable attempt to use the PR methodology to address the issue of poverty in Bangladesh. However, this volume moves beyond poverty analysis to address the perceptions of the poor on the credibility of public interventions targeted to alleviate poverty as manifested in the national budget. Bangladesh's development effort has, over the last quarter of a century, put in place a variety of policies, programmes and projects, targeted to the poor, involving several billion dollars mostly financed by a plethora of aid donors. However, very little is known of the impact of these expenditures on the actual alleviation poverty. Thus, any effort to decompose public expenditure so as to gauge the extent to which such expenditures reach the poor and in the process improve their conditions of life is, in its own right, a valuable contribution to both poverty and budgetary studies in Bangladesh.

The global literature on the impact of aid programmes on poverty suffers from its own limitations because of an imprecise understanding of the causal links between public intervention and poverty. Thus, Bangladesh's literature on the direct impact of public expenditure on the poor remains weak in terms of both conceptions and the availability of direct evidence. The recent research carried out at Centre on Integrated Rural Development for Asia and Pacific (CIRDAP), under the direction of Mustafa K. Mujeri, is a valuable attempt to use quantitative analysis drawing upon a social accounting model which is used to disaggregate public expenditures in such areas as health and education in order to compute its incidence on different household income groups. The nature of the CIRDAP study was, however, exclusively statistical using the available *HIES* and budget data without having to see the face of a poor person. This approach puts a great deal of weight on not just the quality of the data collected but also the methodology of estimating both *HIES* and public expenditure as well as the sensitivity of the model. The present study by the two Rahmans can now test the CIRDAP findings through first hand discussions with the poor on how far different items of public expenditure actually impact on the poor.

The study is also useful because it did not limit itself to participatory research. Since the actual coverage of the participatory enquiries was rather small, the representative character of the reportage needed to be backed by a more comprehensive review of the budgetary expenditure data. The study widens the scope of its enquiry by dissecting the budget to see whether such expenditures actually reached the poor and presents valuable information on the sources of public revenue collection as well as its distributive implications. Such an approach provides an appropriate perspective for the analysis of public expenditure targeted to the poor under such programmes as Test Relief, Food for Work, the Vulnerable Group Development Programme, Food for Education Programme, Rural Development Programme and Women and Youth Development Programme. Such a systematic effort to link all such programmes to their beneficiaries and to examine changing trends in budgetary allocations so as to gauge how far these expenditures serve to alleviate poverty is a valuable contribution to both poverty and budgetary analyses.

The study quite correctly points to the lack of transparency in the budget in general and highlights the problems of relating the budget statement to the needs of the poor. The current method of presenting the budget remains mired in tradition and does little to introduce the new approaches to budget making which are designed to equate expenditure with performance—approaches now in use not just in the developed world but in many developing countries. These manifest limitations in the design of our national budget encourages rhetorical exchanges every year between the government and the opposition about whether the budget will help the poor or aggravate their poverty. Neither side has enough information offered in the budget documents to actually substantiate their respective positions. It is thus essential that the national budget spell out quite clearly its targets, including a precise measure of its objectives for alleviating poverty. It should then relate each budget head and each line item expenditure to the realization of these specifically defined goals. The budget documents should make explicit the link between public expenditure and their outcomes, as enunciated in the previous budget and should report on how far these outcomes were realized as well as the reasons for any deviation. Such an exercise will lend transparency to the budgetary process and provide a basis for meaningful debates in parliament on the budget as well as in civil society.

Improvement in the quality of budget preparation and implementation needs to be matched by a regular exercise in participatory research so as to gauge public responses to the outcome of such public expenditure as it impinges on the circumstances of individual households. For such an exercise to generate an impact both on the government, parliament and civil society, PR should be carried out every year and in order to improve its representative character its coverage should be extended from 60 to at least 400 households distributed over the four Divisions of Bangladesh. This widening of the scope of the participatory process should be reinforced by upgrading the quality of the discussion. Such a move to institutionalize PR would lend greater credibility to the work. A regular public presentation of such findings, preferably through the voices of some of the poor who participated in the research, prior to the publication of the annual budget would provide an important insight to the public as well as to policy makers as to the actual perceptions of the poor about their conditions of life as well as their responses to governmental efforts to improve these conditions. It is presumed that any elected government in Bangladesh would take these publicly voiced concerns of the poor, who make up a plurality of voters, no less seriously than the voices of the business community or the economists of the country which are heard every year by the government.

Dhaka, June 2000

Professor Rehman Sobhan
Executive Chairman
Centre for Policy Dialogue

OVERVIEW

1. The Objectives and Methodology of the Study

The present study examines the impact of the national budget of Bangladesh on the declared goal of poverty eradication. The major objectives of the study are:

i) analysis of financial allocations and actual expenditures in the national budget with a view to understanding its impact on poverty alleviation;

ii) examination of the impact of the budget allocations on the social sector;

iii) monitoring of the performance of a set of macro indicators of poverty;

iv) understanding the perception and knowledge of the poor about the national budget and their attitudes towards it as well as its impact on their conditions of living.

The study uses both primary and secondary information in understanding this interface. The primary information has been collected with the help of both quantitative and qualitative methods.

2. Conceptualization

Poverty may be approached from different perspectives. There are two fundamentally different approaches, namely conventional and participatory. Conceptually, both these approaches look at the constituents and sources of ill-being in different ways. Basic needs deprivation and multiple deprivations are the cornerstones of income/consumption-based poverty-line thinking and participatory poverty assessment respectively.

The conventional approach popularly known as the poverty-line (PL) approach applies its single-scale numerical definition of poverty according to reported levels of income or consumption. This approach is undesirably simplified, reductionist, universal, standardized and quantified. Being unidimensional, the conventional approach misses much and can be misleading as well. There are many aspects of the quality of life which PL thinking and measurement cannot capture. Additionally, as the PL approach essentially represents professionals' realities, the analysis is subject to biases of different types.

The participatory approach, on the other hand, applies poor people's criteria which are basically location-specific, complex, holistic, diverse and unqualified. Based on multidimensional deprivation, the participatory poverty assessment goes beyond the domain of narrow and material aspects of well-being. It takes into account many non-material aspects of ill-being which are hardly amenable to precise quantification. Further, this approach may be used to enable and empower the poor through social consciousness, self-critical awareness and social mobilization.

Methodologically, two approaches have been tried here. The conventional approach employs researchers' analytical framework which is basically unidimensional (income/expenditure levels) and questionnaire survey methods for collection of data whereas the participatory approach makes use of both internal/external and qualitative/quantitative methods where participants' realities are reflected through group consensus in dialogical sessions.

In view of the relative strengths and weaknesses, both the approaches can be judiciously and intelligently applied to appropriate fields where they fit well. Most practitioners, therefore, recommend a 'walking on two legs' strategy in measuring poverty. Rather than engaging in deeper disagreements about the relative merits of these approaches, researchers and policy makers need to develop ways to blend interactively their best aspects in order to make poverty measures more policy relevant.

3. The Budgetary Process

In a developing country like Bangladesh, the annual budget of the government is the main conduit of national resource mobilization and management. The development prospect, inclusive of the widespread poverty alleviation strategy, therefore, depends crucially on the efficiency of the budgetary process.

The major drawbacks of this system are:

- the centralized top-down decision-making process;
- limitations of the macroeconomic models used in the five-year plans for medium- and long-term planning;

- lack of discretion of local policy makers;
- fragmentation of budget responsibilities;
- inconsistencies in the expenditure classification system;
- the opacity of the pattern of sectoral allocations;
- inadequate database and accounting system; and finally
- the incremental nature of budgeting, rather than linking it to performance.

It has been found that the management of the budgetary process is conventional and not sensitive to the needs of the poor. The public sector has not been able to provide incentives for the healthy growth of the economy ensuring participation of civil society at large. The planning system remains highly centralized and inhibits participatory decision-making. The budget maintains an artificial division between recurrent and capital expenditures. Since the major portion of the development budget is financed by foreign aid, national planners have very little control over its design and outcome.

The responsibilities of budgeting remain fragmented and a tug of war between the Planning Commission and the budget wing of the Ministry of Finance cannot always be avoided. There are several budget documents with separate expenditure classifications. This makes the budget even more complicated to an outsider. The pattern of sectoral allocations remains obscure to all but the experienced budget officials. The budget process is, therefore, viewed as a technical exercise which has little to do with the major stakeholders and civil society. The accounting and expenditure control remains complex and, therefore, monitoring public expenditures becomes very difficult.

The budget focuses more sharply on revenue mobilization and fails to prioritize public expenditure for certain specific development goals (eg poverty alleviation). The phasing of development projects is not also done carefully. The complexity of the budget estimates and their documentation makes it difficult to identify how much is really spent for poverty alleviation in the budget.

4. Public Resource Mobilization

As to the revenue side of the budget, four-fifths of public income come from tax revenue. From the perspective of poverty alleviation, the tax system is to be judged on the basis of its redistributive role. Although direct taxes are progressive and hence serve equity, it constitutes merely one-fourth of the total tax revenue. As yet there is no clear indication that this proportion can be substantially increased in the short run. The major portion of tax revenue is currently contributed by indirect taxes which are regressive in nature and, therefore, hurt the poor most. The tax structure in Bangladesh can hardly be used for redistribution of income and poverty alleviation. In the high income countries, a redistributive device is built into the tax system. But in low income countries like Bangladesh, it is primarily intended for mobilization of public resources. The objective is to increase the revenue surplus (revenue income minus revenue expenditures) and to generate a larger amount of domestic resources for financing development expenditures so that aid dependence can be reduced. To all intents and purposes, the development budget is found to be of greater importance for poverty alleviation than the revenue budget.

5. Policies for Poverty Alleviation and Public Expenditure

5.1 Policies for Poverty Alleviation

Policies for poverty alleviation are a part of several macroeconomic policies of development and, in particular, of those associated with the targeted public expenditure programmes. Expenditures under these heads do not appear to be transparent. Besides, the opacity and complicated accounting system of the annual budget makes it difficult to work out the precise amount of public resources devoted to eradication of poverty through suitable projects and programmes. In this context, suggestions can be made to improve the budgetary process, so as to make it more transparent and target-oriented.

However, government plans and policy documents sound rhetorical when the implementation performance falls far short of the pledges made by the government. The impact of these pledges on the conditions of the poor then becomes rather hypothetical. It is, therefore, essential that the policy effects be carefully evaluated on the one hand, and voices of the poor be given a status in public resource management and decision-making on the other. People should be encouraged to start lobbying for their legitimate share of public expenditures.

The key public policies pursued so far appear to have exclusively served the well off. The other social classes, namely the middle, the poor and the poorest have been deprived of the benefits of these policies according to this study. These policies have been assessed by the poor themselves. As perceived by the poor, all these policies have benefited the well off bypassing the poor.

5.2 Public Expenditure for Poverty Alleviation

The review of public expenditure for the period 1978-79 to 1994-95 reveals that the introduction of the Structural Adjustment Programmes (SAP) in 1985-86 has been followed by a higher trend rate of growth of real GDP. The trend rates of growth of revenue and development expenditure have been higher during the post-SAP period than the pre-SAP period. The allocation to the social sectors as a percentage of development expenditure has increased from 17 in 1990-91 to 31 in 1994-95. Within the social sectors, the allocation to education and religious affairs as a percentage of social expenditures has registered significant increase (from 19 in 1990-91 to 45 in 1994-95). Despite increasing allocation to the social overheads, the original budget estimates under this head have been routinely revised and cut. The actual expenditure has been less than the revised allocation every year during 1990-95. Besides, there are several components of development expenditure which are essentially revenue expenditures. The reverse is also true. The volume of the social sector allocation, therefore, needs to be discounted to arrive at its real effects on poverty. As a matter of fact, the segregation of the annual budget into revenue and development budgets complicates the accounting and allocation procedures and makes it difficult to identify the budget components pertinent to the special objective of poverty alleviation. This is a serious impediment to a satisfactory appraisal of the annual budgetary process as far as the poverty alleviation perspective is concerned.

6. Targeted Public Expenditure for Poverty Alleviation

In the last five years, the allocation for the social sectors was not found to exceed one-third of the total ADP allocation despite overwhelming poverty and inability of the poor to get out of the poverty trap by themselves. The major public programmes aiming at poverty alleviation include (a) Test Relief, (b) Food For Works Programme, (c) Vulnerable Group Development Programme, (d) Rural Development, (e) Women Development, (f) Youth Development, and (g) Food For Education. Besides, there are many other programmes in different ministries which indirectly impact on poverty alleviation. Although quite a large amount of money is being spent on these programmes run mostly by bureaucratic agencies, the impact of all of these, has not yet been quite significant. The coverage is yet quite small. The access to this programme remains unequal. The newest of these programmes is FFE. We, therefore, made a special focus on this.

A preliminary assessment report on the FFE programme reveals that:

- the enrolment of students in general and of girl students in particular has increased in all the classes (I-V) after the launching of the FFE programme;
- the enrolment figure is quite high in the FFE schools in comparison with the non-FFE schools;
- the attendance of students as a percentage of total class-days has significantly increased in the FFE schools; and
- the drop-out rates have declined significantly.

These facts have also been confirmed by the sample survey conducted by Shamunnay. In the sample schools, 68.2% of the total students enrolled are from the functionally landless households having less than 0.5 acre of land. Under government rules, 40% of total students enrolled are covered by the FFE programme. The residual 28.2% do not receive wheat under FFE. The coverage of FFE should be expanded to cover all of the target groups toward fulfilling the objective of poverty alleviation.

Members of the school management committees of both the FFE and non-FFE schools opined that the FFE programme:

- increases the participation rate;
- decreases the drop-out rate;
- alleviates poverty; and
- diverts child labour to primary education.

Only 4.17% of the 96 respondents are for discontinuing the programme, while the rest have supported its continuation. They have, however, identified the following problems associated with it:

- small coverage;
- lack of material facilities other than wheat;
- discrimination in wheat distribution among the eligible students;
- deterioration of the quality of education;
- mismanagement in wheat distribution;
- small number of teachers;
- inappropriateness of the selection criterion of potential beneficiaries;
- insufficient wheat supply and allocation;

- inadequate infrastructure; and
- several socio-political problems.

The above allegations against the programme deserve more in-depth investigation for corrective action.

7. Poverty Alleviation (PA) Projects and Public Expenditure

7.1 Allocations for PA Projects

The ADP allocation for 62 'poverty alleviation projects' identified by the Task Forces on the Development Strategies of Bangladesh for the 1990s has fallen from 0.47% of GDP in 1991-92 to 0.36% of GDP in 1994-95. The percentage of revised ADP allocation for these projects decreased from 6% in 1991-92 to 4.5% in 1994-95. There are, however, new poverty alleviating projects apart from these 62 projects which have not been distinguished. Thus, the observations made on the basis of this partial viewing of the budgetary allocations are only tentative and merit further investigation.

According to our study, the findings about the impact of these projects on the poor in the urban slums and rural areas are as follows:

- The role of the government agencies in the provision of sanitation facilities, vaccination facilities, water supply, family planning and other primary health care services are positive and better than those of NGOs except for water supply in the urban slums.

The urban poor are better off than the rural poor with respect to the benefits received from GOs in sanitation, family planning and water supply, while the rural poor are more benefited in terms of vaccination of children.

7.2 The Findings of Qualitative Assessment

Many of the findings of the quantitative assessment have been supported/complemented by our qualitative investigation. In some cases new light has also been thrown. The findings of the qualitative investigation on the budgetary process and sectoral allocations are given here to illustrate the usefulness of the qualitative methodology. Here we focus on two sectors: health and primary education.

7.2.1 Health Sector

Findings and Policy Imperatives

1. The quality of medical care of the major providers, namely government hospitals at the district and metropolitan cities, *thana* and union-level government health complexes/centres and other specialized government hospitals, is found to be very poor.

2. The health sector in Bangladesh including both public and private health care providers is iniquitous. The private health providers serve exclusively the well off bypassing the poor and the poorest. In the urban areas, the major government hospitals and specialized hospitals and local qualified/trained doctors are, in fact, serving exclusively the rich and the middle class. The poor and the poorest are forced to fall back on traditional and homeopathic treatment due mainly to financial constraints.
   In the rural areas, the villagers finding no other suitable options are found to be visiting the *thana* and union-level health complexes/centres for medical care. The quality of medical services provided by the THC and the UHFWC is, however, extremely poor. The doctors at the THC are perceived by the villagers to be skilled but their services are considered to be of very poor quality in terms of promptness and attention.
   These facts suggest that public resources allocated for the health sector is being wrongly spent and, therefore, wasted. A thorough reform in the health sector needs to be undertaken so as to ensure equity, efficiency and economy.

3. As NGOs are found to have made health care accessible to the poorest segments of society, an attempt may be made to formulate a suitable health strategy with effective collaboration with NGOs to ensure the availability of medical services to the poor in both the urban and rural areas.

4. As the government has a fairly good health infrastructure in the rural areas and the majority of the people (including the poor) live in the rural areas, the government should review its prioritization and allocation pattern in the health sector in order to ensure better utilization of this infrastructure to serve the rural people. More fund needs to be allocated for the THC and the UHFWC, and additional manpower needs to be deployed to make these programmes more effective.

5. As the health sector is in shambles, an effective personnel policy needs to be designed to get the best service from the doctors, many of whom are not performing now. A suitable motivation package including accountability provisions needs to be introduced to activate them professionally and morally.
6. As the villagers and, particularly, the poor have easy access to health assistants and local qualified/trained doctors, the government should pay greater attention to utilizing them more effectively to extend medical services in remote rural areas.
7. The government should take measures to extend health care training to the unemployed and educated youths as well as to the pharmacists so that the poor may gain increased access to better health services in both urban and rural areas.
8. The incidence of disease for the poorest households increased sharply in both the urban and rural areas leading to an increase in per capita expenditure on medical treatment.
9. Government hospitals/health complexes are not found to have been in the service of the poorest households. The frequency of the visits of the poorest to the government health-care providers declined during the monitoring period. The poorest patients termed the medical service of these providers as very poor.

7.2.2 Primary Education Sector

Findings

1. The rate of enrolment of primary-age children in the rural areas is increasing among both boys and girls irrespective of the FFE programme. The enrolment is, however, increasing at a higher rate in the FFE villages than in the non-FFE villages. The enrolment of boys is higher than that of girls in the FFE villages but not in the non-FFE villages. Overall, the enrolment of boys is increasing at a higher rate than that of girls.

   The enrolment of poor children is much lower compared to the well off and middle income categories. The enrolment rate of poor students (moderate poor and hardcore poor) is found to be 74% whereas that of the non-poor is 92%. However, the rate of enrolment of girls from poor families is marginally lower: it is 73% compared to 75% for poor boys in the rural areas.

2. It is found that the drop-out rate is lower (1%) in the FFE villages than the non-FFE villages (4%). The drop-out rate is, however, found to be higher at 3% for poor households compared to 1% for non-poor households. It is also found that the drop-out rate is declining in schools under the FFE programmes compared to the non-FFE schools.
3. The rate of child labour is found to be 23%. It is, however, lower (22%) in the FFE villages compared to that in the non-FFE villages (24%). Child labour is found extensive among the poor households. Twenty-seven per cent of the poor school-age children are engaged in child labour compared to 12% of the non-poor children in the rural areas.
4. Students' absenteeism and dropping out have been the major problems at the primary level. Poverty, lack of guardians' awareness /willingness, negligence, child labour and lack of food, books and writing papers are some of the important causes of such absenteeism and dropping out.
5. The main causes of students' failure at this level are guardians' negligence, poverty, lack of books/writing papers, lack of preparation for examinations, absenteeism, etc.
6. After completing the primary level education students find it difficult to continue their studies. Poverty and marriage have been the topmost causes of discontinuation.
7. Some of the problems encountered by the primary level students at the government schools are lack of furniture, books, drinking water, latrine, room for teachers, lack of educational materials, etc.
8. The illiterate person is defined as one who cannot read and write a letter. The rates of illiteracy among the adult men and women remain unchanged during the monitoring period. However, the participation of the children of the poorest households in schooling increased during this period. The participation of boys of the poorest households in schooling is increasing in the study areas. However, the participation rate for girls in schooling is increasing at a much slower pace. The FFE programme is found to have had a significant impact on the participation of both boys and girls in schooling. The programme worked very poorly in the central part in improving children's participation in schooling as compared with the performance of the programme in the northern parts of the country.

Policy Imperatives

1. The increased emphasis on primary education in terms of budgetary allocation and introduction of targeted programmes is in the right direction. The FFE programme has had a positive impact on some of the persistent problems of primary education. This programme has significantly improved the drop-out and child labour situation. Although the overall enrolment ratio has increased in schools covered by this programme, the very poor have not benefited equally. A significant portion of children from the poorest households are still found to be not participating in primary education. Besides, the programme is biased towards boys and not so effective in reaching the girls from the poorest households. More innovative target-oriented programmes need to be introduced to increase enrolment in both the urban and rural areas.
2. The quality of primary education is very poor due to a number of problems faced by the primary schools. Public expenditure in primary education would continue to be wasted if the quality of education is not improved appreciably.
3. Although FFE is targeted to the poorest segments of households, the resources allocated for this programme are leaking to the non-poor in the rural areas. Twelve per cent of the FFE beneficiaries are accounted for by students from the non-poor households. The programme should be monitored more rigorously to avoid such leakages. Greater community vigilance of the programme should be encouraged.
4. The quality of education particularly in the FFE schools is deteriorating. A significant portion of the teachers' time is wasted in the management of the FFE programme. Teachers are found to have been preoccupied more with the programme rather than with their task of teaching. Above all, there is a danger that the programme may degenerate by inviting corruption among teachers. Teachers should be withdrawn from the management of the programme as early as possible and its management may be left with NGOs which have the required capacities.
5. The field-findings provide ample ground to look for more suitable mechanisms of delivering benefits to the poorest households to obviate leakage, wastage of time, etc.

8. Knowledge, Attitude and Perception (KAP) of the Respondents

Major findings on the respondent's KAP are as follows:

- The urban poor are relatively more conscious about the national budget than their rural counterparts. About 55% of the respondents in the urban areas and 81% of the respondents in the rural areas do not know anything about the budget.
- Variations in opinions about the budget depend on the level of education and income.
- Among those respondents who know about the budget, about 95% in the urban areas and 76% in the rural areas had discussions on the national budget with others after hearing about it. However, the scope of their discussion was quite limited (eg hovering around price hike).
- Among the respondents who are aware of the budget, no close association has been found between the opinion level (yes, no) and the educational level.
- To the overwhelming majority of the poor, price hike is the main topic of discussion on the budget.
- Forty-two per cent of the respondents in the urban and 16% of them in the rural areas opined that problems affecting their day-to-day life could be solved through the budget. But a near-overwhelming majority of the respondents in the rural areas and more than half in the urban areas did not know whether this would be possible or not.
- Those who opined that the problems of day-to-day life could be solved through an appropriate budget suggested that higher allocation for education might be an important means. Next came infrastructure and environmental development in their list of priorities.
- Fifty-five percent respondents in the urban areas and 81% in the rural areas indicated that they did not know about the usefulness of the budget. Forty per cent respondents in the urban areas and 16% in the rural areas thought that it was of no use. The remaining 5% in the urban and 3% in the rural areas, that is, very few, opined in favour of its usefulness.

- To the majority of the respondents, the sources of information on the budget are radio and different persons.
- Of those who are aware of the budget speech, 59% of the urban and 69% of the rural respondents do not understand it. The main cause of the difficulty in understanding the budget has been identified as the illiteracy of the respondents.
- Due to difficulties in understanding the budget speech, 61% and 73% of the respondents in the urban and rural areas respectively do not listen to it.
- Sixty-five per cent in the urban and 91% in the rural areas do not feel the necessity to react to the budget. The rest have expressed their reaction. There is a close association between the levels of reaction and one's place of residence.
- Sixty-five per cent in the urban and 91% in the rural areas observed no impact of the budget speech on the market. The rest observed some impact of the budget on the market prices of commodities.

9. Monitoring of Impact of Public Expenditure on Poverty

9.1 Findings from Panel Survey

- The monitoring was conducted through the qualitative method.
- The primary objective of conducting poverty monitoring was to understand the process as to how public expenditure impacts on the lives of the poorest in terms of various indicators of well-being in both the urban and rural areas.
- Instead of a single criterion, community members/villagers used a variety of criteria to categorize themselves into four classes, namely 'well off', 'middle', 'poor' and 'poorest'.
- The findings of the participatory poverty assessment show that in the urban slums, 72% of the households are poor (moderate: 51% and hard-core: 21%) and 28% are non-poor (middle: 19% and well off 9%). On the other hand, 75% of the rural households are considered to be poor (moderate: 20% and hard-core: 55%) and 25% are non-poor (middle: 14% and well off: 11%). Regionally, the incidence of poverty is more acute in the central part (moderate: 17% and hard-core: 60%) than that in the northern part (moderate: 25% and hard-core 47%) of the country.

- A total of 80 poorest households (20 from the urban slums and 60 from the two depressed *thanas* in the rural areas were selected for monitoring progress in terms of a number of socio-economic indicators. The sample was admittedly very small, drawn merely for the illustration of a methodology. Out of the 60 rural households, 30 were drawn from the northern part and the other 30 from the central part of the country. The 30 rural households in each *thana* consist of 10 households under the Food For Education (FFE) programme and 10 non-FFE households in the programme village, the rest are from a village in a control union adjacent to the programme union. These 3 groups of the sample households give 3 different sets of base and impact data for 1993 and 1996 respectively.
- Most of the selected indicators strongly indicate that the poverty of the poorest households worsened over the monitoring period. The spell of poverty is found to have been more serious for both the non-FFE household groups in the programme and the control villages relative to the group of households under the FFE progrmame. The socio-economic condition of the FFE households worsened but to a lesser extent during the monitoring period, largely because of their better resource base compared to the other two non-FFE groups of households. The contribution of Tk. 4.85 a day from the FFE programme to the nominal income of the poorest households is found not so significant (11% of average household income).
- Poverty among the urban slum-dwellers is found less severe than rural poverty. The poorest households are found to have adopted their own long-term strategy through demographic means to cope with socio-economic vulnerabilities and constraints. Regardless of both regional and group differences, the average family size and earning members increased during the monitoring period. This indicates that the poorest households are increasingly falling back on the number of earning members to offset the declining trend of real income and consumption during 1993-1996.
- Although per capita income of the poorest households increased in nominal terms by 7% in the rural areas, it decreased in real terms by 22% during this period. Moreover, the level of income of the rural poorest was very low at Tk. 7.40 (per capita/day) in

1996 compared to Tk. 6.90 in 1993. Real income in terms of coarse rice declined by 24-43% due to a price hike during this period.

- Similar is the case with the real wage rate for unskilled wage labourers in the rural areas. The average wage rate for unskilled wage labourers across the board declined in real terms during the monitoring period.
- Food consumption (rice and wheat) of the poorest households increased in the urban areas from 442 grams (per capita/day) in 1993 to 514 grams in 1996, showing a 16% increase. However, food consumption of the poorest households declined in both per capita and per adult equivalent terms during the same period in the rural areas. The consumption of protein-rich food (non-cereal food, eg fish, beef, chicken, egg, milk, etc) by the hard-core poor in the rural areas declined alarmingly during the monitoring period.
- The poorest people are living in thatched houses, and their housing condition has not improved markedly. The living space available for the poorest is very limited. The condition of overcrowding (members per room) deteriorated during the monitoring period.
- Most of the poor households in the rural areas do not have latrines. There is a very small number have *kutcha* (pit) latrines. In the urban slums, most of the households use *kutcha* latrines and very few have access to water-sealed latrines constructed by the municipality or some other concerned departments/ organizations. The public latrines are found unhygienic due to lack of maintenance.

9.2 Findings from Sample Survey

- Twenty-six per cent of the respondents in the urban areas and 65% in the rural areas assessed their households as chronic deficits. Thirty- seven per cent and 30% of the respondents in the urban and rural areas respectively identified their households as occasionally deficit. Only 1% of the respondents in the rural areas and 10% in the urban areas assessed their households as surplus.
- The poorest households in both the urban and rural areas are deprived of institutional credit. Moneylenders and friends are

their main sources of credit. Recently, NGOs have started lending to them but the coverage has been insignificant during the monitoring period.

In the credit operations for the poor, the role of traditional sources of credit (moneylenders, relatives, shopkeepers) are prominent among the households in chronic deficit both in the urban and rural areas. Moneylenders provided 43% of the deficit households with loans at average interest rates ranging from 103% in the urban to 154% in the rural areas. They are also the main sources of credit for occasionally deficit households. The credit facilities provided by the institutional sources (NGOs and commercial banks) are, in effect, benefiting the break-even and surplus households.

The government assistance to the poor through the channels of NGOs and similar institutional sources by means of the Palli Karmaya Shahayak Foundation (PKSF) do not seem to have reached the bottom end of the hierarchy of the poor masses.

The poorest of the poor are being exploited by the exorbitant interest rates charged by the traditional moneylenders and are expected to have little chance of rising up the income ladder and breaking out of the vicious circle of poverty.

The inadequacy of the knowledge and perceptions of the poor about the budget implies that they can hardly appear as an organized pressure group to influence the budget and allocations in their own favour. Nor can they exert any demand for radical changes in the budgetary process conducive to an all-out attack on poverty. But the fact remains that the budget is the single most important instrument of mobilization and distribution of public resources, and unless due shares of these resources are diverted to the underprivileged and the distressed in a well-planned way there cannot be a major dent on poverty.

10. Policy Implications

1. The budget should be prepared and presented in a simple format so that even the ordinary people can understand its processes. Efforts should be made to rescue the budget from its archaic structural limitations. The informational and analytical contents of the budget, the sectoral allocations of the following year's budget, the demarcation between the revenue and the development budgets

including their recurrent and capital expenditures, the incidence of revenues, etc should be presented in such terms and formats as can be easily comprehensible to an ordinary person.

2. The Finance Minister in his budget speech should reflect the hopes and aspirations of the ordinary people in such a manner as to enable them to relate the fiscal activities of the governmental agencies to some visible outputs. Only then the fear of people about the budget as a mechanism of price hike can be removed.
3. There should be an institutional mechanism to capture the people's own needs. While prioritizing the budget allocations, people's own needs assessment should be seriously considered by those involved in the preparation of the budget. The Finance Minister should find a mechanism to set up regular dialogues with the people's representatives, consumer groups, people's organizations and not only with members of the chambers of commerce and industries and other professional groups. The budget preparation techniques should be modernized using relevant computer-based accounting packages. Apparently, some exercises on this line are going on now and this trend should be enhanced.
4. There is now a move toward the establishment of decentralized local governments. There should be a simultaneous attempt at fiscal decentralization. The local government should be clearly mandated about the nature of their legal rights over certain heads of local resources as well as over a proportion of the central resources. There should also be a mini-parliament at every level of local government where the local budget will be discussed and approved. Besides the elected representatives, representatives of different professional groups, government officials, NGOs, women, youth, etc should be inducted as members of the local parliament. The local government will have to be accountable to this local parliament. They will together formulate local-level plans for poverty alleviation and other development activities.
5. It will be wise for the Finance Minister not to be complacent about the increased allocation of public resources for education and health. If the quality of education and health services does not improve even after increased allocations, this becomes a net wastage of scarce public resources. Adequate institutional mechanisms, therefore, should be designed to regularly monitor the quality of education and health services provided by the government departments. There

should be a greater scope for participatory monitoring of the quality of these services.

6. The task of national budgeting should not merely be a mechanical exercise of resource mapping and sectoral allocations. Its aim should be to see whether the resources mobilized are spent on time and in the intended manner or not. It is widely believed that there is corruption in revenue mobilization and huge wastage in the development programmes and projects. The challenge as to how to reduce corruption and wastage while managing public finance has to be faced squarely. Besides the political commitment to efficient and accountable governance, the entire administration should be motivated for the greater cause of development.
7. There should be an attempt at improving the human expenditure ratio (human priority share of GNP) by allocating more public resources for human priority activities to expand people's choices. In fact, civil society should be invited to initiate a Social Watch to see whether the pledges made by the government and the NGOs for human development are being materialized on the ground or not.
8. The current method of auditing development projects by IMED should be radically changed. The auditing should be done not by 'proforma' checking alone but by the 'programme budgeting' approach where one can clearly identify the 'value for money'. Each and every department/ministry should be required to draw up a financial management plan in a manner so that it can readily answer the question: 'where is the money going and what are we getting for it?'
9. There should be an independent development watchdog with sufficient authority, resources and skilled personnel which should replace IMED and play a crucial role in monitoring the pace and quality of the existing development projects and suggest mid-course revisions of the programmes to the parliament and present its suggestions to the media. All its findings should be publicly debated. This will help the government take corrective action on the shortcomings of any development programme.
10. The annual budgets should not be seen as isolated fiscal events. They should be seen as part of a longer term plan with some fundamental socio-economic guidelines formulated through national consensus preferably at the national parliament taking into consideration ideas proposed by the 'mini-parliaments' at the lower levels.

11 . Poverty alleviation should be clearly conceptualized and should not be allowed to end up as cliches. Indeed this should be more focused on people's capacity to reinvest and go for creative options. The core of this conceptualization should really be equity and not mere palliatives measures.

Chapter 1

THE NATIONAL BUDGET AND POVERTY ERADICATION

1.1 The Setting

The present study is a modest attempt at understanding the effectiveness of the process of mobilization and expenditure of public resources as reflected in the Annual National Budget. This phase of the study is focused on people's perception about the national budget and its impact on the process of poverty eradication particularly in the public sector. It does not discuss in detail the budget-making processes, which will be the focus of the next phase of the study. The aim is to find how the dual objectives of rapid economic growth and poverty alleviation are realized in this regard. The concern for poverty alleviation of the Government of Bangladesh (GOB) is well articulated in various policy documents as well as in commitments made at different international fora. Both the Perspective Plan of Bangladesh (1995-2010) and the recently prepared Fifth Five-Year Plan (1997-2002) have envisaged the target of eradication of poverty by the early years of the next century through the strategy of social mobilization at the grassroots level. The concern for poverty eradication within this stipulated period (2002) has also been reflected in the charter signed by the heads of the government of SAARC countries at the Dhaka summit held in 1993. It is difficult to believe that this target can be achieved within such a short period of time. But even a desire to make a major breakthrough in this matter has immense implications for designing and implementing government's socio-economic policies.

The government of a country is expected to adopt policies with a view to pursuing the national aspirations and translating those into reality. It is all the more necessary when such policies aim at ensuring the well-being of the millions who are at present in utter destitution. For that matter, there is a need for making a serious inquiry into the concept of poverty, its identification, measurement and actions which may be necessary for its eradication. In other words, the drive for poverty eradication has to be made both at the conceptual and implementation levels.

1. 2 Objective, Scope and Methodology of the Study

1.2.1 Objective

The study attempts to analyse the financial allocations and actual expenditures by the GOB in the revenue budget and the Annual Development Programme (ADP) from the perspective of poverty alleviation. The objective of such an analysis is to examine how the allocation of resources over the period would affect investment in the social sectors (education, health and population, social welfare and rural development) and expenditure on Food For Works (FFW), Vulnerable Group Development (VGD), Rural Maintenance Programme (RMP) and Test Relief (TR) as distinct from the 'immediately productive sectors' such as agriculture and industry. Simultaneously, the study tries to monitor the performance of a set of macro indicators (demographic, social and economic) focusing particularly on the state of poverty. It is based on a participatory process involving the living conditions of selected groups of the poor and their knowledge, attitude and perception (KAP) to understand the process and impact of the annual budget.

1.2.2 Scope

In reviewing the National Budget of Bangladesh, the study touches upon the budgetary process, budget allocations and expenditures, and macro information on poverty indicators. It undertakes micro surveys on poverty indicators in selected villages and urban slums to obtain people's perceptions of the budget and of changes in their living conditions, dialogues with policy makers, practitioners and concerned executives.

1.2.3 Methodology

Both quantitative and qualitative methods have been applied in conducting this study. Strengths and weaknesses of both the methods have been considered in order to arrive at a consensus on fruitful integration of the two methods. In a way this is a pioneering effort, particularly in the context of a study which focuses on a macroeconomic issue like the national budget.

Strengths of Quantitative Methods. Quantitative methods are widely used in research. Although particularly needed for research in physical science, the quantitative methods are also used in various fields of social science, especially neoclassical economics.

The quantitative methods are said to have the following desirable characteristics:

1. More objective data are generated by such methods. Large sample sizes are likely to reduce or neutralize various biases/distortions in data/information.
2. They generate 'hard' data referring to the precision of statistics.
3. They require the use of standardized measures so that the varying perspectives and experiences of people can fit into a limited number of predetermined response categories.
4. Aggregation and generalization are the two most important characteristic features of the quantitative methods. In this case, it is possible to measure the reactions of a great many people to a limited set of questions, thus facilitating comparison and statistical aggregation of the data. This gives a broad, generalizable set of findings presented succinctly and parsimoniously.
5. The quantitative data generated through field inquiry may also have some degree of scientific rigour through controlling various activities involved in the data collection process.
6. Scientific research like hypothesis testing can be conducted more easily using hard data.
7. The hard data generated through the data collection process are found to be easily amenable to statistical analysis.
8. These methods are suitable to capture a large area under the study.
9. Sampling on a more scientific basis is possible by using various statistical rules and formalities.
10. Statistical prediction is possible in the case of quantitative methods by applying sophisticated models. Computers can be used for the process of quantitative data.
11. Analysing and processing data are found to be more simple and cost-effective if the latest computer technology is used.

Limitations of Quantitative Methods. However, the conventional approach is usually understood to be a synonym for the quantitative methods. Methodological weaknesses of quantitative methods are dealt with by complementing qualitative methods. Some of the weaknesses of quantitative methods are mentioned below:

1. Quantitative methods require the use of standardized measures so that the varying perspectives and experiences of people can fit into a limited number of predetermined response categories to which numbers are assigned. It might have an undesirable impact upon the quality of data.
2. Validity in quantitative research partly depends on the careful construction of instrument and also on the ability to ensure that the instrument measures what it is supposed to measure. The instrument must then be administered in an appropriate standardized manner according to prescribed procedures. The focus is on the measuring instrument, the test items, survey questions or other measurement tools. As far as the research in social science is concerned, sometimes it is very difficult to comply with the nuances of quantitative research.
3. Data collection activities are usually carried out without the involvement of research subjects (the group of people being studied) in the process. These methods are exclusively characterized by 'experts', outsiders or those external to a situation who gather and analyse information about people, a community, or agency or a situation. Community members are excluded and there is no provision of feedback to the community or agency. People/ informants remain unaware of the research results/findings.
4. Quantitative methods do not involve different stakeholders who have direct and indirect concerns with the research topic.

Rationale for Qualitative Methods. In view of the limitations of the quantitative methods, the qualitative methods are increasingly used to supplement the quantitative investigation. One of the primary reasons for using the qualitative methods is to capture those information which can hardly be dealt with by using the quantitative research tools. The qualitative research methods are, therefore, indispensable for research in social science. Some of the major advantages of these methods are discussed below.

1. Qualitative methods are the first and foremost research methods. Historically, the use of the qualitative methods dates far back in the past (Box 1.1). These are ways of finding out what people do, know, think, and feel by observing, interviewing, and analysing documents (Patton 1990). Direct quotations are a basic source of raw data in qualitative inquiry, revealing respondents' depth of emotion, the ways they have organized their world, their thoughts about what is happening, their experiences, and their basic perceptions.

Box 1.1 *Alexander was a Qualitative Methodologist: An Illustration*

Alexander's military conquests are legends. What is less known and little appreciated is that his battlefield victories depended on in-depth knowledge of the psychology and culture of ordinary people and military leaders in opposing armies. He included in his military intelligence information about the beliefs, worldview, motivations, and patterns of behaviour of those he faced. Moreover, his conquests and subsequent rule were more economic and political in nature than military. He used what we now understand to be psychological, sociological and anthropological insights. He understood that lasting victory depended on the goodwill and moral support of the conquered peoples. He carefully studied the customs and conditions of people he conquered and adopted his policies politically, economically, and culturally to promote good conditions in each locale, so that the people were reasonably well-disposed toward his rule.

Alexander was not only a great general and enlightened ruler, he was an extraordinary ethnographer, and a qualitative methodologist par excellence, using observations and firsthand experience to systematically study and understand the peoples he encountered.

Source: Patton 1990

2. Qualitative methods permit the researcher to study selected issues in depth and detail. Approaching field-work without being constrained by predetermined structured categories of analysis contributes to the depth and details of qualitative inquiry. The qualitative findings are longer, more detailed, and variable in content. The open-ended responses are obtained which permit one to understand the world as seen by the respondents. The purpose of gathering responses to open-ended questions is to enable the researcher to understand and capture the points of view of other people without predetermining those points of view through prior selection of questionnaire categories.

3. Development is a process. Organizational development, community development, human development, etc are process-oriented approaches to facilitating change. Pre- and post-tests do not do justice to a dynamic development process. 'Pre' and 'post' measures imply a kind of linear, ever upward, less-to-more image of growth and development. In reality, development usually occurs in fits and starts, with some upward or forward progress, then backsliding or consolidating. Pre- and post-testing tells us where we started and where we ended up but not what happened along the way. Quantitative measures can parsimoniously capture snapshots of 'pre' and 'post' status, but qualitative methods are more appropriate for capturing the development dynamics.

4. It should be further noted that qualitative inquiry is not concerned with 'representativeness'; rather it seeks to emphasize the process and depth of inquiry.

Methodological Integration of Quantitative and Qualitative Methods. The debate between the qualitative and the quantitative has centered on the capacity of the data, as collected in one or the other method, to describe, understand and explain social phenomena. A growing number of researchers have adopted a more eclectic position from which they claim that no method *per se* has the monopoly on inference. They agree that quantitative and qualitative approaches should not be considered rivals or substitutes, but rather complements.

Within this debate of quantitative versus qualitative approaches, three stereotypes have evolved: the purists, the eclectics and the integrationists or pragmatists.

The purists or segregationists argue that quantitative and qualitative paradigms are incompatible, deriving from different, mutually exclusive epistemologic and ontologic assumptions about the nature of research and society.

From this perspective, methods are based on opposing assumptions and, therefore, lead to profoundly different visions of the world.

The eclectics claim that both approaches are valid. The application of one or the other depends on the situation. Although both sets of methods can be used complementarily for the study of the same subject, they still represent distinct assumptions. Many evaluative studies advocate this perspective, where quantitative and qualitative methods are used in parallel or sequentially as the situation dictates.

Finally, the pragmatists or integrationists maintain that there is a false dichotomy between the quantitative and the qualitative methodologies, and argue for the integration of both methodologies for the same study subject. From this position, polarization is seen as representing the extremes of a continuum along which there is a gradient of possible combinations of quantitative and qualitative methods, both supporting each other and enhancing the credibility of study results. Because quantitative and qualitative methods involve differing strengths and weaknesses, they constitute alternative, but not mutually exclusive, strategies for research. Both quantitative and qualitative data can be collected in the same study. The methodological integration provides *'the quantified bones of the survey with the qualitative flesh'* (Cernea 1992, emphasis added).

There is a growing consensus that applying both sets of methods in an iterative mode can increase the reliability of data and lead to a more complete understanding of the phenomenon under study. The combination of methodologies for the study of the same phenomenon has been coined 'triangulation' (Pedersen 1992).

1.2.3.1 Quantitative Methods

The quantitative part of the study is based on both primary and secondary sources of information. In order to review the national budgetary allocations of Bangladesh, data and information from government documents have been collected. The trends of public expenditures and tax revenues in relation to Gross Domestic Product (GDP) have been analysed to see the efficacy of public resource management. In particular, public expenditures have been reviewed in a disaggregated manner to identify their impacts on poverty alleviation with a special focus on socially disadvantaged target groups. A sample survey for collecting primary data on the Food For Education (FFE) programme has been conducted in the same study areas used for the qualitative investigation. This survey covered 16 primary schools of which 11 are government and 5 are non-government schools. Apart from monitoring the roll strength, attendance and drop-out rates of these schools, the members of the school management committee were interviewed through a questionnaire for their comments on the ongoing FFE programme.

An opinion survey to assess the impact of specified poverty alleviation projects was conducted in both the rural and urban sample areas. The respondents were provided with individual questionnaires to reveal their status in terms of their access to sanitation, health, family planning and drinking water facilities.

The opinion survey was conducted in both the rural and urban areas to assess the level of KAP of the poor about the national budget. The respondents (139 households in the urban and 150 households in the rural areas) were asked to offer their perceptions about certain aspects of the national annual budget. Certainly, such a small number of households cannot represent the entire nation. But this sample size can definitely be considered to be an illustrative exercise for capturing the poor's attitudes towards and perceptions about the national budget. This particular quantitative exercise does not really want to score a point on the quantitative dimension of the national budget. It indeed tries to focus on a process where the poor are not only conveniently excluded, their needs and priorities too are ignored. The issues covered by quantitative methods are given in box 1.2.

The aspects that could not be addressed adequately with the quantitative approach were sought to be covered by the qualitative approach. The two approaches, thus, have been used complementarily.

Box 1.2 Issues Addressed in Quantitative Methods

Topics	Sub-topics	Methods
Public revenue	• Revenue composition • Growth of tax revenue under three heads	• Review of budget estimates • Time series analysis through trend equation
Public expenditure	• Expenditure composition • Growth of revenue and development expenditure • Growth of disaggregated development expenditure	• Review of budget estimates • Time series analysis through trend equation as above
Targeted public expenditure for poverty alleviation	• Foodgrain distribution • Sectoral allocation • Assessment of the FFE programme in terms of enrolment, attendance, drop-out rates, etc.	• Review of published documents and sample survey
Poverty alleviation projects	• Sanitation • Family planning • Health care • Drinking water	• Opinion survey
Knowledge, attitude and perception (KAP) of the poor relating to the public budget	• Knowledge • Attitude • Usefulness of budget • Reaction to the public budget	• Opinion survey

1.2.3.2 Qualitative Methods

Although 'there are no perfect research designs' (Patton 1990) in qualitative research and 'qualitative inquiry is rife with ambiguity' (ibid), the methodology for the qualitative part of this study has been designed following 'purposeful strategies instead of methodological rules' (ibid). However, the 'triangulation norms' (cross-checking of data generated through different methods with varied perspective), the cornerstone of the qualitative research, have been applied to cross-check the accuracy of data and information. Besides triangulation, another objective of applying the qualitative method is to supplement the quantitative data for better interpretation in a more meaningful way. As the qualitative investigation has used the Participatory Rural Appraisal (PRA) tools, it further adds the people's perspective to the interpretation of the data and information generated through other methods/tools. The qualitative part of this study has two components. The first component has been dealt with through PRA tools using the Participatory Rapid Rural Appraisal (PRRA) approach and it generates mainly qualitative data and information in the dialogical sessions at the community level where community members participated to discuss the research issues. The other component is about poverty monitoring and it mainly generates quantitative data. This component monitors poverty on some selected indicators in the same study areas where PRA sessions were held and it used a non-participatory approach. However, instead of group participation, individual participation has been ensured where the investigator's role has been minimum. For facilitating individual participation, a visualized format (questionnaire) has been designed and administered to the selected poorest households in the sample communities. The building blocks of the qualitative inquiry strategy designed for this study are presented below.

Methodology for Qualitative Inquiry Using PRA Tools

Approach. The qualitative inquiry of this study has applied a participatory approach. Semantically, PRRA rather than PRA is more relevant to this study. The focus of PRRA is on data collection whereas that of PRA is on the empowerment of the community. Although PRA tools along with its guidelines and behavioural norms have been followed while interacting with the community to collect data and information rather than promote their empowerment, the purpose of the field exercise amounts to 'extraction'. PRRA not PRA is, therefore, the appropriate term for the approach to qualitative investigation in this study (Mukherjee 1995, Townsley 1996).

Issues. Six broad issues/topics have been addressed under the qualitative part of this study (Box 1.3).

The perception of the poor on all these issues has been the core element of the qualitative investigation. Public expenditure and sectoral prioritization by the poor have been the key issues addressed by the qualitative methods in the first round of this study. Other broad areas of the investigation are various macroeconomic issues, assessment and monitoring of poverty, needs assessment, and some sectoral issues pertaining to education and health.

Selection of study areas. The study has covered both the urban and rural areas (Figure 1.1). Two slums in Dhaka city and two *thanas* each from the northern and central parts of the country have been selected for the study. The two sample *thanas* have been drawn randomly from the

Box 1.3 Issues Addressed in Qualitative Methods

Topics	Sub-topics	Methods	Tools/Techniques
National budget and prioritization by the poor	• Public expenditure and sectoral prioritization by the poor	• Participatory group discussion responses	• Recording direct
	• Perception of budget (ideas and expectations)	• As above	• As above
Various macro-economic/ sectoral issues	• Assessment of public policies	• Participatory group discussion	• Scoring and ranking
	• Assessment of social sectors	• As above	• As above
	• Impact assessment of economic activities	• As above	• As above
Health	• Incidence of major diseases	• Participatory group discussion	• Scoring and ranking
	• Source of healthcare and the poor's preference pattern	• As above	• As above
	• Assessment of health providers	• As above	• As above
	• Reasons for not getting health service at the *Thana* Health Centre	• As above	• As above
Primary education	• Causes of dropping out	• Focus group discussion	• Checklist/ Mapping
	• Causes of failure in examinations	• As above	• As above
	• Causes of absenteeism	• As above	• As above
	• Key problems facing primary students	• As above	• As above
	• Causes of discontinuation of education	• As above	• As above
	• Profile of FFE children	• As above	• As above
Assessment and monitoring of poverty	• Well-being assessment	• Well-being ranking by composite criteria	• Cards sorting
	• Change in basic human development indicators over the last three years	• Standardized open-ended interview	• Visualized format
Needs assessment	• Assessment of socio-economic problems	• Well-being ranking by composite criteria and standardized interview	• Visualized format
	• Listing and prioritizing of needs	• Participatory group discussion	• Scoring and ranking

depressed *thana* list from the Task Force Report prepared under the leadership of Professor Rehman Sobhan in his capacity as an Adviser to the caretaker government of Justice Shahabuddin Ahmed (Task Force 1991) through multi-stage stratification. At the first stage, sample *thanas* were selected randomly from the two *thana* lists. At the later stages the selection process has been purposive. The *thanas* selected for the study have been Katiadi (Kishoreganj district) from the central part and Ulipur (Kurigram district) from the northern part of the country.

Figure 1.1 Sampling for Qualitative Inquiry

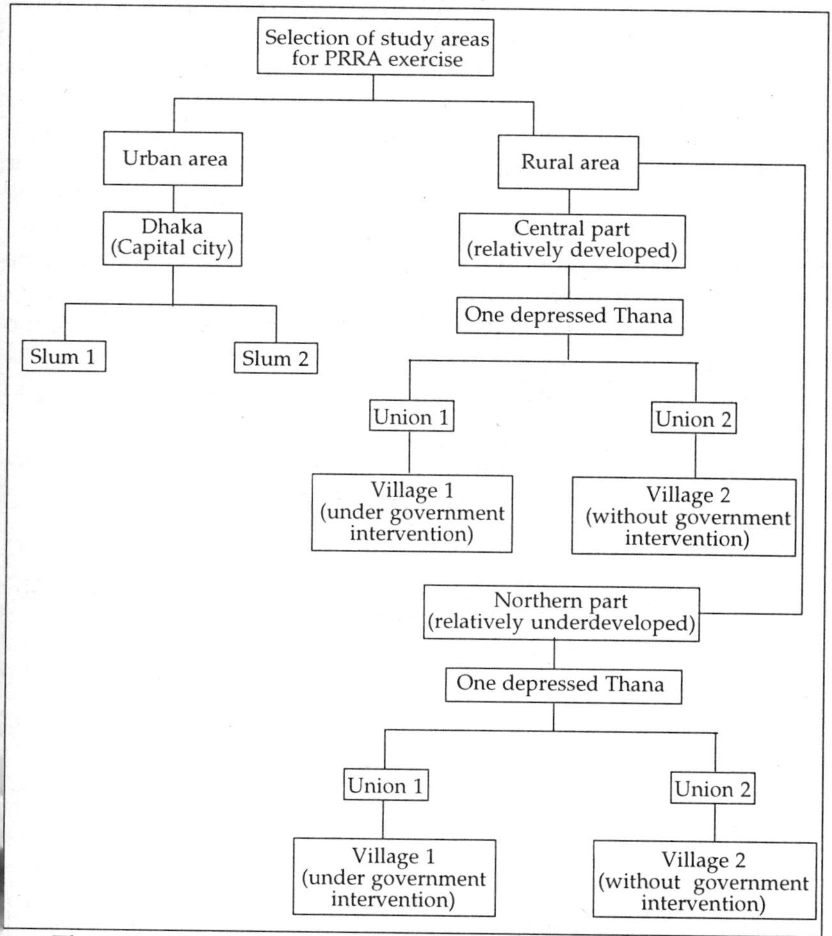

These two parts proxy two characteristics of the country: one representing the relatively developed and the other the underdeveloped areas. It would be interesting to compare the incidence of poverty and the pace of socio-economic progress in these two areas. Two villages from each selected *thana* have been chosen: one from one union under the FFE programme and another from the adjacent union without this programme. One of the two villages has been used as experimental and the other as a control village. The reason for selecting these two villages is that this would serve not only the purpose of monitoring poverty but also of testing the hypothesis that the FFE programme is boosting the primary-level education by encouraging people through counteracting poverty and enabling the poorest households to send their school-age children to primary schools (GOB 1995).

There were two unions under the FFE programme in each of the selected *thanas* at that time. As it was decided that a conventional questionnaire-based survey and participatory exercises including poverty monitoring would be conducted in different unions to ensure wider coverage of the exercise, there was no choice but to select the programme union where any questionnaire-based household survey had not been conducted. After the selection of the programme union, one programme village was drawn in the programme union adjacent to a primary school under the programme in such a way that it lay neither too near nor too far from the school. The selection of the two primary schools under the FFE programme was purposive—one government-operated school in

Figure 1.2 Qualitative Methods and PRA Tools

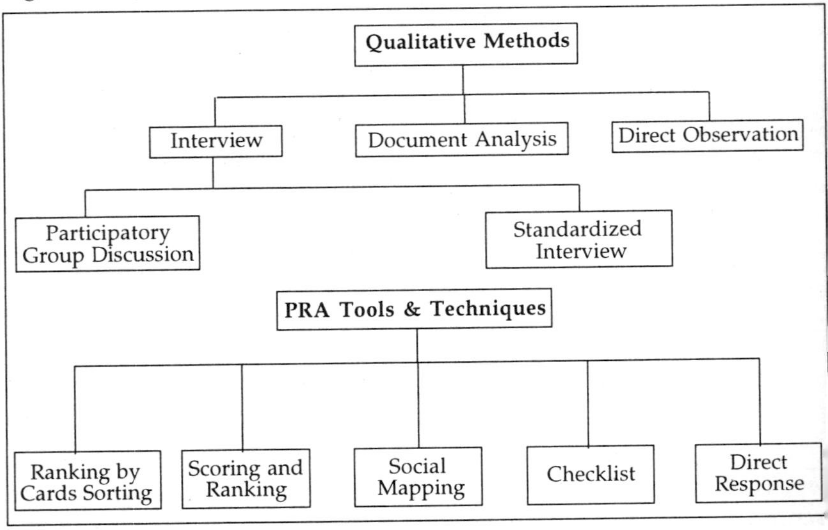

one *thana* and another registered (non-government) school in another *thana*.

After the selection of the programme village in the selected programme union, one control village (without the FFE programme) was selected in the adjacent union where there had been no programme at that time. The selection of the control village had also been purposive. The control village has been near the programme village and was selected on the basis of convenience, eg good transportation, size of the village, etc.

The slums selected for the study are Motaher slum near BNP market of Agargaon slum and Titipara slum in Kamlapur at Dhaka. The selection of these slums was purely purposive. Both these slums are situated in the heart of the city. The Titipara slum is one of the poorest slums in the city. Its environment, housing condition, sanitation system and congestion amply demonstrate that it is one of the few spots in Dhaka city where the poorest of the poor are concentrated. The Motaher slum, on the other hand, is in a better shape. Its condition is not as worse as Titipara slum.

The selected slums also differ in respect of the degree and scale of NGO intervention. NGO intervention was found to be less in Titipara slum than in Motaher slum.

The rationale for selecting the villages from the depressed *thanas* and the urban slums has been to assess the development impacts on the living standard of the poor in order to understand the mechanism of transfer of benefit of public expenditure and the extent of its impacts. The selection of these study areas has further served the research objective of seeing the geographical distribution of development impacts whether development projects/activities implemented so far are effective enough to raise the living standard of the poorest of the poor in the depressed areas in the rural setting and poverty pockets in the urban areas, and also whether there is any difference in the impacts due to some other factors.

Methods. Four major qualitative research methods have been applied in this study (Figure 1.2). These are participatory group discussions, standardized interview, direct observation and document analysis.

PRA tools and techniques. The important PRA tools used in the study have been ranking by cards sorting, scoring and ranking, social mapping, checklist and direct responses (Figure 1.2). These tools are found most effective in communicating with the participants in the PRA sessions and recording data and information.

PRA sessions. Several PRA sessions were arranged in the selected villages/slums to collect data and information. A total of 44 slum-dwellers and 138 villagers actively participated in the PRA sessions to record and analyse their perceptions about sectoral prioritization and other macroeconomic issues of major concern to them. Definitely, these are not representative samples as some readers may expect them to be. The qualitative investigation is not always bogged down with this question of representativeness. It was found rather difficult to arrange PRA sessions in the urban slums due to lack of space, unhygienic environment, lack of time on the part of the slum-dwellers and so on. These problems were found to be the major hindrances to the participatory data gathering process in the urban slums.

Validity and reliability. The quality of data and information generated through the participatory process may be considered good in terms of both validity and reliability because of the use of triangulation methods. Moreover, the free participation of the villagers and slum-dwellers in the process of data generation and analysis further facilitated the cross-checking of the data on the spot through consultation and debate on the issues addressed at the sessions.

PRA team. A PRA team of five facilitators including one female conducted and facilitated all the PRA sessions. All the team members had previous experience of PRA research and they were imparted intensive training on this approach before the field-work.

Interpretation of qualitative data. The role of the researcher is crucial in the conventional approaches (quantitative and qualitative). The dominant role of the researcher in the interpretation of data has been subject to scathing criticism by the proponents of the emerging new approaches like the participatory approach because of the reflection of more bias of the researcher in the interpretation of data and problem (Chambers 1983). In view of the paradigmatic shift, the qualitative part of this study has applied PRA tools instead of conventional qualitative tools for the field investigation. One of the advantages of using the participatory tools is that people themselves play a dominant role in anlaysing and recording data. People's perspectives are captured and reflected in the output of the dialogical sessions. In the participatory approach, the role of the researcher is, therefore, limited.

However, it must be noted that the participatory approach does not completely rule out the role of a researcher in a study. The researcher is not a mechanical observer of the situation. He must not only play a facilitating, enabling and animating role at the field level but also put forward her/his informed judgment and interpretation while documenting the findings of the inquiry without distorting people's perception and analysis. The field insights of the researcher is also a valuable input in interpreting qualitative data in the study. An investigation based on the participatory approach must have some provision for validation of the anlaysis and findings of the study by the people in the dialogical sessions. Validation by the people is an acid test of the researcher.

Diagramming is one of the popular techniques of the presentation of data and analysis. Without the use of suitable diagrams, qualitative data may not be suitably used in a study. Regarding the interpretation of qualitative data, an authority like Peter Oakley suggests:

> Whenever possible the verbal interpretation should be translated into some kind of diagramatic form.... The first point to make is the importance of translating the qualitative material into some kind of visual and diagramatic presentation of what is happening. Without such a form of presentation, the interpretation could well get buried in a mountain of files and words (Oakley 1988).

As a principle, 'Sophistication in simplicity' has been followed while interpreting and presenting the results rather than 'sophistication in complexity' (Chambers 1993). Besides, whenever new interpretations have been shown diagramatically, it has been done beside the presentation of people's own analysis to help the reader to compare and judge the degree of competence and bias of the researcher vis-a-vis people's own analysis.

1.3 Some Methodological Issues for Poverty Monitoring

1.3.1 Typology of Indicators

Poverty monitoring needs a set of carefully selected indicators. The selection of indicators, however, depends on the objective of the monitoring (Carvalho and White 1994). As the assessment of poverty is not an end in itself and assessing the impact of public expenditure on the standard of living of the poor has been the main objective of this study, the indicators have been selected accordingly. The UNDP claims that the indicators of poverty assessment and monitoring can be drawn from five families of indicators, namely 'means' (inputs), 'ends' (impact), 'mixed', 'process' (opportunity) and 'poverty-related' (UNDP 1996). However, they need to be balanced for achieving good monitoring results (Carvalho and White 1994). But it is very difficult to design a clear-cut typology and make a clear distinction between the different indicators.

The choice of indicators necessarily involves a subjective element. An attempt has been made here to make the selection of indicators balanced conforming to the above-mentioned typology of indicators (Box 1.4).

Box 1.4 Indicators Used in Poverty Monitoring

Types of indicators		**Indicators/Variables**
Means	◆ Consumption	▪ per capita daily consumption of food ▪ per household daily consumption of food ▪ per adult equivalent daily consumption of food ▪ frequency of consumption of important food items
	◆ Income	▪ per capita daily nominal/real income ▪ per household daily nominal/real income ▪ earner-member ratio ▪ source of income ▪ wage rate
	◆ Education	▪ participation of children in schooling ▪ expenditure on education
Mixed	◆ Health	▪ incidence of disease ▪ access to health facilities ▪ expenditure on medical treatment ▪ frequency of visits to health care providers
	◆ Drinking water	▪ access to safe drinking water
	◆ Sanitation	▪ type of latrine used
	◆ Fuel	▪ type of fuel used
	◆ Lighting	▪ type of lighting used
	◆ Demography	▪ average family size ▪ age-genderwise composition of family members
	◆ Asset	▪ profile of assets ▪ acquisition of assets
Process	◆ Credit	▪ sources of credit ▪ volume of credit
Poverty-related	◆ Demography	▪ prevalence of female-headed households ▪ prevalence of child labour ▪ prevalence of begging households
Ends	◆ Distress sale	▪ sale of assets
	◆ Health	▪ quality of medical service
	◆ Housing conditions	▪ structure ▪ number of rooms ▪ overcrowding
	◆ Saving	▪ proportion of saving households ▪ per capita savings
	◆ Literacy	▪ rate of illiteracy/literacy

Source: UNDP 1996

1.3.2 Sample Selection for Monitoring Poverty Using Panel Data

For poverty monitoring, 80 poorest of the poor households were selected —20 from the urban slums and 60 from the rural areas—based on the people's criteria and assessment (Figure 1.3). In the urban areas, 20 poorest households from two urban slums, 10 from each, were selected. Out of 60 households selected from the rural areas, 30 have been from each *thana*. Out of 30 poorest households, 20 from the programme village and 10 from the control village were selected. The sample households in the programme village consisted of 10 under the FFE programme and the rest outside the programme. The selected households would allow us to monitor better the poverty trend as well as to compare among the three sub-groups of the poorest households in each *thana*, namely households under the FFE programme, non-FFE households in the programme village and non-FFE households in the control village. These three gorups of the poorest households would give us three different sets of data since the base year 1993. As PRA has a repertoire of tools, the

Figure 1.3 Selection of Panel Households

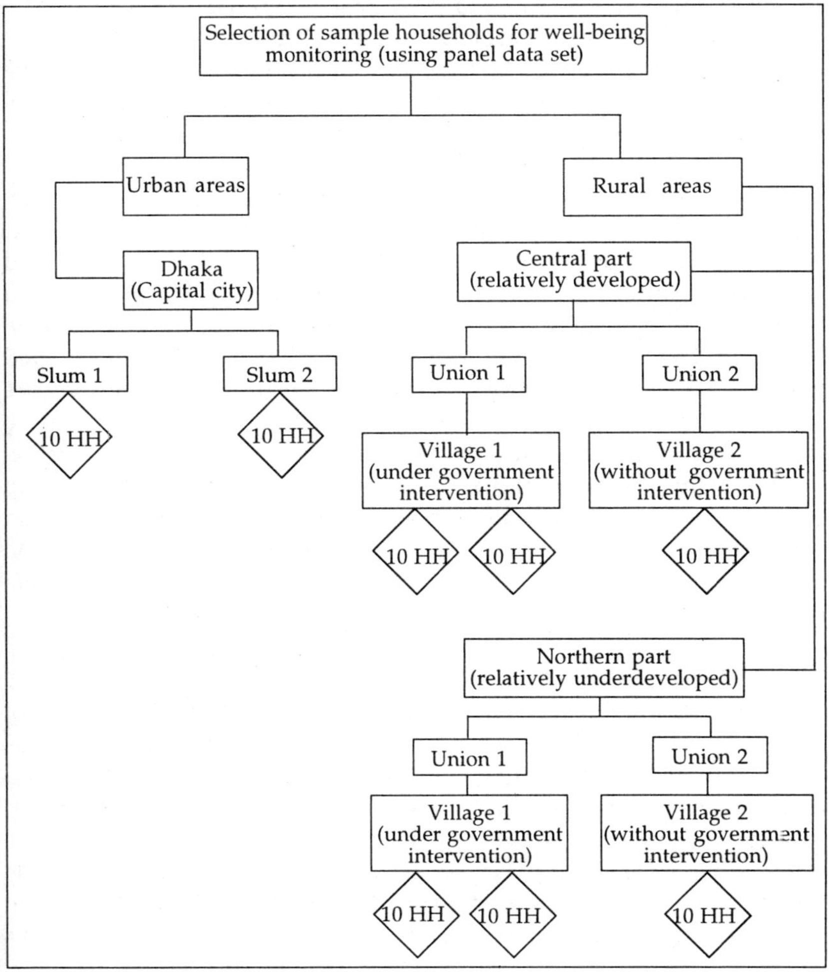

wealth/well-being ranking by cards sorting (IIED 1992 & Grandin 1994) was applied to categorize the slum-dwellers/villagers and thereby to identify/select the poorest of the poor households from the bottom in each slum/ village on the basis of their own criteria and scores given by the participants of the village through consultatioin, debate and consensus among themselves. After deciding on the criteria, they categorized the slum-dwellers and villagers known to them into four social classes viz, well-off, middle, poor and poorest. Four randomly selected different groups of slum-dwellers/villagers of each slum/village actively participated in deciding on the criteria for categorizing the slum-dwellers/villagers and ranking them based on consensus scores.

After the categorization of the slum-dwellers/villagers and selection of the sample households, a visualized format was used for each of the sample households to collect data and information on the various socio-economic indicators in the group environment.

1.3.3 Visualized Format for Collection of Data

A visualized format has been designed for collction of data from the poorest households. The format was highly illustrative and is found effective in communicating with the respondents. The format enabled the respondents to understand the questions and actively participate in recording data in it. Therefore, individual participation has been ensured in the data collection process with the help of the format. The qustionnaire was presented visually with the purpose of enabling the participants to fill it in with their own hands and also to ensure effective communication between the PRA facilitators and the participants in the group environment. The PRA facilitators facilitated the whole process. After the participants filled in the vizualized format themselves, the session was rounded off by a group discussion and cross-checking of the data on the spot.

1.3.4 Validation

The participatory poverty assessment resulting in the categorizatioin of the villagers/slum-dwellers and identification of the sample poor was carried out by four different groups of villagers/slum-dwellers. Based on the average scores worked out for each household using the scores given by the four groups, a list of village households was prepared in the descending order putting the poorest households at the bottom and the well off at the top. The prepared list of villagers/slum-dwellers containing their names, individual scores, average scores, and ranking was presented for validation to the general meeting of the villagers through discussion, modification and finalization of the findings.

1.3.5 Period of Monitoring

The poverty monitoring was conducted over the period from 1993 to 1996. Two sets of data base and impacts were collected for 1993 and 1996 respectively. Impact data for 1996 have been compared with base data for 1993 to see changes in the selected indicators. The data and information for 1993 were collected by recall method.

1.4 Organization of the Report

Apart from other chapters, the report begins with an overview highlighting the key messages of the study. The report has been organized in ten chapters including the introduction. The second chapter presents a conceptual framework for the issue of poverty. This is followed by a chapter on an overview of the existing budgetary process in Bangladesh. The trends and composition of public resource mobilization have been analysed in the fourth chapter. Chapter five highlights the impact of macroeconomic policies on the expenditure pattern of public resources. Chapter six particularly discusses some targeted poverty alleviation programmes of the government. The Food For Education (FFE) programme has been covered specially as a case study in this chapter. Chapter seven focuses on public expenditure on poverty alleviation projects. The quality of public expenditures on health and primary education has been particularly discussed in this chapter. Chapter eight is based on the people's knowledge, attitudes towards and perceptions of the annual budgetary process. Chapter nine illustrates the qualitative approach to monitoring the impacts of public expenditure on poverty. Problems identification and needs assessment by the poor have been analysed in chapter ten. The report concludes by summarizing the major findings of the study with relevant policy suggestions.

Chapter 2

POVERTY: CONCEPTUAL ISSUES

2.1 Introduction

As a buzz-word poverty has been current among development practitioners and agencies at both the national and global levels. The term poverty is being variously used with different connotations by different actors working towards the goal of its eradication. Sometimes the term is used with a hazy notion of what it actually stands for.

The plan documents of the government (The Draft Fifth Five-Year Plan 1997-2002 and the Participatory Perspective Plan for Bangladesh 1995-2010) set 'poverty alleviation' as one of the major development objectives. The government has pompously dubbed the perspective plan to be a 'watershed' in the planning history of Bangladesh in the sense of its being 'participatory', 'a pro-poor plan involving people at the grassroots level', placing 'people at the centre of development' and incorporating as 'inputs the needs and priorities of the people in all strata of society'. But, in fact, the people, let alone the poor, remained excluded as in the past from participating in the discussion of key conceptual issues like poverty while preparing this plan. Notwithstanding its high-sounding rhetoric, the plan document continues to remain as conventional as before. That is why it is neither 'participatory' nor 'pro-poor' as claimed. The recently drafted Fifth Five-Year Plan is no exception so for as the issue of participation is concerned. The poverty research so far conducted in the country is found to have been based on the conventional paradigm with its focus on poverty line-based concepts and measurements. It is, however, heartening to note that the conceptual and measurement flaws with regard to poverty are increasingly being recognized by the mainstream economists and development practitioners all over the world (Ahluwalia 1986; Chambers 1988, 1994b; UNDP 1997). The conventional poverty concept is found to be an anachronism in view of today's increased emphasis on the participatory approach which calls for a new connotation of poverty reflecting people's aspirations, needs and priorities.

The researchers associated with this study having been disenchanted with the conventional approach are trying to mould this outlook to view the world from the people's perspective in general and from the poor's in particular. To fill the conceptual gap in this respect, attempts will be made to answer some of these relevant questions: what is poverty? What are the characteristics of the poor? Why are they poor? Is this poverty situation improving or worsening? How can their poverty be alleviated? How do they evaluate different poverty alleviation programmes undertaken by the GOB and NGOs? How long will it take to alleviate poverty? Who are the beneficiaries of the anti-poverty programmes? These are some of the issues that will be addressed in the subsequent rounds of this study.

The researchers involved in this study feel it most urgent and timely to respond to some of the poverty issues and debate on it, and take a paradigmatic stand on it before we embark on an empirical investigation. This, we hope, would broadly give directions to our research activities in future.

2.2 Poverty Line Approach Versus Participatory Approach

2.2.1 Concepts and Measurement: Conventional Approach

Professional Poverty Trap. The analytical framework used by professionals to study poverty is essentially external. Poverty is viewed a *priori* by a third party, as physical-needs deprivation due to private consumption shortfalls (Shaffer 1996). Poverty is commonly used in two different senses: one, it is used as a broad, blanket word to refer to the whole spectrum of deprivation and ill-being; and the other, in its narrower usage, it has a technical definition for the purposes of measurement and comparison. Conventionally, poverty is defined as low income as it is reported, recorded and analysed; or often as low consumption, which is easier to measure. This is known as income-poverty or consumption-poverty. Poverty defined in these senses are measurable. This permits comparisons worldwide between the income, or more usually, consumption levels of different households, regions and nations. It also makes possible the measurement and assessment of poverty lines. These provide time series measurements to show how income-poverty or consumption-poverty is changing, and for that matter, how well a government can be presumed to be doing in the reduction of poverty in these senses. Despite these advantages of the poverty line (PL) measures, income-poverty is only one measure of many, and it is suspect because it serves the needs of power-prone professionals who hardly emerge from the realities of the poor at the peripheries (Chambers 1988, 1994b). In other words, poverty and deprivation are seen as what are measured and shown in statistics. Deprivation (and poverty) is then defined, not by the changing and varied wants and needs of the poor, but by the more static and standardized wants and needs of professionals. Analysts' needs for numbers narrow their perceptions (Box 2.1). Conceptually, professionals are caught in their own poverty trap (ibid.).

Objective Versus Subjective Measures of Poverty. Proponents of the conventional approach argue that an absolute and objectively determined poverty line is the most appropriate means of measuring poverty (Greeley 1994). In other words, they argue that income/consumption is the best single proxy for poverty (Baulch 1996) and offer the following statistical proof in favour of this approach: i) Its high correlation with income and

Box 2.1 The Underlying McNamara Fallacy of Measurement Bias of the Conventional Poverty Line Approach

Fallacy	Comment
The first step is to measure whatever can be easily measured	This is OK as far as it goes
The second step is to disregard that which cannot be measured or give it an arbitrary quantitative value	This is artificial and misleading
The third step is to disregard that which cannot be measured	This is blindness
The fourth step is to say that what cannot be easily measured really does not exist	This is suicide

Source: Chambers 1988

Note: There is a subtle difference between the steps two and three. In case something is not measurable, the second step allows one the possibility to give an arbitrary value whereas for the third it is totally disregarded for the sake of the researcher's convenience.

expenditure is advanced (Ravallion 1992); ii) The main use of poverty-lines lies in a comparative analysis over time or between groups of households. Precision in setting the line is less important than consistent application; iii) It is absolute and objective poverty lines that provide relevant information on a poverty reduction policy and encourages appropriate resource allocations; iv) The poverty line is not locally determined on a subjective basis but reflects a set of needs that are universal. This implies detachment from any specific individual's assessment (Greeley 1994); v) Quantifiability is usually mentioned to be an important quality of the poverty-line method.

Despite the above-noted merits, the absoluteness and objectivity of the poverty line-based methodology have been countered with the following epistemological/philosophical arguments: i) It simply implies a single 'reality' and is merely an attempt to attribute 'scientific rigour' to something which is only somebody's value judgement. The observation that 'we interpret all other societies in the categories of our own' (Taylor 1985 quoted in Shaffer 1996) underlines the quantitative framework which is the basis of poverty-line-based reasoning. ii) It is true that there is a special seductiveness of numbers in the modern society. Numbers convey a sense of precision and accuracy even if the measurements that yielded the numbers are relatively unreliable, invalid and meaningless. The point, however, is not to be anti-number, the point is to be pro-meaningfulness. Numbers do not protect us against any bias, they merely disguise it. All statistical data are based on someone's definition of what to measure and how to measure it. An 'objective' statistic like the consumer price index is really made up of very subjective decisions about what consumer items to include in the index. Periodically government economists change the basis and definition of such indices. Quantitative methods are not necessarily synonymous with objectivity. Objectivity is sometimes confused with consensual validation of something by multiple observers. In many instances, it was found that the majority of scientists (or other people) were factually wrong (Patton 1990).

Absolute Poverty? There is no absolute poverty line as such. 'Poverty lines vary between climates, cultures, and social and economic environments. The poverty line for the USA is at a substantially higher income level than that for Bangladesh. The US Bureau of Census publishes figures showing that 15% of Americans live below the official poverty line. Clearly they are much better off than the majority of Bangladeshis' (Streeten 1990). This is why 'some authors regard all poverty as relative.... In view of the fact that the absolute poverty is partly a function of average living standards, it is clear that "absolute" does not mean fixed in time. The absolute level of poverty can rise, as incomes increase' (ibid.).

Poverty Measurement Issues. Poverty-line expenditure has two components: food and non-food items. The inconsistency is most likely to crop up in the use of techniques followed to estimate the cost of both food and non-food items. 'The minimum food requirements are derived normatively by calculating how much the minimum food requirements would cost; while the non-food items are determined by observing how much people actually spend. In order to remove the inconsistency we would have to assume that what people actually happen to spend is what they need to spend on non-food items... If the non-food items were also determined normatively, the poverty line would be quite different, probably higher' (ibid.).

In addition to the above procedural complexity, the application of these methods is found to have some common problems:

1. Minimum energy requirements vary from individual to individual due to differences in activity levels, conversion efficiencies and size.
2. The appropriate allowance for non-food consumption also varies between individuals and locations. For example, the share of non-food expenditure in total expenditure is usually much higher for the urban than the rural poor.
3. Unless constant purchasing parity is ensured, poverty lines will not be comparable between locations and socio-economic groups (Baulch 1996).

Identification Problem. Identification means addressing the question : 'who are the poor?' The 'absolute','objective' measures of poverty favoured by the income/consumption approach have numerous identification problems. The poor may, for example, be wrongly identified if incomes fluctuate substantially, or if consumption of state-provided commodities and non-market transactions is under-reported. Conventional income/ consumption measures may also be better for identifying poverty among men rather than among women, because women's poverty is more dependent on the cultural context (ibid.).

Lack of Focus on Inequality. The conventional poverty measures are mainly concerned with the trend, incidence/prevalence, intensity/depth and severity of poverty. 'Head-count' measures, poverty gap ratio and Foster-Greer-Thorbecke index all have various implications centred round the poor below the measured poverty line. They have nothing to do with the non-poor lying above the line. Surprisingly, although these measures offer various policy steps to reduce poverty among the poor they fail miserably as to redirecting income flows from the non-poor to the poor (Rahman 1997, Ravallion 1992).

Static Approach. The poverty-line (PL) appreaet is essentially static. It records changes, but does not itself change (Chambers 1988). Although 'absolute' does not mean fixed in time and 'absolute poverty can rise as incomes increase', the PL measures are not amenable to changes as such (Streeten 1990).

Further, the PL measures tend to provide a 'static description' of poverty and they fail to provide a convincing analysis needed by policy makers for understanding the effectiveness of poverty reduction efforts. They do not focus on the process, i e causes of poverty. Whatever a PL-based analysis tells is nothing but 'outcome indicators, which describe the current poverty situation but tell one little about how one arrived at that state or what may be expected to happen in the future' (Baulch 1996). That is, the PL measures fail to 'track how households income and expenditure vary over time.... To ensure that poverty measurement provides the causal analysis needed by policy makers, more attention needs to be paid to process indicators and the dynamics of poverty' (ibid.).

Reductionist Approach. Poverty is a multi-faceted phenomenon. But the conventional approach applies a single criterion. Complex realities are simplified to manageable figures on a single scale. Sometimes this is done through composite indices with weightings for different dimensions. This approach furnishes a narrow and reductionist view that fails to understand the complex, diverse, local realities in which the poor live. Most professional analyses of poverty use the single, simple scale of consumption. Given the many dimensions of poverty/deprivation, this reductionism over-simplifies. When 10 or 20 dimensions could be listed, the specification of taking just one indicator is not far short of heroic (Chambers 1988, Baulch 1996, Streeten 1990).

2.2.2 Concepts and Measurement: Participatory Approach

The participatory approach aims to elicit local people's own perceptions of poverty/deprivation and to harness their own priorities in the complex and heterogeneous societies in which they live.

Dialogical Process. The participatory approach puts more emphasis on the appropriate process where people can get involved and actively participate in expressing their critical views, conducting fact-finding analysis, articulating their felt needs and priorities, and working out action plans for their collective upliftment (Rahman 1994). The dialogical process can take various forms, namely group meeting, role playing, popular theatre, chorus, camp, people's workshop, etc. The process promotes critical awareness of their environment, self-reliance and self-mobilization of the underprivileged. These indeed empower the people by raising their leaders and establishing their access to the knowledge generation process. Apart from serving as a mechanism to cross-check data and information, the process can facilitate the people's empowerment process as well.

Realities of the Poor. The participatory approach and practices enable the underprevileged to express and analyse their multiple realities. Many poor people's realities are local, complex, diverse, dynamic and unpredictable.

The values and preferences of local people typically contrast with those of the better off, outsiders and professionals. They need and want to be able to take a long view. They can locally manage greater complexity. Their values, preferences and criteria are typically numerous, diverse and dynamic and often differ from those supposed for them by professionals. Local people are themselves diverse, with sharp contrasts of preferences and priorities by age, gender, social and ethnic group, and wealth (Chambers 1997).

The Poor's Perception of Well-being. Poor people view their well-being not in terms of a single aspect but in terms of many. Well-being as perceived by them may be sub-divided into different types: physical, economic, social, psychological and spiritual. Among these, the professionals' tendency is to concentrate on the physical and economic aspects, which are also measurable. This neglects those which are social, psychological and spiritual (Chambers 1988). The critical qualitative dimension of these aspects has some components like: perception of security in livelihood, the sense of freedom from harassment and abuse at home and at work, the feeling of dignity in day-to-day transactions, the belief in the reliability of officialdom, the expectation (or lack of it) that life will improve for one's offspring and so forth (Appadurai 1985 quoted in Chambers 1988).

Poor people's priorities broadly include:

1. **Incomes and consumption:** The importance of incomes and consumption is recognized by professionals and poor people alike, especially the very poor who are said to live 'from-hand-to-mouth.'
2. **Net assets:** The desire of poor people to command and own assets is a common tendency, whether these are land, a hut or house, equipment and tools, livestock, consumable durables, or others. But it is noteworthy that in poverty-line thinking the net asset position of a household is not taken into account. It is more likely that accepting an asset on loan may worsen, not improve, the net asset portfolio of a household even if its income rises. Similarly, it may so happen that the landless labourer households on an average have higher incomes per household than marginal peasants, but their total assets are worth much less. Marginal

peasant households are much better off in terms of assets than landless labourers, though their incomes are lower. Assuming equal average household sizes, the poverty-line thinking, however, identifies the landless labourer households to be better off than the marginal peasants (Chambers 1988).

3. **Independence and self-respect:** The desire to be free of debt is also strong. Poor people, particularly women, have a horror of debt. Debt, as is well known, is often linked with powerlessness, subservience and exploitation. Poor people are found to have a distaste for debt not just because of high interest rates, or forced labour from family members, but also because of 'abuses and insults', 'helplessness, insults and pain', and 'touching the feet' of the lenders. It is striking, though not surprising, that security, independence and self-respect have been overlooked in the numerical poverty measurement. The operational concepts and data of planners and economists exclude these dimensions, so important to the poor.
4. **Vulnerability and security:** These are the neglected aspects of poverty research. People with fewer assets are more vulnerable to contingencies and harder hit by them than those with more. Contingencies include physical incapacity (sickness, the child bearing sequence, accidents and disablement) ; disasters (floods, drought, death of able-bodied household members, etc); social needs (dowry, bridewealth, weddings, funerals, etc); unproductive expenditure (on petty business, a bribe, an offering, a legal fee, etc); seasonal adversity and lack of food; and exploitation (threats, blackmail, violence, imprisonment, fines, etc).

Dimensions of Deprivation. Poor people experience deprivation and disadvantage multi-dimensionally. Deprived people are often thought of as being uniform. But the poor, in fact, are found to have more diversity than the non-poor. The poor usually experience eight types of deprivation in their life (Chambers 1994b). These deprivations capture some of the poor people's realities. Of the eight types of deprivation, the first three, as delineated below, are better recognized:

1. **Poverty:** It refers to lack of physical necessities, assets, and income. It includes the income-poor but it is more than that. Poverty can be distinguished from other dimensions of deprivation such as physical weakness, isolation, vulnerability and powerlessness.
2. **Social inferiority:** It can be ascribed, acquired, or related to age and life cycle. It can be socially defined as genetical inferiority or disadvantaged condition, or being 'lower' in terms of class, caste,

race, gender, ethnicity, social group or occupation, or linked with age, as with children and sometimes daughters-in-law.

3. **Isolation:** It refers to being peripheral and cut off. Poor people can be isolated geographically, living in a 'remote' area; isolated in communication, lacking contacts and information, including not being able to read; isolated due to lack of access to social services and markets; and isolated due to lack of social and economic supports.

   The following dimensions, though prominent in the life of the poor and weak, have been relatively neglected by development professionals.

4. **Physical weakness:** Professionals being dependent on their brains fail to realize the importance of the value of a healthy, strong body and the disadvantage of a body which is sick, weak or disabled. In defining ill-being and well-being, poor people mention physical weakness, sickness or disability, which both are bad in themselves and bad in their effects on others.

5. **Vulnerability:** Sometimes the words 'vulnerable' and 'poor' are used interchangeably. But vulnerability is not the same as income-poverty or other quantitative measures of poverty. It means not lack or want, but defencelessness, insecurity and exposure to contingencies. It has two sides: the external side of exposure to risks, shocks and stress, and the internal side of defencelessness, meaning a lack of means to cope without damaging loss. Loss can take many forms such as becoming or being physically weaker, economically impoverished, socially dependent, and humiliated or psychologically harmed.

   With the increase in vulnerability, livelihoods of the poor may become less sustainable although their incomes may go up. This is why the poor people at the margin often prefer a lower income with less risk of debt and dependence.

6. **Seasonality:** The seasonal dimensions of deprivation are less understood by professionals who are urban based and season proofed. Yet in tropical seasonality, many adverse factors for the poor often coincide during the rains (hard agricultural work, shortage of food, scarcity of cash, indebtedness, sickness, etc).

7. **Powerlessness:** The poor are powerless. Being dispersed, it is difficult for them to get organized or bargain. Often physically weak and economically vulnerable, they lack influence and can easily be ignored and exploited.

8. **Humiliation:** Self-respect, with freedom from dependence, is perhaps the dimension most overlooked and under-valued by professionals. Poor people often have to embrace humiliation in the form of 'abuses and insults', helplessness, 'insults and pain', etc.

Deprivation Trap. Poverty in its broader and popular sense is a synonym for deprivation. Deprivation has many dimensions and connotations. It can be seen as locational or as lack of access to services and resources, etc. Many sets of categories are possible. So far as deprivation is concerned, five core clusters of disadvantage of households are identified, namely poverty, physical weakness, vulnerability, isolation and powerlessness. These can be presented as a composite sketch of the household. These five clusters of disadvantage interlock and reinforce each other to form a deprivation trap. This is variously described as the 'vicious circle of poverty' or the 'syndrome of poverty' (Chambers 1983). Linking the five clusters gives twenty possible relations, which in their negative forms interlock like a web to trap people in their deprivation. The strength of these linkages varies, however (Figure 2.1).

Livelihoods Not Income. Contrary to professional prejudice, the livelihoods of the poorest people are diverse and often complex. There is an ancient Greek saying that 'the fox has many ideas but the hedgehog

Figure 2.1 The Deprivation Trap

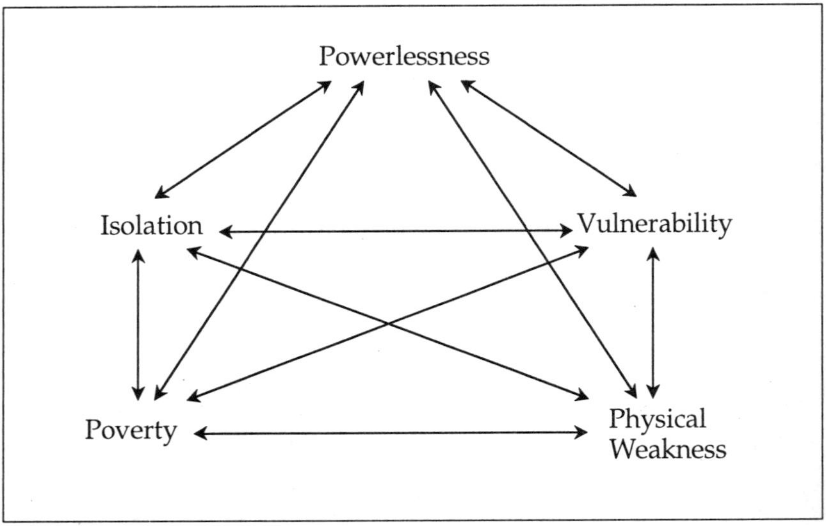

Source: Chambers 1983

has one big idea'. By analogy, most full-time employees found in the North and in industrial sectors in the South are hedgehogs, with one big idea, a job as a source of livelihood. Other hedgehogs are those poor people, often powerless, desperate or exploited, who have but one survival strategy. However, most of the poor people in the South, though, and more now in the North, are foxes. They have not one source of support but several. They maintain a portfolio of activities (Chambers 1997). Fox strategies are rarely completely recognized by outsiders. They are unlikely to be fully revealed, if at all, by conventional questionnaire surveys. Questionnaire surveys tend to construct a standardized, short and simple reality. Besides, many aspects of rural livelihoods are not captured in either income or consumption-based survey data. This is because they are neither commoditized, nor evident enough to the researcher to be allocated 'imputed values' (ibid.).

Poor People's Own Criteria. Investigations, especially questionnaire surveys, almost always start from outsiders' assumptions about the poor, using outsiders' assumptions and indicators. It is rare for poor people themselves to be consulted about their own criteria for well-being.

Unlike questionnaire surveys, the participatory approach elicits the categories and concepts which farmers and villagers are keen to use for assuming changes in their economic status. The number of their criteria may be as many as 30-40 or even more (Box 2.2). The major point is that people's own criteria of well-being can differ from those of a strict PL concept. There are many aspects of the quality of life which PL thinking and measurement cannot capture. Poor people's priorities can differ from those presumed for them by the non-poor. Most obviously, PL-thinking, with its single-scale numerical definition of poverty according to reported levels of income or consumption, misses much and can mislead. Types and sequences of deprivation need better definition and this can be done through applying common sense categories, through identifying relationships which statistics do not reveal and most of all through learning their priorities and their criteria of well-being from poor people themselves.

This is not to assert that the poor people know everything, and the non-poor know nothing. But it is to suggest that one of the least recognized areas of ignorance on the part of the non-poor is poor people's own relative priorities. To overcome that ignorance requires a concerted and imaginative effort (Chambers 1988).

Box 2.2 People's Criteria of Well-being: An Example

(Expressed in a negative form)
The participatory approach aims to elicit local people's own conceptions of poverty/deprivation and to harness their priorities in the complex and heterogeneous societies in which they live. The number of their criteria may be as many as 30-40 or even more.

The following are some of the criteria used by local people in Asia and sub-Saharan Africa for poverty and 'ill-being' which have been drawn from various participatory studies.

- Disabled (eg blind, crippled, mentally impaired, chronically sick, etc)
- Widowed
- Lacking land, livestock, farm equipment, grinding mills etc
- Cannot decently bury their dead
- Cannot send their children to school
- Having more mouths-to-feed, fewer hands-to-help
- Lacking able-bodied members who can fend for their families in the event of crisis
- With bad housing
- Having vices (eg alcoholism)
- Being poor in manpower (in the demographic sense), lacking social supports
- Having to put children in employment
- Single parents
- Having to accept demeaning or low-status work
- Having food security for only a few months each year
- Being dependent on common property resources

These criteria tell us more about local people's multi-dimensional conception of poverty than conventional income/consumption measures.

Source: UNDP 1996a

Reversals: Whose Reality Counts? Self-critical commitment demands personal insight and reflection. If believing is seeing, we have to question belief in order to see well. Learning is then affected through doubt, self-examination and willingness to change, seeking self-correcting engagement with dynamic realities and making learning a way of life. In a phrase, this is epistemological awareness, awareness of how we learn, how that affects what we think, and know, and how we perceive and distort the realities of others (Chambers 1997).

Three lessons stand out. Each entails an up-ending or reversal of the normal condition which generated and sustained the error.

1. The first lesson is to replace dominance with difference and respect, and to reverse positions and sides. The solution is to encourage and enable lowers, so that it is they as lowers, not others as uppers, who appraise and analayse their reality. The lesson is to reverse power relations through changing behaviour.
2. The second lesson is to reduce social and physical distance.
3. The third lesson is to get rid of professional ego.

Reversals of power relations through changed behaviour, through uppers spending time close to lowers, and through redefining the professional ego lead to the synergy of a new professionalism.

The deceptions of power will, however, persist. But we now have approaches and methods, such as those of Participatory Rural Appraisal (PRA), which confront the problems of uppers' behaviour and attitudes, their distance, and their ego, and which provide the tools for lowers to conduct their own analysis, and to define and express their own realities. So the answers to the questions:

- whose categories and criteria count?
- whose values and preferences?
- whose analysis and planning?
- whose action?
- whose monitoring and evaluation?
- whose reality and whose truth?

can now, in practical terms, be more 'their', those of lowers and local people, and less 'ours', those of uppers and of outsider professionals (Chambers 1994a).

2.3 Conclusion

The conventional and participatory approaches are found fundamentally different with regard to poverty research (Boxes 2.3, 2.4 and 2.5). Methodologically, the conventional approach employs researchers' quantitative analytical framework (ie external) which is

Box 2.3 Analytical Approaches to the Study of Poverty

ASPECTS/COMPONENTS		INCOME/CONSUMP-TION APPROACH	PARTICIPATORY APPROACH
	Determination of well-being	External: Third party *a priori* determination	Internal/External: Interactive group determination
	Measurement of well-being	Quantitative: Income/ consumption expenditure levels	Qualitative/quantitative multiple criteria
METHODOLOGY	Stance towards the consumer	Respectful: The consumer is (usually) sovereign	Critical: Discursive examination of given preferences
	Sources of data	Questionnaire survey	Participatory poverty assessment
	Objectives	Description	Critical understanding/ empowerment
CONCEPTIONS	Constituents of ill-being	Basic needs deprivation	Multiple deprivations
OF ILL-BEING	Sources of ill-being	Inadequate consumption of goods and services	Multiple Sources

Source: Shaffer 1996

basically unidimensional (income/expenditure levels) and it employes the questionnaire survey method for the collection of data. Whereas, the participatory approach makes use of both internal/external and qualitative/quantitative methods where participants' realities are reflected through group consensus in dialogical sessions. Multi-dimensionality, diversity and critical group reflection stand out in the participatory approach. As far as the conception of ill-being is concerned, both the approaches look at the constituents and sources of ill-being in quite different ways. Basic needs deprivation and multiple deprivation are the cornerstones of income/consumption-based poverty line thinking and participatory poverty assessment respectively. Moreover, the conventional and participatory approaches are based on two different sets of realities where professionals and poor people play the key roles respectively.

Box 2.4 Contrasting Tendencies in Professional and Poor People's Realities

Professionals' Realities	Poor People's Realities
Universal	Local, specific
Simplified	Complex
Reductionist	Holistic
Standardized	Diverse
Physical	Experiential
Quantified	Unquantified
Income-poverty	Multi-dimensional deprivation
Employment	Livelihood

Source: Chambers 1994b

Box 2.5 Measurement Criteria: Standarized Central Criteria Versus Decentralized Local Criteria

The conventional/PL approach uses standard measures. Most obviously, PL thinking, with its single-scale numerical definition of poverty according to reported levels of income or consumption, misses much and can mislead. There are many aspects of the quality of life which PL-thinking and measurement cannot capture.

Poor people's priorities can differ from those presumed for them by the non-poor. The values and preferences of local poor people typically contrast with those of the better off, outsiders and professionals. People's own ideas and indicators of well-being vary according to locality, region, social group, gender and so on. A concerted and imaginative effort needs to be made to learn the poor's priorities and criteria of well-being from themselves.

Source: Chambers 1988

In view of the emerging consensus among a wide range of development practitioners and partners on there is a pressing need for the participation of the poor in the articulation of their realities to break the age-old elite monopoly over property and knowledge. The monopoly over one reinforces and perpetuates that over the other. As far as sustainability is concerned, it is important to establish people's control over knowledge and its generation process as well as over the means of property. The dual importance of material and non-material (knowledge) production has been elucidated in the following words:

> The dominant view of social transformation has been preoccupied with the need for changing the existing, oppressive structures of relations in material production. This is certainly a necessary task. But (and this is the distinctive viewpoint of Participatory Action Research-PAR) the domination of the masses by the elites is rooted not only in the polarization of control over the means of material production but also over the means of knowledge production including, as in the former case, the social power to determine what is valid or useful knowledge. Irrespective of which of these two polarizations sets off a process of domination, it can be argued that one reinforces the other in augmenting and perpetuating this process. By now, in most polarized societies, the gap between those who have social power over the process of knowledge generation (an important form of 'capital' in as much as knowledge is a form of social power) and those who have not, have reached dimensions no less formidable than the gap in access to the means of physical production. History shows that a convergence of the latter gap in no way ensures a convergence of the former; on the contrary, existence of the latter has been seen to offset the advantages of revolutionary closures of the former and has set off a process of domination once again (Rahman 1994).

The participatory approach enables and empowers the poor through social consciousness, self-critical awareness and social mobilization. It further leads them to achieve progressively greater self-reliance through collective efforts being guided by the new pro-people and pro-poor paradigm. The participatory approach as a guiding approach of the present study will continue to be the same for the next rounds of the same study so as to make it more pro-poor and pro-people.

The inner spirit of this new conceptualization of poverty runs across the entire study though not always so evenly. The chapters on macro data focus on the extent of allocation of resources for the poor and those based on micro investigation try to reflect the reality of poverty as experienced by the poor.

Chapter 3

AN OVERVIEW OF THE BUDGETARY PROCESS

3.1 The Function and Scope of the Budget

The functions of a budget are broadly categorized as:

- allocation and distribution of scarce resources among competing ends;
- stabilization; and
- growth.

Given the acute constraint of resources, both national and foreign, there are considerable trade-offs between and among these goals. The accommodation of these trade-offs in line with the development priorities is the challenge encountered by the policy makers.

Although the annual budget of the government is the most important fiscal event which affects the living conditions of all social groups, the process of budget preparation and implementation does not appear to be a transparent exercise. While organized richer groups (eg chambers of commerce and industries) with better access to the bureaucracy and political tents can lobby for their interests before the finalization of the budget, the organized poor not to speak of the unorganized, can hardly influence the mechanism of budget preparation. As such they have no control over the macroeconomic policies envisaged in the budget although they cannot escape the effects, whether positive or negative, of those decisions.

It is usually observed that most Finance Ministers make over-optimistic pledges for public revenue and expenses. They seem to rely mostly on the submission of the revenue officials without taking into account the capacity of the economy to respond to the high revenue demands. As a consequence, the government invariably lands into budget deficit. The so-called 'surplus budget' is deceptive in the sense that it only refers to the surplus in the revenue budget; more than half of the development budget is still financed from external resources despite the spectacular increase in domestic resource mobilization in recent years.

Furthermore, the scope of the ADP is often curtailed due to unforeseen fluctuations in the external resource flow. This is done by adjusting public investment in the immediately productive sectors as well as social sectors. These measures widen the gap between the targets and the achievements of the poverty alleviation programmes.

The budget is the financial statement of the government intended for a fiscal year from July 1 of the 'current year' to June 30 of the following year. Usually, it is presented at the Parliament by the Finance Minister by mid-June and approved in its entirety by mid-July. The budget is structured by two broad components: the consolidated fund and the public account of the Republic. The consolidated fund covers all revenues, borrowings and recoveries of loans on the receipt side and all disbursements other than those chargeable to deposits, reserve accounts and remittances. On the other hand, the public account of the Republic comprises transactions in respect of remittance and suspense heads of account. We shall concentrate our attention entirely on the consolidated fund.

3.2 Structure of Budget Documents

Different documents of the budget are presented in typical forms. Government's expenditure proposals in the budget are presented under the head of 'demand for grants'. Usually, 'demand for grants' in the current budget includes expenditure proposed in terms of organizational units and objects of expenditure. The 'demand for grants' in the ADP shows allocations for expenditure against projects. In the case of social sectors, expenditure projects are synonymously called programmes.

The classification pattern in the budget as a whole can be described as a functional-cum-objects classification. But there is an absence of programme and performance classification which would give a break-down of programmes and activities in each broad functional area along with relevant performance units.

3.3 Major Heads of ADP

Allocations in the ADP are shown by sectors/sub-sectors and for projects under each sector/sub-sector. It is found that all the allocations cannot be identified under two major heads categorized as productive sectors and social sectors. So another sector is shown as infrastructure support for productive activities (PSI). But this classification cannot make all the sub-sectors very distinct. The ADP includes certain programmes which cover productive, infrastructure as well as social sector activities like the Annual Technical Assistance Programme (ATAP), the Self-Financed Programme, Development Assistance to *Thanas*, etc. These are included in different sectoral heads according to their nature of activities.

3.4 Major Heads of the Revenue Budget

Not all the allocations in the revenue budget can be classified unambiguously. Allocations and expenditures under defence, various organs of the government, public order and safety, subsidies, etc can be accounted neither in the directly productive sectors, nor in the social sectors. Such items are separately classified as non-productive overheads (NP). The revenue budget has a large part called 'unexpected expenditure' which comes down significantly in the Revised Estimates as funds are allocated out of this head to different ministries during the financial year.

3.5 Other Major Heads

Government operates some programmes which are purely development-oriented but are not included in the ADP, eg the FFW and the VGD. The financial impacts of FFW and VGD activities are reflected in the overall budget outcome through the net position of the food budget.

3.6 Administrative Structure

Though the Ministry of Finance administers the whole budget process, it does not bear the sole responsibility for budget preparation. Various ministries and divisions are involved in the budgetary process as shown in Annex II Table 3.1.

3.7 Formulation of the Budget Estimates

3.7.1 Revenue-Expenditure Estimates: Formulation

The administrative units where the expenditure takes place send the respective estimates to the Comptroller/Auditor General of Accounts and the Ministry of Finance through their respective controlling authorities. Usually, these estimates present the revised (latest) estimates for the current year and the budget estimates for the forthcoming year.

These initial estimates are formulated on the basis of trends in the actual expenditure during the first quarter of the ongoing financial year (July-September), and the designated deadline for their submission to the Ministry of Finance is October 31. An important feature of the expenditure estimates in recent years has been the priority attached to the operation and maintenance of existing assets, especially those in the areas of health, education, public works and roads and highways.

3.7.2 Revenue-Expenditure Estimates: Scrutiny

After receiving the estimates from the controlling officers, the Ministry of Finance checks their completeness. The process of checking and scrutinizing becomes easier when the Ministry of Finance receives the actual expenditure documents from the Comptroller General who by this time reprocesses the actual estimates. Any expenditure to be included in the budget must be approved by the competent authority according to the existing delegation of financial powers.

After completing its scrutiny, the Ministry of Finance sends the estimates to the controlling authorities with a brief explanation about the new estimates. The controlling authorities then study these explanations and argue with the Ministry of Finance in the budget meeting which is usually held in the months March-April. By this time, the second quarter of the ongoing fiscal year is passed. The estimates are given the final shape at the budget meetings after taking into consideration the actual expenditure of these six months and other relevant factors.

The final decisions are taken on the basis of judgments about the trends revealed by the actual expenditure and receipts of the past six or eight months and the acceptability of specific items outside the trends.

3.7.3 Revenue-Budget-Receipt Estimates: Formulation and Scrutiny

a. Non-tax revenue. The estimates of non-tax receipts (profits from nationalized institutions, enterprises, net receipts, various fees, user charges, etc) are formulated by the respective agencies and ministries concerned and their scrutiny and finalization are done by the Ministry of Finance in the same manner as has been discussed earlier. An important point is that the mobilization of revenue receives less attention than the estimation of expenditures as is evident in the chronic losses incurred by the public sector corporations.

b. Major taxes, land revenues and other minor taxes. The National Board of Revenue and the Ministry of Land formulate the major tax estimates on the basis of the existing trends in the actual collection and, in some cases, relating some tax receipts and the variables that determine the magnitude of these receipts. An intensive and direct interaction takes place between the Ministry of Finance and the National Board of Revenue during the Budget months (January-May).

c. Foreign loans and grants. Bangladesh receives foreign loans and grants in three forms: project aid, commodity assistance and food aid. The Economic Relations Division (ERD) is responsible for the formulation of estimates of project and commodity assistance, and estimates of food aid are formulated by joint collaboration between ERD and the Ministry of Food.

The estimates of project aid and technical assistance receipts are largely based on information about the likely progress of ongoing and new projects covered by the existing commitments. The estimates of commodity assistance are based on information about the utilization rate of the existing commitments and a proportion of forthcoming commitments in consonance with past trends.

The Food Department is responsible for formulating the estimates of expenditure or food procurement to be financed by food aid as well as by domestic resources. Some payments in kind (eg FFW and VGD) are also incorporated in these estimates.

3.7.4 Annual Development Programme Formulation

The implementing agencies of the ADP and the Planning Commission proceed parallelly to formulate and scrutinize the estimates in the revised ADP and the expenditures to be proposed for the forthcoming year. These are projectwise estimates formulated by different incumbent agencies in the light of guidelines provided by the Planning Commission in regard to priority and phasing. After the initial scrutiny carried out by the Planning Commission, the agencies formulate revised estimates on the basis of assured foreign aid financing, completion of projects and those which were marked earlier as 'core'projects. All these procedures take place in November. The final shape of the ADP, both the revised one for the current year and the proposed one for the forthcoming year, depends on the availability of resources as determined by the Resource Committee of the Government.

Estimates of the ADP are submitted to the National Economic Council (NEC) for final approval with some modifications made at the interministerial meeting. After its approval the ADP is forwarded to the Ministry of Finance for recasting it as 'demand for grants'.

3.8 Comments on the Budgetary Process

The management of the budgetary process is conventional, and in most respects, unsatisfactory. We shall discuss below some of the limitations of the budgetary process.

3.8.1 Planning

a. It has been recognized that the public sector has a limited capacity to direct aggregate resource flows and that excessive reliance on discretionary actions can inhibit growth by restraining private sector initiatives and encouraging wasteful rent-seeking activities. Hence, most countries (including Bangladesh) now place emphasis on policy reforms to create a macroeconomic climate which provides incentives for growth while using detailed planning procedures primarily for the public expenditure programmes. However, the planning system used in Bangladesh remains highly centralized which sustains a top-down decision-making process and inhibits participatory decision-making.

b. The macroeconomic model used for the five-year plans is complex and does not provide a flexible tool for medium-term economic forecasting.[1] The five-year plan itself contains an extensive discussion of sectoral strategies, but in practice it is used primarily to set allocations for the ADP and provide a list of new projects to be included in the ADP over the five-year planning period.[2]

c. The project planning framework fails to address a number of important issues, such as defining an optimum project pipeline and enlisting new projects within the given resource constraint.

d. The expenditure classification system for the budget maintains an artificial division between recurrent and capital expenditures, which contributes to the neglect of the need for the budgetary allocations for operations and maintenance (O&M).

e. As long as a major proportion of the Development Budget is financed by foreign aid which is very often tied and meant to give special

---

1. The Third Five-Year Plan (TFYP) used a 36-sector general equilibrium model.

2. Many of the projects on the TFYP list were defined by given new names to the old projects. New projects are added to the list and existing project names are often adapted to suit other purposes.

advantages to donor economies, local planners cannot fully exercise their authority in expenditure planning. As a result, although the ADP is approved by the concerned ministries, it has to be revised considerably in accordance with the availability of foreign resources and the will of the donors. This is the reason why the development budget diverges from the ADP, and the development priorities are compromised.

3.8.2 Budgeting

a. One crucial problem in the process of budgeting is the fragmentation of budget responsibilities. The Planning Commission is at present responsible for setting budget allocations for the ongoing projects. But this process is unsatisfactory as it often relies on outdated cost estimates of the project proposals rather than on realistic estimates of current requirements. In addition, the Planning Commission's role overlaps with that of the Development Wing of the Ministry of Finance, which is responsible for translating the ADP into a statutory budget document (the Development Budget) and maintaining expenditure control over the investment programme. The Finance Division of the Ministry of Finance also prepares the Revenue Budget and the Budget Summary Statements. The preparation of the Revenue Budget is done on an incremental basis, with the Expenditure Control Wing scrutinizing the budget requests in detail. Since the objective is expenditure control rather than programme performance, this process has contributed to a general decline in operating funds over the years. Moreover, because of the fragmentation of responsibilities and differing objectives for each part of the budget process, the sectoral ministries are discouraged from taking an active role in trying to influence the expenditure priorities.

b. Each of the major budget documents utilizes its own expenditure classification system which is often inconsistent with the other documents.

c. The ADP uses a rudimentary programme budget format. None of the expenditure classification systems can be reconciled with others without substantial efforts and without facing considerable ambiguity. As a result, the pattern of sectoral allocations remains obscure to all but the experienced budget officials. This contributes to developing a situation where the budget process is viewed as a technical exercise rather than an important means for expressing the government's priorities in the public expenditure programme. As a result, many relevant stakeholders cannot participate effectively in the process of budget making.

3.8.3 Accounting and Expenditure Control

a. The current procedures for expenditure monitoring are inadequate for tracking and controlling public expenditures totalling in the order of US $ 3 billions annually. In the course of the budget year, the Ministry of Finance monitors its financial position by looking at its cash balance held with the Bangladesh Bank. More detailed information on expenditures at a ministerial or departmental level is available only after lengthy delays and at too aggregate a level to permit the data to be used to monitor the detailed outcome of the expenditure programme. In order to prevent over-spending, the Ministry of Finance relies on a detailed system of line-item expenditure controls backed up by strict authorization procedures, rather than monitoring expenditures on a broader basis. This system hinders the delegation of responsibility and accountability to the respective ministries and agencies. Moreover, there is a growing concern that the present system cannot cope with the increasing complexity of the expenditure programme, leading to opportunities for misappropriation of public funds.

The Ministry of Finance introduced a plan in 1983 to deal with this situation. The centralized functions of audit and the preparation of accounts were to be separated with the responsibility for pre-audit and preliminary preparation of accounts delegated to the operating ministries, while the Comptroller and Auditor-General retain authority for the preparation of combined accounts and post-audit procedures. However, no provision was made for the introduction of improved data processing facilities, so that the government's skilled accounting personnel continue to be preoccupied with maintaining manual data procedures, rather than concentrating on improving accounting systems and information flows. As a result, the primary focus of the accounting system has remained confined to the preparation and auditing of final accounts, rather than developing a flexible management information system for monitoring the outcome of the public expenditure programme.

In recent times the government has initiated the development of the budgetary process with the help of computer technology under a project entitled Reforms in Budgeting and Expenditure Control

(RIBEC). The government is storing the last five years' budget documents into a computerized database system which will later help analyse expenditure and revenue earning trends and other aspects of national budgets. This will enable the government to allocate its resources more efficiently. This will also upgrade the financial management capability of the government offices.

The 15 million dollar project funded by British Overseas Development Administration (ODA) and GOB is expected to increase the transparency, accountability and efficiency of the central and local level officials. This project has also proposed a new budget classification system which would ensure the accountability of the ministries and local governments involved in the budget-making process. The new classification follows an International Monitory Fund (IMF) outline which is a standard procedure for preserving and providing statistics.

b. The annual budget exercise currently focuses more on revenue mobilization than on prioritizing expenditure. The estimates of revenues are not linked to any formal macroeconomic model, and the major objective of the exercise is to decide on the allocation of resources between the Revenue Budget and the ADP. No further breakdown in resource allocation is provided, and sectoral allocations are determined largely on an incremental basis using the five-year plan guidelines for the ADP and approved staffing and operating requirements for the revenue budget. Thus the government does not make use of the opportunity provided by the budget cycle to monitor decisions on public resource flows to the various sectors, which is the primary focus for expenditure decision-making and control processed in most countries.

Instead, the project approval mechanism serves as the focus for determining public resource flows over the medium term. Project approval procedures are an important tool in public expenditure planning, and the Planning Commission has made a useful contribution by improving the standard of project preparation. But this approach has a number of limitations, namely emphasis on new projects rather than the implementation of existing ones, neglect of recurrent cost requirements and a tendency to focus on individual projects rather than on sectoral investment priorities.

c. The phasing of development projects is not always done carefully. It is reported that there are several projects in which two phases are going on simultaneously although they were planned to be implemented successively. This is another factor that contributes to the misappropriation of public resources. Besides, one objective of phasing, ie to take lessons from the experience of the earlier phases for the later phases and achieve greater efficiency in resource utilization cannot be realized.

3.8.4 Poverty Alleviating Components in the Annual Budget

It is not very easy to capture the exact estimates for poverty alleviation from the conventional budget documents which are by nature very complex. Nevertheless, in the subsequent chapters this study attempts to examine the broad categories of the revenue and development budgets focusing particularly on the budget components under social sectoral heads targeted to the poor.

Chapter 4

PUBLIC RESOURCE MOBILIZATION

4.1 Introduction

The history of economic planning in Bangladesh has not been one of spectacular success. Even after implementing several development plans and budgets, Bangladesh still finds itself in the bottom league of the world economic atlas. All the more disturbing is the fact that an extremely skewed distribution of national income at a low level has created a staggering problem of poverty. The budget, being a short-run instrument for implementing long-run objectives of development, has two fiscal measures: revenue collection and expenditure. The mode of using the fiscal apparatus is determined by the development philosophy of the government. Despite the widely held notion that government expenditure affects the overall poverty scenario, revenue collection has no less important bearing on the poor.

Tax revenue, which is the major source of total revenue, has a corresponding negative impact on the income of the taxpayer. Taxes, therefore, not only provide resources to be invested in economic development, but also reduce the purchasing power of the people. A concern for eliminating poverty, reducing inequality along with pursuing the goal of maximizing economic growth would suggest that the distributional impact of taxation cannot be separated from its other impacts.

The objective of poverty elimination has a natural bearing on the distributional implication of the tax. This interest is generally reflected in the question, 'who pays the tax?' and 'whose income is reduced as a result?' The answer to these crucially important questions lies in a rigorous analysis of the revenue composition and tax structure of Bangladesh.

4.2 Revenue Structure

The most salient feature of the revenue structure of Bangladesh has been a greater dependence on tax revenue than on non-tax revenue. Annex II

Table 4.1 shows that the contribution of tax revenue has consistently been more than 80% of the total revenue for the period from 1975-76 to 1992-93. The percentage share of tax revenue declined to 78% during the fiscal years of 1993-94 and 1994-95. This decline in tax revenue and the corresponding rise in non-tax revenue collection are explained by higher yields from government-managed commercial profit-seeking organizations on the one hand, and by the gap between expected tax receipts and actual tax collections on the other. The discrepancy between the expected target and actual collection of taxes in these fiscal years is evidenced by the budget speech of the then Finance Minister:

> In FY 1992-93 the highest tax rate for individuals was reduced to 25%. This is one of the lowest rates in Asia. It was hoped that more tax payers will disclose higher income with the reduction of tax rates and the increase in tax will make it possible to review future tax rates. Unfortunately this expectation did not materialize (budget speech 1995-96).

The large contribution of taxes to the total revenue means that the government is meeting her revenue and development expenditures by diverting money from individuals who could otherwise spend the money. Thus the present revenue structure is prone to reducing the purchasing power of people and has far-reaching implications for the demand structure of the economy.

4.3 The Tax Structure

Total taxes can be divided into direct and indirect taxes. Direct taxes consist of taxes on income (income tax, corporation tax, agricultural income tax) and taxes on property (wealth tax, gift tax, estate duty, capital gain tax, urban property tax, house rent, land revenue, registration, non-judicial stamp). Indirect taxes may be broadly divided into taxes on domestic goods and services and taxes on foreign trade. Annex II Table 4.2 shows that direct tax covers around one-fourth of the total tax revenue and indirect tax accounts for around 75% of the entire tax revenue of Bangladesh. The poor contribution of direct tax (income tax) is also conceded by the Finance Minister in his budget speech (1994-95):

> The share of income tax in total revenue increases with the improvement in the level of economic development. In Bangladesh income tax collection constitutes about 1.6% of GDP; in neighboring India the ratio stands at 2.8%.

The incidence of a direct tax has no poverty augmenting implication unless the poor are directly taxed, since it has no scope of being shifted.

But an indirect tax has possibilities of being shifted and can have important bearing on changing inequality and poverty depending on the person or socio-economic group who effectively bear the burden of the tax.

The low contribution of direct taxes to total tax revenue and continual upward shifting of the exemption limit for income tax exhibit that the present philosophy of taxation has little concern for equity (Annex II Table 4.3).

The income tax structure in Bangladesh is very complicated. The legislative structure, developed through different tax ordinances, consists of different types of exemptions, eg deductions, exclusions, concessions, tax holiday, etc. These provisions give immense discretionary powers to the tax officers and pave the way for rent seeking and corruption. A corrupt tax administration reduces the government revenue and strengthens the oligarchy among the high income group. The indirect effect of such unfair dealings is that the government imposes more and more indirect taxes to affect the leakages of direct taxes. The incidence of such taxes falls more sharply on the poor. In the recent years, some reforms have been undertaken, eg the four-fold reforms in financial year (FY) 1992-93 which have resulted in an increase in the percentage share of direct tax from 22.85% to 30.98% during 1992-93 to 1993-94 (Annex II Table 4.2). But its fall in FY 1994-95 to 27.11% creates doubts about the effectiveness of these reforms. It may be apprehended that these reforms might be abortive unless supported by complementary policy measures.

4.3.1 Indirect Tax Structure

Indirect taxes account for about three-fourths of Bangladesh's total tax yield which, in turn, contribute nearly 80% of the total revenue earnings of the country. The share of indirect taxes in total revenue income of the country is around 60%. It is difficult to ascertain how the burden of this large contribution to public revenue is distributed among individuals due to the possibilities of shifting such tax liabilities. Economists have long recognized that indirect taxes generally impose burdens on the consumers and producers. The burdens often exceed the amount of revenue obtained by the government. The so-called excess burden of indirect taxation reflects the loss of welfare that results from tax-induced distortion effects on the economy. The nominal tax rate, therefore, does not reflect the real incidence of tax which has serious consequences on poverty in the long run.

The concept of effective tax incidence is an indispensable tool for distributional investigation. The link between the two is intimate because tax incidence is the direct result of a fiscal action, even in the absence of conscious redistributional policies. No matter whether the budget is used for any of the three 'Musgravian' purposes (stabilization, distribution, resource allocation), taxation reduces real resources available to individuals.

Indirect taxes are broadly composed of taxes on domestic goods and services and taxes on foreign trade. Annex II Table 4.4 shows that taxes on international trade form the lion's share of total indirect taxes. The introduction of the value added tax (VAT) from July 1, 1991 marks a major tax reform in Bangladesh. Under the new system, the excise duty on domestic production at the production stage and sales tax on imports at the import stage are replaced by VAT at the basic rate of 15%. The important features of VAT are that it is uniform and non-discriminatory. It, therefore, does not address the problem of distributive injustice. Since indirect taxes in Bangladesh were regressive, their replacement by VAT can only sustain the regressivity.

4.4 Growth of Tax Revenues

Since 1985-86, Bangladesh has been undergoing the structural adjustment (SA) programme with the aim of market-oriented transformation of the economy and efficient resource management. This programme has entailed a major shift in the policies of the GOB and can be expected to affect the fiscal performance of the government.

In order to examine and compare the trend rates of growth of direct taxes (DT), taxes from international trade (TIT) and taxes from domestic services (TDS) between the pre-SA and post-SA period as well as between the periods before and after the imposition of VAT in 1990-91, we have fitted the following annual trend equation to the data of the period 1978-79 to 1994-95:

$$\text{Log}Y_t = a_1 + a_2X_t + b_1T + b_2(X_t.T_t) + u_t \quad ..... (4.1)$$

where,
- Y = dependent variable (DT, TIT and TDS)
- X = dummy variable which assumes the value 0 for pre-SA years and 1 for post SA years
- T = time variable which runs from 1978-79 to 1994-95 and takes the value 1 for 1978-79 and onwards up to 17 for 1994-95 in that order
- t = time subscript
- u = error term

a_1, a_2, b_1 and b_2 are the parameters to be estimated.

In this model the slope and the intercept are allowed to change and the variance of the error term is assumed to be the same in both the pre-

SA and post-SA periods. The estimated parameter a_2 shown in Annex II Table 4.5 on account of DT and TIT indicates that the levels of direct tax and taxes on international trade fell after SA was launched in 1985-86, while that of taxes on domestic services shows an increase in the post-SA period (a_2 is positive but insignificant). The trend rates of growth of DT and TIT were higher during the post-SA period compared to the pre-SA period (b_2 is positive and significant at a higher level).

The trend rate of growth on account of TDS was, however, found to be lower during the post-SA period (b_2 is negative but not significant). Similar trend behaviour is observed when we compare the size level and the trend rate of growth before and after the imposition of VAT. The fit of equation as indicated by adjusted R^2 is quite good for all the models. The D W statistic satisfies the condition of absence of auto correlation.

The increased trend growth rate of DT and decreased trend growth rate of TDS in the post-SA period may apparently indicate that the tax structure has become more progressive. Simultaneously, TIT contributing no less than 60% of total indirect taxes increased more rapidly in the post-SA period compared to the pre-SA period. As far as the possibilities of shifting the burdens are concerned, the latter trend can be presumed to have worked against redistributive justice. The net impact of the SA programmes or income redistribution is, therefore, ambiguous, if not regressive. The income distribution scenario in the post-SA period, however, is more unequal.

Deseggregating indirect taxes into taxes on international trade and taxes on domestic goods and services is not sufficient to arrive at any conclusion with regard to the regressivity of indirect taxes and their impacts on different income groups. To delve deeper, we need to distinguish between the proportions of indirect tax revenue coming from luxuries and necessities. The underlying logic of such disaggregation is that taxes on luxurious items do not touch the poor while affecting the rich, and those on necessities curtail the purchasing power of all income groups, although the marginal disutility of such loss in disposable income is greater for the lower levels of income. The luxury and necessity items covered by the tax net may be classified on the basis of the income elasticity of demand for each good. Usually, those with inelastic demand are considered necessities and those with elastic demand are taken as luxuries which are unaffordable to the poor. This analysis has been extended in the subsequent phases of the study.

4.5 Taxation and Equity

While expressing its concern for poverty alleviation, the government pays the least attention to the burden that is imposed on the poor through indirect taxes. The selection of the commodities and fixation of tax rates are highly against the poor. The commodity bundle that constitutes the day-to-day subsistence of the poor is taxed and thus the purchasing power of the poor is reduced (eg daily necessities like edible oil, salt, pulses and items for mass consumption invariably come under indirect taxation). Although a lower price of rice benefits the landless and other poor people, this, too, can be construed as a form of indirect taxation of the small and marginal farmers who are forced to sell rice at a lower price to buy consumable items at a higher price. Indeed this group of rural people belong to the category of tomorrow's poor and remain largely unattended by ongoing poverty alleviation programmes.

No equity concern is reflected in the government's indirect taxation policies. Due to the launching of the import-substitution policies of the government at the initial stage, all the consumer goods used to be taxed. Within a short span of time after the change in the political regime in the mid-seventies, the development approach changed dramatically and associated itself with the new trend of liberalization. The existing high import tariff was lowered and at the same time domestically produced goods were brought under taxation through the introduction of VAT. High income groups benefited from the reduction of import tariff, while the poor whose consumption bundle consists mainly of the domestic goods were adversely affected by the second change. Thus the indirect tax structure has been made more regressive in nature. In fact, it is clearly regressive in the rural areas where the incidence of indirect taxes rises as income falls, and in the urban areas the poorest group bear a relatively higher tax burden compared to the middle income groups. The indirect tax structure also has virtually no impact on narrowing the substantial rural-urban income differential (Chowdhury 1994). In sum, the concern for poverty and equity is totally missing in the reliance on indirect taxation as a safe source of revenue.

4.6 Today's Achievements, Tomorrow's Predicament

Having a very poor contribution from the non-tax revenue sector, the government has to rely on tax revenues for financing fiscal and development activities. At the same time the government has to borrow from the overseas moneylenders in the guise of 'foreign aid'. The economy of Bangladesh is still largely non-monetized. So the subsistence agricultural sector plays a very little role in mobilizing direct taxes. But this sector pays heavily the indirect taxes. This certainly exerts a negative impact on savings and capital accumulation by the rich on the one hand, and worsens the condition of the people struggling at the edge of subsistence on the other. Borrowing from the overseas agencies has a long-term effect on the economy. A lion's share of our export earnings is being spent for servicing the debt liabilities. To that extent the country is deprived of the growth-augmenting effect of export earnings. The nature of use of foreign aid yields very little benefit to the poor, although they have to share the ultimate burden of foreign debt in one form or the other (Sobhan 1989, 1992).

4.7 From Politics to Economics

The budget is nothing but the numerical documentation of the political ideology of the government which is to be implemented through a suitable economic framework. Revenue collection is also affected by the development philosophy of the government. The development philosophy of the governments of Bangladesh has not been seriously anchored on the strategy of poverty reduction. However, there has been no dearth of rhetorics. Though the five-year plans contain the slogans of poverty eradication and inequality reduction, the annual financial budgets could not conform to these slogans. Among the socio-economic groups, the poor have no scope for exerting pressure on the government. Government functionaries, therefore, have no urge to have any consultation with them, although the budget-makers have been routinely consulting members of more powerful socio-economic groups. The government imposes taxes and other fiscal measures which adversely affect the poor and households who marginally escape the poverty trap. No forward nor any diagnostic analysis has been undertaken by the government to track the effect of its fiscal measures on the poor with a view to redesigning its economic policies.

The political character of the government restricts not only the launching of pro-poor fiscal policies but also the implementation of other progressive policies. The collection of income tax is one good example. In order to retain the support of the high income groups who command much of the economic and political power of society, the government is unable to take any serious action against them for tax evasion. In the budget speech of 1994-95 the then Finance Minister mentioned:

> Though 5 lakh households are supposed to pay the income tax in the country, in 1992-93 only about 2 lakh and 16 thousand households paid it.

What the Finance Minister did not mention is the type of punitive measures that are needed against the tax evaders.

Chapter 5

MACROECONOMIC POLICY IMPACTS ON PUBLIC EXPENDITURE

5.1 Qualitative Assessment

The incidence of the national budget needs to be qualitatively assessed as well. As the traditional cost-benefit analysis does not look at distributional weights, the impact of alternative expenditure allocations on fulfilment of the needs of the poor needs to be taken into account in order to ensure that the composition of government spending meets the poverty alleviation objective (Pradhan 1996). In the quantitative exercise this is accomplished through the most commonly used method of benefit-incidence analysis. One of the comparable methods applied in qualitative research is participatory impact assessment which has been carried out through the 'scoring technique'. Key macroeconomic policies have been investigated in this section because it is these policies which largely affect and determine the distributional impact of public expenditure on the various social classes. The questions that have been addressed in this section are: what are the key public policies that have been pursued so far in the country and who are their beneficiaries? What are the various socio-economic development projects/programmes that the government has implemented so far and what are their impacts on the major social groups? What have been the overall development impacts of these policies and programmes on the poor during the last three years?

5.1.1 Public Policies and Their Beneficiaries

A set of eight different public policies has been selected for investigation, ie trade, industry, agriculture, food, fiscal issues, employment, decentralization and participation (Figure 5.1). The key aspects of these policies were presented to the poor for obtaining their responses to them. It is found that among four classes, namely 'well-off', 'middle', 'poor' and 'poorest', in the perception of the poor, the benefits accruing from all

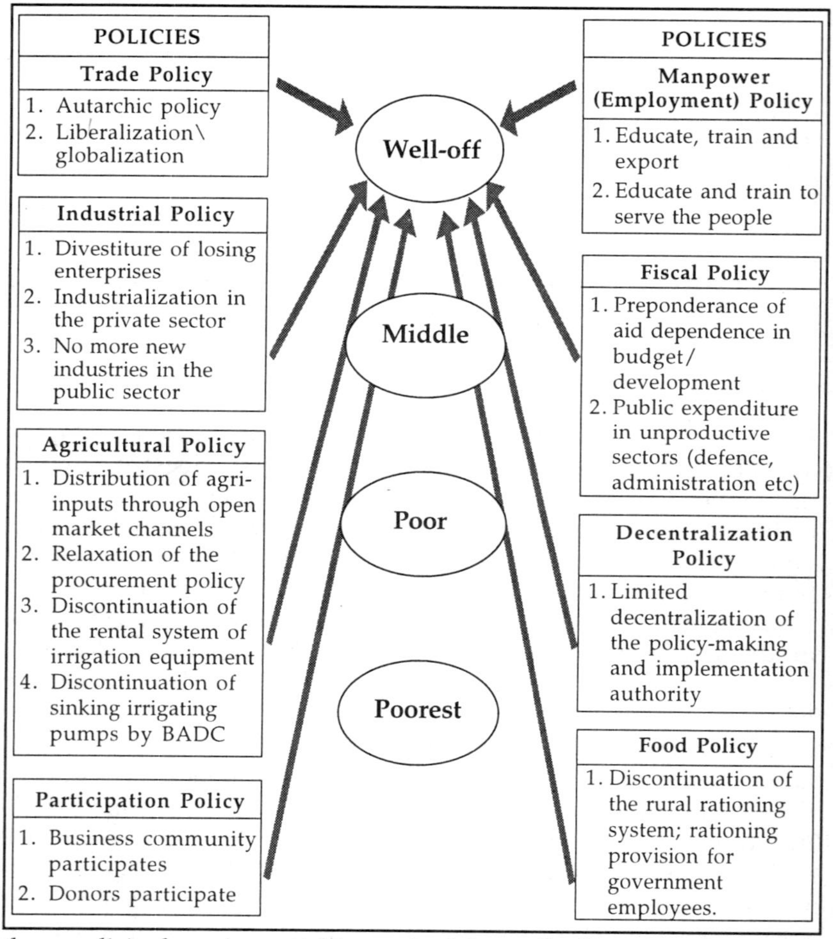

Figure 5.1 Public Policies: Whose Interests Served?

these policies have inequitably reached the well-off section of society to the neglect of other groups.

These findings, while reflecting the perceptions of the poor, convey a meaningful message for the policy makers and call for a rethinking on these dominant policies currently under operation in the country.

5.1.2 Impacts of Development Activities

For analytical convenience, key development activities carried out in various sectors by the government have been arranged under two broad heads, namely, 'social sectors' and 'non-social sectors'. Social sectors include both targeted and non-targeted programmes ranging over a sample of 21 development programmes under various sectors/sub-sectors, namely health, education, social welfare, etc. Non-social sectors, on the other hand, include 20 different types of activities considered for our investigation. As perceived by the poor, all the targeted and most of the non-targeted programmes benefit both the poor, including the poorest segments of society and the non-poor (Figure 5.2). It is found that out of 21 development activities/programmes (targeted and non-targeted) under the social sector, 20 (95%) reach the poorest (including the moderate poor) and 10 (47%) reach the well-off (including the middle). On the other hand, the findings are almost reverse in the case of the non-social sectors. As far as the non-social sectors are concerned, out of 20 development activities/programmes, the poor are found to have benefited from only 11 (52%) and the non-poor from 16 (80%) programmes. These findings confirm the contention that public expenditure in the social sector activities/programmes with a thrust on its targeted components are more likely to reach the people lying at the lower end of the resource distribution scale of society compared to those under non-social sectors (Bardhan 1995, Sen 1995).

5.1.3 Trends in Socio-Economic Development in the Lives of the Poor

Although there has been some improvement in the condition of the poor in some respects, namely the wage rate, education, etc their condition has deteriorated in other respects over the last three years. The same pattern of changes was noted with regard to the poor both in the urban and rural areas.

The urban poor assessed their own socio-economic development during the last three years in terms of 13 indicators (Figure 5.3). They placed themselves on a four-point scale from 'very happy' to 'very unhappy'. The poor were not found 'very happy' in any of the instances. They were, however, found 'happy' with their development in respect of the wage rate, credit, development of the marketplace, education and institutional development. The urban poor witnessed very little progress during the same period in respect of construction/repair of roads, employment opportunities, electric connection, poverty/crisis and the living standard. They were found to be 'very unhappy' with the law and order situation prevailing in their locality and also the pressure of out-migration for jobs which forced them to leave behind the parental homesteads.

Figure. 5.2 Beneficiaries of Socio-Economic Development Activities in Rural Areas

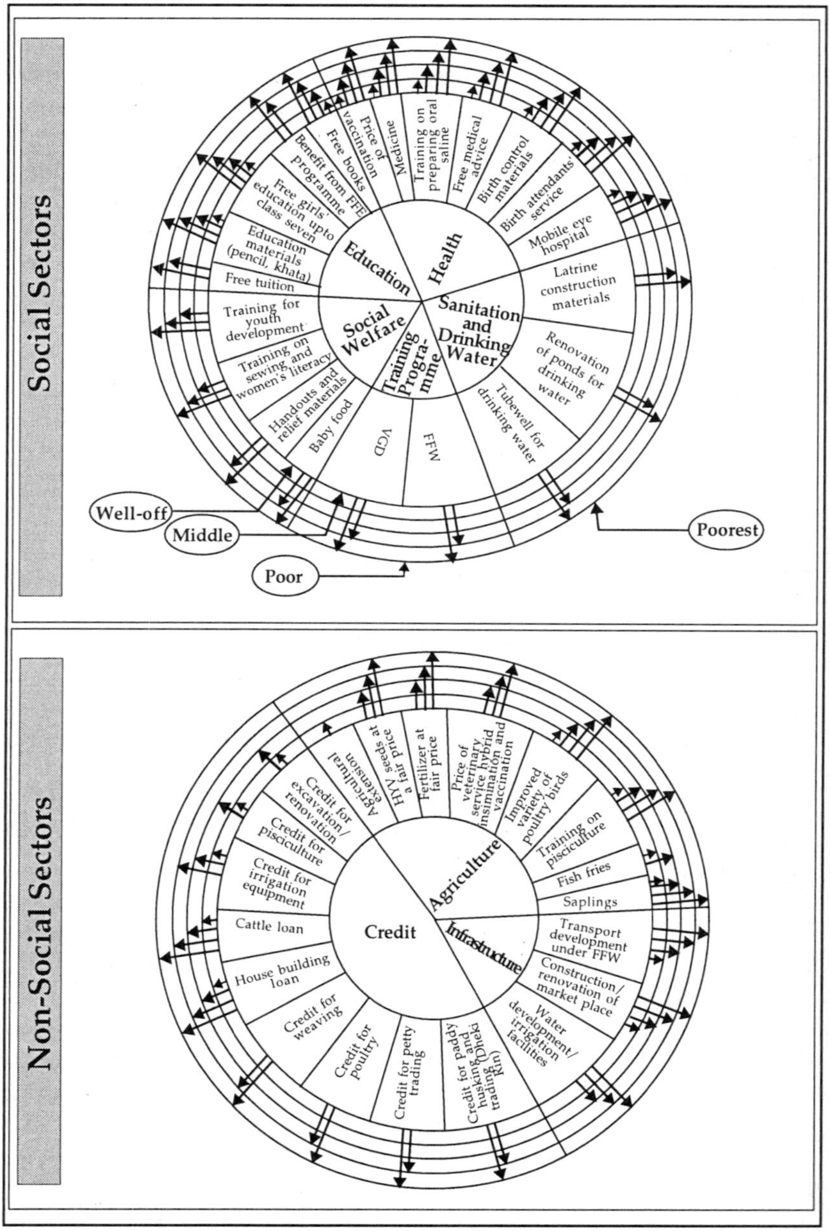

The rural poor, on the other hand, were requested to express their perceptions about their socio-economic development in respect of 15 indicators on the same scale (Figure 5.4). By and large, the poor were found 'happy' with the wage rate and education, although they were found worse off with these indicators in other parts of the rural areas. About the law and order situation in the rural areas, the findings do not show any general pattern. Out of the four sample villages, the law and order situation was perceived to be 'very happy' by the villagers in two villages. However, among the remaining two it was assessed to be 'very unhappy' in the one and 'unhappy' in the other. On the other hand, the rural poor expressed unhappiness with their progress with respect to out-migration for job, credit, banking, living standard and health. They were found 'very unhappy' with the meagre development in construction/repairing of rural roads, electric connection, irrigation system, institutional development, poverty/crisis, employment opportunities, supply of agricultural inputs and market-place during the last three years.

The above findings of the qualitative investigation demonstrate that the benefits from most of the macroeconomic policies and development activities have either missed the poor or have had a marginal impact on them. Except in respect of wage rates and education, only a small portion of the rural poor have benefited from major development programmes. However, in the case of the targeted programmes, the poor are found to have benefited most. As the share of the targeted programmes in the overall public expenditure is minimal, the total benefit reaching the poor is also insignificant. These findings also support the quantitative findings reported later in the section on poverty monitoring.

5.2 Quantitative Assessment

5.2.1 The Background

The management of public resources affects macroeconomic factors such as productivity, income, investment, savings, terms of trade, human resource development, etc through a complex socio-economic fabric spread all over the country. A close look at the composition, volume and growth of public expenditures reveals the adequacy and efficiency of the macroeconomic policies with respect to socio-economic goals—to be more specific, with respect to the alleviation of poverty.

As we have observed, the development strategies of the government are purportedly aimed at promoting economic growth and reducing poverty. In order to achieve these goals, public resources are channelled through two distinct ways to the directly productive and social sectors

Figure 5.3 Poor People's Perceptions of Their Own Socio-Economic Development over the Last Three Years (BNP Market Slum, Dhaka)

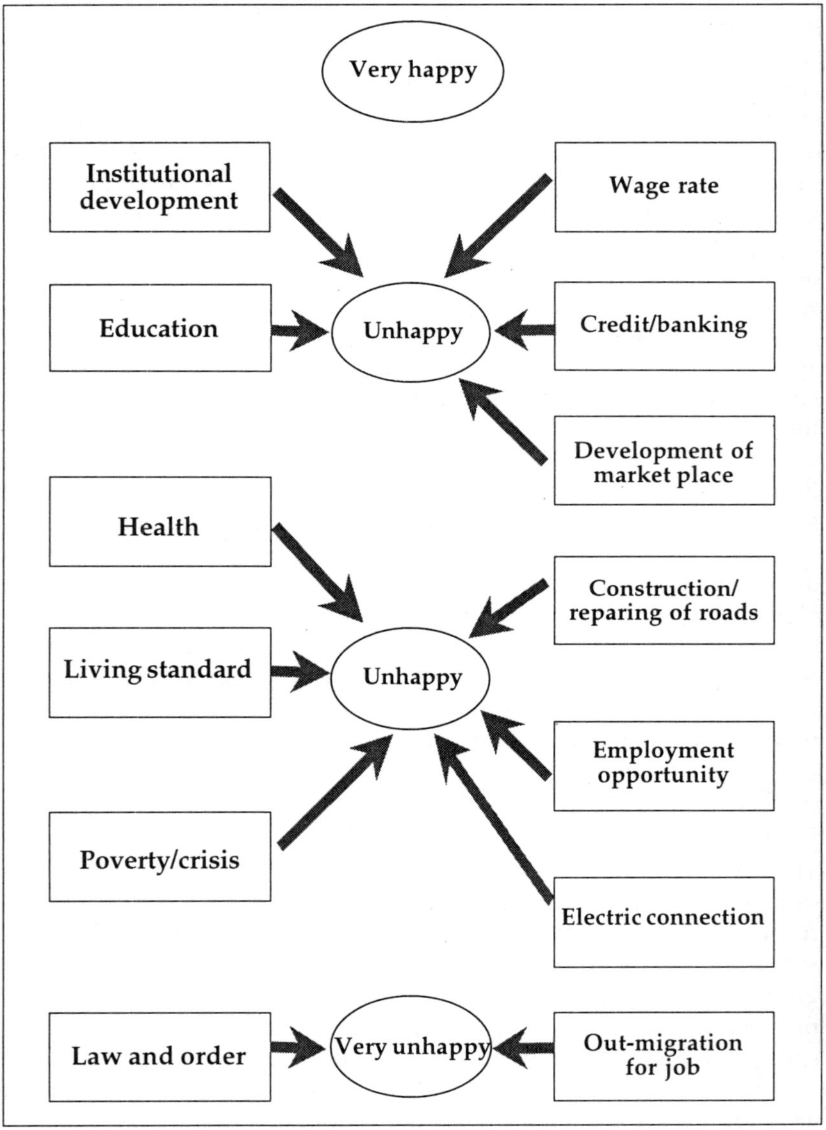

Note : 'Happy' means those who are either better off or have received benefit. 'Unhappy' means those who are either worse off or have received no benifit.

Figure 5.4 Poor People's Perceptions of Their Own Socio-Economic Development over the Last Three Years (Rural Areas)

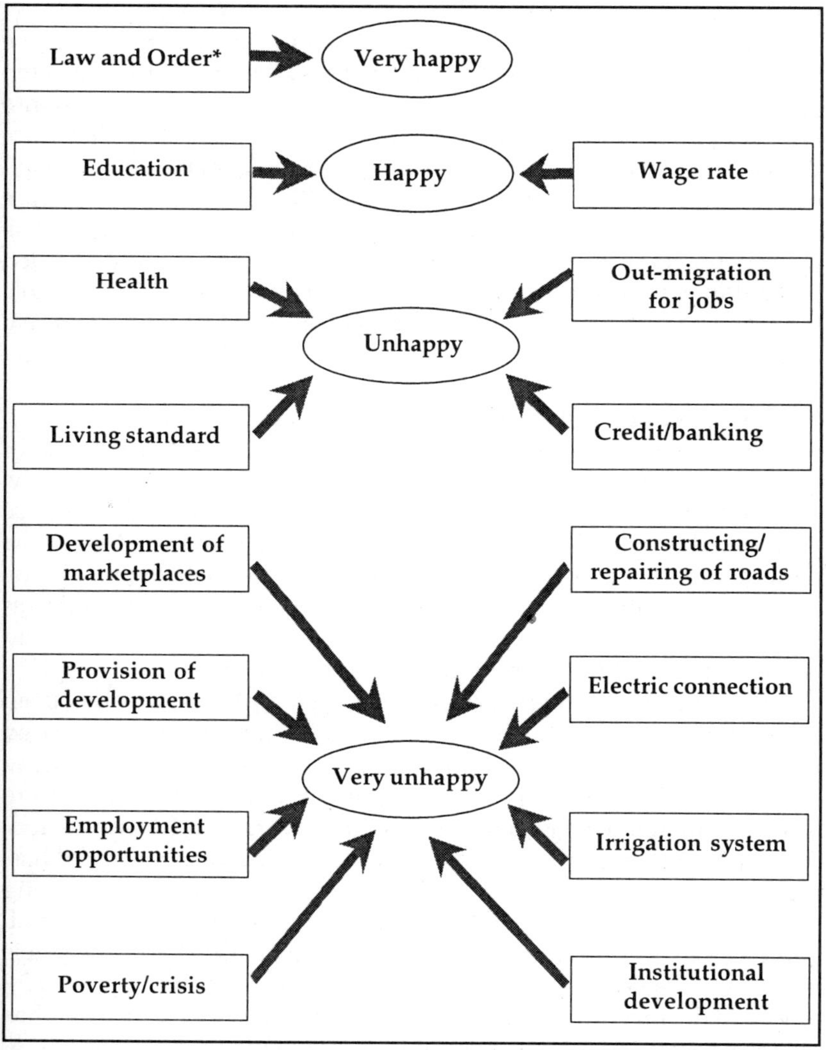

Note : 'Happy' means those who are either better off or have received benefit. 'Unhappy' means those who are either worse off or have received no benifit.

* Out of the four sample villages, two were found 'very happy', and the other two 'very unhappy' and 'unhappy'. The word 'happy' should not be taken literally. It comes close to the word 'tolerable'.

on the one hand and the target groups comprising the poor and underprivileged on the other. Public expenditures under the directly productive sectors benefit all groups although in a varying degree. Usually, the more unequal is the distribution of income, the less is the share of benefits of growth that the poor receive. The target-group oriented policies, which are intended solely for the poor, may be classified into two categories: indirect and direct policies. The indirect policies are designed to enhance the income-earning capabilities of the poor through education, skill development, various health services, infrastructure development, etc. The direct policies are meant to directly bring income to the poor. These policies are implemented mostly by way of food-aided programmes such as Food for Work (FFW), Test Relief (TR), Vulnerable Group Development (VGD), Food For Education (FFE) and other social welfare programmes.

5.2.2 Pattern of Public Expenditure

The level and composition of public expenditure reflect the role of government in economic development to a large extent. More importantly, these determine the extent to which the benefits accrued from growth are distributed among the various social groups. In order to observe the patterns of public expenditure, it is necessary to look at both the revenue and development expenditures. The disaggregated public expenditures in terms of revenue and development expenditures are shown in Annex II Table 5.1 for the period 1990-91 to 1994-95.

The total public expenditure (as a per cent of GDP) has been consistently increasing but at a slow pace. In nominal terms, it increased from Tk. 124.98 billion in 1990-91 to Tk. 217.0 billion in 1994-95 showing on the average about 15% increase per annum. The revenue expenditure has stagnated between 8.6 to 9.4% of GDP over the reference period. Although the development expenditure as a proportion of GDP has, registered almost 4 percentage point increase (from 6.3 to 10.0%) during this period, its impact on poverty alleviation is yet to be firmly established. Although the development expenditure has increased marginally, it is in the FY 1994-95 that development expenditure as a percentage of GDP exceeded the revenue counterpart for the first time. But this increase has not been translated into greater public investment.

5.2.3 Composition of Revenue Expenditure

The revenue expenditures may be classified into two main sectors, viz (a) economic sectors, and (b) social sectors. About 59% of the net revenue expenditures in the economic sectors was accounted for by 'goods and services' in 1990-91, which rose to 63% in 1994-95 (Annex II Table 5.2). About 12% of the total was accounted for by 'interest payment' in 1990-91 and 11.5% in 1994-95. The share of subsidies and other current transfers to total revenue expenditure fell from 33% in 1990-91 to 23% in 1994-95. The cut in subsidies and transfer payments has released resources for allocation to the productive heads in the revenue budget.

The revenue expenditure on the social sectors has risen from Tk. 16.34 billion in 1990-91 to Tk.26.33 billion in 1994-95 indicating about 12.5% average increase per annum (Annex II Table 5.3). The allocation of total revenue expenditure to the social sector has risen from 23% in 1990-91 to 27% in 1992-93 but declined to 25% in 1994-95. Of the total expenditure in the social sectors, more than 70% has been spent on education alone. Health and population have received around 25% of the total revenue expenditure during 1990-91 to 94-95. The rest is shared by youth, sports and cultural affairs, social welfare and women's affairs. In nominal terms, the per capita revenue expenditure in the social sectors consistently increased during 1990-91 to 1994-95. But in real terms, although it increased during 1990-91, the trend reversed thereafter in a row.

5.2.4 Composition of Development Expenditure

The budget and revised estimates as well as the actual spending in the development budget have been rising during 1990-91 to 94-95 (Annex II Table 5.4). But the original allocation has been revised downward in the final quarter of the fiscal year and the actual expenditure has been less than the revised allocation in every year of the 1990s except 1994-95. The rate of utilization nosedived in 1992-93 but recovered soon, exceeding 100% by 1994-95 as shown by the trend of actual expenditure as a percentage of the revised target.

The underutilization of the development budget confirms that the needed institutional base has not yet been created to implement the ADP fully. There are other structural bottlenecks like bureaucratic sloth, inefficient management, corruption and a host of administrative complexities that tend to slow down the rate of utilization of the provisions of the development budget.

Although the social sectors (education, health, etc) merit particular attention in view of the urgency of poverty alleviation, at most 31% of the development expenditure was allocated for the social sectors in 1994-95 which was significantly higher than the 1990-91 level

(17%) (Annex II Table 5.5). Moreover, the development expenditure-GDP ratio of Bangladesh, which has been a maximum of 10% in 1994-95, is one of the lowest in this region. Among the social sectors, educational allocation has gained momentum with a marked hike from 3.3% of total ADP in 1990-91 to 13.8% in 1994-95 out of the total development allocation (Annex II Table 5.6). The remarkable increase in the ADP allocation for the social sectors does not necessarily imply that the targeted social expenditure for poverty alleviation has risen significantly as the development budget includes a number of components of revenue expenditures which are intended to support the development projects or are spent otherwise.

A detailed breakdown of the social sector allocation of development expenditure has been provided in Annex II Table 5.5. The emphasis on education and religious affairs is clearly evident in this table which shows that allocation under this head has galloped from 19% of the total social expenditure in 1990-91 to 45% in 1994-95. Again, this is a lumped figure and does not clearly indicate the sub-sectoral allocations. In the fiscal year of 1994-95, the budgetary concentration in terms of allocation of public funds has been greatest in education and religious affairs followed by rural development, family welfare, health, public administration, social welfare and women and youth development, and 'others' in that order. The per capita ADP expenditure in the social sectors has increased significantly over the reference period. Due to the inadequacy of appropriately disaggregated data it is, however, not very clear from this trend whether such increase in social expenditure per head implies an increasing thrust of the poverty alleviation drive. A mere allocation of additional resource for the social sector does not, however, always imply a strong interest in poverty alleviation.

5.2.5 Growth of Public Expenditure

In order to examine the impact of structural adjustment on the levels and trend rates of growth of GDP, revenue expenditure (RE) and development expenditure (DE), we have fitted the trend equation as expressed in section 4.4 of chapter IV. The estimated value of a_2 (Annex II Table 5.7) corresponding to GDP at 1989-90 constant prices shows that the level of GDP fell after SA since 1985-86 (a_2 is negative but insignificant) but the trend rate of growth was found to be higher during the post-SA period compared to the pre-SA period (b_2 is positive and significant). The level as well as trend rate of growth of RE (adjusted by 1989-90 GDP deflator) was higher during the post-SA period compared to the pre-SA period (a_2

and b_2 are positive) but the test showed both a_2 and b_2 to be insignificant. The level of development expenditure adjusted by the 1989-90 GDP deflator fell after the introduction of structural adjustment (a_2 is negative) but the corresponding trend rate of growth was higher in the post-SA period compared to the pre-SA period (b_2 is positive and significant). The fit of equation as indicated by adjusted R_2 is quite good for all the models except for development expenditure. The D W statistics satisfies the test of absence of auto-correlation.

The development expenditure has been further disaggregated by major functional categories, viz (i) economic services (agriculture, water, industry); (ii) social services (education and religious affairs, population control and family planning, health, social welfare, sports and culture); (iii) infrastructure; and (iv) others. The disaggregated data have been obtained from the Implementation Monitoring and Evaluation Division (IMED), Planning Commission and are reproduced in Annex II Table 5.8. The total of disaggregated figures may not exactly tally with the current development expenditure shown in Annex II Table 5.9. However, the estimated trend equation (Annex II Table 5.10) indicates that the level of development expenditure on account of economic services (ES) increased during the post-SA period (a_2 is positive but insignificant), while social services (SS) and the infrastructure development sector (IDS) fell after structural adjustment (a_2 is negative and significant). The trend rate of growth was, however, higher in the post-SA period compared to the pre-SA period (b_2 is positive and not significant) for the social services and infrastructural development (Annex II Table 5.10). The trend rate of growth of economic services was found to be lower during the post-SA period compared to the pre-SA period. The trend equations under consideration show good fits as can be noticed from the estimated value of R_2. The D W statistics used for the test of auto-correlation points to an inconclusive decision regarding the presence or absence of auto-correlation.

The faster growth of development expenditure and, within the development expenditure, the faster growth rate of expenditure in the social sector points to the fact that the SA programmes have not been apparently biased against poverty alleviating public expenditures, although they are basically not meant for poverty alleviation. As a matter of fact, SA entails a gradual shift to the market mechanism and to a reduced role of government in resource allocation. Providing additional resources to the social sectors without ensuring the quality of public expenditure does not mean much for poverty alleviation. Indeed, the additional expenditures may end up in larger wastage and corruption.

Chapter 6

TARGETED PUBLIC EXPENDITURE FOR POVERTY ALLEVIATION

This chapter assesses the efficacy of the poverty alleviation and safety net programmes operated by the government. The main findings obtained from both sample survey and secondary sources to evaluate the performance of the 'Food For Education' (FFE) programme are also reported here. This chapter only reports the main observations relegating detailed analysis in Annex I. The major components of the 'safety net' programme are: i) skill development; ii) Test Relief (TR); iii) Food For Work (FFW); iv) Vulnerable Group Development (VGD); v) Food For Education (FFE) and other programmes specially designed for poverty alleviation. These are mainly food-aided programmes which include TR, FFW, VGD and FFE.

6.1 Test Relief

TR is a nationwide programme aiming at creating employment opportunities for the poor and simultaneous transfer of income to them during slack seasons. However, the contribution of this programme to augmenting the income of the beneficiary group is negligible. A survey on TR conducted in 1989 by BBS indicates that the TR programme augmented only 5% of the household income of the beneficiary households.

6.2 Food For Works (FFW)

FFW is a rural development programme where labourers are paid food instead of cash in exchange of their physical labour. The programme generally reaches the target group and also plays a positive role in providing employment to the target group during lean seasons. However, some weaknesses of the programme have been reported by BBS (1993 and 1986). According to BBS (1993), more than 75% of the total 520 respondents opined that the programme could not yield much tangible benefit due to misappropriation of wheat and improper selection of sites. A Bangladesh Institute of Development Studies (BIDS) study reported that 25.30% of the allotted foodgrain did not actually reach the intended beneficiaries.

6.3 Vulnerable Group Development Programme

Destitute, widowed and divorced women with undernourished children and women with handicapped husbands are the target groups of the VGD programme. The objective of this programme is to enhance the income generating capabilities of destitute women by providing them with training. It is generally assumed that this programme generally reaches the target group. This has been assessed positively in creating self-employment activities for the hard-core poor women. Though the coverage is not very large, this programme at least generates some income for the very poor women who are normally excluded by both government and NGO programmes.

6.4 BBS Evaluation of Food Aided Programmes

A BBS survey (1993) on food-aided programmes made some important observations: i) the average income of the beneficiary and non-beneficiary groups is not markedly different as they are both submerged in the sea of poverty; ii) the contribution of FFW and TR programmes to total income is estimated to be only 4% while about 23% of the total income of the beneficiary groups is contributed by the VGD programme; iii) the food-aided programmes appear to have less income augmenting effect except the VGD programme. However, they all have an important employment effect during the pre- and post-harvest lean periods, and iv) one major problem is that the operational cost of these programmes is high and not really sustainable (WB 1992).

6.5 Some Other PA Programmes

In addition to these 'safety net' programmes, specific programmes have also been undertaken to improve: i) the rural economy embracing agriculture and rural development; ii) the condition of women; and iii) the employment and income earning capabilities of the youth. In recent years, gradual withdrawal of input subsidies, privatization of the distribution of fertilizer and irrigation equipment have significantly affected the agriculture sector, especially the small and marginal farmers. Despite these shortcomings, agricultural production has increased significantly, thanks to the favourable weather and additional efforts of the farmers. But the government has failed to provide the farmers with adequate price support hurting them in both fronts: input and output. The government must provide adequate price support to the farmers and thereby, help them to improve their situation. They will then contribute even more to the growth of the agricultural sector.

6.6 Rural Development

The rural development strategies of GOB have focused on the diversification of the rural economy beyond agriculture, through investment in human resource development, and appropriate technology to provide integrated production and employment opportunities. The implementation of the rural development programmes rests with Bangladesh Rural Development Board (BRDB) which was established in 1972. BRDB has been implementing these programmes through various projects. It has been observed from a BRDB report (1994) that 86% of the total members under these programmes were women and 70% of the total credit was targeted to them. The rate of recovery of the loans has been over 95%. However, whatever may be the success story of BRDB, the coverage of the programme is very small. The expansion of the coverage of BRDB has been impeded by the rather small allocation of fund for rural development programmes. It has also been recognized by the report that increasing financial allocation, better planning and efficient management are urgently needed for the improvement of the rural poverty situation.

6.7 Women Development

In order to improve the socio-economic condition of the rural women, special programmes have been undertaken by GOB. A separate ministry named Ministry of Women's Affairs (MWA) has been formed and assigned the responsibility of organizing the socially and economically disadvantaged groups of women and helping them develop as skilled and productive forces. Although GOB has given great importance to women development for reducing poverty, ADP allocation for the ministry does not really match this assertion. During the period 1990-91 to 1994-95, the ADP allocation for women's affairs hovered around 0.20% of ADP and 0.02% of GDP. Although there is no comprehensive quantification of the impact of these programmes, the general impression is that the impact of the programmes on the overall poverty situation is very little, specially in a country where there are a huge number of poor and destitute women.

6.8 Youth Development

Although a comprehensive assessment of youth development programmes is still awaited, the available information tends to suggest an effective role of these programmes in poverty eradication. The official reports of the Department of Youth Development (DYD) indicate that about 3,25,000 unemployed young men and women have been trained for skill development upto June, 1995. Out of the total trained youth only 60% are self-employed. The DYD also reports that upto June, 1995 a total of 21,189 young men and women have become economically self-reliant under the poverty alleviation programmes. These numbers in relation to the target population of 20 million unemployed youth does not indicate any substantial contribution towards youth development. Moreover, there is no evidence of the sustainability of these programmes. We, however, could not make any in-depth primary investigation to assess the impact of these programmes. But the available data from secondary sources do not give much room for complacence either.

6.9 Food For Education Programme

Another food-aided poverty alleviation programme is the Food For Education programme. The aim of the programme is to encourage the poor households to send their children, specially female, to schools rather than engaging them as child labourers. An incentive package of distribution of wheat from the public sources has also been built in this programme. The FFE programme was spread over 460 unions and it covered all government and registered non-government primary schools, and a certain number of madrasas in each selected union. An early assessment by Ahmed (1994) reveals the following aspects of the FFE programme:

i) The enrolment of students in general and girl students in particular has increased in all classes after the launching of the FFE programme. ii) The enrolment figure is higher in the FFE school compared to the non-FFE schools. iii) The attendance as percentage of total class-days has increased significantly in the FFE schools, compared to the non-FFE schools. iv) The drop-out rates have also declined significantly after the implementation of FFE programmes. v) Leakage of wheat from the FFE programme was about 6.5% of the total allotment of wheat. vi) It appears to be an expensive programme compared to other programmes. It is found that to transfer Taka 1 of income benefit it costs Taka 1.59 as against Rural Maintenance Programme (RMP) where the per unit transfer cost is Taka 1.32. Thus, the analysis suggests that even though the FFE programme appears to be successful, to some extent there is room for improvement in terms of reducing leakage and transfer cost. With a view to assessing the impact of the FFE programme, under the present study an opinion survey was conducted in two sample *thanas* (eg Tanore of Rajshahi District and Rupsha of Khulna District) covering 16 primary schools, half of which was non-FFE schools. The major findings are as follows: i) The total number of students enrolled in the FFE-funded schools is higher than the non-FFE schools for both boys and girls. It implies that the programme has been able to attract more students perhaps at the cost of non-FFE programme. ii) The proportion of female students is greater in the FFE schools than in the non-FFE schools. This is in line with the bias towards girls in wheat distribution. iii) There is a disparity between the enrolment figures of the FFE and non-FFE schools.

A sample survey on the representatives of the School Management Committee (SMC) including community leaders, headteachers and parents was conducted to solicit their opinion on the effectiveness of the FFE programme. Some interesting insights have been given by the respondents. They noted a number of weaknesses of the programme:

i) small coverage;
ii) lack of material facilities other than wheat;
iii) discrimination in wheat distribution among the eligible students;
iv) deterioration in the quality of education;
v) mismanagement in wheat distribution;
vi) inefficiencies of teachers;
vii) inappropriateness of the criterion for selecting potential beneficiaries;
viii) insufficient wheat supply and allocation;
ix) inadequate infrastructure;
x) several socio-political problems; and
xi) diversion of students from non-FFE to FFE schools.

Some of the respondents have delivered useful suggestions for improving the effectiveness of the programme. The majority has, however, asked for the expansion of FFE coverage and the provision of free extra facilities relevant to education.

Chapter 7

PUBLIC EXPENDITURE ON POVERTY ALLEVIATION PROJECTS

7.1 Introduction

A number of interventionist projects have been launched by the government for poverty alleviation, particularly in the rural areas over the last two decades. The Task Forces on Bangladesh development strategies for the 1990s identified 62 projects of direct intervention for poverty alleviation. These projects are mainly targeted to the poor and disadvantaged and cover a wide range of activities which include agriculture, rural development, social welfare, women's development, youth development, education, health, family welfare, etc. Annex II Tables 7.1, 7.2 and 7.3 provide details of some key aspects of the projects including the budgetary allocations for those.

7.2 Financial Implications of the Projects

Almost all the projects mentioned in Annex II Table 7.1 are expected to benefit the rural poor. The table shows the financial aspects of these projects. The total allocation for these projects increased from Tk. 3,741.14 million in 1991-92 to Tk.4,248.17 million in 1994-95 showing a 14% annual growth at the 1989-90 constant price. The revised ADP for 1991-92 allocated Tk. 3,022.84 million, and in 1994-95 the allocation was Tk. 3952.56 million, showing a rise of 31% over 1991-92. The revised allocation was, however, always considerably lower than the original allocation. As a ratio to GDP, total ADP allocation to these projects has actually fallen. It has fallen from 0.47% of GDP in 1991-92 to 0.36% of GDP in 1994-95. The ADP allocations since 1990-91 onwards show an increased emphasis on poverty alleviation but as a share of GDP these are rather small. The percentage of the revised ADP allocation for the different poverty-related projects decreased from 6.12% in 1991-92 to 4.99% in 1994-95. The share of the allocation for the social sector in the ADP has, however, increased from 17% in 1990-91 to 31% in 1994-95.

The 62 poverty alleviation projects do not reflect the whole of the annual budget pertaining to poverty alleviation. This is because over the period 1991-92 to 1994-95, certain projects have been discontinued and also a number of new poverty alleviating projects have been launched. It is, however, difficult to distinguish all these components from the budget documents. Nevertheless, attempts can be made to assess the impact of these projects on the poor. One such attempt has been made in this study through a sample survey.

7.3 Socio-Economic Impact of the Projects

During the sample survey conducted in the urban slums and in the rural areas, poor people were asked to express their views regarding public contribution towards the betterment of their life, particularly in respect of sanitation, drinking water, family planning, and health care. The purpose was to inquire whether they have adequate access to these basic amenities.

7.3.1 Sanitation Facilities

As it appears from Annex II Table 7.4, about 71% of the total respondents in the rural areas have no latrine, while about 25% use *kutcha* latrines and 4% use sanitary latrines. The sanitary latrines have been provided by the government organizations (GOs) and NGOs at a subsidized rate. The situation is better in the urban slums. About 55% of the respondents use *kutcha* latrines, 37% use sanitary latrines and the rest (9%) have no latrine at all. Most of the sanitary latrines have been built up by the city corporation, and thus the contribution of the government in the urban slum areas is better than the rural areas. The estimated value of $\chi^2 = 143.58$ indicates that the association between the two criteria of classification is significant as it stands at 0.001%, that is, the use of sanitation (with levels: *kutcha,* sanitary and no latrine) and residence (with levels: urban and rural) are interdependent.

7.3.2 Family Planning

The overpopulation problem has been identified by the government as the most acute problem of the country in general and among the poor in particular. As about 85% of the total population live in the villages, the family planning programme is an appropriate vehicle for addressing the population problem as a part of a strategy of poverty alleviation in the rural areas.

Regarding the source of information about family planning, the majority of the respondents (about 89% in the urban and 93% in rural areas) are found to know about family planning through government publicity (TV, radio, newspapers, etc) (Annex II Table 7.5). The NGOs as sources of this information are not really significant—9% in urban areas and 6% in rural areas.

7.3.3 Drinking Water Facilities

With different sources of water, the government can surely take credit for ensuring almost universal access to drinking water. In the urban areas 35% of the households have access to tap water. Another 50% have access to tubewells. In the rural areas 83% of the respondent households have access to tubewells (Annex II Table 7.6).

The NGOs play an important role in supplying drinking water to the urban areas. Forty-two per cent of the respondent households have access to these sources. NGO contribution in this regard is almost insignificant in the rural areas (Annex II Table 7.7).

To sum up, the role of the government in the provision of basic facilities like sanitation, water supply, family planning and primary health care is positive and wider than that of the NGOs except in the case of water supply in the urban slums. As illustrated above, the poor in both urban and rural areas are getting more benefits from public resources, though the quantification of spending from public resources has not been done at this stage. But the coverage is partial and is, therefore, not satisfactory. It should be noted here that sanitation and hygiene, safe drinking water, family planning and vaccination are considered to be indispensable basic needs for a healthy and active life. Although problems related to health have a direct bearing on the earning capacity of the poor, the public health facilities are not adequately accessible to them. As a matter of fact, merely 12% of sicknesses in rural areas is treated in the public health centres and the rest is taken care of by private medical practitioners, pharmacists and quacks (Rahman 1996). This figure raises serious questions about the effectiveness of the public health infrastructure. It indicates that increasing allocation of public resources for public health would not suffice unless complemented by proper utilization of these resources. Most of these findings of the quantitative survey have been supported by qualitative assessment by the poor themselves.

7.3.4 Health Care

With respect to the contribution of the government to the provision of primary health care facilities, about 61% respondents in the urban and 75% in the rural areas have said that their children have been vaccinated. It is interesting to note that the coverage of vaccination is higher among the rural respondents than among their urban counterparts (Annex II Table 7.8).

Furthermore, it appears from Annex II Table 7.9 that about 61% of the respondents who have had their children vaccinated have completed the full course and the rest have not, due to the unavailability of primary health workers. Some of them have said that time is not yet over for the completion of the full course.

Annex II Table 7.10 shows that about 58% of the respondents in the urban and 74% in the rural areas have received vaccination facilities from government health workers and about one-fourth respondents have got the facilities from family planning welfare workers. NGOs perform very little role in this regard as only 16% of the respondents in the urban and 1% in the rural areas have received vaccination facilities from NGO workers. The quality of public expenditure on health care has been studied more intensively using qualitative methods.

7.4 Monitoring the Effectiveness of Public Expenditure: Some Illustrations

The quality of public spending in any sector in terms of effectiveness and equity largely depends on the accessibility and quality of services, and the categories of beneficiaries whom public spending serves. As test cases, the health and education sectors have been selected to assess the effectiveness and equity of public spending. The budget review reveals that nearly one-fourth of total public spending goes to these two important social sectors.

As regards the health sector, the following questions have been addressed in this study: what major diseases afflict the urban and the rural poor? Is the health care system provided by the public providers accessible to the poor? What is the quality of health care with respect to the availability of doctors, medical equipments, etc?

Regarding primary education, the study focuses on the following questions: what is the enrolment status of boys and girls ? What are the drop-out rates? Does the FFE programme have any impact on the participation of the primary-age children? Is the programme effective in improving the drop-out rate of children? Is the programme effective in reducing child-labour? Such issues have been investigated using qualitative techniques, the findings of which are given below.

7.4.1 Health

The members of the communities were approached in dialogical sessions to reflect on some common issues relating to health and health care providers. After discussions and debate they gave a consensus on those issues. The following are the findings derived from the sessions.

7.4.1.1 Incidence of diseases: The incidence of diseases is found to be almost the same among both the urban and the rural poor (Figures 7.1, 7.2 and 7.3). Most commonly suffered diseases are: diarrhoea, dysentery, asthma, jaundice, fever, intestinal pain, chickenpox, typhoid, etc. In the urban slums, ringworms, worms, itching, indigestion, cardiac diseases are the most common ones.

7.4.1.2 Medical care providers and beneficiaries: Medical service providers are available in both the urban and rural areas. In addition to government and private health care providers, NGOs have emerged as new sources of health care for the poor in the urban areas (Figure 7.4). However, NGOs do not seem to have been able to expand health services so markedly in the rural areas (Figure 7.5).

Although there are several modern health providers in the urban areas, particularly in Dhaka city, most of them are not accessible to the poorest segment of the urban population. Both the urban and the rural poor are found not to have benefited at all from the private hospitals and clinics. The well-off persons are found to be the only beneficiaries of these providers. As the urban poor cannot afford modern health services, they are found to fall back on cheap and traditional health providers, namely herbalists, and homeopaths. Besides, the urban poor obtain health care from NGOs, diarrhoeal hospitals and government health assistants. It must be mentioned that government health assistants have very limited services to offer. Government general hospitals and other specialized hospitals are also found to have failed to make their services available to the poor.

In the rural context, the medical profile of the poor is found to be somewhat different. The rural poor are found to have accessed medicare from both the *thana* and union level health complexes/clinics. Additionally, the rural poor take medicare from herbalists, pharmacists/drug-sellers and local trained doctors. Like the urban poor, the rural poor are found to be excluded from the accessibility of medical

Figure 7.1 **Incidence of Diseases among the Slum Poor (in Dhaka City)**

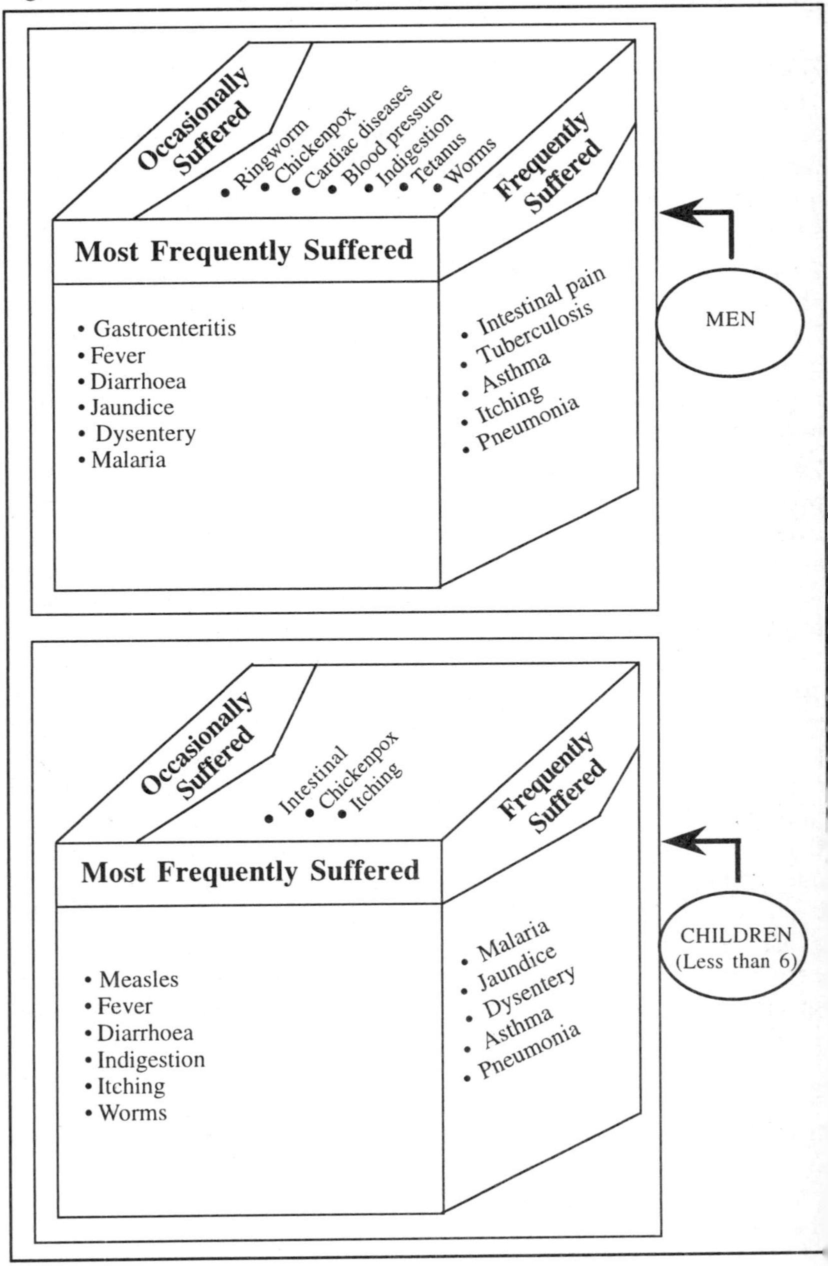

Figure 7.1 (Continued)

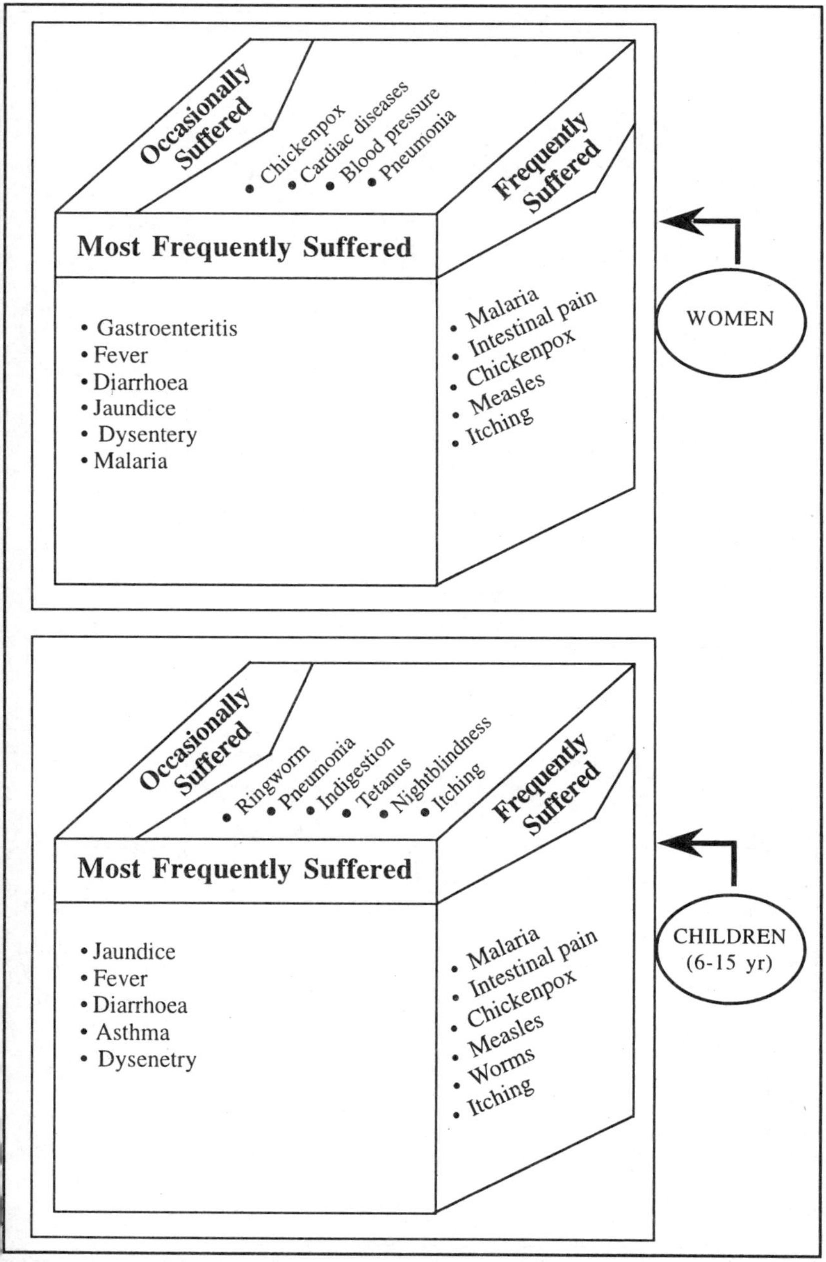

Figure 7.2 Incidence of Diseases among the Poor (in Rural Areas)

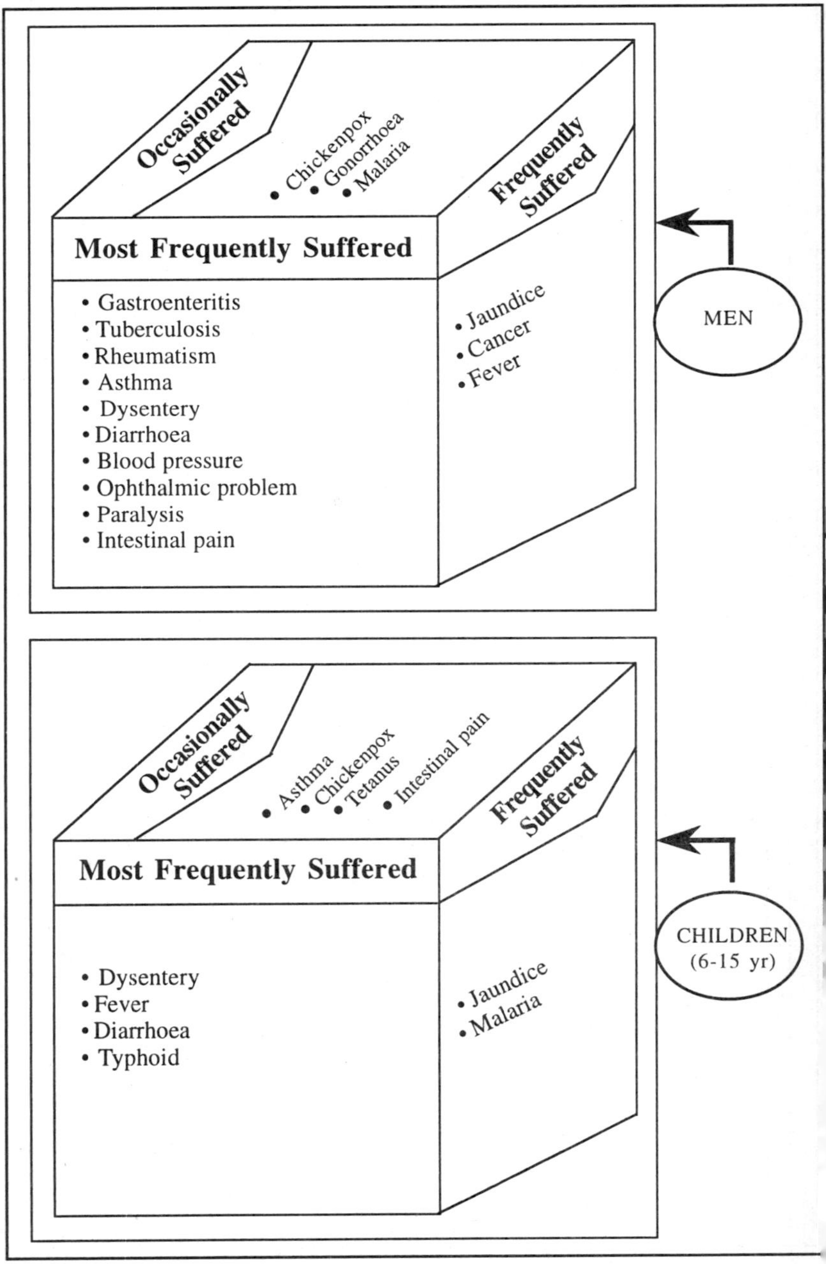

Figure 7.2 (Continued)

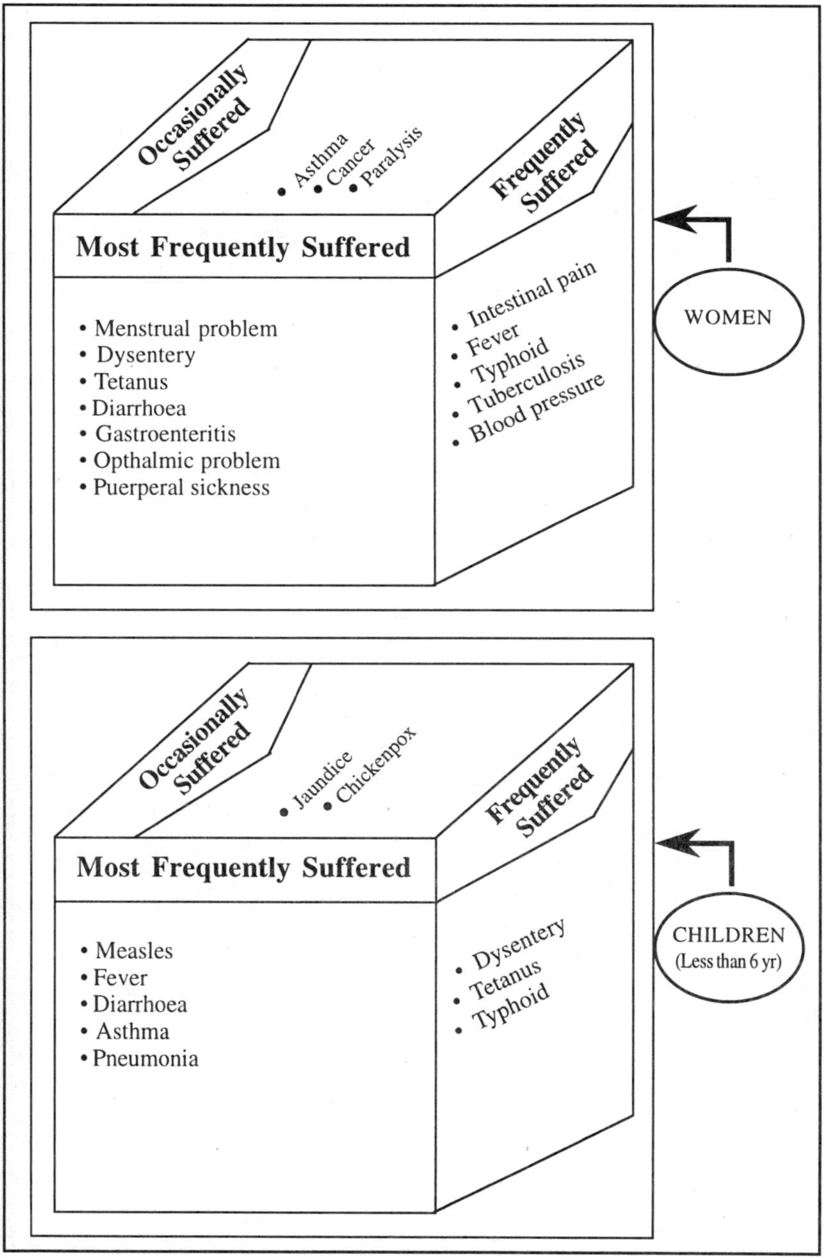

Figure 7.3 Diseases of Topmost Incidence

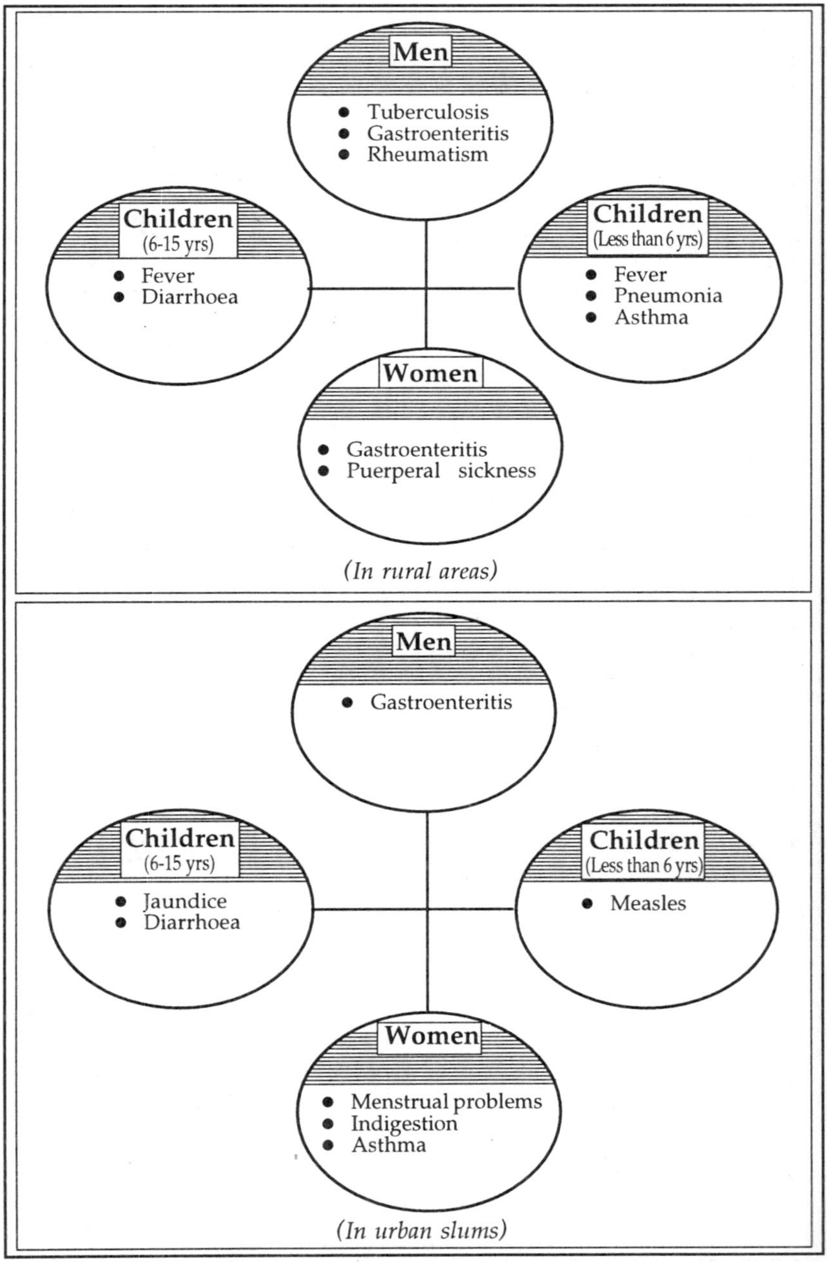

Figure 7.4 Urban Beneficiaries and Health Service Providers (as Perceived by Slum Dwellers in Dhaka City)

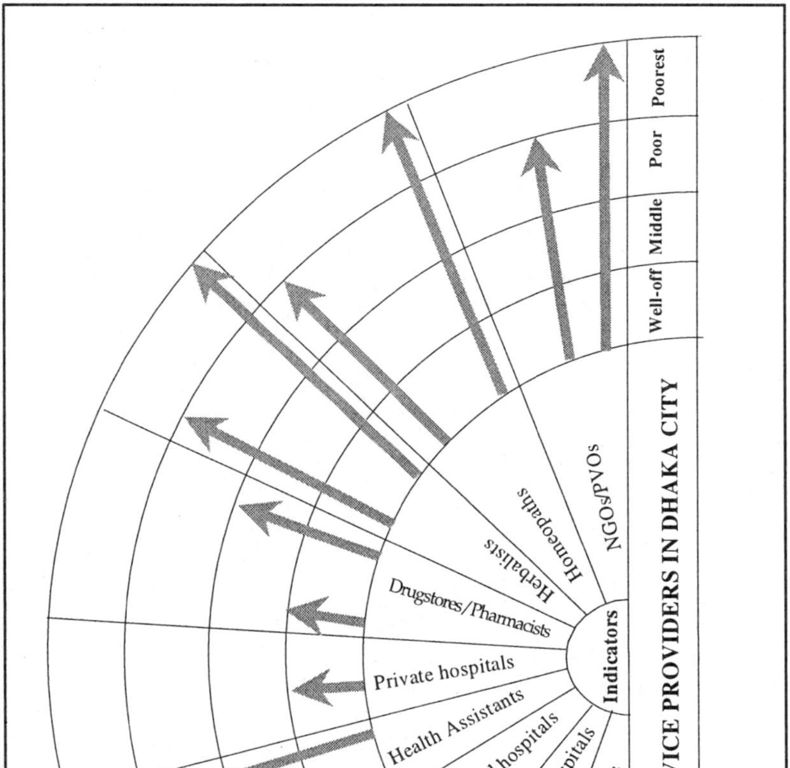

Figure 7.5 Rural Beneficiaries and Health Service Providers (as Perceived by the Poor)

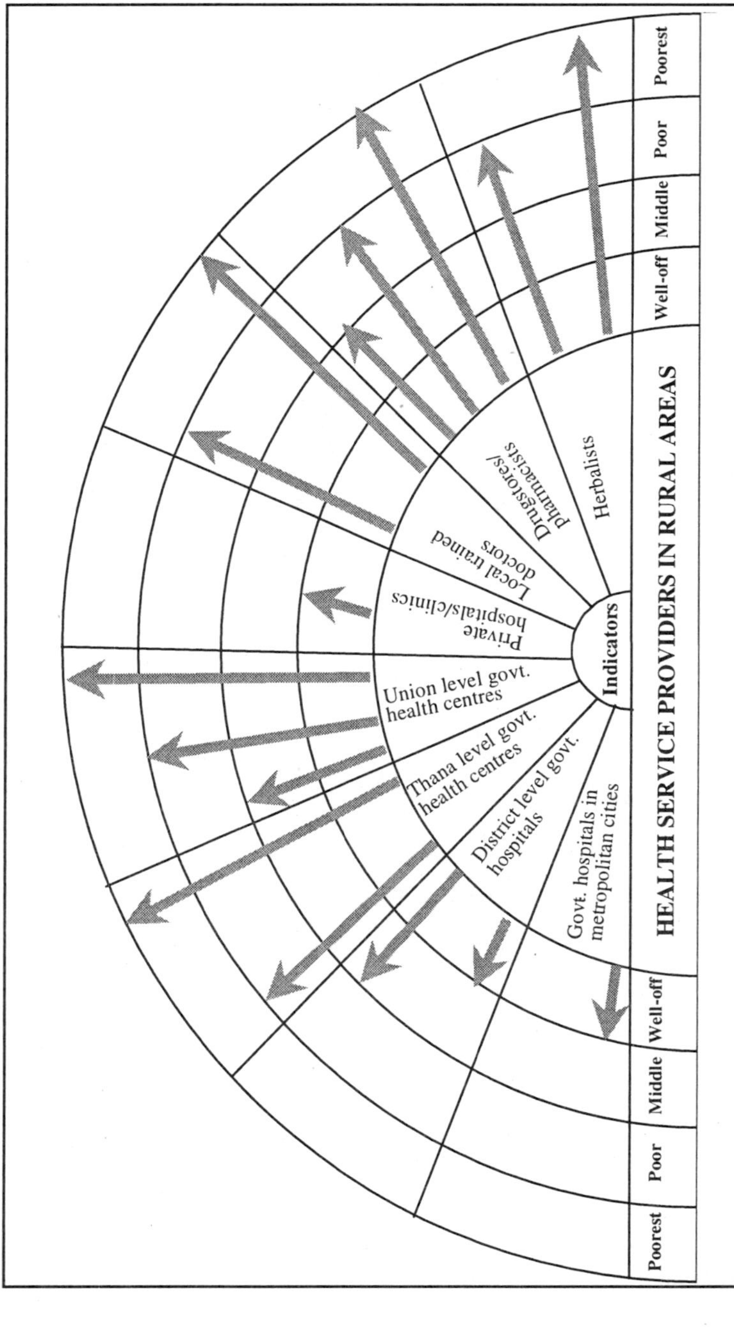

Note : Health services regularly and frequently used by the four social classes have been presented here facilities of the government hospitals in the metropolitan cities, private hospitals and clinics.

7.4.1.3 Quality of medical care: The poor in both the urban and rural settings have expressed their feelings about the overall services rendered by the major medical care providers. The poor have expressed their perceptions in terms of 12 indicators, such as the number of doctors, the quality of doctor's services, the number of medical instruments, the quality of instruments, etc.

Three major types of medical care providers, namely the government hospitals/health centres, private hospitals/clinics and health programmes of NGOs were put to participatory assessment by the poor. Regarding the overall quality of medicare provided by the government and private providers, the poor were found strongly dissatisfied at giving more ratings for 'very bad' and 'bad' on a four-point rating scale (very good, good, bad and very bad) in terms of the selected indicators (Figure 7.6). On the other hand, the medical services rendered by NGOs received more favourable appreciation from the poor than the services of the government and private health care providers.

However, as assessed more specifically by the urban poor, the medical care of government hospitals is satisfactory in terms of the number of doctors and the number and quality of medical instruments (Figures 7.7 and 7.8). In the case of the private hospitals/clinics, their services were also found to be satisfactory regarding the number of specialized doctors, their skills, the number of instruments and their quality. As for the NGOs, the quality of medicare provided by them is assessed as very good in other terms, namely the quality of physicians' advice. Their physicians are more prompt, attentive and skilled. Above all, their services are accompanied by a supply of the medicines needed for treatment.

In the rural areas, the quality of medical services at the *thana* and union level health complex/clinic is perceived by the villagers to be extremely poor in terms of most of the indicators (Figure 7.9 and 7.10). The villagers are found satisfied with the beds in the Thana Health Centre.

In some parts of the rural areas, the number of doctors and the quality of their services, as well as the number of instruments and their quality at the *Thana* Health Complex were assessed as satisfactory. However, the quality of doctors' services was found universally, and extremely poor in terms of promptness and attention. The condition of the union level health centres was found worse in every respect, everywhere in the rural areas.

Figure 7.6 The Poor's Perceptions about Various Health Service Providers

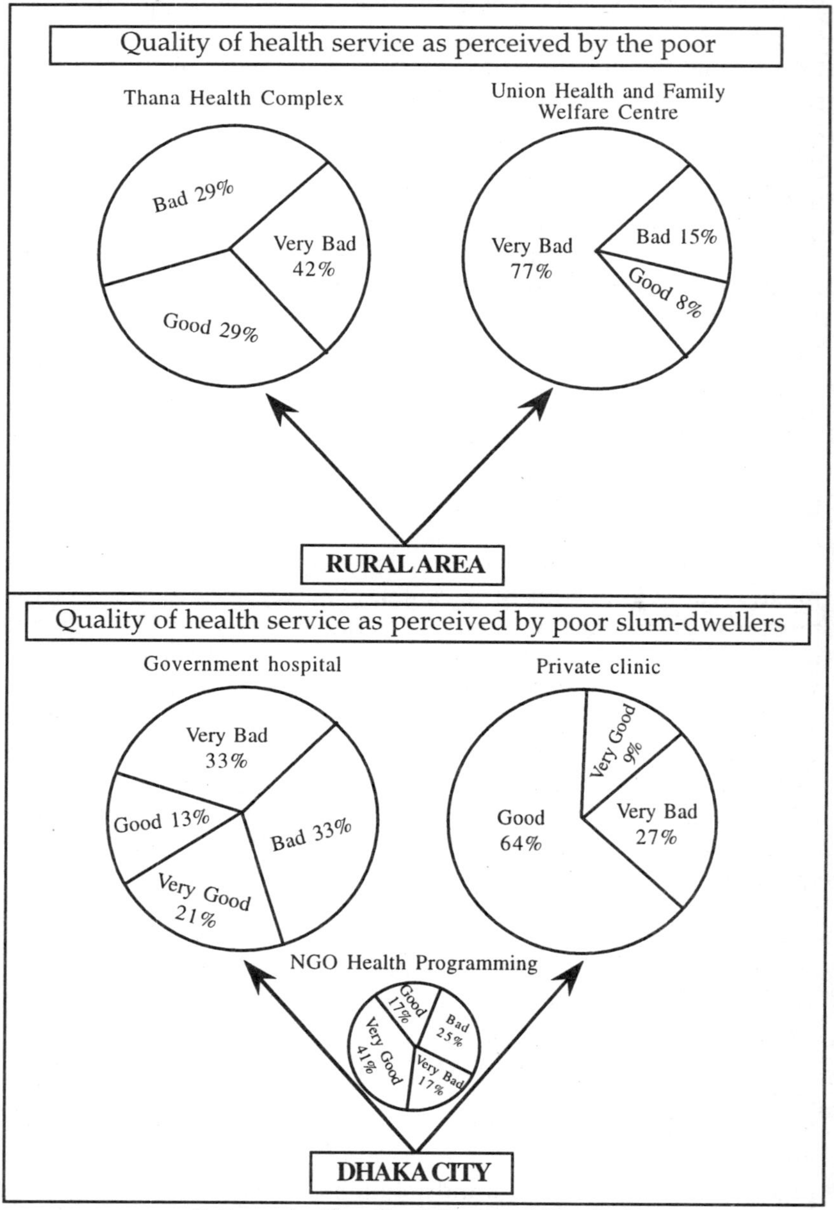

Rating scale : Very Good; Good; Bad; Very Bad.
Note : Percentage implies the percentage of the poor.

Figure 7.7 Quality of Medical Services of Government Hospitals/Clinics (as Perceived by the Residents of Motaher Slum in Dhaka City)

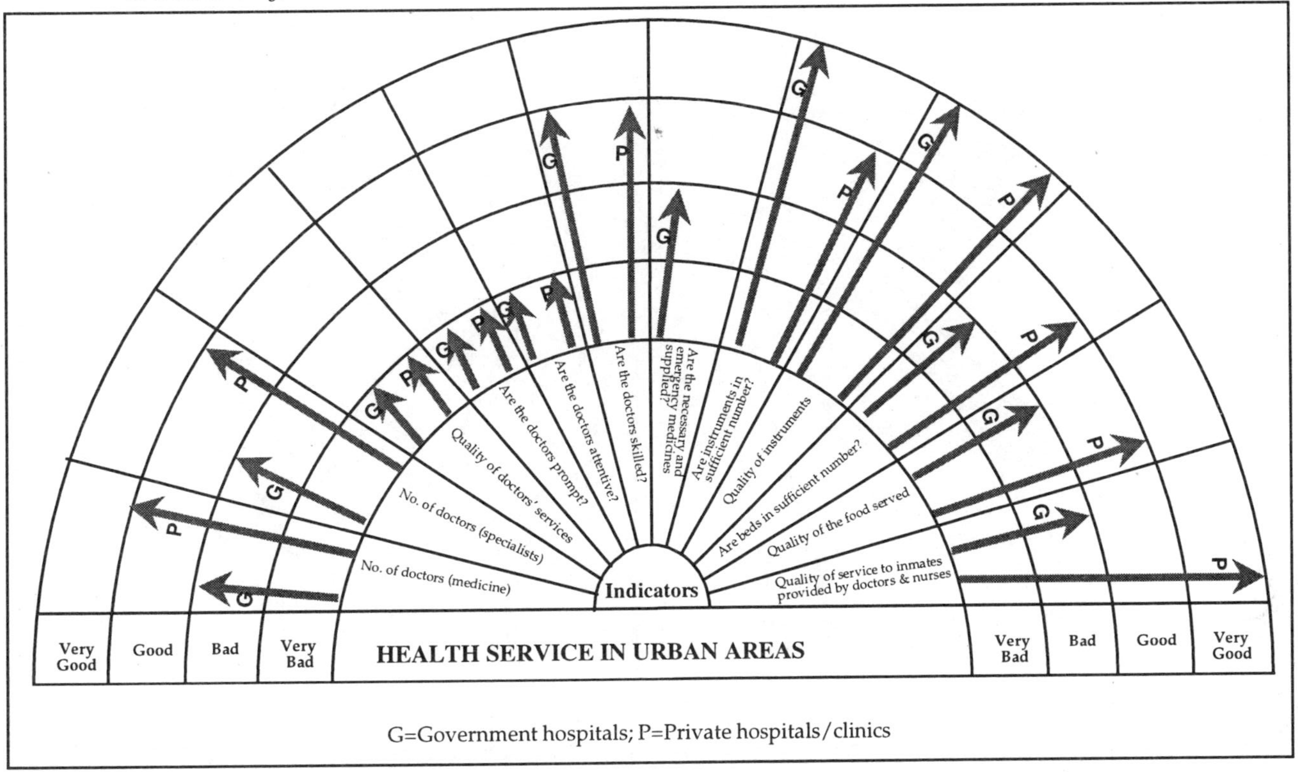

Figure 7.8 Quality of Medical Services of Government Hospitals and NGOs (as Perceived by the Residents of Titipara Slum in Dhaka City)

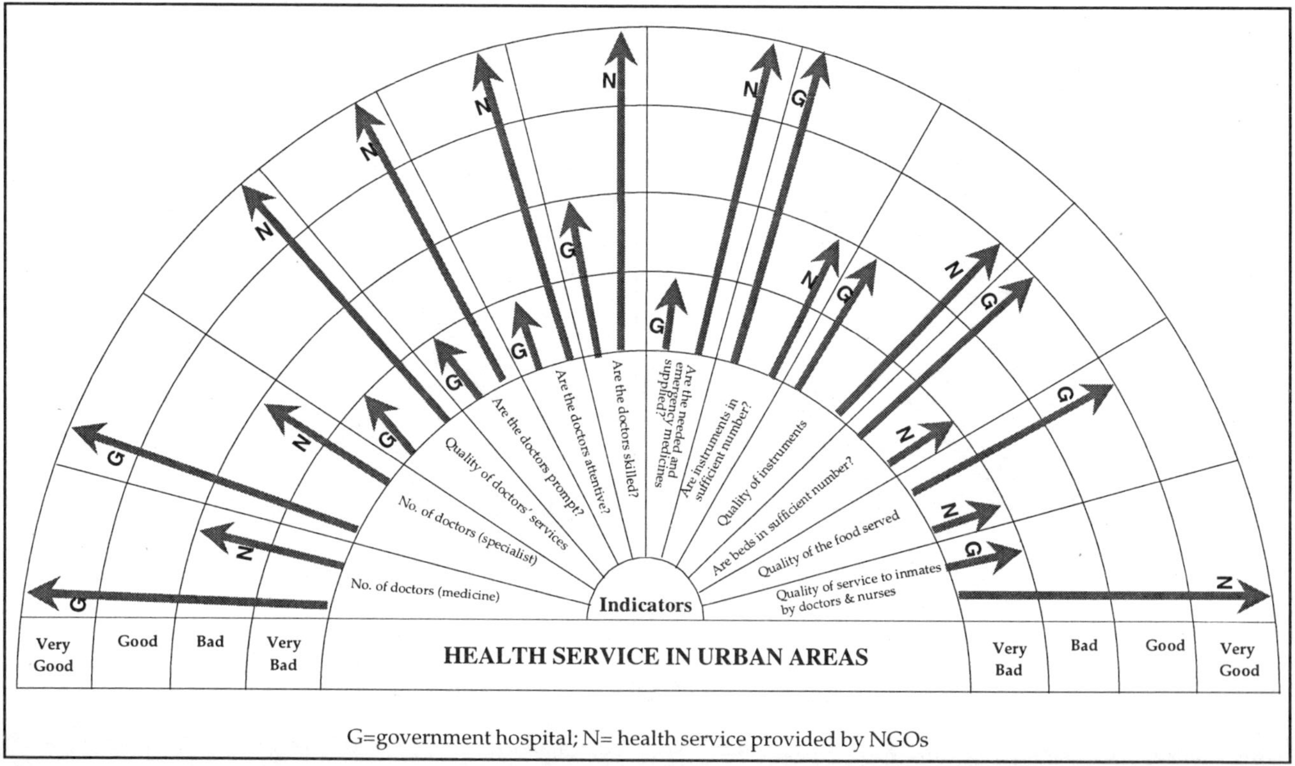

Figure 7.9 Quality of Medical Services of Thana and Union Level Government Health Centres (Kotiadi Thana)

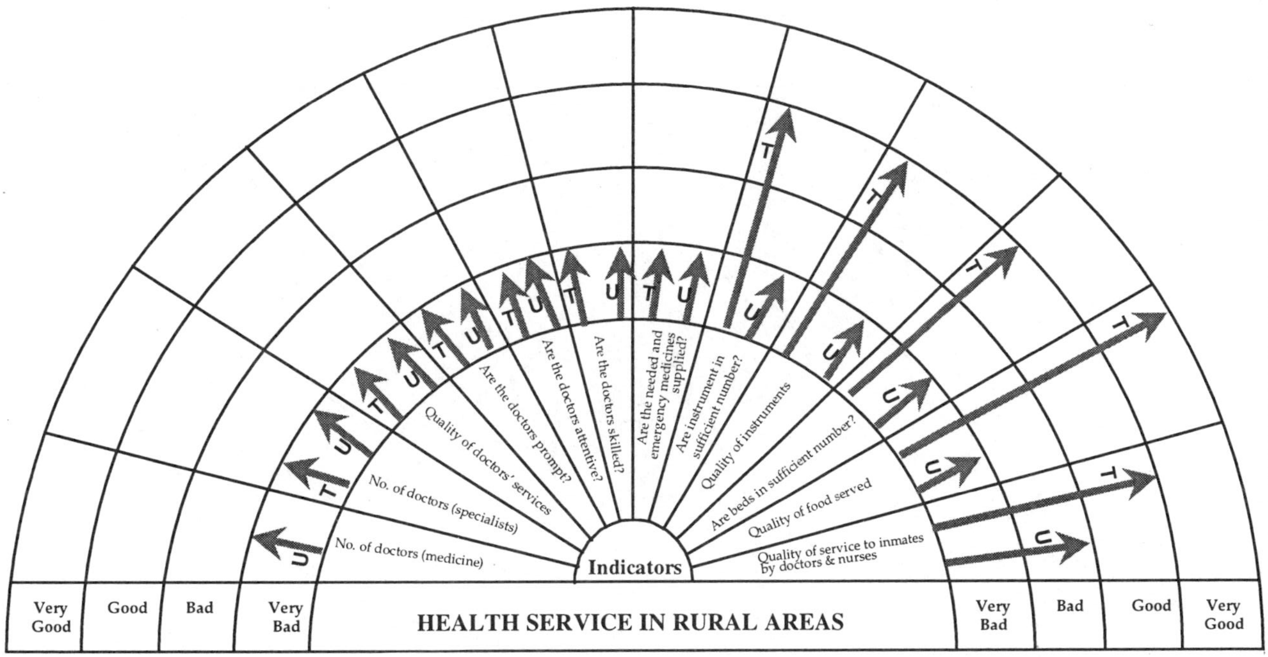

T=*Thana* Health Complex; U= Union Health Family Wealfare Centres

Figure 7.10 Quality of Medical Services of Thana and Union Level Government Health Centres (Ulipur Thana)

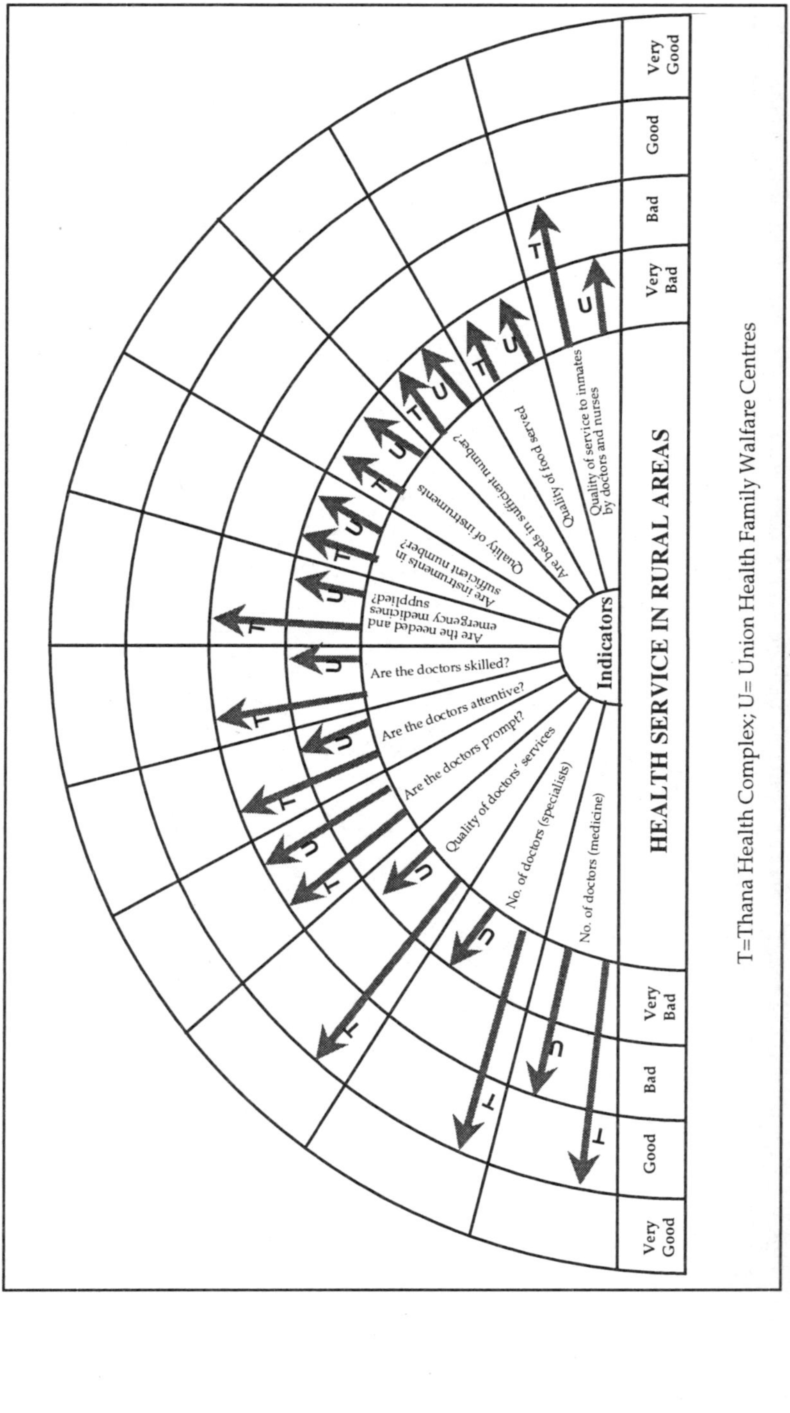

Figure 7.11 Causes of Not Getting Health Service at Thana/Union Health Centres

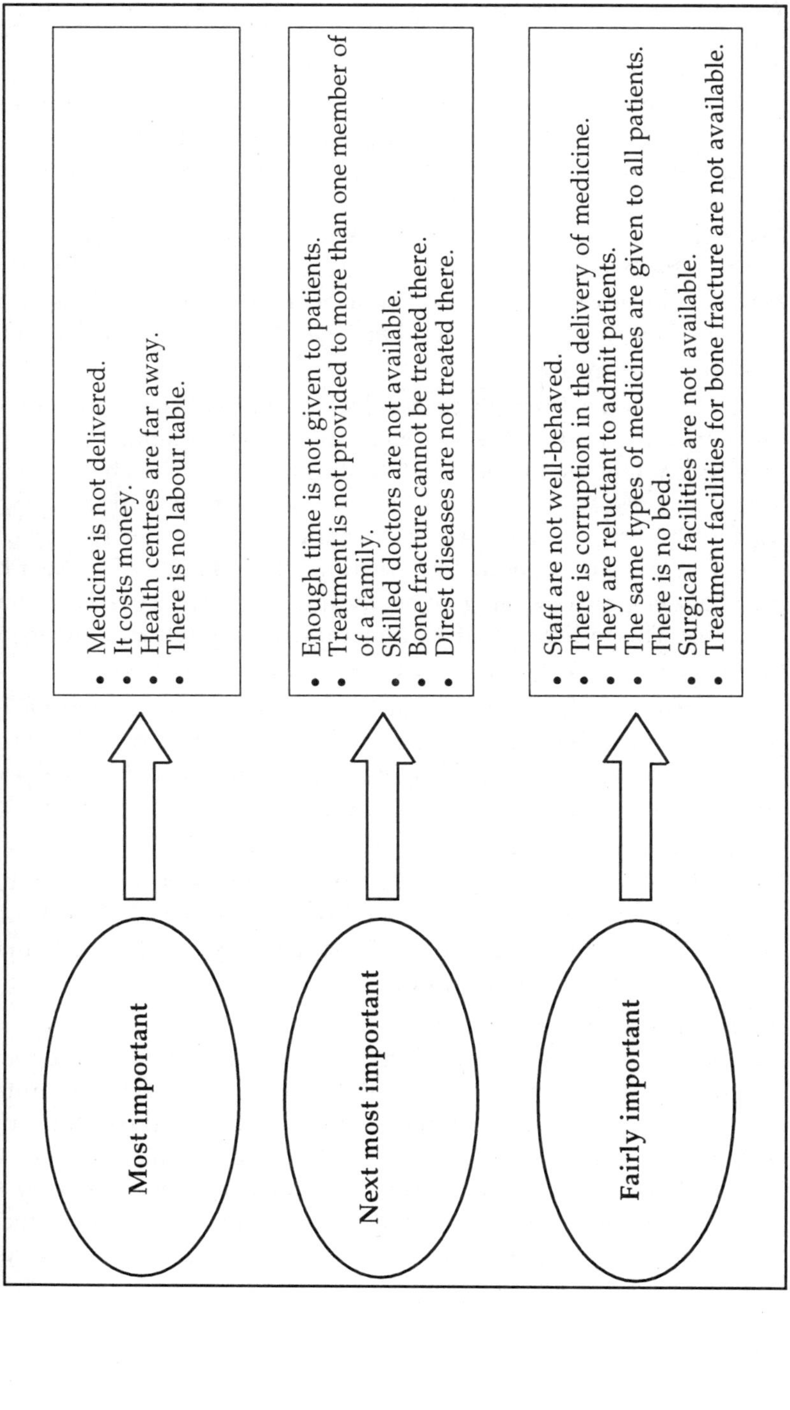

7.4.1.4 Causes of not utilizing medical services: Despite the high incidence of diseases, the rural people are found unwilling to avail themselves of medical care at the *thana* and union level government health complexes/centres (Figure 7.11). The most important causes of this are: the health centre is far away; there is no labour table; the services entail costs; medicine is not supplied; the doctors are reluctant to admit patients; surgical facilities are not available, and so on.
In the rural areas, despite many weaknesses of the health care system, the poor have to visit the government health complexes/centres at the *thana*/union level, because the skill of the doctors at this level are perceived by them to be better than that of other medicare providers available in the locality.

7.4.1.5 Preference for medical service providers: The urban poor and villagers have ranked the key medical care providers based on five criteria, namely 'quality service', 'prompt service', 'less hassle', 'easy access' and 'less costly' (Figures 7.12 and 7.13). In the urban area, private doctors (homeopaths) and government hospitals are preferred by poor people in terms of the above criteria (Figures 7.14 and 7.15). The urban poor have had mixed feelings about the quality of care at the government hospitals. This indicates that the government hospitals are still meeting the health care of a segment of the poor in the urban areas.

7.4.1.6 Health of the poorest of the poor: some findings from 1993-96 poverty monitoring: Poverty is being monitored by the study team in terms of some socio-economic aspects of the poorest people in both rural and urban areas (Chapter 9 for details).

A. Access to Drinking Water

The poorest households both in the urban and rural areas have almost universal access to drinking water (Annex II Tables 7.11 and 7.12). Tubewell water is the only source of portable water for them in both the areas during the reference period.

B. State of Sanitation

The poorest households in both the urban and rural areas are found lacking in safe sanitation during the monitoring period. Insanitary conditions are more acute in the rural areas than in the urban slums (Annex II Tables 7.11 and 7.12). In the urban slums, 100% of the households were using *kutcha* (pit and fenced) latrines in 1993 and the figure declined to 50% in 1996 showing encouraging improvement during the period. The rest of the latrines were water-sealed. But in the rural areas, 92% of the poorest households did not have any latrine and 8% used *kutcha* latrines in 1993. The situation improved marginally to 87% and 13% respectively during the monitoring period.

So far as the geographical distribution is concerned, the state of insanitation (regarding latrines) is more acute in the central parts than in the northern parts during this period. The relatively encouraging situation in this respect in the northern parts is, however, mainly due to the better resource endowments of the programme (FFE) households than those of the non-FFE households.

C. Health

Regarding the health conditions of the poorest people, four aspects, namely morbidity, medical expenditure, utilizing medical services of government hospitals/health clinics and the quality of the medical service of government hospitals/health complexs, have been investigated under the poverty monitoring. The findings are as follows:

i. Morbidity

The morbidity of the members of the poorest households irrespective of age and sex shows alarming signs. The overall incidence of diseases regardless of age and sex has registered about 137% growth over the 1993-96 period (Annex II Table 7.13). The change in the incidence of diseases is at on alarmingly higher level among children and women han among men. The poorest people are found to have mostly suffered seven diseases/health problems, namely fever, diarrhoea, gastroenteritis, intestinal pain, asthma, skin diseases and feeling of weakness which accounted for 74% of all the incidence of diseases during he monitoring period. These diseases are mainly caused by socio-conomic and environmental factors.

The differences in the incidence of diseases among men, women nd children were not so remarkable in the urban slums compared to hose in the rural areas during the monitoring period (Annex II Tables .14 and 7.15). However, in the rural areas, there is a significant difference n the growth in the incidence of diseases among these groups of people f the poorest households during the same period.

Regional difference in the incidence of diseases was also significant uring the monitoring period. The central parts of the country had an larmingly higher incidence of diseases (75) than that in the northern arts (36) (Annex II Table 7.15). As insanitation was alarmingly higher n the central parts, this might be the cause of the higher incidence of iseases in the area.

Figure 7.12 Preference Ranking of Medical Service Providers by Urban Slum Dwellers

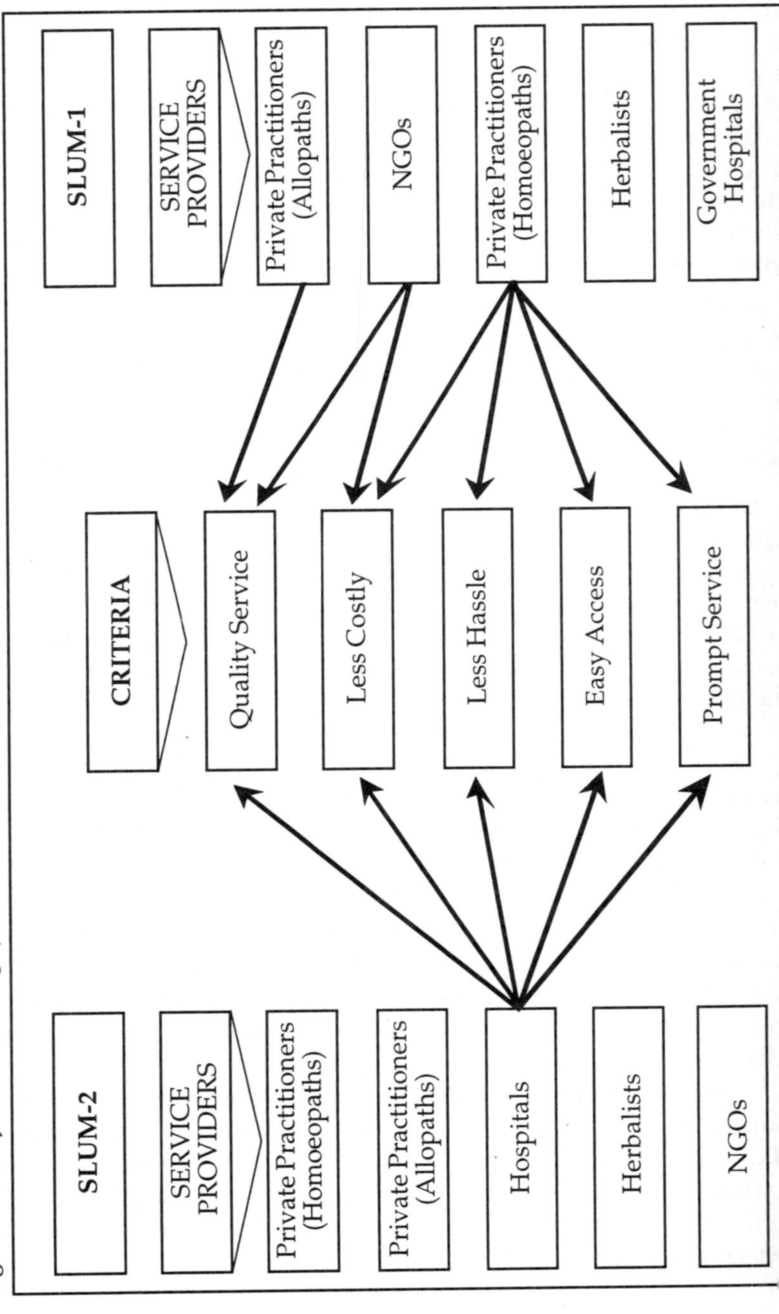

Figure 7.13 Preference Ranking of Medical Service Providers by the Rural Poor

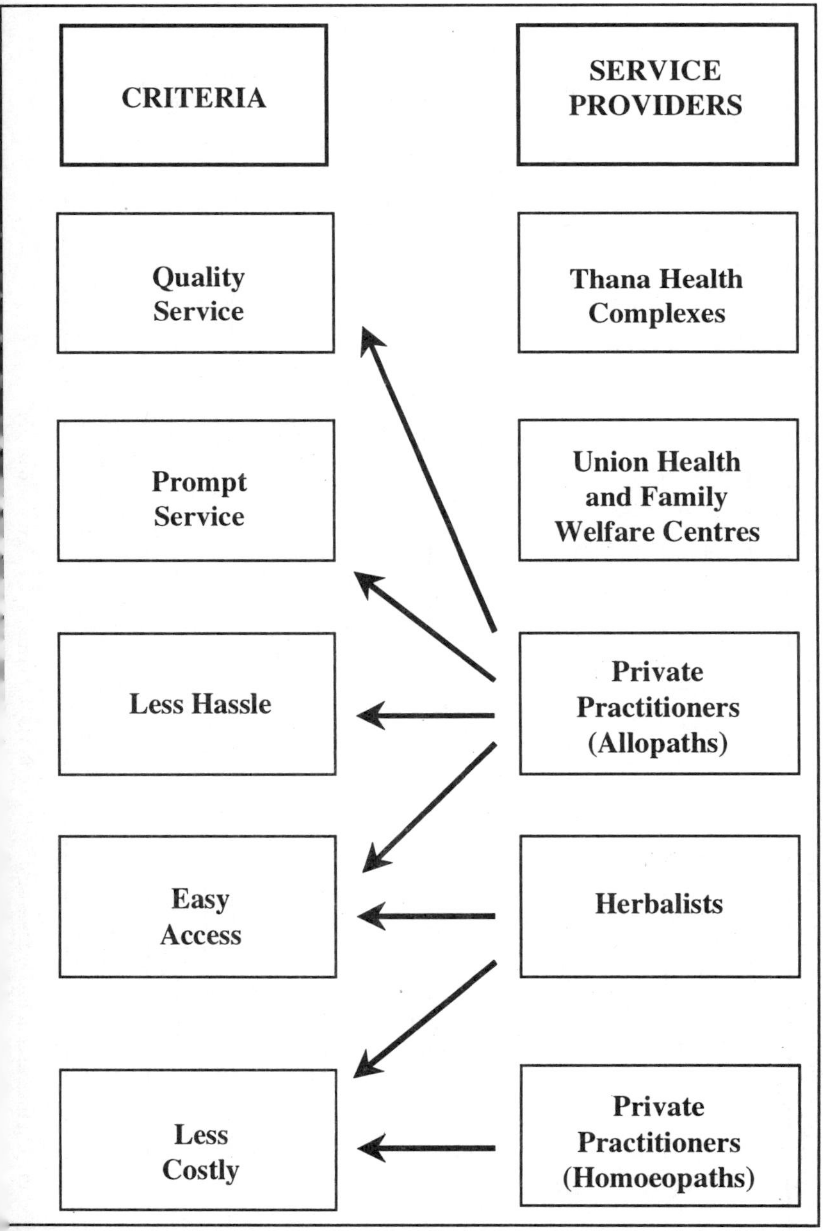

Figure 7.14 Preference Ranking of Medical Service Providers by Slum Dwellers in Dhaka City

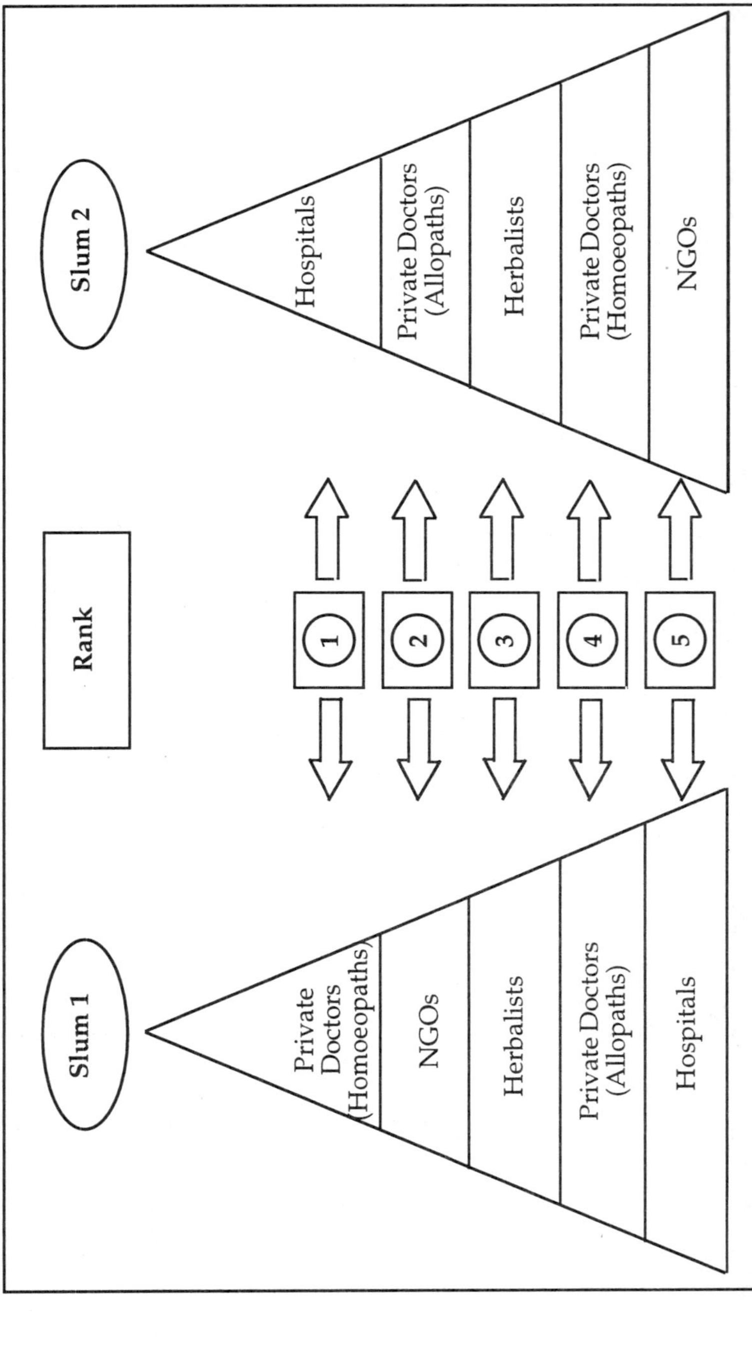

Note : On the basis of total scores against five criteria (for criteria, see figures 16 or 17)

Figure 7.15 Preference Ranking of Medical Service Providers in Rural Areas

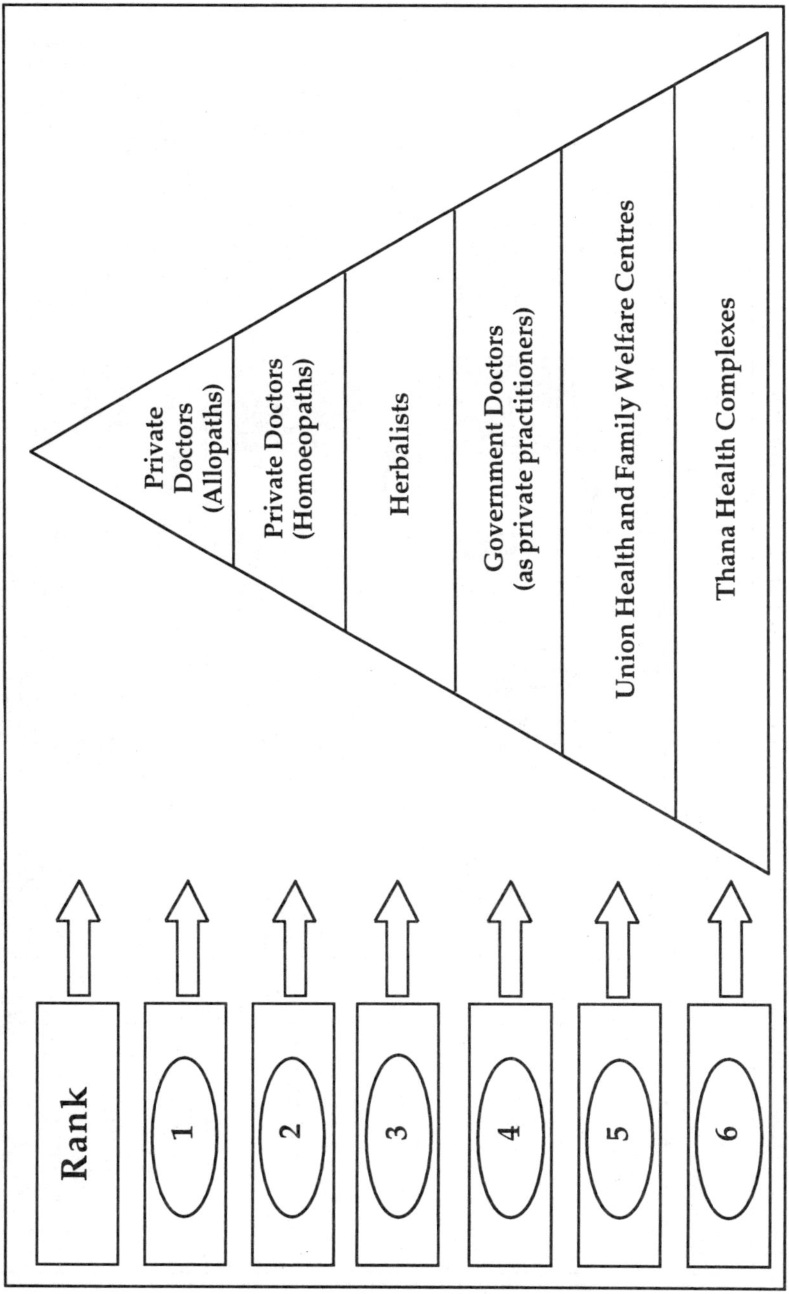

Figure 7.16 Enrolment/Participation Growth Before and After the FFE Programme

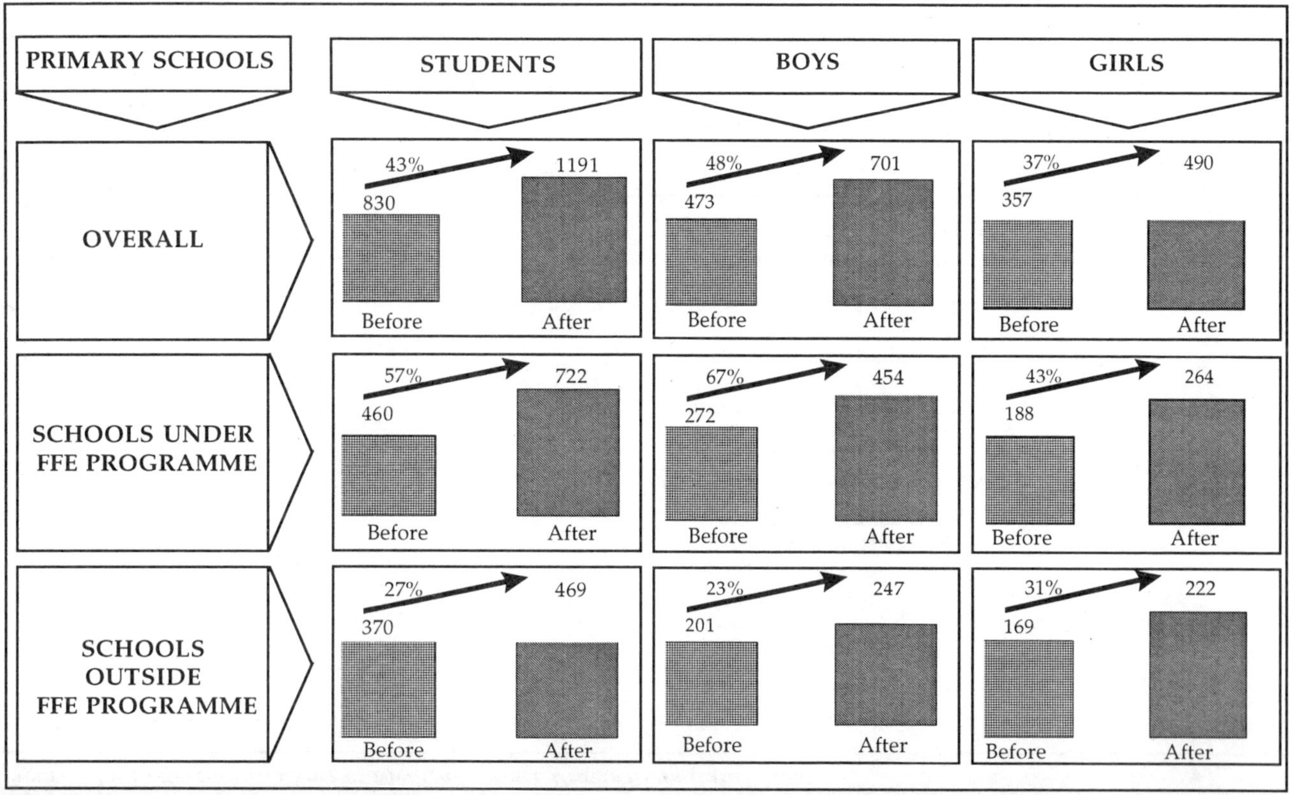

Figure 7.17 Enrolment/Participation Growth (Average No. of Students Per Year)

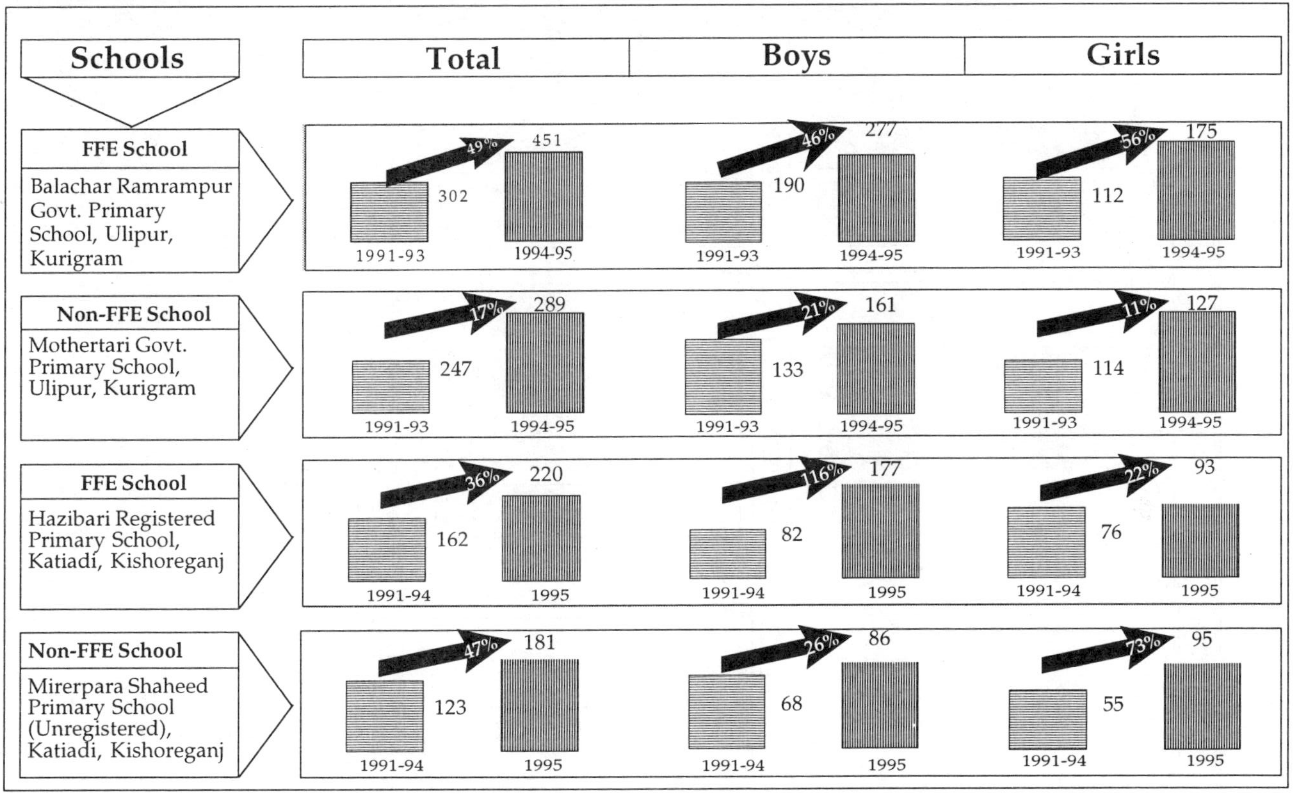

***Figure 7.18** Enrolment Rate at the Primary Level by Social Categories and Gender*

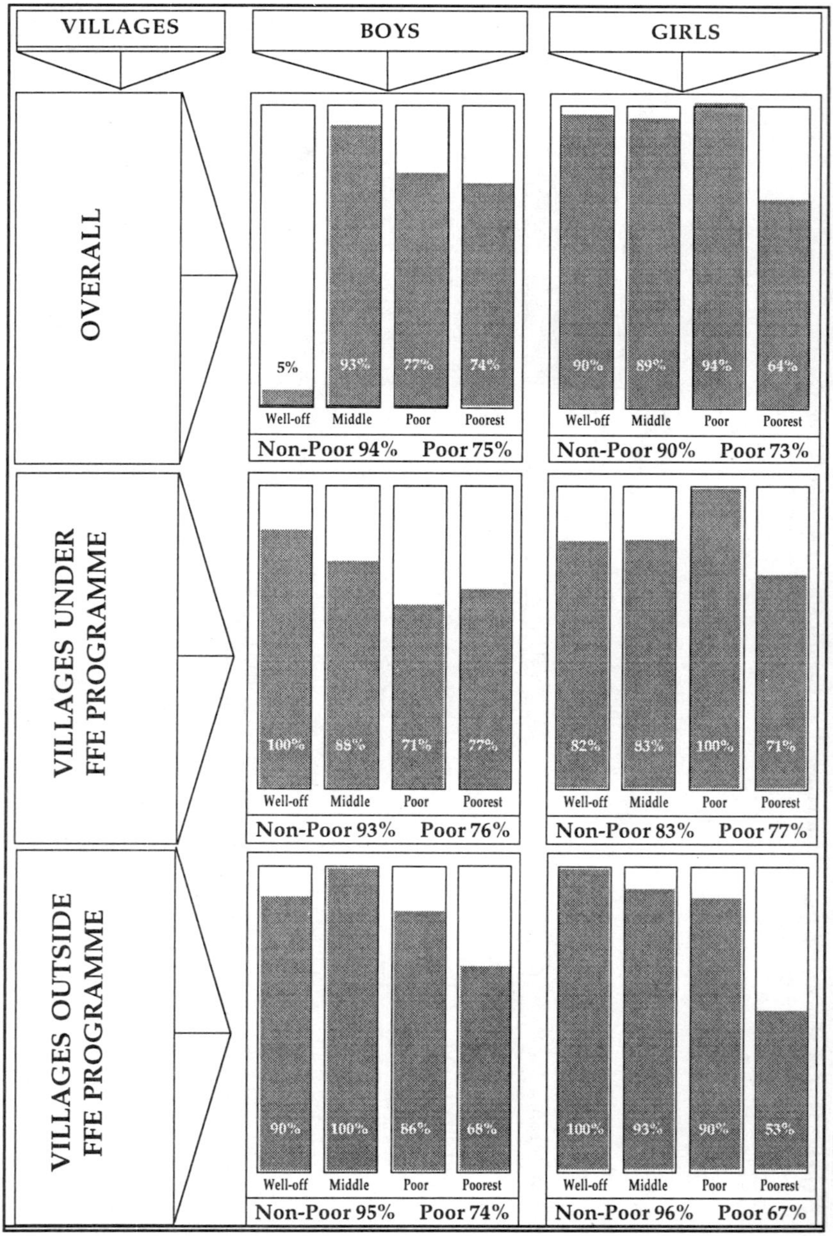

ii. Medical expenditure

The medical expenditure incurred by the poorest households escalated sharply due to high morbidity during the period, which appears to be abnormal (Annex II Table 7.16). The overall per capita expenditure on medical treatment is found to have increased by 245% from Tk. 38 in 1993 to Tk. 131 in 1996. In the case of urban slums, per capita medical expenditure, decreased (-32%) but it recorded a sharp increase (383%) in the rural areas.

A gender and age bias is found to have been present in the distribution of medical expenditure of the poorest households. Intra-household disparity in this matter shows that adult male members have spent the lion's share (87%) of the total medical expenditure of the households, and this share increased over time leaving very little for the women (6%) and children (7%). Although children and women had a higher incidence of diseases, they had a disproportionately lower share in health expenditure indicating highly inequitous intra-household resource distribution during the monitoring period. The inequity has been more stark in the rural areas than in the urban areas. The urban-rural differences in intra-household resource distribution for medical treatment may be explained by the relative difference in the control of women and children over household resources due to their different levels of engagement in income-earning activities. As women and children are engaged in income-earning activities in a higher proportion in the urban slums compared to the rural areas, they have faced less discrimination in this regard (Annex II Table 7.17). Medical expenditure varied among the three groups of households during the monitoring period (Annex II Table 7.18). The per capita medical expenditure has been much lower for the FFE households than the non-FFE households. The non-FFE households in the control villages had to incur the highest expenditure probably due to the poor health condition and high morbidity of these groups.

iii. Utilizing medical services of government hospitals/health clinics

The government hospitals/health centres are found to have provided very little to the poorest people in the country. In the rural areas, the average number of visits per poorest household to a government hospital/health clinic was 1.5 times only in 1993.This further declined to 1.2 times in 1996 (Annex II Table 7.19). In the urban slums, the poorest households hardly get any medical service from government hospitals in Dhaka city (Annex II Table 7.20). The number of visits to government hospitals by the urban poor is also found to have been very insignificant although this increased during the monitoring period from 0.1 to 0.6 during 1993-96. Similarly, the average number of visits to the poorest households by the Family Welfare Assistants and Health Assistants is also found to have declined during the same period (Annex II Table 7.21). In the urban slums, the frequency of their visits, however, has remained unchanged.

iv. Quality of the medical service of government hospitals/health complexes
More than one-third of the members of the poorest households could not say anything about the medical services provided by government health complexes in the rural areas because they hardly made visits to the health complexes during the monitoring priod (Annex II Table 7.22). The quality of care at the government health complexes has been assessed to be extremely poor by the poorest people in the rural areas. Barring a large number of non-responses, the majority of them (51-61%) felt that the quality of the care was highly unsatisfactory (bad and very bad) in terms of adequacy of doctors, services of doctors, availability of medicine and beds and serviceability of instruments in 1996. Very few of them were found, however, satisfied with the quality of the care. The findings indicate that the quality of the care in terms of the above indicators is improving, although at a very slow pace during the same period. Regionally, no remarkable variation is observed with regard to the quality of medical services of the government health centres in the rural areas (Annex II Table 7.23).

In the urban slums, as the poorest households did not have enough experience of the services of the government hospitals in Dhaka city, they expressed their inablity to assess the medical services provided by these hospitals (Annex II Table 7.24).

In the rural areas, the poor got medical services from the government's domiciliary service delivery system. The poor beneficiaries were asked to assess the services of the health and family planning domiciliary personnel. Close to one-third (32-37%) of the poorest households could not give their perceptions of them in 1996 (Annex II Table 7.25). This indicates that they did not have any interaction with the Family Welfare Assistants (FWA) and Health Assistants (HA) during the monitoring period. More than half of them are found to have been satisfied with their services (good and very good: 60-62%). Only 5% of the poor graded the services of the Health Assistants as highly unsatisfactory. These findings, therefore, suggest that barring the excluded households, those who got the domiciliary services were satisfied with them. However, failure to provide services to a considerable portion of the poor is found to have been one of the major problems in the delivery system of domiciliary services.

The same problem is also found in the urban slums (Annex II Table 7.26). The poor households in one of the sample slums is found to have been completely outside the service network of FWAs and HAs. Out of the two, only one slum is found to have been under the domiciliary service delivery system.

7.4.2 Primary Education

7.4.2.1 Enrolment: The rate of enrolment of primary-age children is increasing among both boys and girls in all primary schools irrespective of the FFE programme (Figures 7.16 and 7.17). The enrolment is increasing at a higher rate in schools under the FFE programme than in other schools. Overall, the enrolment of boys is increasing at a higher rate than that of girls. However, the enrolment of boys is found to be more than that of girls in the FFE schools but not in the non-FFE schools.

It is found from the village-level investigation of both the programme (under FFE programme) and control villages (without FFE programme) that 79% of primary-level school-age children are enrolled (boys: 81% and girls: 77%) on the average (Figure 7.18 and Annex II Table 7.27). However, contrary to what one might have expected, the enrolment rate (79%) in the programme village is found not that much different from that (78%) in the contol villages.

The impact of the FFE programme on the enrolment of children classified by social categories has also been investigated. The village-level PRA findings reveal that the programme does not appear to have had a significant impact on the poorer households with regard to the enrolment of children. It is found that 76% of the school-age children of the poorer households are enrolled in the programme villages as against 70% in the control villages (Annex II Table 7.27).

The programme seems to have some positive impact on the enrolment of girls of poorer families which is evident from the difference in their enrolment rates in the programme (77%) and control villagers (67%).

7.4.2.2 Drop-out: The FFE programme seems to have had some positive impact on the drop-out trend among primary-level students in the programme villages (Figure 7.19 and Annex II Table 7.28). In the programme villages, 1% of the primary level students are found to be dropping out compared to 4% in the control villages. The drop-out rate for the poorest households is found to be 2% in the programme villages compared to 4% in the control villages.

The incidence of drop-out for girls was nil among the poorest households in the programme villages whereas in the control villages the drop-out rate was 3% in 1996.

7.4.2.3 Child labour: The incidence of child labour is more widespread among the poor households (27%) than among the non-poor (12%). The pattern is true of both the programme and control villages. Overall, the prevalence of child labour seems to have been positively affected by the FFE programme in the programme villages (Figures 7.20 and Annex II Table 7.29). It is found that 22% of the primary school-age children are taking part in income-earning activities in the programme villages compared to 24% in the control villages. The incidence of child labour is much less (11-14%) among female children than among male children (30-39%) in the study villages. As far as the poorest households are concerned, the prevalence of child labour follows the general pattern both by gender and age in the study villages. The incidence of child labour for boys and girls of the poorest families has been 42% and 19% respectively in the programme villages as against 57% and 18% in the control villages.

This indicates that, although the FFE programme may have had some positive impact on the prevalence of child labour among boys, this is not so among the girls.

7.4.2.4 Beneficiaries of the FFE programme: The findings arrived at through the village-level PRA exercises reveal that the FFE programme, although it is meant for the poorest segment of the households, is benefiting the non-poor households in the villages as well (Annex II Table 7.30). It is found that 45% of the primary students from the poor households have been covered under the programme along with 18% students from the non-poor households under the same programme.

Gender-based distribution of the programme beneficiaries indicates that the FFE programme is still more biased towards boys (51%) than girls (38%) among students from the poor households compared to the distribution among students from the non-poor households (4% for boys and 37% for girls).

The coverage of the programme among the primary school-age children is found to be very low ie 29% (34% for poor households and 16% for non-poor households). The programme coverage among the children from the poorest households is also very low (37%).

7.4.2.5 Causes of drop-out and failure in the examinations: Students' absenteeism and dropping out have been the major problems at the primary level. Poverty, guardians' negligence, child labour, assisting

Figure 7.19 ***Drop-Out Rate at the Primary Level by Social Categories and Gender***

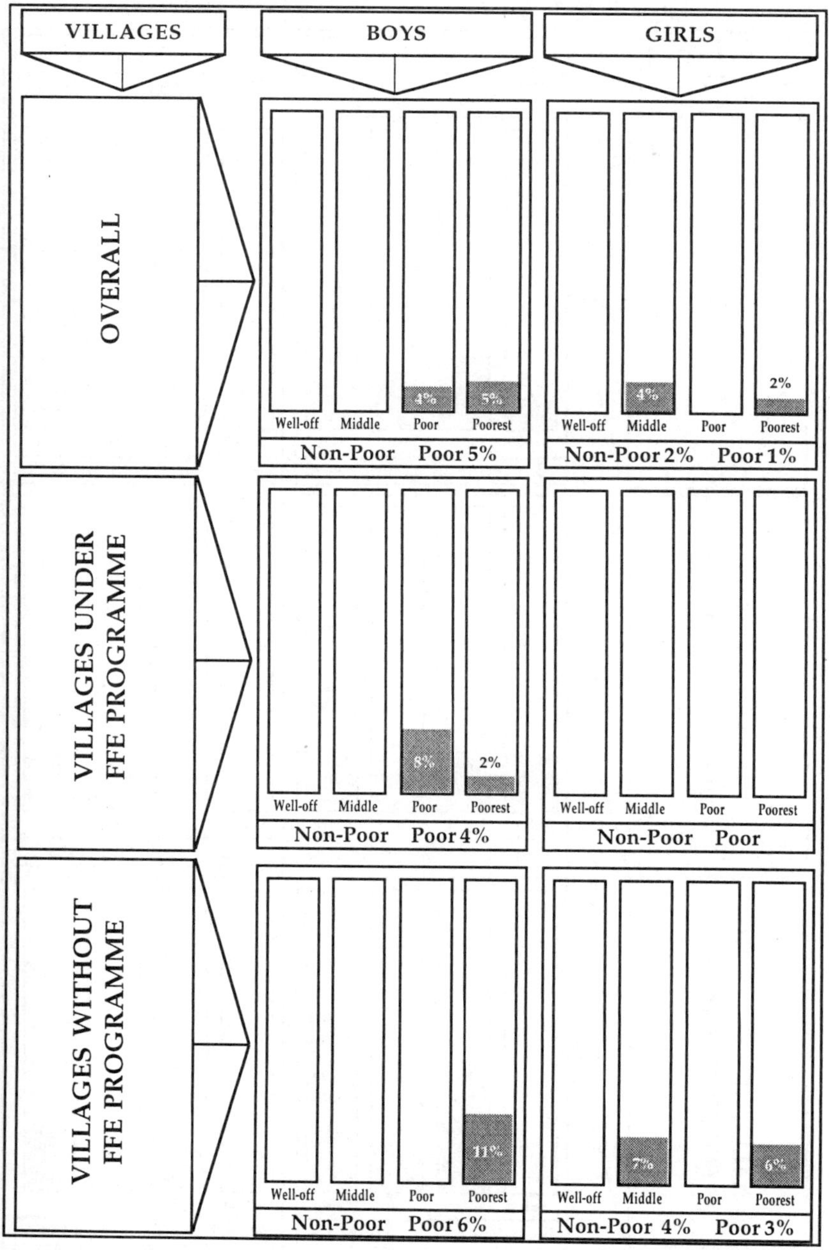

Figure 7.20 Prevalence of Child Labour at the Primary Level by Social Categories and Gender

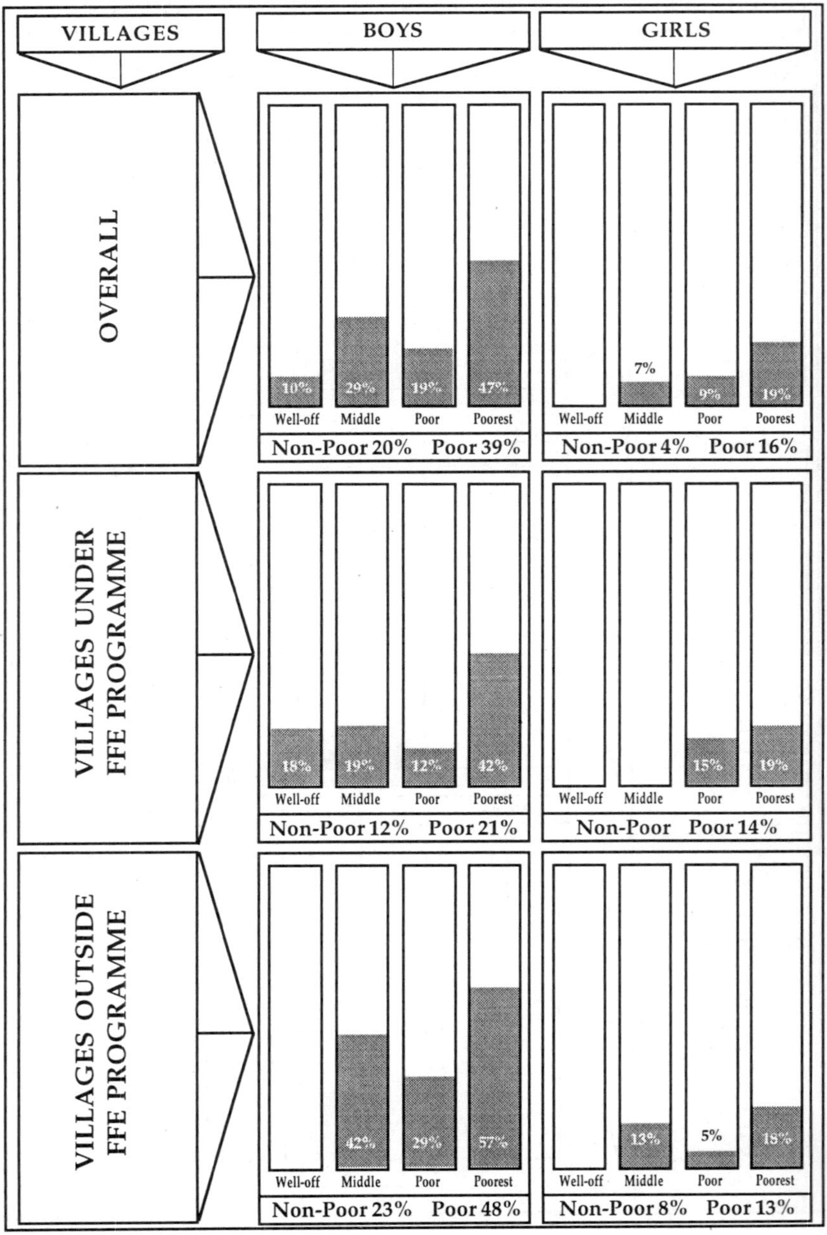

the father in cultivation, early marriage, lack of congenial environment at home, lack of food/books/writing papers, etc are some of the important causes of students' absenteeism and dropping out at the primary-level schooling (Figures 7.21 and 7.22).

The main causes of failure of unsuccessful students at the primary level are guardians' negligence, poverty, lack of books/writing papers, poor preparation for examinations, absenteeism, etc (Figure 7.23).

7.4.2.6 Causes of discontinuation of education: Students face difficulty in continuing their studies after completing their primary level education. Poverty and marriage have been the topmost causes of the discontinuation (Figure 7.24). Assisting fathers in their own farms and working in others' farms as labourers are found to be other causes which are, in turn, the outcome of abject poverty.

7.4.2.7 Problems faced by students: Primary students face a number of problems. Some of the problems encountered by the students at the government schools are: paucity of teachers, lack of educational materials/ furniture/books/drinking water/latrine, inadequate space, lack of rooms for teachers, etc (Figure 7.35).

7.4.2.8 Education of the poorest of the poor: some findings of 1993-96 poverty monitoring: Like other aspects, the education profile of the poorest households is also grim. Only three aspects of education have been looked into, namely illiteracy of the adults, children's participation in schooling and expenditure on education. The findings of the 1993-96 poverty monitoring about these aspects are furnished below.

a. Illiteracy

Illiteracy has been defined in this study as the inability to read and write a letter. Most of the adult members of the poorest households (96-100%) were found illiterate and the rate of illiteracy was found unchanged in the monitoring period (Annex II Tables 7.31 and 7.32). In the urban slums, 100% adults including women are illiterate. In the rural areas, the illiteracy rate for men and women were 96% and 100% respectively in 1993 and it remained unchanged till 1996.

b. Children's participation in schooling

In the rural areas, children's participation in schooling is increasing on the average with a variety of trends. Increase in the participation of boys in schooling is found to be a common trend in the study area among the FFE households (Annex II Table 7.31). The participation rate for boys is found to be 46% in 1993 and it increased to 52% in 1996. The rate of participation for boys is, however, found to be higher in the northern parts (59-68%) than in the central parts (36%) of the country.

Figure 7.21 Causes of Students' Absenteeism

Most Important	Next Most Important	Fairly Important
1. Guardians' negligence and lack of awareness	1. Lack of congenial environment in the family	1. Assist father in cultivation
2. Poverty	2. Students' negligence	2. Sickness
3. Child labour		
4. Lack of pen and paper		
5. Lack of food and clothes		
6. Not getting FFE benefits		
7. Class tasks not prepared		
8. Migration to nearby schools		

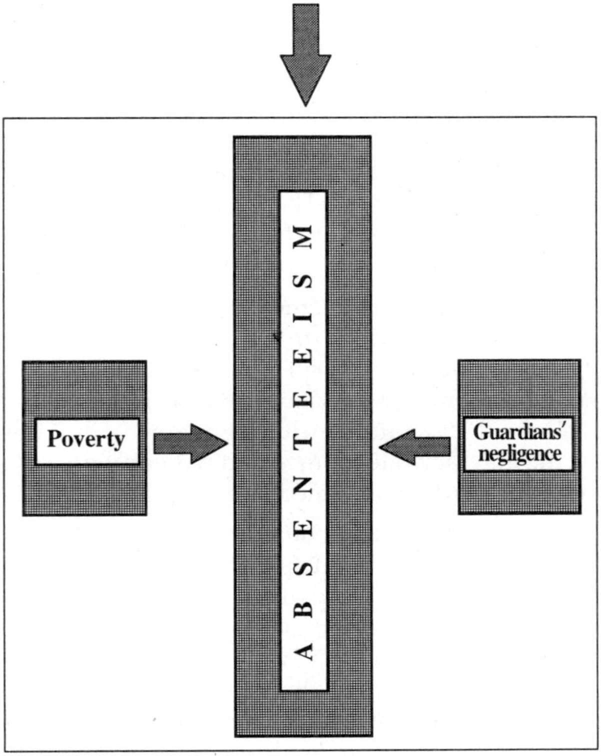

Figure 7.22 Causes of Students' Drop-Out at the Primary Level

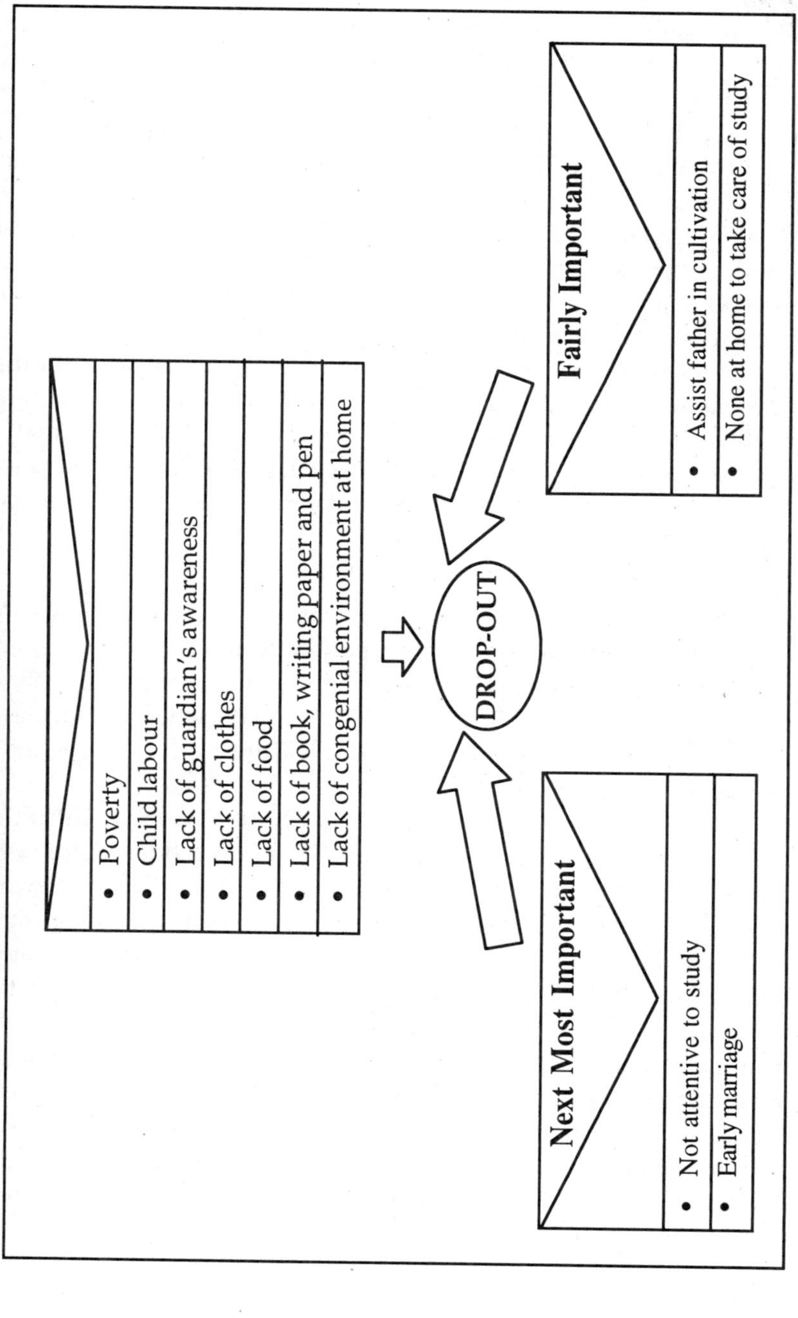

Overall, the participation of girls in schooling is found to be rising at almost a similar rate (49-53%). The difference in the participation rates for boys and girls has been widening with the passage of time. The participatioin of girls in schooling is found to be very low (14) in the central parts compared to that (81%) in the northern parts in 1996.

Overall, the Food For Education programme is found to have had a significant impact on the participation of both boys and girls during the monitoring period. However, the programme seems to have worked very poorly in the central parts in improving children's participation in schooling although it had a considerable impact on children's participation in the northern parts of the country.

The participation in schooling of the children of the poorest urban households was at a deplorably lower level (11% for boys) compared to their rural counterparts in 1993 (Annex II Table 7.32). The situation deteriorated during 1993-96. Children's participation in schooling was not only low but also declined during this period. Alarmingly, no school-age girl attended school in 1996.

c. *Expenditure on education*

The annual average expenditure on education for school students more than doubled during the monitoring period (Annex II Table 7.33). In the rural areas, the annual expenditure on education per student is found to have increased from Tk.95 in 1993 to Tk.200 in 1996 whereas it increased at a much higher rate from Tk.600 to Tk.1,800 during the same period in the case of the urban poor.

In the rural areas, genderwise distribution of expenditure on education reveals a bias towards boys. The poorest households spent Tk.235 for a boy as against Tk.129 for a girl in 1996. The gap between average expenditure on education for male and female students (primary and secondary) is found to have increased over the monitoring period (Annex II Table 7.34). The distribution of expenditure on education also shows wide differences for different groups of the poorest households in the rural areas. In 1996, non-FFE households in the programme villages are found to have spent much more on education (Tk.600 per student) compared to FFE households (Tk.198 per student) and other non-FFE households (Tk.104 per student) in the control villages. The available data is not, however, adequate to explain the differences in expenditures on education by the different categories of households.

Figure 7.23 Causes of Failure in Examination at the Primary Level

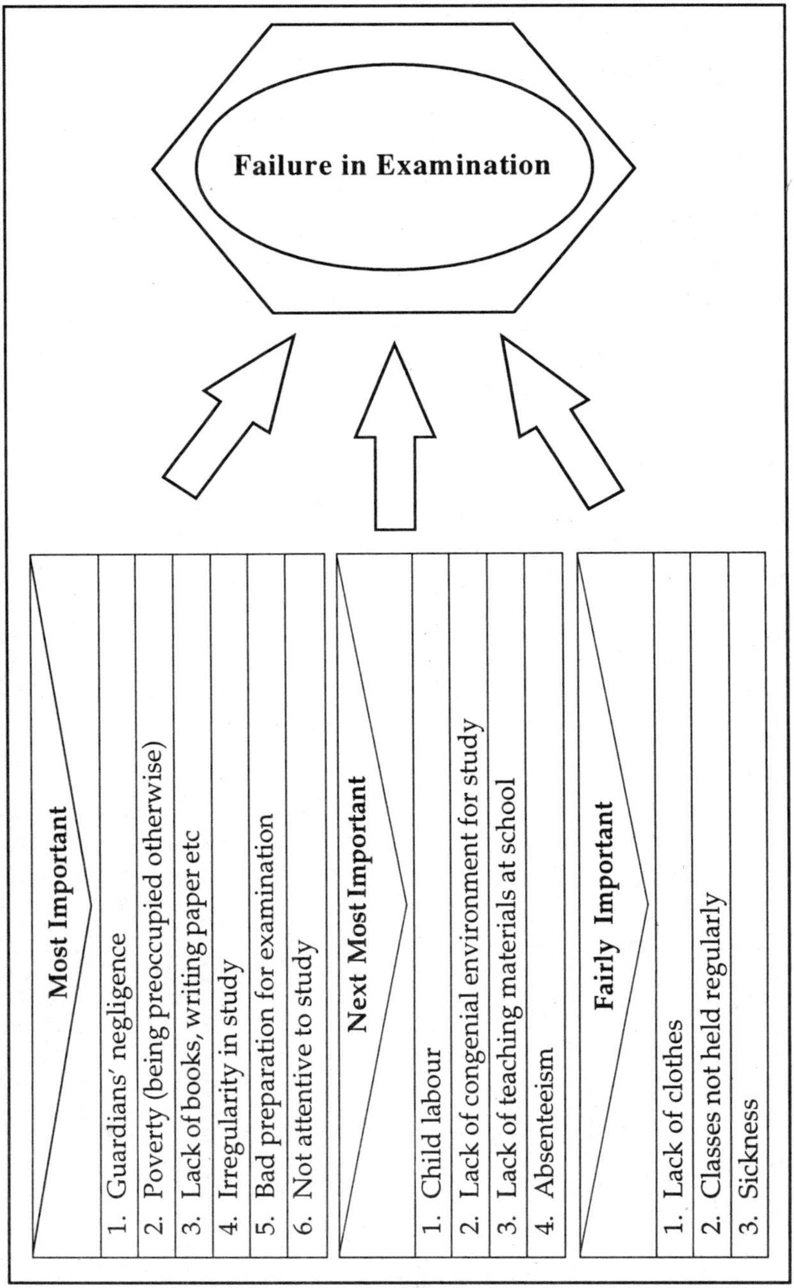

Figure 7.24 Causes of Discontinuation of Education After Completing the Primary Level

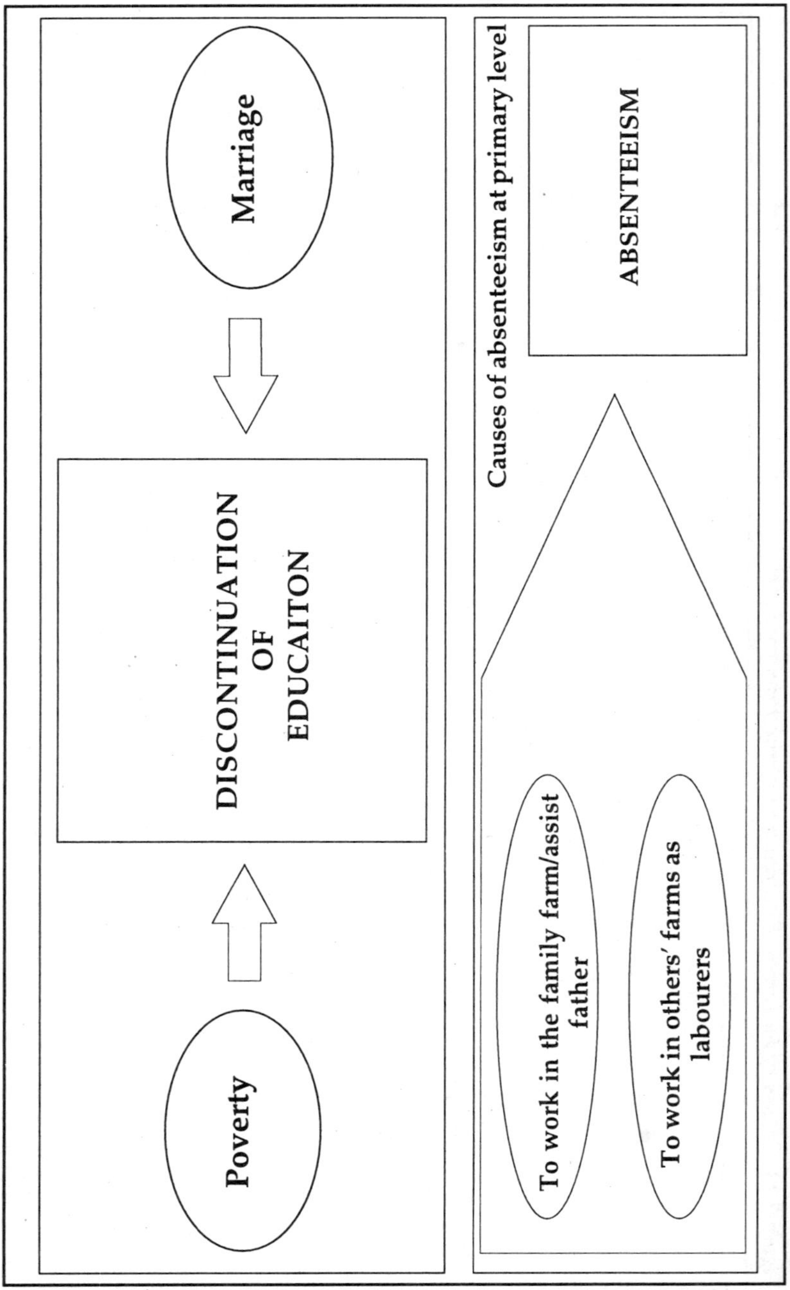

Figure 7.25 Educational Problems in Government Primary Schools (in Rural Areas)

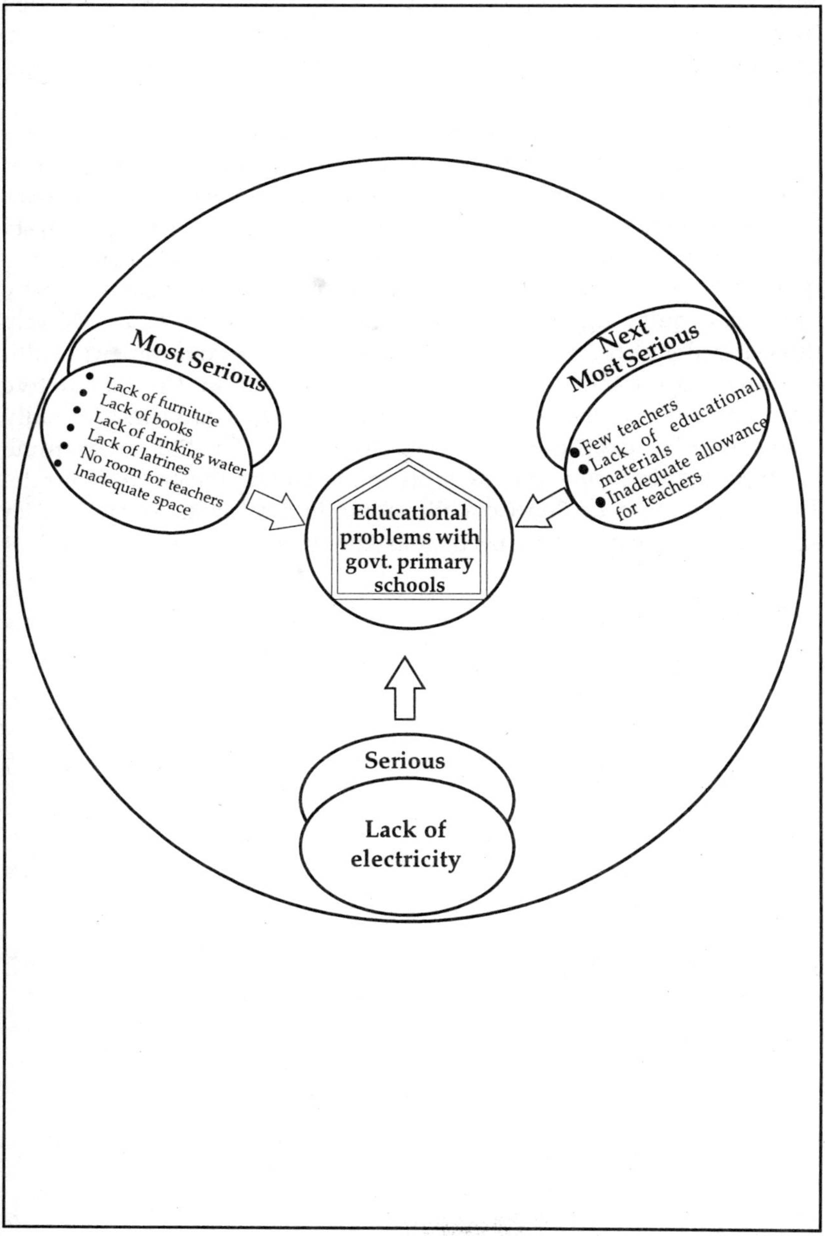

7.5 Summary

As revealed through the survey, the quality of health services provided by governmnet-run medical centres is very poor. The private medical practitioners, pharmacists and quacks still constitute the major sources of health service.

Our qualitative investigation has confirmed the above findings. The respondents were strongly dissatisfied with the quality of services provided by the government health centres, specially in the rural areas. Morbidity remains very high in the rural areas. However, the per capita expenditure on health has increased in such areas. Further, the qualitative study reveals that immunization of children against deadly diseases is quite high (61% in urban and 75% in rural areas). Nearly three-fourths of the providers of this service are government health workers. As for the state of the primary education, the qualitiative investigation reveals that the rate of enrolment has been gradually increasing. The drop-out rate is also decreasing. The FFE programme has been playing some positive role in improving the enrolment rate. There is still some incidence of child labour in rural areas. The per capita expenditure on education has increased with a bias towards boys.

Chapter 8

THE NATIONAL BUDGET: KNOWLEDGE, ATTITUDES AND PERCEPTIONS (KAP) OF THE POOR

8.1 The National Budget and Prioritization by the Poor: Findings of a Qualitative Investigation

Setting expenditure priorities in the context of limited resources is one of the basic challenges facing all governments. Priorities, in fact, represent the interests and concerns of certain specific economic classes or social categories. Theoretically, the class character, interests and concerns of the ruling class are reflected in their priorities. Against the background of the emerging consensus of the elites that their interests would continue to remain unsustainable and under constant risk and threat from the other 'half' of society (Toye and Jackson 1996), and as the realization of the interests of the poor is ostensibly declared to be the sacred task of the non-poor (WB 1992), the need to know the poor's perceptions and priorities with regard to sectoral allocations of public expenditure is increasingly being felt by the policy makers, donors and other concerned sections of society.

The present budgetary process is altogether archaic, non-transparent and mechanical. There is neither any scope for reflecting the people's perspectives in the budgetary process nor is there any need felt by the 'public servants' to ascertain the people's priorities, let alone the poor's. There is a strong reason to believe that the present budget reflects the preferences of those who are in charge of preparing it. The existing budgetary process is poised to reflect 'elite perceptions', not the poor's perceptions.

What are the public expenditure priorities from the perspective of the poor? This core question has been addressed in this phase of the study. Besides, some other questions have also been addressed in the study which include: which sectors should be given more priority and which ones less? How to quantify their priorities? To what extent the poor's perspectives are different from those of a typical recent budget? Are the priorities articulated by the urban poor different from those articulated by the rural poor? How do the poor reflect on the importance of the various economic sectors and give relative weights to them ? These are the questions that have been asked in trying to obtain the poor's perspectives in the following paragraphs.

The budget as viewed by the poor. The poor, in both the urban and rural areas, do not understand the budget. Many of them have not even heard of it. Those who are aware of it can equate the budget with price hike. They have observed that the budget benefit the well off, not the poor and even the budget is perceived as an instrument to put the poor into trouble. They have, however, expected that their needs like food, shelter, stable price level, employment, drinking water, latrine, clothing, agriculture, industry, education, communication, fishery, etc should get priority in the budgetary allocation (Figures 8.1 and 8.2).

The budget's inclusions and exclusions. The present budget is viewed by the poor to be highly inequitable in terms of its distributional impacts. Through public expenditure, the national budget in Bangladesh by and large has been benefiting the non-poor to the exclusion of both the urban and the rural poor (Figure 8.3). The desired budgetary allocations as prioritized by the poor are expected to have fair distributional impacts on them in the long run. It is, however, true that mere reprioritization of sectoral allocations is no guarantee of a fair distribution of resources, but it is expected that this might benefit them in the long run.

Sectoral prioritization. The poor have revealed their prioritization pattern for sectoral allocations of the national budget in the PRA sessions (Box 8.1). The poor's prioritization significantly differs from that of the government budgets in recent times (Figures 8.4 and 8.5).

Out of 15 sectors, agriculture has been identified by both the rural and the urban poor to be the most important sector receiving the topmost priority. The transport and communication sector—the topmost priority sector in the government budget— has been reprioritized next to agriculture in the poor's budget. Industry has been put in the third important position in the budget desired by the poor. The education and religion sector—the second most prioritized sector in the government budget—has been ranked fourth in the poor's desired budget.

Figure 8.1 The Urban Poor's Perceptions of the Budget

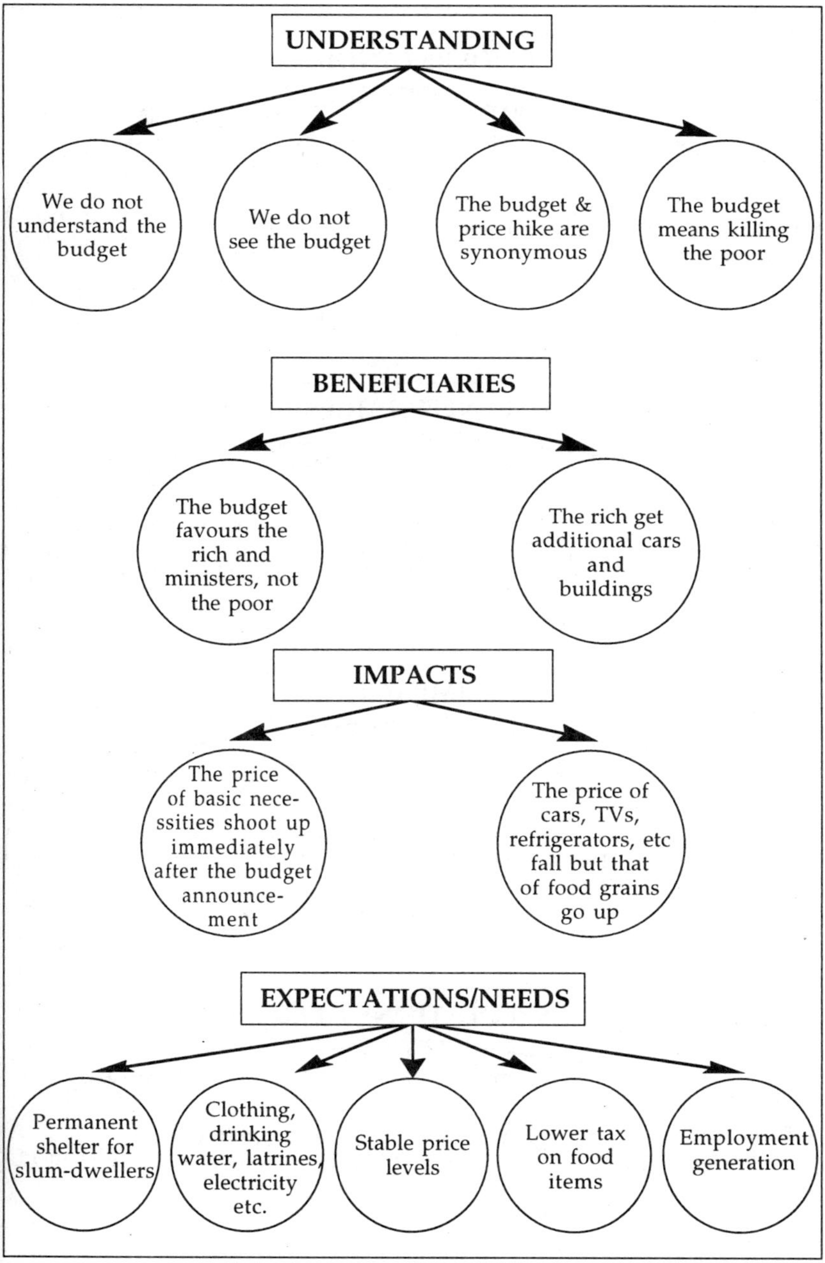

Figure 8.2 The Rural Poor's Perceptions of the Budget

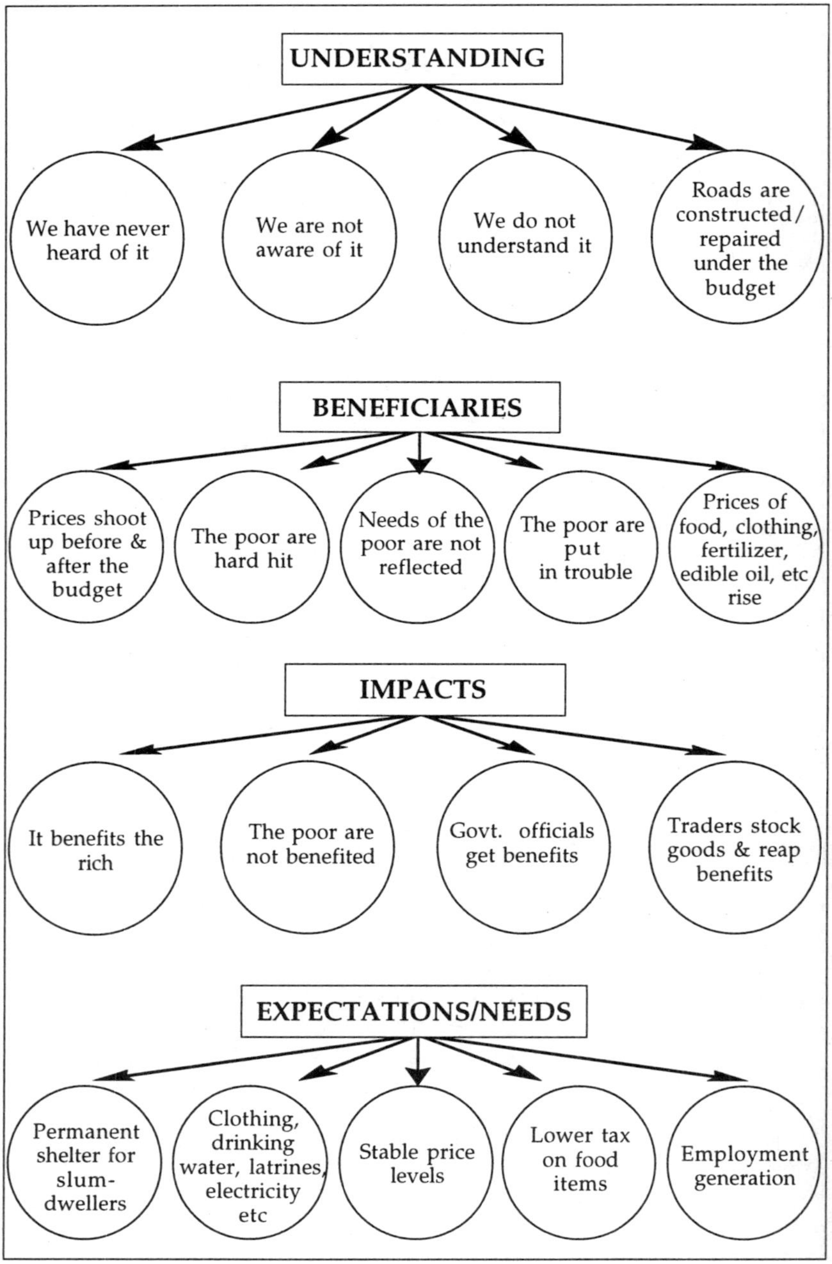

Figure 8.3 ***Beneficiaries of Actual and Desired Public Expenditure***

ACTUAL BUDGET

Sl. No.	Sectors
1.	Transport & Communication (17)
2.	Education & Religion (15)
3.	Power,Oil,Gas & Natural Resources (9)
4.	Defence (9)
5.	Administration (9)
6.	Health, Population & Family Planning (7)
7.	Debt Service (6)
8.	Physical Planning, Water Supply & Housing (5)
9.	Agriculture (5)
10.	Rural Development (5)
11.	Water Resources (4)
12.	Upazilla (2)
13.	Industry (2)
14.	Subsidy (1)
15.	Others (4)
16.	Total (100)

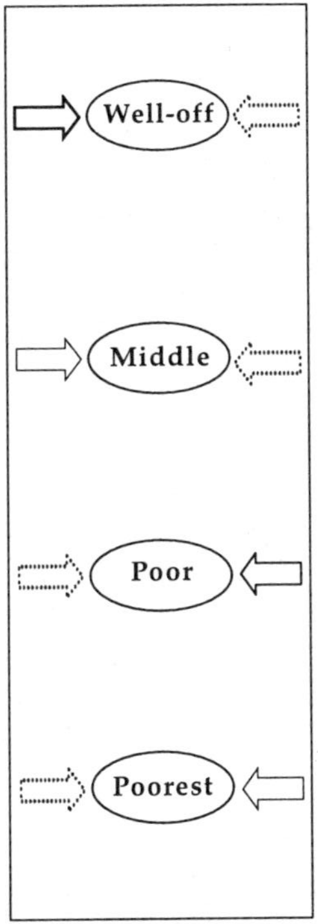

DESIRED BUDGET

Sl. No	Sectors
1.	Transport & Communication (10)
2.	Education & Religion (9)
3.	Power, Oil, Gas & Natural Resources (8)
4.	Defence (3)
5.	Administration (3)
6.	Health, Population & Family Planning (7)
7.	Debt Service (2.5)
8.	Physical Planning, Water Supply & Housing (6)
9.	Agriculture (14)
10.	Rural Development (8.5)
11.	Water Resources (6)
12.	Upazilla (2.5)
13.	Industry (9.5)
14.	Subsidy (8)
15.	Others (3)
16.	Total (100)

Note: Thick arrows show stronger flows of benefits and broken arrows indicate weaker ones.

Figure 8.4 Public Expenditure Patterns—Actual and Desired

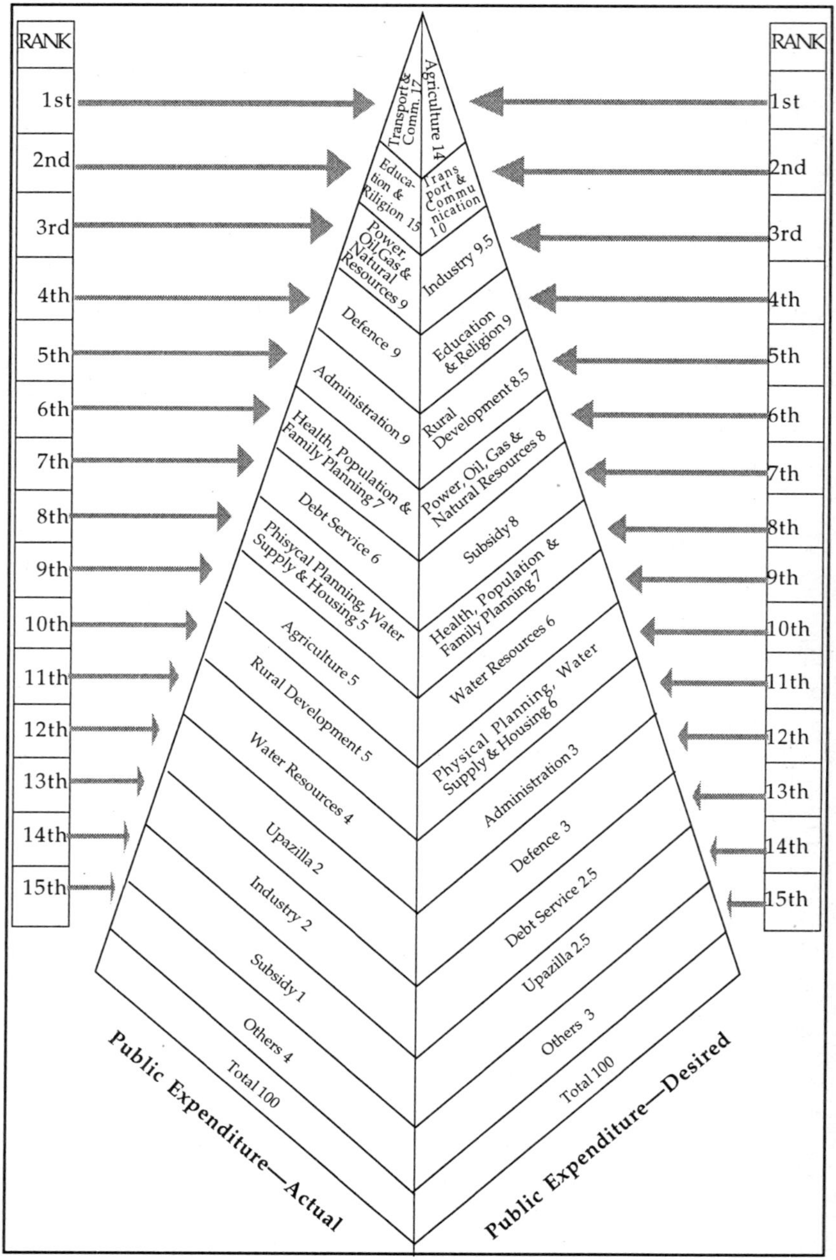

Problem identification and needs assessment by the poor

Problems facing the poor were identified by the poor themselves, and a list of 'felt needs' were the outcome of the participatory discussion, debates and consensus among themselves. Two sets of problems and needs were assessed in a participatory manner, each for the urban and rural areas.

Urban setting

To the urban slum poor, homelessness and eviction from slums are the topmost problems. Other serious problems identified by the poor include lack of good health and water facilities, employment opportunities, security, education, latrines, gas, etc (Figure. 8.6).

By way of needs assessment, the urban poor listed and prioritized their felt needs. Some of the most important are latrines, shelter, drinking water, electricity, gas, security, rationing, employment and so on (Figure 8.7).

Rural setting

Agricultural inputs, irrigation and culverts are considered to be the topmost problems by the rural poor. Apart from these, some other most serious problems mentioned by them are related to health, electricity, unemployment, flood, drinking water, industrialization, veterinary facilities, silting up of rivers, etc (Figure. 8.9).

According to the needs assessment and prioritization by the rural poor, some of the most important needs as articulated by themselves are industries for employment, agricultural inputs at a fair price, rural roads, irrigation, electricity, schools and madrasas, medical facilities, etc (Figure. 8.10).

The poor's emphasis and de-emphasis. The budget charted by the poor has clearly shown their own allocation pattern laying added emphasis on five sectors: agriculture, industry, rural development, water resources, and subsidy (Figure 8.11). On the other hand, five other sectors including defence, administration, transport and communication, education and religion, and debt service have been relatively de-emphasized in the desired budget compared to the actual expenditures on the same sectors in the government budget.

The poor's budget is balanced. The largest chunk (14%) of public expenditure has been allocated for agriculture in the poor's budget as against the largest share (17%) in the total expenditure accounted for by transport and communication in the government budget. The standard deviation of sectoral public expenditure has been found higher in the government budget than in the poor's budget. This indicates that the budget prepared by the poor is more balanced than the government budget so far as the sectoral expenditure/allocation pattern is concerned.

Sectoral reallocation. An analysis of the expenditure pattern shows that all the sectors except health, population and family planning have been subjected to reallocation in the case of the poor's budget. Out of the four

Figure 8.5 Socio-Economic Problems/Privations as Identified by the Urban Poor

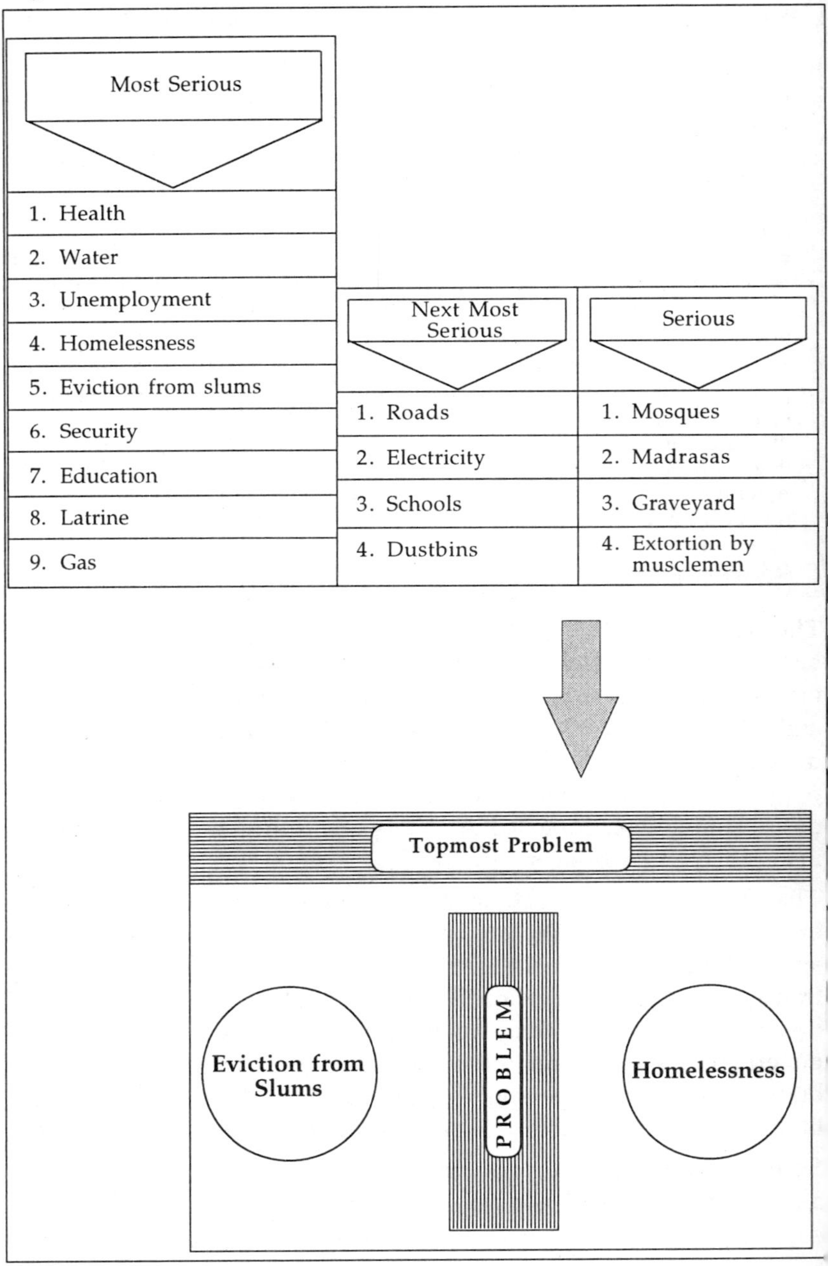

Figure 8.6 Needs Assessment and Prioritization by the Urban Poor (Slum Dwellers)

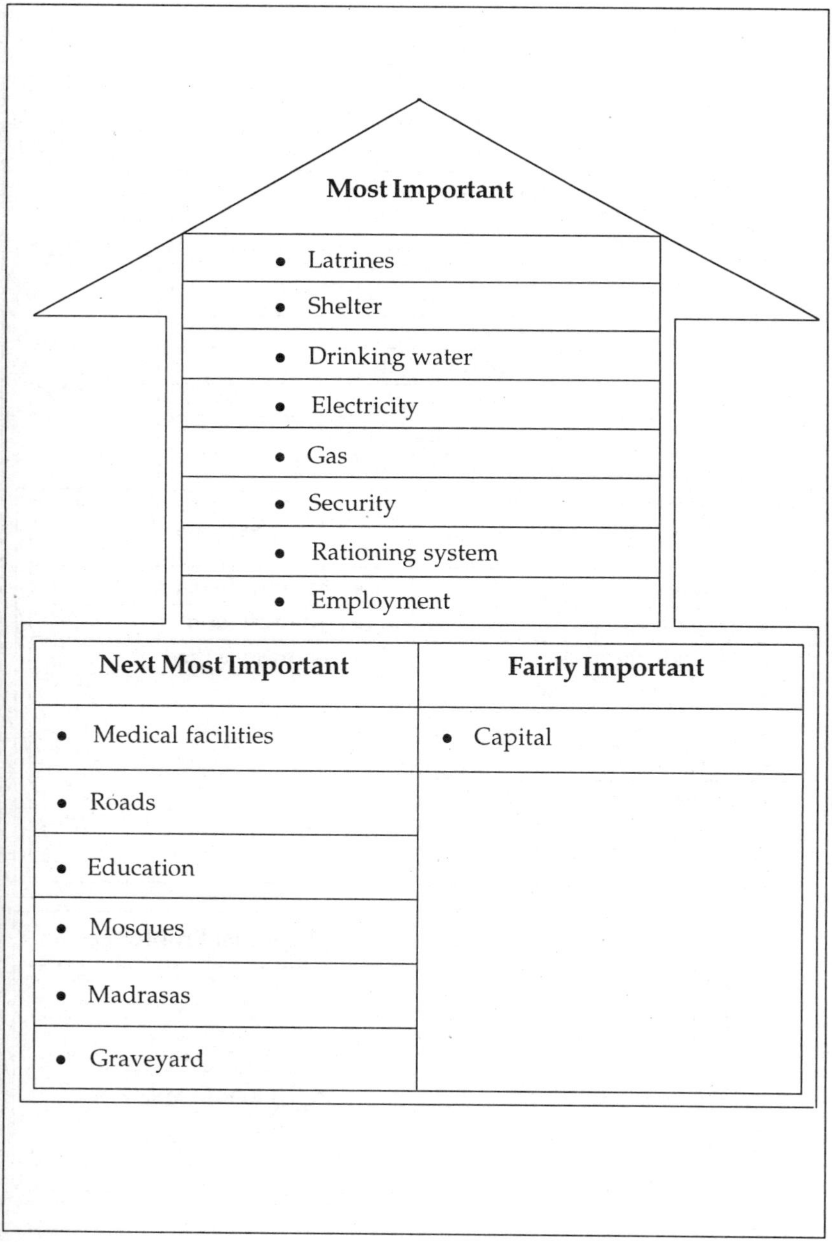

Figure 8.7 Socio-Economic Problems/Privations as Identified by the Rural Poor

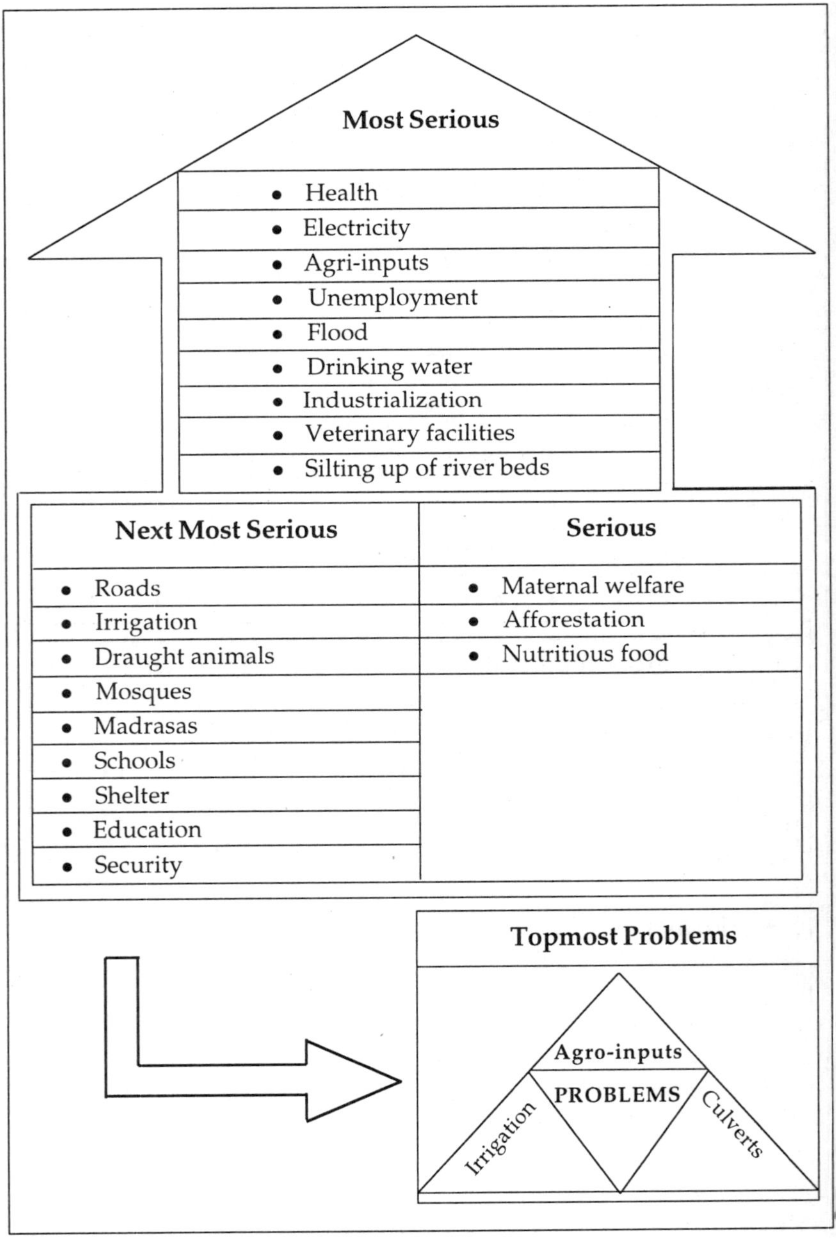

Figure 8.8 Needs Assessment and Prioritization by the Rural Poor

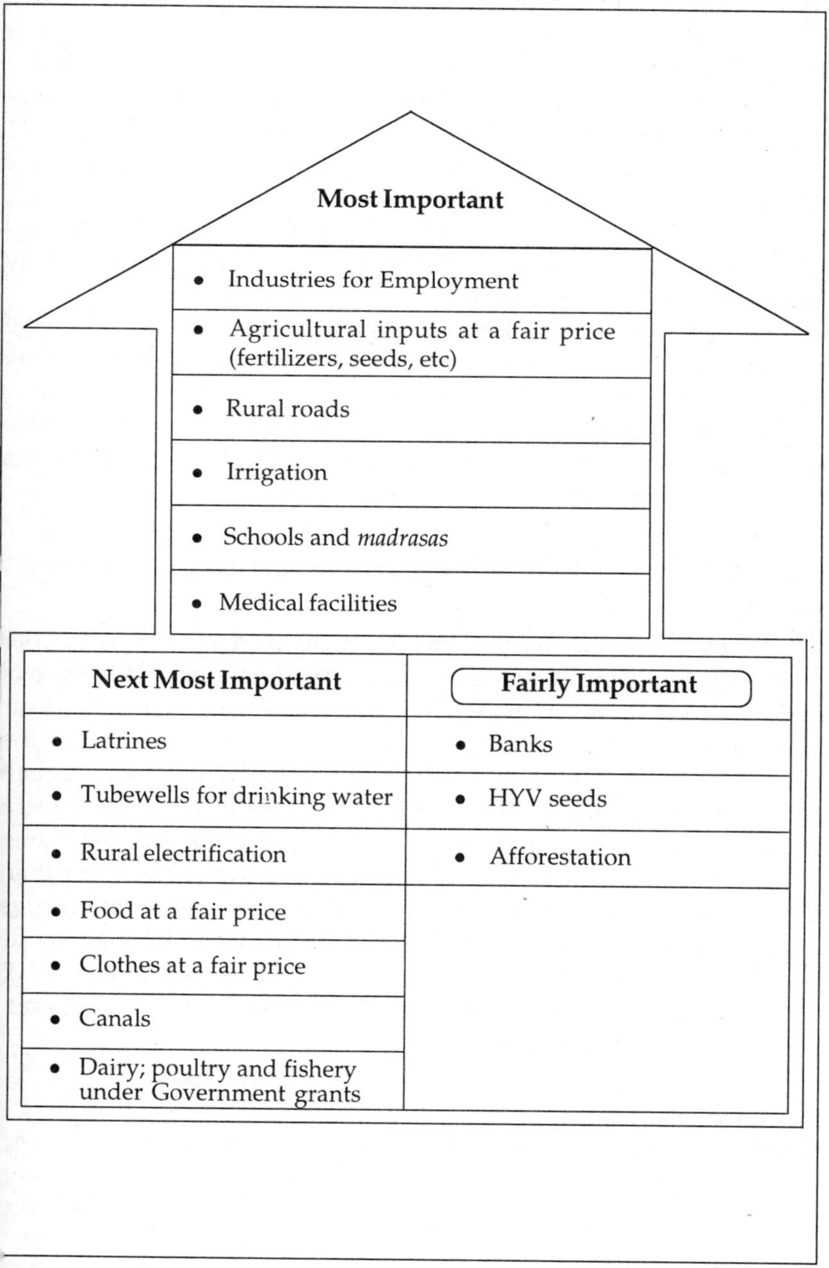

broad sectoral categories: infrastructures, directly productive sectors, social sectors and miscellaneous sectors, the government budget makes higher allocations for infrastructures, social sectors and miscellaneous sectors and lower allocations for directly productive sectors than the poor's one. The infrastructure sector has received the topmost budgetary allocation in the recent past in the government's budgets (Figures 8.11 and 8.12). On the other hand, the poor's budget has laid the topmost emphasis on the directly productive sectors which include agriculture, industry and subsidy. The poor are in favour of a reduction of budgetary allocation for all other sectors under the three sectoral groups, namely infrastructures, social sectors and miscellaneous sectors.

The prominent feature of the poor's budget is that it demands a large cutback on the budgetary allocation for non-economic sectors, namely defence, administration and debt service.

The perceptions of the poor about the budgetary process have also been captured by a quantitative knowledge, attitudes and perceptions (KAP) survey. The findings of this survey are given below.

8.2 KAP of the Poor: Findings of a Quantitative Survey

8.2.1 The Coverage

It has already been emphasized that information on the KAP of the poor people regarding the budget is essential for planners and policy makers in their efforts for meeting people's aspirations through the five-year and perspective plans and the annual budgets. In order to know the KAP of the poor, an opinion survey was conducted both in the urban and rural areas. Households in the slum areas in Dhaka city were considered as poor and taken as the final sampling units for conducting a KAP survey on the public budget. Households having land less than 0.50 acre were considered as rural poor and were selected for interviews in the rural areas. In all, 139 households in the urban and 150 households in the rural areas were selected and interviewed to know their KAP regarding the government budget. The sample size was, however, constrained by time and finance.

8.2.2 Test of Association

Based on the opinion survey data, the selected households have been classified according to two criteria and arranged in a rectangular array. This has been done to ascertain whether there is any relationship between

Figure 8.9 The Poor's Perceptions of Prioritization of Sectoral Allocation

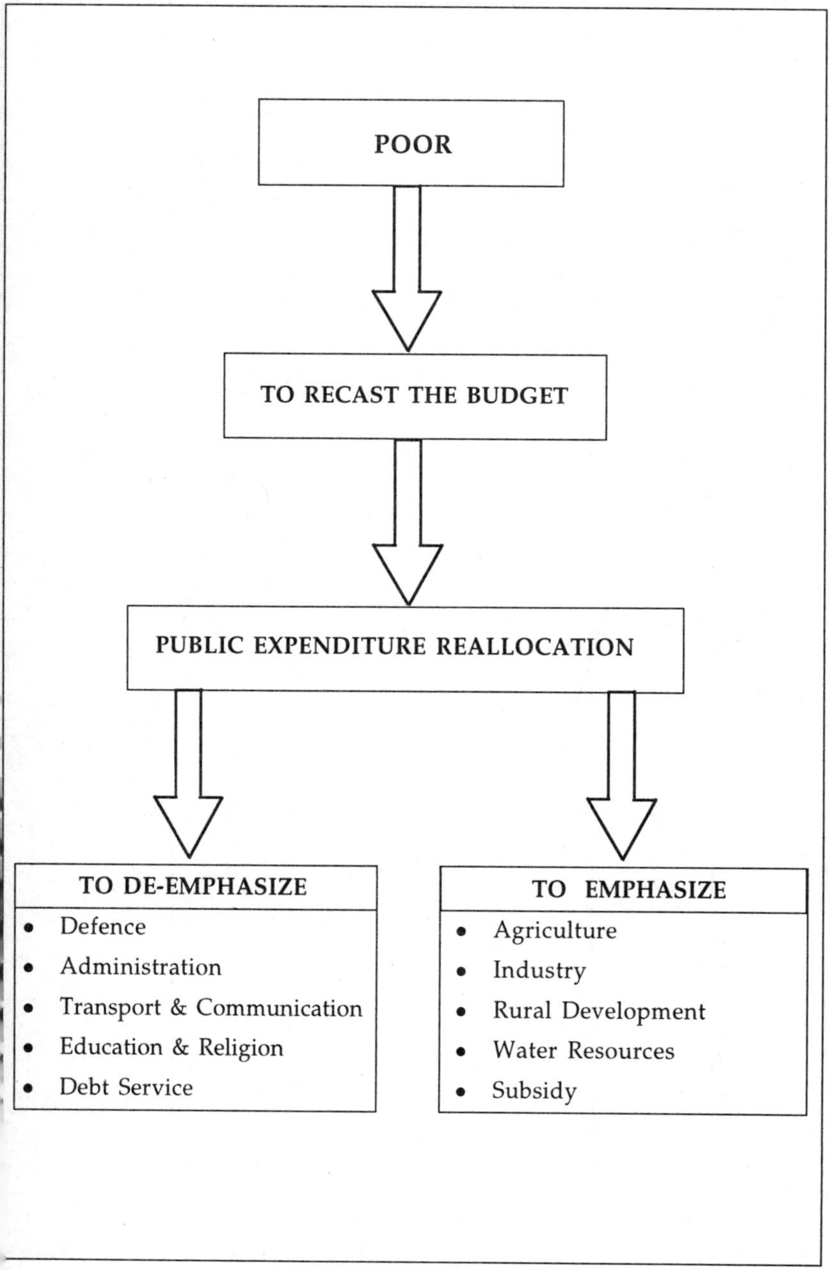

Figure 8.10 Analysis of the Public Expenditure Pattern

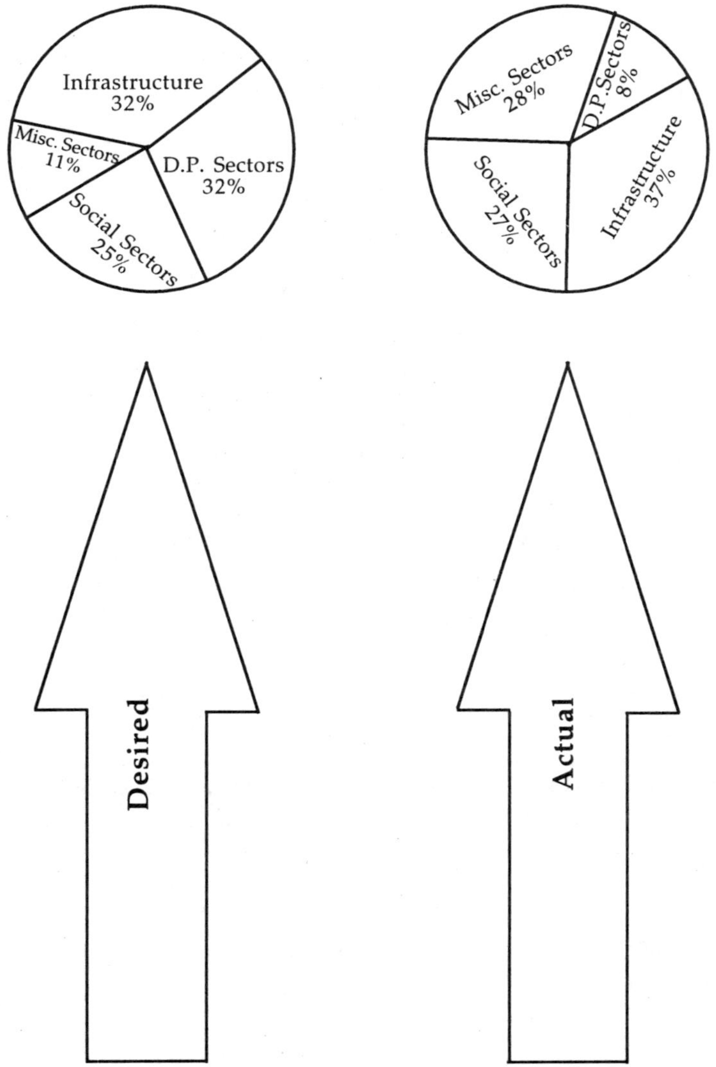

Note: D.P.=Directly Productive sectors

***Figure 8.11* Detailed Analysis of the Public Expenditure Pattern**

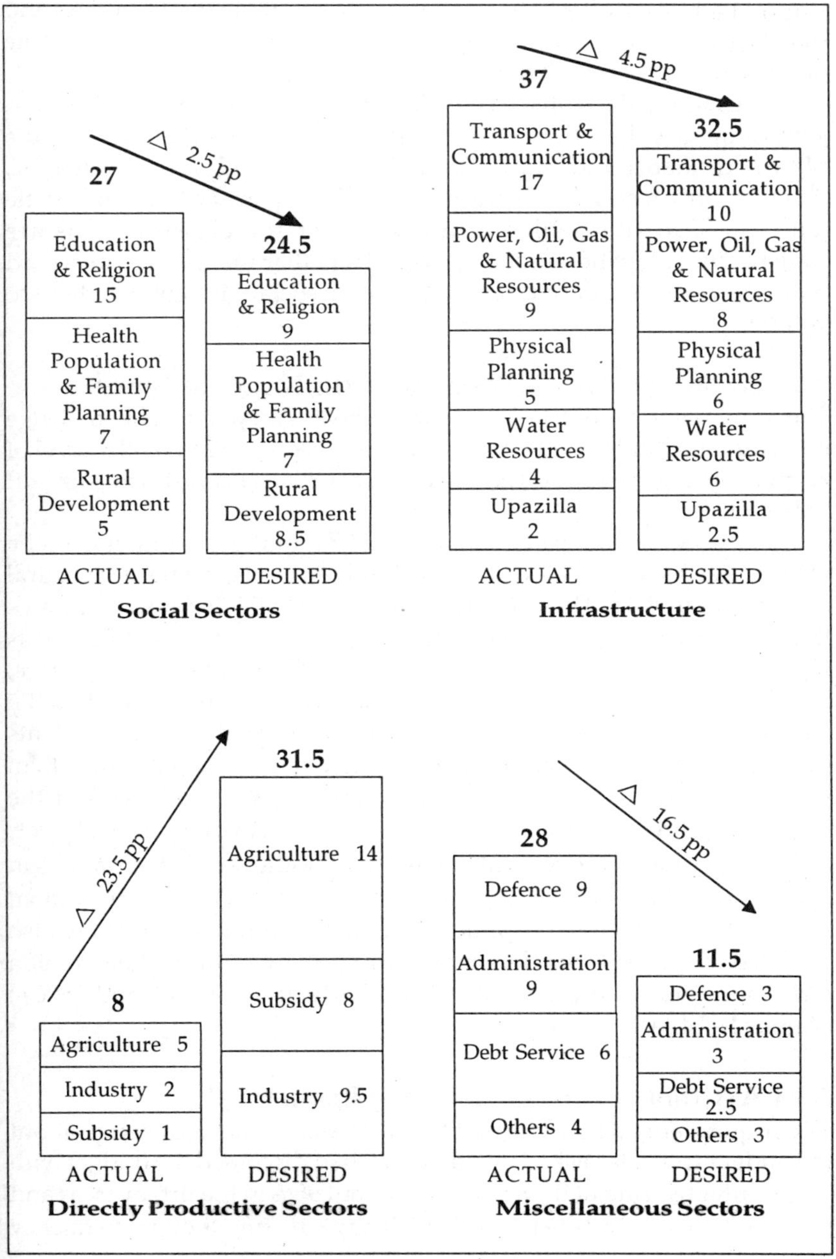

the two mutually exclusive classifications. For instance, we may classify respondents according to their knowledge about the public budget and the place of residence (urban and rural) of the respondents or use some other criteria of classification.

To examine the statistical relationship between the classifications, joint frequency distribution of the respondents in accordance with the place of residence and knowledge regarding the budget has been done. A significance test is then made by using Chi-Square (χ^2) statistic for the joint classification tables to test whether the classifications are statistically independent, that is, to test whether the data are in accord with the desired null hypothesis (H_0) of association between the two criteria.

8.2.3 Knowledge of the Poor about the National Budget

The respondents were asked to answer whether they had any knowledge regarding the budget, and their answers were arranged by the level of knowledge (eg 'Yes', 'No') and residence (urban and rural) in Annex II Table 8.1.

It appears from the table that about 55% of the respondents in the urban areas have not heard about the budget, while this figure for rural areas is about 81%. The estimated value of χ^2 is 21.36 which indicates that the association between the two criteria of classifications is significant as it stands at 0.001% level. The null hypothesis is, therefore, rejected which means that the level of knowledge is dependent on the location of the sample respondents. A higher percentage of respondents in the urban areas have some knowledge about the national budget than their rural counterparts. When the opinions ('Yes' and 'No') of the respondents are classified according to their respective educational levels (illiterate, literate), the estimated value of χ^2 indicates that variations in opinion about the budget depend on the variations of the educational levels of the respondents (Annex II Table 8.2). Similar results are also obtained when the respondents are distributed according to their opinion ('Yes' and 'No') and income levels (Taka 1000, 1000-2500 and 2500+) (Annex II Table 8.3).

8.2.4 Attitudes of the Poor to the Budget

The respondents who indicated that they had some knowledge about the budget were also asked whether they had discussed the budget with others after hearing of it. In response, about 95% in the urban areas and about 76% in the rural areas said 'Yes'. It appears from the joint frequency distribution (Annex II Table 8.4) and the estimated value of $\chi^2 = 7.52$ that the null hypothesis is to be rejected, ie variation in knowledge depends on the variations in the locations of residence of the respondents. But when this table is classified according to the levels of opinion and the levels of education (illiterate and literate), we do not find any association between the two criteria of classification. Actually, the level of education among the poor in the sample area is very low so that the impact of education on the attitudes of the respondents is not found to be significant. As a result, in most of the cases we do not find any significant variation in the answers with the variation of the educational levels (Annex II Table 8.5).

It seems from the findings that there is no difference in the topics of discussion on budget among the poor, irrespective of the level of literacy. An overwhelming majority of the respondents mainly discussed the issue of price hike (Annex II Table 8.6).

8.2.5 Solving Problems through the Budget

The respondents were asked to indicate whether the problems of their day-to-day life could be solved through the budget. The answer is given in Annex II Table 8.7 which illustrates the distribution of respondents by levels of answer ('Yes', 'No' and 'Do not know') and residence (urban and rural).

It can be seen in the table that about 55% of the respondents in the urban and 81% in the rural areas said 'do not know', while about 42% in the urban and 16% in the rural areas said 'yes'. The rest said 'no'. The value of $\chi^2 = 23.60$ indicates that there is a strong association between the criteria of classifications, which implies that there is a variation in the levels of reply due to the variation in the levels of residence.

A section of the respondents thought that the national budget, if properly designed and prioritized, could help solve the problems identified by them. The order of intervention, according to this group, should be employment creation, infrastructure and environmental protection (Annex II Table 8.8).

8.2.6 Usefulness of the Budget

The classification of the respondents according to their answers on the usefulness of the budget ('useful', 'not useful' and 'do not know') and their residence (urban and rural) has been shown in Annex II Table 8.9.

It can be seen from the table that about 55% of the respondents in the urban and 81% in the rural areas have indicated that they actually do not know about the usefulness of the budget. On the contrary, about 40% of the respondents in the urban and 16% in the rural areas have opined that the national budget does not serve their interests. However, the value of $\chi^2 = 21.88$ indicates that the level of usefulness and the category of residence of the respondents are not independent.

Next, they were asked to indicate wherefrom they received information about the budget. A majority (80% in urban and 73% in rural areas) of the respondents have said that they have come to know of the budget through radio and different persons (Annex II Table 8.10). The variation in the levels of opinion regarding whether they hear or read the budget speech depends on the variations in both education and income levels (Annex II Tables 8.11 and 8.12). The estimated value of χ^2 supports this statement. Regarding the understanding of the budget speech, about 59% of the respondents in the urban and 69% in the rural areas have said that they do not understand the budget speech (Annex II Table 8.13). They have also explained their inability to understand the budget speech. The answers in this respect have been presented in Annex II Table 8.14. The main reason for not understanding the budget speech appears to be the illiteracy of the respondents. Fifty per cent respondents in the urban and 11% in the rural areas said that the budget was not easily understandable.

8.2.7 Reasons for Not Listening to the Budget Speech

The respondents have been arrayed in Annex II Table 8.15 according to the reasons for not listening to the budget speech (lack of radio/TV sets, illiterate and 'do not understand'/'busy with work') and residence (urban and rural) The main reason for not listening to the budget speech appears to be the difficulty in understanding it and lack of time. About 61% of the respondents in the urban and 73% in the rural areas have said that they do not understand the budget speech and so they do not listen. Seven per cent of the respondents do not listen to the budget speech for not having access to radio/TV and 24% for not having education. The estimated test statistic $\chi^2 = 5.71$ is significant at the 5% level which implies that the level of reasons is dependent on the level of residence of the sample respondents.

8.2.8 Reaction to the Public Budget

Among the respondents, about 65% in the urban and 91% in the rural areas do not seem to react to the budget. However, about 35% of the respondents in the urban areas have expressed their reaction to the budget (Annex II Table 8.16). The estimated $\chi^2 = 28.43$ rejects the null hypothesis that there is no association between the level of reaction and the level of residence. Ignorance about the budget is found to be the main reason for not reacting. When asked to identify the immediate impact of the declaration of the national budget, about 65% of the respondents in the urban areas and 91% in the rural areas have said that they do not observe any impact following the budget speech (Annex II Table 8.18). The rest have stated that they do observe some impacts in the form of rise of the market price of commodities.

The implication of the inadequacy of the knowledge and understanding of the poor about the national budget is serious and worthy of deep reflection. This implies that the poor can hardly act as an organized pressure group to influence the budget decisions in favour of their upliftment, to voice any demand for radical changes in the budget process, despite the fact that the budget is the only conduit for public resources to be channelled to the underprivileged and distressed masses.

Chapter 9

MONITORING THE IMPACT OF PUBLIC EXPENDITURE ON POVERTY

9.1 Objective

The primary objective of monitoring the impact of public expenditure on poverty in this chapter is to understand the living conditions of the poor. This is more of an illustrative exercise rather than a whole sector monitoring of poverty. The issue of representativeness has to be, therefore, viewed in this context. One of the stated objectives of the development strategy of both the present and previous governments is to reduce poverty. A growing share of public expenditure is claimed to have been allocated for the development activities ostensibly aiming at poverty reduction in the recent past, and this is likely to be continued in the future.

Against this background of increasing the public expenditure allocation for poverty alleviating projects, it is necessary to know the effects and impacts of these expenditures on poverty alleviation. In this section a number of key questions have been addressed: does the benefit of the public expenditure reach those lying at the bottom of the income scale? Is there any sign of improvement in the conditions of the poorest of the poor? How do the selected poverty indicators behave? Do they improve, deteriorate or oscillate? In case of improvement, at what pace do they improve? Based on these questions, an attempt will be made to assess the quality of public expenditure in terms of a set of selected indicators. To understand the trend of the impact of public expenditure on poverty, we started monitoring the behaviour of some selected indicators of poverty in both the urban and rural areas since 1993, the base year. The qualitative and quantitative data generated through the participatory tools have been used for this poverty monitoring. This is the first round of the periodic monitoring of poverty in a participatory manner.

9.2. Participatory Poverty Assessment (PPA) and Monitoring: People's Views

The poverty assessment carried out under this study has two components. The community members actively participated in the assessment of their well-being by listing and categorizing all the households by themselves in several groups based on their own criteria. This is, in fact, a 'subjective' assessment. Secondly, after the categorization, all households were arranged in the descending order on the basis of well-being scores of each of the households resulting in the identification of the poorest of the poor in the respective communities lying at the bottom of the scale with quantitative precision which was again validated by the community members/participants. The poverty of some of the poorest households in the community has been monitored with the selected indicators. As this monitoring is based on hard data, it, therefore, gives us an 'objective' assessment of

Figure 9.1 Process of Poverty Monitoring

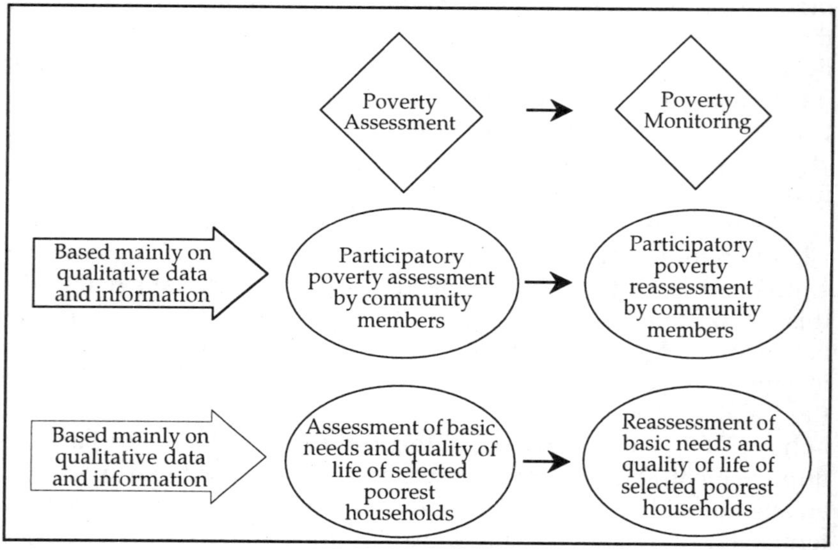

the living standard of the poorest (Figure 9.1). The poverty situtlon in the urban and rural areas has been assessed in a participatory manner. Instead of applying any pre-conceived ideas, standards, measures or categories by the researchers to measure poverty, as is done conventionally, the criteria used in this study have been developed by the people at the community level. The basic question relating to poverty measurement or assessment is who is poor and how to identify him/her.

Criteria. Unlike a single standard or formula as applied in the conventional methodology, the community members consider it appropriate to use a set of socio-economic criteria to assess the economic and social status of a household. For this purpose, the researchers and facilitators involved in the study initiated a series of group-level discussions and community-level validations. The community people developed their own criteria to assess the status of their own members and also to categorize them into a set of social classes (Box 9.1).

The more important criteria developed by the rural people in the selected villages are, among others, the amount of land owned and cultivated, the number of earning members, the cash in hand, the housing conditions, the amount of fixed assets, the family size, other sources of income, whether a household is female- or male-headed, etc.

9.2.1 Prevalence of Poverty (Qualitative)

Based on the above criteria, the community people identified the 'moderate' poor and the poorest ('extreme' or 'hardcore' poor) households in their own community. As poverty was assessed at the household level, the status of all the households in the community was assessed and categorized into four classes, namely well-off, middle, poor and the poorest.

In the urban areas, 72% of the households in the two sample slums were found poor (moderate: 51%, hardcore: 21%) and 28% non-poor (middle: 19%, well-off: 9%) (Annex II Tables 9.1 and 9.2). The incidence of poverty was, however, found to be widely different in different slums. In one sample slum there were no well-off households in 1996, although there were many in another sample.

In the rural areas, 75% of the households in the sample villages were classified as poor (moderate: 20% and hardcore: 55%) whereas 25% were classified as non-poor (middle: 14% and well-off: 11%) (Annex II Table 9.3). Regionally, the incidence of poverty was more acute in the central part (moderate: 17%, hardcore: 60%) than in the northern part (moderate: 25%, hardcore: 47%).

The findings reached through the PRA exercises were further validated by the people in the respective communities. So the scope of subjective bias, if any, was greatly reduced.

9.2.2 Poverty Monitoring Using Panel Data Set (Quantitative)

Being a value-loaded term, poverty as such can hardly be measured quantitatively/'objectively'. Debates on the issue abound in the relevant literature. But the symptoms and aspects of poverty can be understood and monitored by means of a series of socio-economic indicators that proxy the level of well-being of people. That is why, an attempt has been made in this section to specify a number of indicators and monitor poverty through those indicators/variables in two different years, ie 1993 and 1996. Most of the indicators used for monitoring were suggested by the community members (Box 9.1). The indicators used here are meant to have satisfied the desirable criteria, namely, unambiguity, consistency, specificity, sensitivity and ease of collection of data and information (Carvalho and White 1994).

Box 9.1 Criteria Used by Community Members to Categorize Households

Urban Slums	Rural Areas
1. Family size	1. Amount of land cultivated
2. Amount of income	2. Amount of land owned
3. Number of meals eaten daily	3. Cash in hand
4. Polygamy / monogamy	4. Number of earning members
5. Housing condition	5. Employment in salaried jobs
6. House owned or rented ?	6. Housing condition
7. Ability to let in house	7. Involvement in trade
8. Involvement in trade	8. Number of cattle
9. Amount of cash in hand	9. Family size
10. Involvement in money-lending business	10. Amount of fixed assets
11. Begging or not	11. Other sources of income
12. Employed in stone-crushing, catering, domestic services, etc.	
13. Widowed or not	
14. Women-headed household or not	
15. Rickshaw, owned or rented ?	
16. Number of earning members	
17. Number of rickshaws owned	

9.3 Change in Demographic and Socio-Economic Profiles of the Poorest Households During 1993-96

9.3.1 Demographic and Social Characterstics

Family size and composition. The population of the poorest households and their average family size grew by about 5% over the monitoring period 1993-96 (AnnexII Table 9.4). However, the population growth rate is found to have been higher at 7.2% for the urban poor compared to 4.4% in the rural areas over the same period. The family size of the poorest households in the rural areas is, however, found to be higher at 4.2 in 1993 and it increased further to 4.4 in 1996. The family size of the urban poor was lower at 3.5 in 1993, and it grew to 3.7 in 1996.

In the rural areas, the family size of the FFE-households is found to be much higher at 6.0 on an average in both the central and northern parts compared to 3.7 and 3.5 for the non-FFE households in the programme and control villages respectively in 1996 (Annex II Table 9.5).

Another important demographic characteristic of the poorest households is their family composition. In 1996, the FFE households are found to have a male majority of 61% compared to 49% and 41% for the non-FFE households in the programme and control villages respectively. The family composition is, however, found reverse for the poorest families in the urban slums. The poorest households had a female majority of 62% in 1996 (Annex II Table 9.6).

The above findings pose some questions challenging the appropriateness of the main thrust of the development strategy being pursued by the government in the country. The much-publicized motto 'two children are enough' seems to have been irrelevant so far as the poorest people are concerned in both the urban and rural areas. The increasing growth rates in population and family size suggest that under the existing socio-economic conditions, their economic and social security lies not in smaller families but in larger ones.

Earning members and incidence of child labour. The poorest households and their different groups are found to have peculiar characterstics in the composition of their earning members. Overall, close to half of the earning members are men, and one-fourth each are women and boys in 1996 (Annex II Table 7.17).

Against this general distribution of the earning members, the poorest families in the urban and rural areas are found to have different compositions of earning members by age and gender. In the urban slums, female earning members accounted for 43% (women: 36% and girls: 7%) among all the earners compared to 24% (women: 23% and girls: 1%) in the rural areas (Annex II Tables 7.17 and 9.7). Female children were not found to have been as active in income-earning activities previously as they are in 1996. The preponderance of male income earners is found to be more prominent among the poorest households in the rural areas. At the disaggregate level, the difference is more revealing in the rural areas. The participation of girls in income-earning activities is found to be very minimal throughout the rural areas (Annex II Table 9.8). Among the FFE-households, women's participation in income-earning activities is very small (3%), but it is widely observed (33-36%) among the non-FFE households.

Among the FFE households, the preponderance of male child labour is observed, and this remained unchanged throughout the monitoring period despite the programme intervention in the rural areas. The incidence of child labour among the earning members of the FFE households is found to be 40 and 41% in the central and northern parts respectively of the country, and this remained unchanged in both the areas during the period 1993-1996. The insignificant impact of the FFE programme on the incidence of child labour at large in the rural areas is also revealed sharply if we focus on the trend in the incidence of child labour. Overall, 25% of the boys of all ages were involved in income-earning activities in 1993, and this remained almost at the same level (24%) in 1996. Like the boys, the incidence of female child labour among the earning members is found to be at a much lower level (1.2%) in 1993 and this remained at that level in 1996 as well.

The above findings brings an important question to the fore: why is the FFE programme found to be ineffective in reducing the incidence of child labour ? The answer to this question should be searched not in the programme itself but in the economics. For the poorest households, the opportunity cost of sparing a boy for education was around Tk. 14 a day (wage rate) in 1996 (Annex II Table 9.9). The financial benefit gained from the FFE programme by a rural poor household is found to be at Tk. 4.85 (Tk. 0.81 per capita per day) a day for a boy which is not so significant (Annex II Table 9.10). The participatioin of a poor family in the FFE programme causes a substantial income loss to that family. As the benefit under the programme cannot offset the income loss that an extremely poor family has to incur, the appeal of the programme to a precariously asset-poor family is found to be weak. This finding is also found consistent with that of other studies (Ahmed and Billah 1995).

Female-headed households. One of the important demographic features of the poorest households is that close to one-third of them were female-headed during the reference period (Annex II Table 9.11). More than half of the sample households (55%) are found to be female-headed in the urban slums compared to 23% in the rural households during the same period.

Another important demographic feature of the three groups of the poorest households is that only 5% of the FFE households have been female headed compared to 25% and 40% for the non-FFE households respectively in the programme and control villages in 1993 (Annex II Table 9.12A). This composition remained unchanged even in 1996.

The above findings suggest that the FFE households are found to be relatively stable not only in respect of assets (presanted later) but also demographically. The preponderance of female-headed households among the non-FFE household groups implies that these households are not only asset-poor but also subject to a higher degree of vulnerability and defencelessness both economically and socially.

In the urban slums, a significant portion of the poorest households happened to be female-headed during the monitoring period (Annex II Table 9.12B). The gender focus of poverty is found more pronounced among the poorest segment of the slum-dwellers than those in the rural areas. Annex II Table 9.11 shows that more than half (55%) of the sample households have been female-headed as against the 23% female headed households among the rural counterparts during the same period.

Begging households. Altogether, 6% of the poorest households are found engaged in begging. In the urban slums, none of the poorest households is found in this category and all begging households under our sample belong to the rural areas (Annex II Table 9.13). Besides, all these households are found among the non-FFE groups (Annex II Table 9.14). These households are more vulnerable and extremely poverty-ridden mainly due to some unfavourable demographic factors. The households engaged in begging are relatively small (3.8) in family size compared to the sample average (4.2) in 1996. Moreover, the dependancy ratio for the begging households was lower (2.7) than that for the sample households (3.0) in 1996.The predominance of women among the earning members points to the poor income level of these households. As the dependency ratio is very low, it implies that most of the family members are forced to go for earning activities due to their poverty.

9.3.2 Income

Sources of income. The poorest households have limited sources of income. The urban poor are usually engaged in unskilled manual labour. Similar is the case with the rural poor as well (Annex II Table 9.15). Sale of labour was the main source of the rural poor accounting for 82% of their total income in 1993. It marginally increased to 84% in 1996. Agriculture was the second most important source of income making up only 12% of the total income of the rural poor in 1993 and 10% in 1996. Only 1% of the income of the rural poor was derived from livestock, a new source of income, in 1996.

Nominal income. In the rural areas, the income of the poorest households has been found to be miserably low during the monitoring period. The per capita daily income of these households was Tk. 6.9 in 1993. This increased to Tk. 7.4 in 1996 showing a 7% growth (Annex II Table 9.16). Their daily income per household grew by 12% from Tk. 29 in 1993 to Tk 33 in 1996. The higher growth rate of nominal income is mainly due to a positive growth of the nominal wage rate (12%) along with a growth of the number of earning members (5%) of the poorest households. The low per capita income is partly due to the large family size and its growth over the monitoring period. The low income of the poorest households is the result of a number of socio-economic factors, eg low wage rate (Annex II Table 9.9), poor asset base, poor human capability due to illiteracy (Annex II Tables 7.31 and 7.32), low access to economic opportunities, etc.

The impact of the FFE programme does not seem to have been appreciable on the level of income of the programme households. Although the programme has had some positive impact on the growth of income (15% in per capita and 18% in per household terms during 1993-1996), its contribution to the growth is difficult to ascertain. However, other findings indicate that the contribution of the programme to the income of the programme households is insignificant (Tk. 0.81 per capita/daily, Tk. 4.85 per household/daily, 15% of the average household income) (Annex II Tables 9.10 and 9.16).

The per capita nominal income of the poorest households in the urban slums was Tk. 12 a day in 1993 and it increased to Tk. 19 a day in 1996 representing a 31% growth (Annex II Table 9.17). The per household daily income of the urban poor increased by a higher rate of 40% from Tk. 41 a day to Tk. 58 during the same period.

The income of the urban poor increased by a much higher rate than that of the rural poor in both per capita and per household terms because of the higher growth rates of wage (29%) (Annex II Table 9.9) and of earners per household (17%) (Annex II Table 9.7), lower family size (3.7), etc. Moreover, gainful economic opportunities are greater in the urban areas relative to the rural areas.

Real income. The income of the poorest households in real terms (in kilograms of coarse rice) is found to have declined across the board during the monitoring period. In the rural areas, the per capita real income of the poorest households declined by 22% on an average from 0.9 in 1993 to 0.7 kilograms of coarse rice in 1996 (Annex II Table 9.18). Barring the FFE households, the per household real income has registered a sharp decline during the same period irrespective of differences in regional diversity. Due to the income support under the FFE programme, the FFE households could avoid the sharp fall of income. The per capita real income for the FFE households has declined by 13% against a 20 to 25% decline for the non-FFE households over the same peiod. Overall, despite a 7% increase in per capita income in nominal terms on an average during 1993-96 (Annex II Table 9.16), the corresponding real income took an appreciably higher downward turn (-22%) (Annex II Table 9.18) caused by a 24 to 43% price hike of coarse rice in the rural areas during the same peirod (Annex II Table 9.19).

The per capita real income of the urban poor remained unchanged, whereas the per household real income marked an upward trend (5%) during the monitoring period (Annex II Table 9.20). The per capita real income of the urban poor was almost double (1.4 kg a day) that of the rural poor in 1993 which remained almost unchanged during the same period. The per household real income of the poorest households in urban slums stood at 4.7 kg and 5.0 kg a day in 1993 and 1996 respectively recording a 5% growth. The poorest households in the urban slums are relatively better off than their rural counterparts in respect of per household real income which declined by 16% for the latter during the same period (Annex II Table 9.18).

Wage rate. The unskilled wage rate is considered to be an important indicator for monitoring poverty. The wage rate for all categories of unskilled wage labourers is found to have increased in both the rural and urban areas (Annex II Table 9.9). In the rural areas, the daily nominal wage rate increased by 11.7% from Tk. 17.2 in 1993 to Tk. 19.2 in 1996 (Annex II Tables 9.21 and 9.24) The wage rate is found to be much higher for the urban slum-dwellers, and it grew by 29% from the level of Tk. 35.8 in 1993 to Tk. 46.1 in 1996 (Annex II Tables 9.21 and 9.22).

Although the wage rate for unskilled labourers increased during the monitoring period, the purchasing power of the poor labourers did not rise due to a higher rate of price increase in the case of coarse rice. The average wage rate for unskilled wage labourers, in fact, declined across the board in real terms during the monitoring period. However, the poor in the northern part had to sustain a much higher rate of fall (22%) in real wage rate as against 14% for those in the central part during this period (Annex II Table 9.24).

9.3.3 Consumption

Consumption of food. The consumption of rice and wheat—the staple food items of the poorest households—is found to have recorded opposite trends among these households in the urban and rural areas. In the urban slums, the per capita daily consumption of food (rice and wheat) was 442 grams in 1993 and it rose to 514 grams in 1996 representing a 16% growth (Annex II Table 9.25). The increase in the consumption level of food in terms of both per adult equivalent unit and per household units has also been substantial, 18 and 25% respectively during the monitoring period. These findings, however, conceal the substantially low level of food intake observed in one of the slums where poverty is found to be more acute (Annex II Table 9.26).

In the rural areas, the trend in food consumption is, however, found to have consistantly sunk during the monitoring period in per capita and per adult equivalent terms (Annex II Table 9.27). The per capita daily consumption of rice and wheat declined from the level of 585 grams in 1993 to 566 in 1996 showing a 3% decrease. The food consumption per adult equivalent unit is found to have been at a much higher level—797 grams in 1993 and 786 grams a day in 1996—recording a relatively small fall during the period. The declining trend in food intake is true of both the programme and non-programme households during the same period. The consistent fall in the level of consumption of food is largely due to the fall in real income and expansion of the average family size of the poorest households during the monitoring period.

Box 9.2 Food Security: A Quantitative Assessment

In order to assess the poverty status of sample households, the heads of the households were asked to make self-assessments in respect of poverty. Their self-assessed status may be categorized as follows:

(i) Chronic deficit households reporting food shortage throughout the year;
(ii) Occasional deficit households reporting food shortage occasionally in a year;
(iii) Break-even households reporting neither shortage nor surplus; and
(iv) Surplus households reporting food surplus throughout the year.

The distribution of sample households by poverty status are arranged in Table 9.28. It appears from the table that most of the sample households are characterized as year-round or occasional deficit households and very few are surplus households. About 26% among the urban and 65% among the rural household heads have said that they had chronic food deficit in the previous year as against only 10% in the urban and 1% in the rural areas who have assessed themselves as surplus households. The proportion of occasional deficit households is about 37% in the urban and 30% in the rural areas. The break-even households comprise about 27% in the urban and 4% in the rural areas. The situation of the poor in respect of food availability seems to be more deplorable in the rural areas than in the urban areas.

Shift from rice to wheat. In the rural areas, some consumers of the poorest households seem to have switched over to wheat from rice and have increasingly consumed wheat, an inferior substitute for rice during the reference period (Annex II Table 9.29). It is found that wheat accounted for 8% of total cereal food (rice and wheat) in 1996 compared to only 3% in 1993. The shift from rice to wheat in the composition of the food basket has been more pronounced in the central part than in the northern part of the country. The change in the composition of cereal food seems to be largely due to poverty and the availability of wheat under the FFE programme.The shift took place in the cases of FFE and non-FFE households alike. There is a likelihood that a part of this wheat provided to the beneficiaries of the programme might leak to other non-FFE households through sale or other channels. This might contribute to the process even for the non-FFE households in the control villages. The urban poor are not found to consume wheat and no shift from rice to wheat took place during the reporting period (Annex II Table 9.30).

Consumption of non-cereal items. The consumption of protein-rich non-cereal food like fish, beef, chicken, egg, milk, etc by the hardcore poor in the rural areas declined alarmingly during the monitoring period (Annex II Table 9.31). The consumption of these nutritious food items is, however, found to have been unchanged in the urban slums (Annex II Table 9.32). On an average, the poorest households eat fish less than 6 times a month, meat twice a year, chicken less than once a year, milk less than once a month and so on, showing the extremely poor level of consumption of such nutritionally-rich food items (Annex II Table 9.33). More alarmingly, the consumption level of these important food items has tended to fall further since the base period. Although the rural poor do consume fish, chicken, egg and milk more frequently during certain periods in a year such as festivals, the frequency of consuming these items went down in 1996 in comparison with the base period 1993. The urban poor have eaten beef and vegetables more frequently during the monitoring period.

At a more disaggregate level, the consumption of these protein-rich food by the poorest households is much worse in the central part than to the northern part of the country. A similar difference is observed among the urban slums as well. Although the consumption of these nutritious food items by the FFE-household group recorded a downward trend with respect to almost all the above items except egg, chicken and milk, they ate more frequently than the two non-FFE household groups during the same time because of their higher levels of income and resource base.

9.3.4 Housing Conditions

Structure. In the rural areas, the housing conditions of the poorest households improved marginally during the monitoring period. In 1993, 87% of the poorest households had completely thatched (F-type) houses, the figure decreasing to 80% in 1996 (Annex II Table 9.34). On the other hand, 13% of their houses were thatched with corrugated iron-roof in 1993, the figure improving to 20% in 1996. Whatever improvement took place during the monitoring period, the northern part accounted more for the improvement than the central part. Similarly, most of the benefit resulting from the improvement in the housing structure accrued to the poorest households under the FFE programme (Annex II Table 9.35). This suggests that the FFE progamme may have contributed to an improvement in the living standards of the poorest, albeit minimally. The causality, however, is difficult to prove.

In the urban slums, the houses of the poorest households were completely thatched ones and no improvement took place in any manner during the monitoring period (Annex II Table 9.36).

Living space. It is not only the structure of the houses that the poorest people lived in were the worst, but the space of these houses was also very limited in both the urban and rural areas. In the urban slums, 95% of the houses that the poorest lived in were single-roomed and only 5% were double-roomed in 1993 (Annex II Table 9.36). The housing conditions of the urban poor relating to living space did not improve in any respect during the monitoring period.

In the rural areas, the housing problem facing the poorest is found to have been a bit less acute. Single-, double- and tripple-roomed houses of the hardcore poor accounted for 88, 8 and 3% respectively in 1993 and this improved marginally to 85, 10 and 5% respectively in 1996 (Annex II Table 9.35). As in the case of the structure of the houses, the housing condition of the poorest households in terms of living space also shows some signs of improvement, though not significant, in the rural areas during the monitoring period.

It must be mentioned that the benefit by the way of improvement in the housing conditions in terms of both the structure and living space, is found to have gone to the FFE-households only. The non-FFE households could not improve their housing conditions during the period from 1993 to 1996.

State of overcrowding. The shortage of availability of living space for the household members can be better appreciated in terms of the average number of members per room. In the rural areas, the state of overcrowding is showing no sign of improvement (Annex II Table 9.37). The condition of the urban poor has aggravated during the monitoring period (Annex II Table 9.38). The finding that the housing condition of households under the FFE programme have improve in during the reference period is also supported by another finding in this regard. Although the FFE-households had a worse state of overcrowding due to their higher family sizes (5.3 in 1993 and 5.6 in 1996), the overcrowding problems faced by these households eased marginally from 4.4 persons/room in 1993 to 4.1 in 1996.

The overcrowding problem has become worse for the non-programme households because of their more precarious economic conditions.

Regionally, the overcrowding problem facing the poorest households is found more acute in the central part compared to the northern part during the monitoring period. In the central part, the burden of overcrowding increased irrespective of the programme and non-programme households. However, in the northern part, the FFE-househods had some improvement in respect of this problem during this period, although no improvement accrued to the non-FFE households.

9.3.5 Fuel and Lighting

In the rural areas, the poorest households mostly used dry leaves (98% of the households), firewood (10%) and cowdung (33%) as fuel for cooking (Annex II Table 9.39). The urban poor, on the other hand, commonly used firewood (50%) and rags (pieces of cloth) (50%) for cooking purposes during this period (Annex II Table 9.40). Although, as a whole, cowdung was found to be the second largest source of fuel for cooking, households in the northern part are much more dependent (60%) on it than those (7%) in the central part. This is probably due to the better asset position (livestock) of the poorest households in the northern part. There has been no change in the type of fuels used during the monitoring period in both the urban and rural areas.

The poorest households in both the areas are found to be completely dependent on a single type of lighting, namely uncovered kerosene lamp. They did not have any access to electricity in both the areas in the monitoring period (Annex II Tables 9.39 and 9.40).

9.3.6 Assets Profile

Land. The poorest households in the rural areas are found to be extremely land-poor in terms of both cultivable land and area of homesteads. Only 17% of them are found owning cultivable land (Annex II Table 9.41). The average size of landholding cultivated by them is found to have been 68 decimals in 1993 which subsequently shrank to 64 decimals in 1996. However, the average size of cultivable land per household is found to be insignificant: 11.4 decimals in 1993, falling further to 10.6 decimals in 1996.

Although most of the poorest households in the rural areas owned homesteads, the size of their homesteads is found to be very small. Eighty-two per cent of the poorest households owned homesteads built on 7 decimals of land on an average, and this remained unchanged throughout the monitoring period. However, the average size of land for a homestead per sample household amounts to 6 decimals in 1996.

There have been differences in the landholding pattern in the rural areas. The average holding size of cultivable land was much larger (93 decimals) in the central part compared to that (57 decimals) in the northern part, although the per household cultivable land was strikingly much lower in the central part than that in the northern part. This indicates the existence of more skewed patterns of landholding (10% of the owned cultivable land) among the poorest households in the central part than those (23%) in the northern part.

Annex II Table 9.41 shows that the poorest households under the FFE programme have much more land compared to those outside the programme. The FFE-households have on an average 23.6 decimals of cultivable land compared to 3.1-5.3 decimals for the non-FFE households in 1996. With respect to the area of homesteads, the FFE households are also found in a better position than the other groups. The average size of homestead is found to be 13 decimals for the FFE households as against 5 and 2 decimals for the non-FFE households in the experimental and control villages respectively. The better resource endowments of the FFE households relative to the non-FFE households seem to be the real cause of the better performance by the FFE households in respect of some of the indicators mentioned elsewhere.

The poorest households in the urban slums are found to be completely detached from land. They have neither cultivable land nor homesteads of their own. This shows that the asset base of the urban poor is more weak compared to their counterparts in the rural areas.

Livestock. In the rural areas, livestock is an important asset of the rural people. But the poorest households are found to be bereft of this asset (Annex II Table 9.42). It is strange to observe that on an average 7-8% of the poorest households have had less than two cows and goats on an average, 8% have had 2 ducks and 22% have had less than 2 chickens in 1996. The livestock size of the poorest households has improved at a very slow pace during the monitoring period.

The resource base of the poorest households in the central part is terribly low not only in terms of cultivable land but also in terms of livestock too. Only 3% households had cows and goats in the central part as againist to 10-13% in the northern part.

In the urban slums, the poorest households are found to be completely bereft of livestock in the monitoring period.

Buying and selling of assets. Regarding consumer goods, the only asset that the poorest households purchased during the monitoring period are utensils. In the rural areas, 35% of the poorest households bought utensils whereas 3% of them sold the same in 1996 (Annex II Table 9.43). So far as producer goods are concerned, namely rickshaws, rickshaw vans, bicycles and cows, 5 and 10% of the poorest households bought and sold each of these items during the monitoring period. No systematic pattern of buying and selling goods is found among the FFE and non-FFE household groups during the reference period.

In the urban slums, a considerable number of the poorest households bought both consumer and producer goods during the monitoring period (Annex II Table 9.44). Forty per cent and 20% of these households bought consumer and producer goods respectively in 1996. The urban poor could not buy any kind of producer goods whatsoever in the base year.

9.3.7 Credit

The poor's access to credit improved considerably in terms of both the number of borrowers and the volume of credit in both the urban and rural areas during 1993-96. In terms of the volume of credit, their access to credit grew by 457% in the rural areas and by 135% in the urban slums during this period (Annex II Table 9.45). Their access to credit in terms of the number of borrowers (net) registered 63% and 233% growth in the rural and urban areas respectively (Annex II Tables 9.46, 9.47 and 9.48) (See also, Box 9.3).

The volume of credit per poorest borrower increased markedly from Tk.1,156 to Tk.3,963 in the rural areas but declined from Tk. 4,500 to Tk. 3,170 in the urban areas during the same period. The average volume of credit per poorest household is found to have been very low (Tk. 400) in 1993, and it soared to Tk. 1,684 in 1996. The main financiers of credit to the poorest households are moneylenders, friends and NGOs. In 1993, moneylenders and friends were the main sources of their credit. As a new window for credit, NGOs started lending to the poorest households in the study areas in 1996.

Moneylenders have been the top-ranking financiers of the poorest households both in the rural and urban areas. Although the credit from this source escalated in absolute terms, it declined proportionately during the monitoring period. Despite that, moneylenders are found as the largest deliverers of credit who meet the credit needs of the largest number of poorest borrowers. NGOs have emerged as a new and potential source of credit to the poorest in both the urban and rural areas. As the poorest households in both the areas have been deprived of institutional credits, NGOs are marginally filling the gap as an alternative source of institutional credit for them. NGOs are coming forward to meet the credit need of the poorest households albeit at a lower pace. Although NGOs have emerged as an important source of credit for the poor in the study areas in 1996, the access of the poorest households to NGO credit in terms of coverage (10% of the poorest households) is still at a much lower level. The poorest households are found to have borrowed for a variety of purposes, namely consumption, repairing of houses, financing agricultural activities, purchase of rickshaws/push carts, repayment of loans and medical treatment. In the urban areas, the poorest households used the overwhelming portion of their credit (63%) for health in 1993 compared to 61% for buying rickshaws in 1996 (Annex II Table 9.46). Credit used for the consumption purpose declined during this period. In the rural areas, although the credit used for consumption declined, health claimed an increased volume of credit during the same period (Annex II Table 9.47). The percentage shares of the total credit used for consumption, health and agriculture have been to the extent of 76, 0 and 22% in 1993 compared to 40, 28 and 24% respectively in 1996. In the face of a high incidence of diseases, the rural poor had to borrow money for meeting medical expenses in 1996.

Box 9.3 Household Credits: Quantitative Findings

Majority of the respondents (72%) replied affirmatively to the question whether they had taken credit from any source. Their opinions are summarized and shown in Table 9.48. It appears from the same table that households that took credit during the year preceding the enumeration were 60% of the total respondents in the urban and 83% in the rural areas. Distribution of respondents by the source of credit is shown in Table 9.49. It is interesting to note that the interest rate of credit taken from usurers and relatives is found to be exorbitantly high and it varies from 102.8% in the urban areas to 153.6% in the rural areas for credit from usurers, while the interest rate of credit taken from relatives varies from 103.2% in the urban and 110% in rural areas.

Credits from institutional sources like commercial banks were about 8% for the chronic deficit households in the rural areas, 2% for the occasional deficit households, and 17% for the break-even households. On the other hand, credit from NGOs were about 15% for chronic deficit, 13% for ocassionally deficit, 39% for the break-even and 30% for the surplus households in the urban areas and 19%, 30%, 33% and 50% respectively in the rural areas (Table 9.50). Of the traditional credit sources, money-lenders, relatives and shopkeepers were prominent particularly among the chronic deficit households both in the urban and rural areas. Among the 130 chronic deficit households, money-lenders provided credit to as many as 52 households (43%) with average interest rates ranging from 103% in the urban and 154% in the rural areas. On the other hand, 30% of the surplus households received credits from the urban areas from NGOs with the interest rate of 17% per annum and only one household out of two surplus households in the rural areas received credit from NGOs sources. NGOs as a credit source were available more to the break-even and surplus households. On the other hand the money-lender was reportedly the main source of credit for chronic deficit and occasionally deficit households. Similar results were reported by the BBS in its poverty monitoring survey report on 2,235 rural households.

In the rural areas, the poorest households are found to have increasingly utilized credit for directly income-yielding activities like agriculture, purchase of rickshaws, etc instead of consumption and other purposes. This is why credit used for consumption declined appreciably from 76% in 1993 to 40% in 1996 in the rural areas, although it increased in absolute terms during the same period (Annex II Table 9.45). As regards the urban poor, credit for consumption is found to have reduced from 38% in 1993 to 12% in the terminal year of the monitoring period. Credit utilized for directly productive activities, on the other hand, escalated during the same period. The change in credit utiliztion took place mainly due to the impact of the new source of credit, namely NGOs who are providing credit to the poor for income-yielding purposes.

9.3.8 Savings

Savings by the poorest households have been insignificant during 1993-96. Not only the volume of their savings has been low, but the number of saving households is also very few (Annex II Table 9.51).

In 1993 there was no saving households. However, the number of households participating in the savings programmes increased to 22% of the poorest households in the rural areas. In the urban slums, no poorest household is found to have saved during this period. In the rural areas, the poorest households who participated in the savings programme could save only Tk. 21 on an average in 1996. However, the average savings per household was much lower (Tk. 7 and Tk. 3 to 4 for the programme and non-programme households respectively) in 1996 (Annex II Table 9.52). The poorest households in the northern part regardless of groups could save nothing during the monitoring period.

The difference in the amounts of savings of the three groups of the poorest households is found to have remained unchanged, because their saving is largely determined by the difference in the resource bases of these households. The FFE households could save more than the non-FFE households, because their resource base was better than those of the non-FFE households.

Limitations

The poverty monitoring carried out under this study has the following limitations:

1. The main objective of this monitoring is not to analyse the dynamics of poverty as such, but rather to highlight the interface between the poorest households, and public expenditure and public policies. In the first round of the monitoring, two sets of data base and impacts on the socio-economic profile of the poorest have been gathered for 1993 and 1996 respectively. As the base data were generated through the recall method by the participants, its quality may not, therefore, be as good as that of the impact data. Instead of 1993, 1996 should be used as the base year in future because of the better quality of data. The monitoring in the years ahead against 1996 would, therefore, be more valid and reliable than that in 1996 against 1993.

2. As the present monitoring is based on a small sample (n=80), it may not suffice for generalizing of the findings. However, it must be re-emphasized that this monitoring exercise is primarily meant

not for generalization but for understanding the process of the qualitative approach. Qualitative inquiry typically focuses on relatively small samples (Patton 1990).

3. As already mentioned, this monitoring is part of a broad qualitative investigation interfacing between public expenditure and public policies on the one hand and the poorest on the other. Under this monitoring, the 'quantified bones' have been provided so far but not the 'qualified flesh' (Cernea 1992) as much as needed to interpret the changes in quantitative data in depth which will be attempted in the next rounds of monitoring. In fact, there are several questions which remain unanswered in this round of monitoring.
4. Public expenditure impacts upon the poor through a number of channels, direct and indirect. This round of monitoring has been focused on the direct aspects of impacts only while indirect impacts remain unaccounted for. The monitoring to be followed in the years ahead would be focused on both.
5. As the definition of poverty and the criteria used in the participatory approach are completely different from those of the conventional poverty line based approach, the prevalence rates of poverty for these two approaches may not be strictly comparable.
6. The prevalence of poverty has been measured in a participatory manner for 1996 only so that no comparison has been made against any year because of the data gap in respect of this measure over the period 1993-96. The prevalence rate would, however, be measured in the next rounds of monitoring using the figures for 1996 as the base data.

The major trends identified in the qualitiative assessment

The pauperization process in Bangladesh, particularly in the rural areas, is in full motion. Poverty is degenerating into indigence and pauperism. In the rural areas, 75% of households were poor in 1996 including 55% in extreme poverty. The comparable figures for the urban slums were 72% and 21% respectively. This is one aspect of poverty. The prevalence of poverty as such cannot reveal the 'intensity' and 'severity' of poverty. The base and impact data under this study confirm that the living standard of the poorest is deteriorating as a part of the declining trends of the economy, particularly in the rural areas where the majority of them live.

To counteract the gradual alienation from land and decline in real labour wages, the poorest households are reducing the consumption of those food items which are badly needed for the maintenance of the physiological existence. They are trying to offset the declining trend in real income by increasing the family size and the number of earning members. To them, a larger family size means more earning members and more income for the family. The total income of a household is increasing but per capita income in real terms is declining. The pace of development taking place in the rural areas is so slow that the poorest have to bear the brunt of the stagnation. They are trying to cope with their socio-economic uncertainities and insecurities by resorting to demographic solutions. Some of them are falling back on humiliating activities like begging. The income-earning capacity of the poorest households remains at the lowest level due to a lack of gainful opportnities in the rural areas. Although NGOs have recently entered the field in the study areas with their credit package, the access of the poorest households to NGO credit is still at a low level. The poorest households are found outside the network of institutional credit. Public policies including budgetary policies are totally ineffective in transferring the benefits to them through traditional channels. Only targeted programmes are found effective in transferring some benefits despite leakages and wrong targeting.

Comments

The findings from the study provide some empirical ground to raise questions about the rationale of public expenditure in the two important social sectors, namely health and education. From the perspective of poverty, the benefit of the huge public expenditure for the health sector does not reach the poorest in either the urban or the rural areas. The same is the case with the education sector. Although targeted programmes are providing some benefits to the poorest, they fail to ensure the sustainability of such benefits so as to link human capability with economic opportunities.

Public policies and public expenditure seem to have failed to satisfy the basic principles of social justice. The ongoing pauperization process is forcing the hardcore poor to out-migrate to urban cities for sheer survival. The failure of the public policies in this regard is not only pointing to the inapplicability of the current strands of economic policies but also raising questions about the legitimacy of the political and economic governance because of the forced displacement of the poorest from their paternal homesteads in a stagnant rural economy.

Chapter 10

CONCLUSIONS AND POLICY SUGGESTIONS

Conclusions

The annual budget being the most important fiscal document of a government significantly influences the living conditions of all the sections of people. In a way, it is also the most important political document since the main objective of government budgeting is to mobilize and distribute scarce resources. In more specific terms the budget purportedly aims at:

- mobilization of domestic resources through tax and non-tax revenues;
- allocation of scarce resources among competing needs;
- distribution of costs and benefits of economic development;
- stabilization of macroeconomic trends;
- sustainable growth; and
- equity.

There are considerable trade-offs between and among the above goals, mainly because of the severity of resource constraints.

The Finance Minister can face the above challenges squarely only if the entire budget process is transparent, participatory and performance-oriented. If the overriding consideration is poverty eradication, the job becomes all the more difficult. Poverty eradication calls for greater transparency and accountability in the process of budget-making and its implementation. With this perspective in mind, the annual budget (1990-91 to 1994-95) has been monitored to see how much the poor are involved in the process and how far their needs are reflected in it. Both quantitative and qualitative tools have been applied while conducting this monitoring exercise.

The major findings of the exercise are:

- Budget-making in Bangladesh continues to be an archaic process which is centralized, top-down, not linked with the long-term development goals and performance of the economy, not responsive enough to the needs of the poor and not based on adequate data sources. It continues to believe in incremental budgeting which is mostly decided on the thumb's rule.
- The revenue budget is very rigid. It depends mostly on indirect taxes and lacks a built-in redistributive mechanism for social justice.
- Though the size of public expenditure has been consistently increasing, the overall living conditions of the poor have not improved appreciably. While public expenditure in the social sectors has been increasing in quantity, specially in the original estimates and not so much in the revised ones, the quality of such expenditure has not been improving significantly. The proportion of such expenditures has been hovering around one-third of the ADP over the monitoring period.
- Many components of the development expenditures are in fact revenue expenditures or the vice-versa. A clear segregation between the two has not yet been seriously attempted. Moreover, there is no effective monitoring of the development budget. The ADP is still a 'black hole' and nobody knows where the money goes. Nor has this been brought under public scrutiny by the Members of Parliament (MP), professionals and development agencies.

The macro indicators of poverty present a dismal picture of the poverty situation of Bangladesh compared to other countries. There is, however, no alternative to growth in GDP and per capita income for sustainable poverty eradication. The social sector allocation is claimed to be aimed at the empowerment of the poor so that they can be engaged in sustainable income-earning activities. In the last five years, however, the allocation for the social sectors was not found to exceed one-third of the total ADP allocation despite a widespread incidence of poverty.

A close review of the components of the social sectors confirms the dismal picture provided by the macro indicators. For instance, employment generated under the FFW and TR programmes shows an absolute decline during 1992-94. Similarly, the number of beneficiaries under the VGD programme also declined by 26% during 1990-95. Such a drastic decline in the food-aided programmes (FFW, TR, VGD, etc) has a deleterious impact on the already acute poverty situation in the country. On the other hand, the BRDB programme targeted to the poor has contributed to an increase in the average income of the beneficiaries, and the ratio of public expenditure on rural development to GDP has increased over the period 1990-95. However, BRDB activities have not significantly improved the rural poverty situation in terms of social and demographic indicators.

The sample survey indicates the efficacy of the FFE programme in terms of (i) increasing the participation rate, (ii) decreasing the drop-out rate, (iii) alleviating poverty, and (iv) diverting child labour to primary education. However, the level of investment in education appears to be inadequate as reflected by the adult literacy rate of 33%. The survey also suggests that the role of government agencies in both the rural and urban areas in the provision of sanitation facilities, vaccination facilities, family planning and other primary health care services is positive and greater than those of NGOs except for water supply in the urban slums. It is also observed that the urban poor are better off than the rural poor with respect to the benefits received from GOs in sanitation, family planning and water supply, while the rural poor have more benefited in terms of vaccination of children.

On the other hand, findings of the opinion survey of knowledge, attitudes and perceptions (KAP) of the poor relating to the public budget reveal that the urban poor are more aware of the national budget than the rural poor.

The qualitative survey complements most of the above findings. This survey also confirms that the quality of primary education is very poor. While the access of students from the poor households to primary education has been improving due to the Food For Education programme in recent years, this did not make a substantial impact on the quality of education. The delivery system introduced by the programme has a number of loopholes which encourage corruption and waste of the teacher-student contact period.

The qualitative assessment indicates that the performance of the primary health sector is not encouraging either. The delivery system of the health sector at the grassroots level is inefficient, unequal and often biased towards infrastructure building rather than toward improving the quality of service. The rural poor get maximum health services from pharmacists and existing indigenous providers like *kaviraj*.

When a set of qualitative tools for monitoring public expenditures were applied to find out their impacts on poverty a number of interesting findings were noted:

- seventy-one per cent of urban and 74% of rural households were categorized by the respondents themselves as poor;
- the poverty situation has been worsening over time;
- the real income of the poorest households has been declining over time; and
- the condition of the very poor households was not encouraging when judged by indicators of poverty like the housing condition, incidence of common diseases, availability of improved sanitary facilities, etc.

Policy Suggestions

Given the above findings, one may be tempted to make a number of policy suggestions for improving the quality of budget making in Bangladesh, specially for responding to the needs of the poor.

1. The budget should be prepared and presented in a simple format so that even the ordinary people can understand its processes. Efforts should be made to rescue the budget from its archaic structural limitations. The information and analytical contents of the budget, the sectoral allocations of the following year's budget, the demarcation between the revenue and the development budget including their recurrent and capital expenditures, the incidence of revenues, etc should be presented in such terms and formats as can be easily comprehensible to an ordinary person.
2. The Finance Minister in his budget speech should reflect the hopes and aspirations of the ordinary people in such a manner that they can immediately relate the fiscal activities of the governmental agencies to some visible outputs. Only then the fear of the people about the budget as a mechanism of price hike can be removed.
3. There should be an institutional mechanism to capture the people's own needs. While prioritizing the budget allocations, the people's needs assessment should be seriously considered by those involved in the preparation of the budget. The Finance Minister should find a mechanism to carry out regular dialogues with people's representatives, consumer groups, people's organizations, members of the chambers of commerce and industries as well as other professional groups. The budget

preparation techniques should be modernized using relevant computer-based accounting packages. Apparently, some exercises are now going on along this line and this trend should be strengthened.

4. There is now a move toward the establishment of decentralized local governments. There should be a simultaneous attempt at fiscal decentralization. The local government should be clearly mandated about the nature of their rights over certain heads of local resources as well as over a proportion of the central resources. There should also be a mini-parliament at every level of local government where the local budget will be discussed and approved. Besides the elected representatives, representatives of different professional groups, government officials, NGOs, women, youth, etc should be inducted as members of the local parliament. The local government will have to be accountable to this local parliament. They will together formulate local-level plans for poverty alleviation and other development activities.
5. It will be wise for the Finance Minister not to be complacent about the increased allocation of public resources for education and health. If the quality of education and health services does not improve even after increased allocations, this should be treated as a net wastage of scarce public resources. Adequate institutional mechanisms, therefore, should be designed to regularly monitor the quality of education and health services provided by the relevant government departments. There should be a greater scope for participatory monitoring of the quality of those services.
6. The task of national budgeting should not be seen merely as a mechanical exercise of resource mapping and sectoral allocations. Its aim should be to see whether the resources mobilized are spent in time and in the intended manner or not. It is widely believed that there is corruption in revenue mobilization and huge wastage in the development programmes and projects. The challenge as to how to reduce corruption and wastage while managing public finance has to be faced squarely. Besides the political commitment for efficient and accountable governance, the entire administration should be motivated for the greater cause of development.
7. There should be an attempt at improving the human expenditure ratio by allocating more public resources for human priority activities to expand people's choices.

8. The current method of auditing development projects by IMED should be radically changed. The auditing should be done not by 'proforma' checking alone but by the 'programme budgeting' approach where one can clearly identify the 'value for money'. Each and every department/ministry should be required to draw up a financial management plan which can readily address the question: 'where is the money going and what are we getting for it ?'
9. There should be an independent development watchdog with sufficient authority, resources and skilled personnel which should replace IMED and play a crucial role in monitoring the pace and quality of the existing development projects, suggest mid-course revisions of the programmes to the parliament and present suggestions to the media. All its findings should be publicly debated. This will help the government take corrective action on the shortcomings of any development programme.
10. The annual budgets should not be seen as isolated fiscal events. They should be seen as a part of a longer-term plan with some fundamental socio-economic guidelines formulated through national consensus preferably in the national parliament, after careful consideration of ideas proposed by the 'mini-parliaments' at the lower levels.

Annexes

ANNEX I: TARGETED PUBLIC EXPENDITURE FOR POVERTY ALLEVIATION

Introduction

It is widely held that a country like Bangladesh cannot afford to allocate a major share of its total public expenditure for such social overheads as education, health, medicare, etc although the returns on such investment may in the long run outweigh those on alternative investments. But to make a journey along a sustainable and equitable growth path, the social sectors merit large public resource allocations.

The only assets a poor woman or man has are her/his labour and brain power. S/he does not have a wide choice of employment opportunities because s/he lacks education and health which can turn her/him into a productive worker. Increasing expenditure in social sectors can thus help improve human capital formation leading to poverty eradication.

To emphasize increased allocations in the social sectors in public resource management is not to say that the directly productive sectors (agriculture, industries, etc), the physical infrastructure or non-productive sectors are less important from the perspective of poverty alleviation. In reality, as an economy grows, people across all socio-economic strata are benefited, either directly or indirectly. But what is more desirable is that the sources of this growth, instead of only the benefits, should be more equitably distributed. The trickle-down effect does hardly take place in an unequal society. If a participatory growth process is in place involving all these sectors, it can generate mutually reinforcing forces for the reduction of poverty. But given the acute resource constraint, what is needed is to strike a balance between the allocations for the targeted and non-targeted poverty alleviating programmes. Improvement in the poverty situation can create effective demand and increase the profitability of the productive sectors of the economy, thereby invigorating the growth potential. Rapid economic growth, in turn, strengthens the positive impact of the poverty alleviating measures. In fact, there is no trade-off between growth and poverty alleviation. Given proper support, the poor can be more productive and efficient and can save at a high rate in participatory group initiatives.

Resources invested for poverty alleviation, therefore, assist the process of growth itself, provided that the poor are animated and assisted to take participatory development initiatives. In such initiatives, they will not only have shares in the incremental pie but also contribute to the expansion process. In this manner, the poor can benefit both ways and the pace of poverty alleviation can be accelerated by releasing the dormant productive potential of the poor.

Indeed, if we really want to make a significant impact on the poverty front, the poor should get a greater share of the public resources under appropriate institutional frameworks. The rate of growth of income of the lower echelons of society should be significantly greater than those of the upper echelons. Such a transfer of income will not only ensure social justice but will also lead to a higher rate of growth of GDP.

Looking into the allocation for social development in different budgets, it is observed that nearly one-third of the total budget has been going into this sector. This is still far short of the UN recommended allocation for social sectors (the public expenditure ratio is around 25%, the social allocation ratio more than 40% and the social priority ratio more than 50%), (HDR 1991). The allocation for targeted projects/programmes involved in poverty alleviation (including food aided projects, youth development, women development, rural development, etc) has certainly increased over time. But one cannot be so definite about the actual achievement in poverty alleviation even after such an increased allocation.

More allocation of funds for the social sectors does not guarantee any improvement in the economic condition of the underprivileged in society. It is only a necessary condition but not sufficient for effective utilization. The funds allocated for the social sectors may not bring about the desired results due to the following reasons:

1. The composition of the funds channeled to the social sectors may have a bias against the social priority sectors which an economy in tight budgetary condition may not afford. According to the HDR it should not be less than 50% of the total social sector spending.
2. The quality of social spending may be very poor leading to a reduction in its value in terms of efficiency and effectiveness. This may be due to large-scale corruption, wastage, misutilization, non-utilization, etc of the allocated resources.
3. Large spending in the programmes under the social sectors may not reach the underprivileged if the major share of it is ultimately diverted to the better-off section of the society. Lack of access to facilities by the poor, lack of participation of the community members, lack of decentralization, etc lead to a diversion of resources and facilities away from them.

4. The lessons learned from the experiences of the Indian states, 'suggest that mere provision of funds is not enough and organization and administration machinery are equally or more important in order to reach the poor more effectively. Decentralized delivery systems are important in this context... the role of public participation and local leadership is also important... ' for their success (UN 1996).

Assessment of the efficacy of public expenditure in alleviating poverty merits both quantitative and qualitative enquiries. In such enquiries, both the allocative and distributive consequences of public expenditure need to be reviewed. Though the Finance Ministers of Bangladesh stated repeatedly in their budget speeches that poverty alleviation was the prime goal of the government, allocation for the social sectors in the last five years did not exceed one-third of the total ADP allocation. Certainly the allocation for social sectors has increased substantially but this is still quite insufficient given the magnitude of poverty in the country. Within the social sectors, the distribution pattern of expenditure does not seem to have tilted towards the lower segment of the income groups, let alone the poor masses at the bottom. One plausible explanation of such a maldistribution of public resources is that the poor, even constituting half of the total population of Bangladesh, have not been able to represent themselves as a strong political pressure group. They, therefore, were unable to force an organized approach to the government demanding their due share of national resources. Their lack of capacity to force the public authority to reallocate resources to meet their needs is attributable to illiteracy, morbidity, crisis proneness and insecurity of income. In this context the inadequate social sector investment of the government only accentuates the vicious circle of poverty in Bangladesh.

In addition to its allocations in the social sector, GOB has some 'safety net' (one kind of transfer mostly given in terms of food assistance) programmes targeted for poverty alleviation. It is claimed that these programmes focus on: i. skill development, and ii. special programmes/projects for poverty alleviation. We have described a set of food aided 'safety net' programmes in sub-sections 6.2, 6.3 and 6.4.

Public Expenditure

Public Expenditure in Terms of Foodgrains. There are two types of Foodgrain Distribution System: monetized and non-monetized. There are 13 public foodgrains distribution channels of which 8 are monetized and 5 are non-monetized. The Statutory Rationing (SR), Modified Rationing (MR), Essential Rationing (ER) for armed forces, other priorities

(OP) for government employees, large employers (LE), Flour Mills (FM), Open Market Sales (OMS), Marketing Operation (MO) and Free Sales (FS) are the monetized channels. The non-monetized channels are: Food for Work (FFW), Test Relief (TR), Vulnerable Group Development (VGD) Programme, Gratuitous Relief (GR) and Food for Education (FFE) [CIRDAP, 1994]. The monetized channels for foodgrain distribution are not intended for the poor as such. However, foodgrains distributed through the non-monetized channels are particularly made available to the target groups in return for their physical labour and in some cases as a relief. Foodgrain under the non-monetized programme is channeled mainly through the Ministry of Relief and Rehabilitation and the Ministry of Women Affairs. Such programmes are envisaged primarily as a transfer of income rather than as a strategy for increasing the income earning capability of the beneficiaries.

Until 1990-91, the monetized channels received foodgrain, amounting to about twice as much as those received by the non-monetized channels. This implies a clear bias against the poor in the public expenditure on foodgrains. Later, the proportion started to decline. The trend has been reversed thereafter. In 1994-95, non-monetized channels received twice as much foodgrain as distributed through the monetized channels.

Trends of Channelwise Public Foodgrain Distribution. The government imports generally large quantities of wheat and rice and distributes them through the PFDS channels. In addition to usual foreign assistance for the Annual Development Programme (ADP), the government also receives a sizeable amount of food aid such as wheat, rice, edible oil, etc from different donor agencies. With these food aids, the GOB prepares a separate food budget and launches various rural development programmes for employment and income generation for the rural poor. Under PFDS, about 66.36% of the total foodgrains were distributed at subsidized prices through monetized channels in 1994-95 (Annex II Table 6.1). The main reason behind this decline is that Bangladesh has now moved towards a market oriented economy and is hence gradually withdrawing subsidy from foodgrain for distribution through monetized channels.

The economic subsidy[1] of foodgrains declined substantially in recent years as may be seen in Annex II Table 6.3. This table shows that the economic subsidies on account of foodgrains have fallen consistently

1. Economic subsidy is defined as the difference between border prices, inclusive of distribution cost, and the issue price [CIRDAP, 1994]

throughout the period 1990-91 to 94-95. It declined from Tk. 3,727 million in 1990-91 to Tk. 1950 million in 1994-95 showing about 48% decrease over the period. On the other hand, the proportion of foodgrains distributed through non-monetized channels has risen consistently over the period. It increased from 34% in 1990-91 to 68% in 1994-95 (Annex II Table 6.1). The average annual growth rate of public expenditure in terms of foodgrains distribution through non-monetized channels for poverty alleviation has been 6.69% over the reference period.

Annex II Table 6.1 shows that at the peak of the foodgrain distribution through monetized channels in 1990-91, as much as 1,574 thousand tons were distributed. The quantity distributed through this channel has been consistently declining in recent years reaching the level of 508 thousand tons in 1994-95. Thus the scope of distribution of foodgrains through the monetized channel has been curtailed. The table also shows that after 1991-92, when 924 thousand tons were distributed through non-monetized channels, the non-monetized foodgrain distribution fell to 617 thousand tons in 1992-93, rising again to 845 thousand tons in 1993-94 and 1,065 thousand tons in 1994-95. The total amount of foodgrains has, however, declined by 34% during 1990-91 to 1994-95 at an annual average rate of about 10%.

Food-Aided Government Programmes for Poverty Alleviation. Food is the only staple item in the consumption basket of the poor. Any unforeseen disaster in the supply of foodgrain or exorbitant rise in food prices has a deleterious effect on the very survival of the poor. This is why food security is the foremost concern in the poverty alleviation drive. Lack of adequate food consumption leads to nutritional deprivation and retards the healthy growth of a population and its development as a strong labour force. And here comes the issue of entitlement or the capability of the deprived sections of the people to establish a secure command over food. This is not ensured by the mere availability of food in the market.

The target group-oriented programmes through the non-monetized channels are undertaken as a direct intervention for poverty alleviation through a provision of food to the poor in return for their physical labour. This, however, does not guarantee food security for the target group. Foodgrains distributed under this head is essentially a kind of welfare measure of the government to improve the living standard of the economically-deprived population. As most of these programmes are supported by foreign donors, the programmes may not be sustainable if the donor agencies withdraw their support. Moreover, the possibility of capital formation through these programmes is insignificant and these programmes may be treated as public charity programmes instead of poverty alleviation programmes.

a. Test Relief (TR) programme

TR is a nationwide programme for the creation of employment opportunities for the poor and simultaneous transfer of income to them. Under this programme, food aids are provided to the target groups instead of cash payment for the repair and maintenance of newly built roads, culverts, earth cutting for educational institutions, etc. This programme is usually administered in the rural areas in order to create employment opportunities for the rural poor to keep the price level of foodgrains stable and to sustain the nutritional status of the rural poor during the

Figure A-1 Public Foodgrain Distributed under the TR Programme

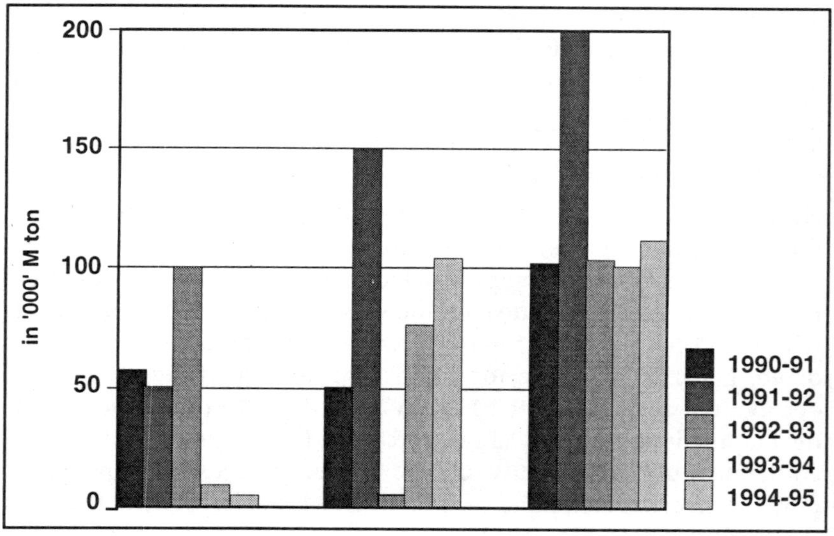

Source: Database on Food Situation Bangladesh, FPMU, June 1995.

lean periods. A survey of TR by the Bangladesh Bureau of Statistics (BBS) conducted in 1989 indicated that the programme contributed only 5% of the household income of the beneficiary households. Its contribution to total household income is higher in the lower income brackets in comparison with the higher income ones. The higher contribution of the TR Programme to poor households (beneficiaries) may be attributed to the increased employment opportunity this programme brings to these households during the lean periods when they are in most precarious conditions. The public foodgrain distribution on account of TR public stock is shown in Annex II Table 6.3.

The Table shows that after 1991-92, when 1,97,000 MT of foodgrain was distributed, the volume of distribution fell to the lowest level of 1,01,00 MT in 1993-94, rising again slightly to 1,27,000 MT in 1994-95. The trend in the distribution of foodgrains under TR is illustrated in Figure A-1. This programme gives only a palliative support to a small section of the poor in tiding over their crisis at a given period of time.

b. Food For Work (FFW) programme

FFW is a rural development programme of the government. Under this programme labourers are paid food instead of cash in exchange for their physical labour. The prime objective of the FFW programme are: i) to develop rural infrastructure such as the construction of link roads, embankments, culverts, digging of canals and ponds, re-excavation of ponds, etc; and ii) to help the rural poor by creating job opportunities for them during the lean seasons. The FFW programme generally reaches

Figure A-2: Public Foodgrain Distributed under the FFW Programme

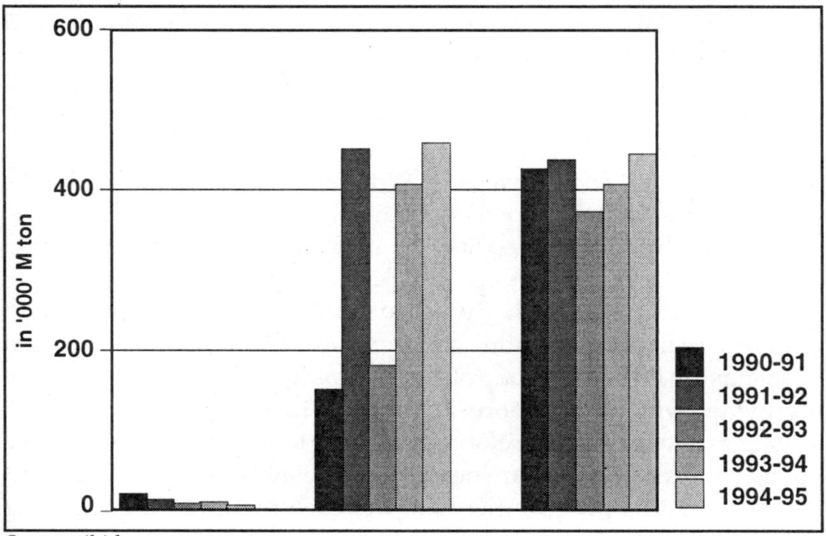

Source: ibid

the target-group and plays a positive role in solving the problem of unemployment in rural areas. However, an opinion survey report on food aided programmes conducted by BBS identified some weaknesses of the programme. More than 75% of the total respondents (250 persons) opined that these programmes could not yield much tangible benefit due to misappropriation of wheat and improper selection of sites for the programme [BBS 1993]. An evaluation study by BIDS in the early 1980s reported that 25—30% of the allotted foodgrains does not actually reach the intended beneficiaries. Annex II Table 6.4 shows the volume and value of foodgrain distributed under the FFW programme.

Annex II Table 6.4 shows that over the 1990-91 to 94-95 period, the total quantity of rice and wheat distributed has increased by merely 9% with an annual average growth of 2%. However, the share of wheat in total distribution has increased significantly due to the higher price of rice which is about 1.5 times higher than that of wheat. The value of foodgrains is estimated at an average wholesale price of rice and wheat as reported by the Department of Agriculture Marketing [FPMU 1995]. The trend in the distribution of foodgrains under the FFW programme may be observed in figure A-2.

c. Vulnerable Group Development (VGD) programme

The VGD was started as a programme for destitute women. Later a training component was added to it. Now it is one of the largest multidimensional food-aided programmes of the government aimed at the distressed women in the country. This programme is composed of the following four components:

i) the Union VGD programme managed by the Directorate of Relief and Rehabilitation (DRR);
ii) the Women Training Centre (WTC);
iii) Group Leader Extension Workers (GLEW), managed by the Directorate of Women's Affairs (DWA); and
iv) the Institutional Feeding Development Project (IFDP), managed by the Directorate of Social Services (DSS).

Destitute, widowed, divorced and seperated women with undernourished and lactating children and women with handicapped husbands are the target group of the VGD programme. Each beneficiary is provided with food support at the rate of 31.25 kg of wheat per month as long as she qualifies. Preference is given to poor women who have young children and who are heads of households. Another important objective of this programme is to increase the income-generating capabilities of destitute women by providing them with skill training such as sewing, knitting, rearing of livestock and poultry, etc encouraging the accumulation of seed capital through savings and giving them access to institutional credit. They are also given functional knowledge, literacy and numeracy. At least 30 women in a union get wheat at the rate of 31.25 kg per month per head.

During the period 1990-95 a total of 8,55,226.090 MT wheat was targeted for distribution among 23,84,606 VGD women including WTC and IFDP. Of the targeted amount of wheat a total of 7,84,091.139 MT was distributed (Annex II Table 6.5). During the same period a total of 17,99,155 VGD members deposited a sum of Tk. 45,98,82,728 in their individual and joint accounts in the post offices/banks under the saving schemes at the rate of Tk. 25 per month/per person (Annex II Table 6.6). Subsequently, women belonging to the VGD programme utilized large amounts of seed capital in different income-generating activities to earn income for their livelihood. There are 343 women training centres under the VGD programme of which 61 are run by the DWA.

In addition to the DWA, BRAC is also co-ordinating a training programme on different income-generating activities and providing credit to VGD members for the enhancement of their socio-economic condition. During the period 1990-95, a total of 3,65,893 out of the targeted number of 3,68,991 VGD card holders were trained in different activities such as sericulture, poultry, etc under the framework of the rural development programme (RDP). During the same period BRAC has received Tk. 13,84,24,428 as revolving fund and disbursed an amount of Tk. 34,94,12,200 as loan to 2,30,891 VGD members in 74 *thanas*. This programme generally reaches the target group and is, therefore, important for creating self-employment activities and for providing nutritional supplement to the hardcore poor women.

The number of beneficiaries and the distribution of wheat together with the volume of savings made by VGD members in the last five years are shown in Annex II Tables 6.5 and 6.6.

The number of beneficiaries under the union VGD programme shows a decreasing trend. It decreased from 5,25,124 in 1990-91 to 3,86,951 members in 1994-95 revealing a decline of 26% over the period 1990-95. The incidence of this programme has declined in recent years reaching its lowest level in 1994-95 when 1,49,659.125 MT of foodgrains was distributed. A similar trend is also observed in saving made by the beneficiaries of the programmes. It decreased from about Tk. 103 million in 1990-91 to Tk. 64 million in 1994-95 showing about 38% decrease. Both the number of beneficiaries and the amount saved by them have been declining during 1990-95.

The insignificant growth of decline in the volume of non-monetized foodgrain distribution does not necessarily imply that the need for public assistance to the poor has been reduced during 1990-95 or that the poverty situation has actually improved. To all intents and purposes, the volume of foodgrains available for distribution is dependent on the external resource flow and in turn on the will of the donors. So it depicts a supply-side situation.

Income and Employment Generation under FFW, TR and VGD. Under the FFW and TR programmes a beneficiary gets 2.5 kg of rice or 5.25 kg of wheat as wages per day for six hours of work (GOB 1994). Based on these rates and on the actual distribution of foodgrains, the estimated employment opportunities created through the FFW and TR programmes is presented in Annex II Table 6.7. The food stocks could not be built up through local procurement for these programmes due to lack of budgetary provision of the GOB to create employment opportunities and to meet the needs of the rural poor and destitute women by other targeted programmes. The survey report on food aided programmes including the VGD programme conducted by BBS (1989) pointed out that the average income of beneficiary and non-beneficiary groups is not markedly different where members of both groups live in poverty. The average income of the beneficiary groups is still one-fourth of the rural average. The contribution of FFW and TR programmes to total income is calculated to be only 4% while about 23% of the total income of the beneficiary groups is contributed by the VGD programme. The food aided programmes appear to have less income augmenting effect except the VGD programme. But they have an important employment augmenting effect during the pre-and post-harvest periods. The VGD programme plays an important, albeit limited, role of income augmentation of a temporary nature for the VGD beneficiaries, and the food aided programmes appear to have no lasting effect on the long-term livelihoods of the target groups.

The employment opportunities created under the FFW and TR programmes show an absolute decline during 1992-94 with a marked fall in 1993-94, despite the fact that in recent years these programmes had been an important source of work for the hard-core poor and of nutrition for the poor rural women. Employment generation by the FFW and TR programmes have, however, risen in 1994-95 by 19.14% over the 1993-94 figure.

It is found that PFDS has a bias towards the well-off urban population. In order to reduce PFDS's original bias in favour of the relatively well-off urban population, efforts have been made to improve the development impact of the VGD programme, for example, by including credit and training components. Policy recommendations for streamlining the effectiveness of the food aided programmes are provided in a report of the special Task Force on strengthening institutions for food-aided development (SIFAD). Though the financial costs in terms of food subsidies in the budget are declining, it is still a major head of account. The World Bank, the dominant actor in the field of foreign aid in Bangladesh, feels that food aid in future should focus on utilizing imited resources in a cost effective way if these programmes are to remain viable options for poverty alleviation (WB, 1992).

Agriculture and Rural Development. Agriculture is the dominant sector in Bangladesh which contributes about 38% of GDP. Eighty-five percent of the total population who live in rural areas, are directly and indirectly engaged in various stages of agricultural production, processing and marketing. About 65% of them are small/marginal farmers, landless labourers, fishermen, artisans, etc. This large population cannot generate marketable surplus through agricultural production. The growth rate of agricultural value added is declining. During the period 1973-76 the growth rate of agricultural output was 6.0% which came down to 2.9% during 1976-87 and was negative (-1.0) in 1994.

In view of the preponderance of agriculture in the national economy, it is clear that a stagnating agricultural sector would hold back the growth of income and employment in the national economy as a whole. Therefore, unless a growth dynamics is generated in this large sector, rural poverty alleviation will remain a far cry.

Agriculture. The agricultural policy of Bangladesh has justifiably emphasized the achievement of self-sufficiency in foodgrain production. The widespread adoption of the HYV seed-water-fertilizer technology across the board by all classes of farmers has contributed substantially to the growth in rice production. But this achievement is not sufficient for sustainable agricultural growth. This is because the population growth along with the fragmentation of land is creating ever-increasing pressure on the limited land resources which has resulted, to an increasing extent, in a decline in agricultural productivity and increase in the cost of production. In addition, the ever increasing use of fertilizer, irrigation and pesticide has been causing serious damage to the fertility of soil and groundwater. The environmental cost of this careless drive for food self-sufficiency may be heavy and irreversible. Even then the agricultural sector may not be capable of accommodating the expanding pool of the unemployed and the underemployed labour force in the rural areas.

Against this backdrop, there may be some ways of coping with this impending crisis in agriculture. We point out only a few of them:

i) technological development, something as great as the Green Revolution of the past decades but not degrading the environment;
ii) diversification of agriculture through the encouragement of non-farm activities like livestock and poultry raising, fisheries, etc;
iii) broadening the export base of the agricultural sector to yield higher returns on agricultural investment;
iv appropriate pricing policies of agricultural inputs and output; and
v) encouraging farmers to adopt bio-fertilizer by giving some incentives to the farmers, if necessary, for adopting ecological agriculture.

The positive effects of the introduction of a new technology is predicted to be stronger for the marginal and small farmers than the large farmers, because the former in general tend to be better adopters than the latter (Hossain 1995). This implies that the poorer farmers' needs to be prioritized in spreading a new agricultural technology to reap the highest aggregate benefit. The new technology should again be not negligent of the environmental imperatives of our soil and water.

That the promotion of non-farm activities can moderate the incidence of poverty is indisputable, as it has been found that land-poor households engaged in non-agricultural activities manage to raise their per capita income substantially (ibid.). Anti-poverty policies and strategies should, therefore, emphasize targeted self and wage employment generation programmes. This type of programmes have already been undertaken on a large scale throughout the country without adequate evaluation of the performance of the beneficiaries. That is why the effectiveness of these policies and strategies is not yet very clear, no matter how enormous these programmes are in terms of public expenditure or coverage.

In course of the Structural Adjustment policies, the subsidies on agricultural inputs have gradually been withdrawn. The distribution of fertilizer and irrigation equipments has been transferred to private hands. This policy was primarily taken as an adherence to the market economy principle and was aimed at gaining efficiency in resource allocation. But the experience is just the reverse. The private distributors are amassing abnormal profits by creating artificial shortage of fertilizer. Though the

GOB is marketing locally produced fertilizer at a price below the international level, the intended farming communities are being deprived of this subsidy. The scarcity premium is going to the pockets of the intermediaries. Similar is the case with the distribution of water. The so-called waterlords, who are mainly large farmers and locally influential persons, are exploiting the small farmers by charging unfair prices for water. These are serious impediments to the augmentation of agricultural income and the economic emancipation of the struggling farmers. There is, therefore, a need for rethinking our agricultural policies if we really want to ensure both the sustainability of the sector and equity in the distribution of gains from agricultural activities. The environmental context should not be forgotten as well.

All these observations call into question the validity of the privatization policy in the case of agricultural inputs. The government needs to give a second thought to the policy in seeking a way to stimulate agricultural growth. The GOB has, however, expressed its concern for enhancing investment opportunities for the intensification and diversification of farm production and expansion of non-farm activities by accelerating the development of rural infrastructure in its policy agenda for agriculture. To this end, an IDA sponsored study is being carried out in collaboration with the GOB to explore the potentials of an agricultural breakthrough. The outcome of such a government step is expected to be in the betterment of the poor.

Rural Development. The stated objectives of the rural development policies of Bangladesh throughout the 1980s have been:

i) to bring 10% of the rural poor above the poverty line;
ii) to ensure better access of the rural poor to means of production—both farm and non-farm—through the creation of production activities;
iii) to ensure participation of the rural poor in the development process and their fair share in its fruits; and
iv) to improve the quality of life of the rural people by fulfilling their physical and social needs.

The rural development strategies of the GOB have focused on the diversification of the rural economy beyond agriculture, through investment in human resource development and appropriate technology to provide integrated production and employment opportunities. Targets were set to construct feeder roads, bridges, Rural Growth Centres at the *thana* level; to provide electricity for the growth centres and to expand irrigation facilities to include micro-level drainage, and flood protection projects. How much progress has been made in this respect is worth investigating in assessing the progress in poverty alleviation.

The development of rural physical infrastructure is important in four respects:

i) it curtails the unit cost of production and transportation and thereby stimulates productive activities;
ii) it expands employment opportunities for the local people, for example, the building of metalled roads and bridges is followed by an increase in the use of motor vehicles which can be driven by locally trained people;
iii) it facilitates labour mobility which is particularly beneficial for the poor because they can travel to distant places in a shorter time than before to find temporary jobs during lean agricultural seasons and come back during peak seasons; and
iv) it quickens the transfer of information from the urban centres to the rural peripheries and thereby facilitates the transfer of new technology and knowledge.

All these factors can add to the potential of income generation of the poor who lack rightful access to resources. 'These poverty-alleviating effects of rural infrastructure is found to be even higher compared to the impact of the new agricultural technology ' (ibid.).

Despite the formulation of eloquent policies, poverty appears to be one of the most serious threats to economic development in Bangladesh. The drawbacks need to be searched not only in the policies, but also in the implementation. Ever since independence in 1971, the Bangladesh Rural Development Board (BRDB) has been playing the leading role in executing rural development programmes such as the Rural Works Programme, Training and Development, Integrated Rural Development Programme (IRDP), etc. But these institutions are visibly the extension of the bureaucratic top-down mechanism which does not permit the effective participation of the rural poor in decision-making. The bottom-up process involving participatory development programmes is accepted as the best strategy for poverty alleviation. The perspective plan has also envisaged this strategy which clearly calls for a reshuffling of the entire administrative machinery. Perhaps, a strong local government system could have helped achieve such a strategy.

Role of BRDB. BRDB was set up by the GOB in 1972 as the main government agency for rural development. The main thrust of this organization is to promote agricultural production through institutionalizing two-tier cooperatives like Krishi Samabay Samiti (KSS) and to channel agricultural inputs, especially irrigation equipments and agricultural credit to small and marginal farmers. During the mid-1980s, the scope of BRDB was expanded to promote cooperatives as well as informal groups such as landless and rural poor groups for their socio-economic development. By the end of 1980s, BRDB became the largest organization of the GOB in the field of rural development. Many donors collaborated with the BRDB to undertake various projects for the socio-economic development of the rural poor. The main projects of the BRDB in recent years have focused on poverty alleviation. The following are the main BRDB projects which are directly concerned with poverty alleviation: i. Rural Development (RD)-5, ii. Rural Development (RD)-9. iii. Rural Development (RD)-12. iv. Rural Poor Cooperative (RPC) and v. Project for Women (PFW). These projects are important for skill development, operation of credit for income generation and self-employment, formation of cooperatives and, through all these, for poverty alleviation.

Coverage of BRDB Projects. The coverage of BRDB projects intended for poverty alleviation in terms of the number of group members and the number of credit borrowers up to June 1994 is shown in Annex II Table 6.8.

As of June 1994, 2,66,362 group members across 279 *thanas* have benefited from these programmes and half of the these members have benefited from the BRDB credit programme. The number of beneficiaries compared to the target group members in Bangladesh is very small. However, about 68% of the total members under these programmes were women and more than 70% of the total credit was targeted to them. The rate of recovery of the loans was 99% in RD-5, 99.6% in RD-9 and 97% in the RD-12 projects [BRDB, 1994]

Impact of the Project on Poverty Alleviation. Although the programmes under BRDB have been evaluated by different agencies, researchers and scholars at different times, the impact of these programmes on poverty alleviation has not been examined systematically. However, according to the annual report, BRDB claims that these programmes have had substantial employment and income generating effects. Upto 1994, about 0.12 lakh man-days of employement were created from RD-5 and RD-9 projects for 40,000 group members for construction of roads, planting of trees, etc. Employment to the extent of 58,000 man-days was created for 646 group members for re-excavation of derelict tanks. A sample survey on 535 men and 465 women borrowers pointed out that on the average an annual net income of Tk. 3,089 was generated from a loan of Tk. 2,126 given to a woman. This figure was Tk. 4,721 from a loan of Tk. 2,242 given to a male member. An analysis of village survey data indicates that rural wages were higher in RD-12 programme villages than in non-programme villages [Khandkar 1995]. But this does not change the social milieu. Still there is a wide disparity between the rural male and female wage rates. And there has been no institutional attempt at reducing the disparity. Since the rural society is highly patriarchal, the rural development programmes, although successful in absolute terms, have not proved very effective in ameliorating the gender bias against women. The survey also shows that the household income of credit borrowers from the RD-12 programme was 48% higher than the income of the non-borrower households. But the survey does not mention how many households have been able to cross the poverty threshold income, nor does it mention the cost-effectiveness of this programme. Is a mere increase in income and employment opportunities sufficient to alleviate their poverty? These questions are yet be looked into for drawing any valid conclusion regarding the positive impact of the project on poverty alleviation.

In fact, the operations of BRDB have to be analysed from different angles. Though the average income of the poor has increased in absolute terms and the proportion of people below the poverty lines has decreased, the disparity of income between the rich and the poor is still large. The Gini-coefficient in Bangladesh is 0.39. The infant mortality rate is still alarming (84.0). The prevalence of morbidity is highest for the marginal landowners (174.9) and lowest for the large landowners (144.0). The same disparity is found in terms of diarrhoeal morbidity, the crude death rate (CDR), and the crude birth rate (CBR) [GOB 1995]. Thus it is evident that the improvement in rural poverty trends only on the basis of the income criterion is misleading. Most social indicators suggest that some of the dire needs of the rural poor are yet to be attended to on a priority basis.

The ADP allocation on account of rural development for poverty alleviation has been showing an upward trend since 1990-91 (Annex II Table 6.9). The allocation for this sub-sector has risen from Tk. 2.22 billion in 1990-91 to Tk. 6.34 billion in 1994-95 growing at an annual average rate of 37.12% in 1994-95. As ratio to GDP at the current market price, it was only 0.266% in 1990-91, 0.386% in 1992-93 and 0.567% in 1994-95.

Despite this higher allocation for rural development, the mission of poverty alleviation remains unfulfilled. BRDB has not been able to manage its fund properly. Except a few projects under the direct supervision of the donors, most of the projects have failed to impact positively on the conditions of living of the poor.

Women Development

Women's Affairs Policy

Women comprise almost half of the total population in Bangladesh. In 1995, the estimated female population was about 48.61% of the total population. Without the integration of this large number of female population in the mainstream development process, balanced socio-economic development cannot be claimed. Gender differentials in the social indicators are quite pronounced in Bangladesh. For instance, only 26% of the female (7 years and above) population were literate in 1991 as against 39% of the male population. Female participation in the official labour force is also very low compared to male participation. This backwardness of women not only impedes the women development process but also accentuates the incidence of poverty.

In 1988-89, the proportion of people below the hard-core and ultra poverty lines was also higher among female-headed households than the male headed ones. For the absolute poor, the proportion was higher for female-headed households in the urban areas but lower in the rural areas, and the national figure was also lower. As of 1991-92, the incidence of poverty (absolute, hard-core as well as ultra) is found to be proportionately higher for the female-headed households than the male-headed ones in both the rural and urban areas (Annex II Table 6.10). This picture reflects the backwardness of women compared to men as well as their vulnerability which constrains their capacity to get out of the poverty trap. The percentage of female-headed households has remained broadly constant at 5% during 1990-94 (Rahman 1995). That the number of poor female-headed households is lower than that of male-headed ones is a reflection of the patriarchal social structure where males predominate in most households. The number of female-headed households below the poverty line (absolute, hard-core and ultra) has almost doubled over the three years from 1998-89 to 1991-92.

The economic emancipation of women requires purposive government efforts. The women's affairs policies adopted by the Ministry of Social Welfare and Women's Affairs aim at:

i) the expansion of educational opportunities for women including non-formal and vocational education, specialized training for development of managerial and entrepreneurial abilities;
ii) formation of women associations for formulation of policies and promotion of activities for women's emancipation from poverty, for organization of training for rehabilitation of uprooted women in society;
iii) generation of jobs for women through programmes tailored to make the home the basic unit of production where household-based cottage industries can be developed; and
iv) providing rural women with easy access to credit through the rural banking system.

All these efforts have no doubt accrued some benefits to women, for example, the female labour force participation rate has increased considerably in recent years. This outcome implies that upon gaining access to resources, women can turn out to be more productive despite their socially disadvantaged position. Since poor women are among the most distressed of the poor, they need to be assisted on a priority basis.

Women's poverty in Bangladesh has multi-dimensional features constituting their social, cultural and economic oppression and deprivation. Their state of deprivation is age-old and deep-rooted in the socio-economic structure of Bangladesh. Hence, poverty alleviation for women may not simply be a matter of resource transfer to the vulnerable female section of the population. The perception of society about women as inferior human beings needs to be changed. This is indeed a matter of change of mindset both at the policy makers' and women's own levels. With this aim in view, each distressed woman must be individually addressed in the poverty alleviation effort so as to keep up the momentum of this effort. The distressed women also need to be empowered socially and politically to promote gender balance.

Over the past two decades of planned development in Bangladesh, the government claims that women's programmes have gradually shifted from the consumption-oriented approach to a development-oriented approach. The government has introduced special stipends to encourage female education and has been able to reduce the drop-out rate of the girl students. Secondary education for girls up to class X has been made free in the rural areas. As a result, the literacy rate for women has increased from 16% in 1990 to 24% in 1993. But an increasing female literacy rate must be complemented by appropriate opportunities for productive activities for women in the rural areas.

Experience, however, shows that women are not always ensured equal rights with men in terms of remuneration, let alone prioritization. There is a wide range of wage discrimination between male and female labourers. It, therefore, appears imperative that society be pulled up for sex discrimination, and antipathy against women in particular. The security and rights of women need to be ensured through appropriate legal sanctions and their strict enforcement.

To support legally the destitute rural poor women some legal measures such as the Muslim Family Law Ordinance, the Dowry Prohibition Act, the Cruelty to Women (Deterrent Punishment) Ordinance, the Family Courts Ordinance, the Child Marriage Restraint Act, the Muslim Marriage and Divorce Act have been enacted. But rural poor women cannot get legal redress because of the poor implementation machinery of the government. All development ministries have been asked to formulate Women in Development (WID) projects. Focal points in 30 relevant ministries have been identified to ensure inclusion of WID components in their multi-sectoral projects. But these are mostly ornamental and have very little tangible impact on the women's living conditions.

Bangladesh has supported the strategies and plans for action sponsored by the United Nations through the World Conference on Women. It has also endorsed the recommendations adopted through the convention on the elimination of all forms of discrimination against women. Recently, some efforts have been made by both government and organized women's groups to take stock of what has been going on in the policy arena of women development. A national policy on women development has already been drafted. All this indicate an improvement in the overall social consciousness for a better gender balance. But the implementation of the policies is yet far from satisfactory.

The effectiveness of the various policies related to women can be assessed by a comparative scenario (Annex II Table 6.11). Compared to the welfare state of Sweden where women enjoy utmost freedom and opportunities, the status of women in Bangladesh seems to be miserable. Although this comparison may appear extreme, this has been done to highlight the relative status of women in two democratic countries, though placed in different contexts.

Analysis of the poverty situation in Bangladesh for 1991-92 indicates that while about 47.31% of the population in male-headed households lived in absolute poverty, in female-headed households this figure was about 51.35%. In the case of hard-core poverty the difference is wider (Annex

II Table 6.10). Keeping these facts in view, the GOB has expressed its commitment to women development and mainstreaming them into the development process. A seperate ministry known as the Ministry of Women's Affairs (MWA) has been formed and has been assigned the responsibility of organizing the socially and economically disadvantaged groups, particularly rural women and helping them develop into skilled and productive forces. The MWA has identified the following specific programmes for them:

i) Skill Development Training Programme;
ii) Women's Credit Programme;
iii) Poverty Alleviation;
iv) Support Service; and
v) Special Women's Programme.

The main thrust of these programmes is to promote income-earning opportunities for rural poor women through skill development training on various farm and non-farm activities and through ready access to resources and services.

In addition to MWA, other ministries such as Social Welfare, Livestock, Education, Health and Population Control, Relief and Rehabilitation and Food have taken up certain integrated programmes in order to involve women more productively in economic activities.

Public Expenditure on Women Development

During the Forth Five-Year Plan period, the government sanctioned Tk. 880 million for women development. Of this, Tk. 200 million was allocated for poverty alleviation. This amount is only 22.7% of the total budget for women development. The total ADP allocation for women's affairs has been spelt out in Annex II Table 6.12. It appears from the table that ADP allocation under this head in real terms (adjusted by 1989-90 GDP deflator) increased over the period from 1990-91 at an average annual growth rate of 24.5%. The ADP allocation for women's affairs hovered around 0.20% of ADP and 0.02% of GDP over the reference period.

Coverage of Women Development Programmes

The coverage of women's training on various poverty alleviation projects up to June 1992 may be observed in Annex II Table 6.13.

There is no comprehensive quantification of the impact of these programmes of self-employment generation, poverty alleviation and socio-economic development of women. Thus, we have not been able to draw upon any actual impact of the women's development programme on the poverty status of its beneficiaries. However, the above table suggests that the impact of the programme on the overall problem is very little compared to the huge bulk of poor and destitute women.

The gender-differentiated impact of a policy or programme is difficult to assess. Moreover, the impact of the same policy or programme on different classes of women are also different. We can, however, draw some conclusions relating to policies, programmes and projects intended for women development.

i) It is found that specific women-based policies have far less impact on women than macro policies and programmes which are gender- neutral. The forces that are leading large number of women to seek wage employment outside the home, and the factors that are facilitating women's introduction into the wage labour market are the by-products of overall development strategies and macro policies.

ii) Macro planning, policies and programmes generally fail to recognize women's actual and potential roles in the productive sectors. In many of the sectors where women predominate as producer, ie in homestead agriculture, livestock, poultry and agro-processing there is a high potential which could be realized by adequate policy and programme support. Yet these sectors do not receive the needed policy and programme support.

iii) Many of the special skill training and income-generating projects for women initiated by the government as well as the NGOs are ill-designed without adequate consideration given to inputs, capital and market linkages. For instance, sewing, knitting and handicraft projects often add to the poor women's work burden and accrue only marginal income benefits to them (UNDP 1998).

iv) Directly targeted investments are an interventionist strategy. Evidence from successful initiatives shows that women are responsive and responsible when economic investments are directed at them. Although women tend to invest in low-risk low-return activities and their need for consumption loans is high, they also tend to save at a higher rate than men (Jahan 1989).

v) Giving women income-earning opportunities and control over their income is an effective strategy to enhance their households' health and nutritional well-being. Women tend to spend a greater portion of their income than men in improving their children's literacy, health and nutrition status (UNICEF 1978).

That donors have emphasized the development of women is evident in the increasing dependence of the women development programmes on aid. According to an estimate, between 1980 and 1986, about 19% of project allocations by donors went to projects where women were targeted as beneficiaries. Of these, 55% went to population and family planning projects, 2% to health, 8% to education, and 25% to self-help projects (Hamid 1995). In view of the world-wide recognition of the potential of the women workforce, there seems to be immense scope for the expansion of women development programmes.

Targeted Public Expenditure on Education

Importance of Education in Poverty Alleviation

Direct policies or target group oriented programmes for the rural poor have for many years been adopted by both GOs and NGOs to alleviate rural poverty. Besides direct interventions, appropriate social policies indirectly affect the human resources and they can contribute a lot toward alleviation of poverty. Among the social policies, investment in education is one of the most powerful weapons in the fight against population growth and poverty. A study in 88 countries indicated that increase in the literacy rate from 20% to 30% was associated with an increase in real GDP by between 8% to 16% difference in per capita income growth rates (ibid.). The enrolment at different levels of education in Bangladesh is considerably lower in comparison with other developing countries with a comparable socio-economic status. As observed in the study, most of the children from poor households do not attend school. Even if they as, they are irregular or frequently drop-out of the class because they cannot afford to continue or they are engaged in livelihood earning activities. Unwillingness of the children, poor economic conditions and ignorance of the parents due to poverty have been identified as the major causes of the poor enrolment in schools, irregularity of attendance and high drop-out rate of poor children (Rahman 1993).

Despite much rhetoric of the government about the importance of primary education, its share in the educational budget has not reflected any such priority. However, since July 1993, the FFE programme has been launched by the government for rural poor children on a pilot basis. It is one of the important direct interventions by the government for increasing enrolment, promoting attendance and preventing dropping out from schools, enhancing the capacity of the poor to earn and empowering them in the long run. The FFE programme is designed for transferring income to the poor as well as for enhancing the earning capacity of the poor children through development of their human potentials. Based on our primary serveys, we want to focus below some issues related to education. We will first evaluate the performance of FFE programme which was specially designed to benefit the poor. This will be followed by a more focused discussion using qualitative methods on the participation of poor children in education and the related public expenditure incurred by them.

Target Group for the FFE Programme
Poor household heads who send their primary school aged (6-10) children to such schools are the target group of the FFE programme. The criteria for selecting the beneficiary households are:

i) Landless or near landless condition (households having less than 0.50 acres of land)
ii) The household head's earning livelihood mainly as a day labourer
iii) Female-headed households (headed by women who are widowed, separated from husbands, divorced or have disabled husbands), and
iv) Low-income professions (fishermen, potters, blacksmiths, weavers and cobblers)

A household that qualifies according to the above criteria but is not covered by any other food aided programme such as the Vulnerable Group Development Programme (VGD), Road Maintenance Project (RMP), etc is entitled to receive wheat under the FFE programme.

Selection of Beneficiaries
On the basis of the above set of criteria, the School Management Committee (SMC) and the Compulsory Primary Education Ward Committee (CPEWC) jointly prepare a list of beneficiary households for each school under the FFE programme. The list is then recorded in a register which is kept under the custody of the headmaster. Each listed beneficiary household is given an identification card to receive free wheat ration at the rate of 15 kg. per month for sending a primary school aged child to school. A beneficiary household may get maximum 30 kg. of wheat ration per month for sending more than one child to school. Each enrolled student of the beneficiary household must attend 85% of the total classes in a month. The headmasters prepare the list of beneficiaries for their respective schools by the third day of each month. Accordingly, the SMC calculates the wheat requirement for the respective school and submits the requirement statement to the Thana Nirbahi Officer (TNO) for clearance of wheat. Each school receives a maximum cash transport

allowance of Tk. 185 per ton of wheat plus the proceeds from selling the empty bags that contained wheat, to cover the cost of transporting wheat from the Local Supply Depot (LSD) to the school.

Coverage of the FFE Programme

The FFE programme has been started entirely by the initiative of the government. The programme is spread over 460 unions. One union is selected from each of 460 rural *thanas,* and the programme covers all government and registered non-government primary schools and a certain number of *madrasas* in each selected union. A total of 4,787 primary schools and 877 *madrasas* are currently covered under the programme. A total of 1.48 million children have been enrolled in the FFE schools and *madrasas*. Of the total enrolled students, 698 thousand students (47%) in primary schools and 782 thousand students (53%) in *madrasas* are currently receiving aid under the FFE programme. The year-wise distribution of beneficiaries of foodgrain under the FFE programme is shown in Annex II Table 6.14 and Annex II Table 7.15 respectively.

Impact of the Programme

It is too early to assess the impact of the FFE programme on primary education because it has been started only in 1993-94. However, an early assessment report (Ahmed 1994) indicates that the enrolment of students in general and girl students in particular has increased in all classes after the launching of the FFE programme. The enrolment figure is quite high in the FFE schools in comparison with non-FFE schools. The changes in school enrolment of girl students in the FFE and non-FFE schools before and after the launching of the FFE programme are shown in Annex II Table 6.16. The attendance as percentage of total class days has increased in the FFE schools. It shows quite a high rate of attendance among the FFE beneficiaries as compared to the non-beneficiaries (Annex II Table 6.17). This has happened through a diversion of students from the non-FFE schools to the FFE schools mainly for additional food support to the latter. The drop-out rates have also declined after the implementation of the FFE programme. Annex II Table 6.18 shows the difference in drop-out rates in the FFE schools as well as in the non-FFE schools before and after launching the FFE programme. The survey report also indicates that the leakage of wheat from the FFE programme was about 6.5% of the total wheat allotted to the programme. The cost effectiveness analysis reveals that to transfer Taka 1 of income benefit to the beneficiary household costs Tk. 1.59 considering the leakage of 6.5%. If there were no leakages, Taka 1 of income could be delivered to the beneficiary at a cost of Taka 1.48 which apears to be the cheapest among the food aided programmes except the RMP. Under the RMP programme, it costs Taka 1.32 to deliver taka 1 of income benefit to a beneficiary household, while it is Taka 6.55 for the former Rural Rationing Programme (Ahmed 1994).

Findings of the Opinion Survey of the FFE Programme

With a view to assessing the impact of the FFE programme of the GOB on poverty, the Shamunnay wing of Unnayan Shamannay conducted an opinion survey in two sample *thanas,* namely Tanore of Rajshahi District and Rupsa of Khulna District, during February-March, 1996. This survey covered 16 primary schools—6 in Rupsha and 10 in Tanore—of which 11 are government and 5 are non-government schools.

The roll strength of these 16 schools is 5,739 of which 48% are male students and the remaining 52% are female. The higher enrolment of girls signals the expansion of female education. As Annex II Table 6.19 shows, as many as 2,323 students, accounting for 40% of the total enrolled, are the beneficiaries of the FFE Programme. Of those who receive wheat, 47.4% of the beneficiaries are male and the majority, that is, 52.6% are female. This bias towards girl students in the distribution of wheat explains much of the greater participation of girls in the Universal Free Primary Education Programme.

The gradewise percentage distribution of primary school students in the sample schools also shows the predominance of female participation in primary education in all the grades (Annex II Table 6.20).

Within the 6 schools surveyed in the Khulna district, 3 are under the FFE-Programme and 3 are not. The distribution of students in these two types of schools as shown in Annex II Table 6.21 reveals that the total number of students enrolled in FFE-funded schools is higher than those in the non-FFE funded ones for both sexes. It implies that the distribution of wheat has been able to attract more students and this is precisely what underlines the objective of the FFE programme. The proportion of female students is greater in the FFE-schools than that in the non-FFE schools. This finding is in line with the bias towards girls in wheat distribution. In effect, grils need more incentive than boys to enrol in schools because girls are traditionally associated with household chores and are not as easily allowed to go to schools as boys.

There is, however, a marked disparity between the enrolment figures of the FFE and non-FFE schools. Enrolment in the FFE schools is 5.7 times as much as that in the non-FFE schools. The figures, however, may be taken with some degree of caution because of the smallness of the sample size on the one hand and the perceived tendency of school authorities to inflate the enrolment figure to attract more aid on the other.

In the 10 schools surveyed in Rajshahi District, it has been found that the number of students whose parents have less than 0.50 acres of land and (self-cultivated or rented) accounts for as high as 68.2% of the total number of students enrolled in these schools (Annex II Table 6.22). This means that 68.2% of the students enrolled have come from the functionally landless category of households in these villages. The proportion of students receiving wheat is 40% of the total enrolled which is less than the proportion of the landless category. It can, therefore, be deduced that the FFE does not cover all the households in the lowest strata.

The FFE programme has not completed 5 years yet. Considering the fact that it takes at least 5 years to complete primary education, it seems too early to assess the qualitative performance of the programme. Nevertheless, it is worthwhile to keep track of the quantitative performance, such as the number of students enrolled, the number of beneficiaries, the number of repeaters and drop-outs and the like. These indicators are showing positive signals according to an early assessment (IFPRI 1994). This has also been affirmed by the opinions expressed by the members of the school management committees regarding the FFE. For example, Out of 71 respondents from 3 FFE-funded schools in Khulna, all have agreed that the FFE has increased the participation rate in primary education and 67 are of the opinion that the incidence of child labour has fallen due to this programme as more children now go to school. Most of the respondents from the non-FFE school have also felt that the FFE programme helped increase the enrolment ratio (Annex II Table 6.23).

In the sample survey of primary schools, the members of the SMC (including 16 presidents, 16 headmasters and 64 parents) were asked to make general comments on the FFE programme apart from the specific question. This open-ended part of the survey questionnaire has provided a wide range of valuable insights for the analysis. These comments have been classified into 13 broad categories which may be summarized as follows (Box 1).

The total frequency of the comments is not necessarily equal to the number of respondents because each respondent was allowed to give

Box 1. Comments on the FFE Programme

	Comments	Percentage of respondents
a.	At the present state, the FFE programme can make a very insignificant contribution to poverty alleviation as it covers merely 40% of the total roll strength. To eradicate illiteracy, a major symptom of poverty, the FFE needs to be extended to all (or 70%) poor children and all schools in the poverty-stricken localities.	60
b.	The FFE programme can be made more effective by increasing the amount of wheat entitlement per head above 15 kg. per month and providing brick-built school houses, free school dress, study materials, medical facilities, library facilities, sports materials, tiffin meals and other extra curricular facilities.	98
c.	FFE is likely to perpetuate the begging tendency and dependence of poor children.	5.21
d.	Students are shifting from non-FFE to FFE-funded schools in response to the food incentive. In some cases, they are even leaving their own villages if there is no FFE-funded school there. The discrimination between FFE and non-FFE schools is unacceptable.	8.33
e.	Students are tempted by the receipt of wheat rather than education. This motive debases the quality of education. Efforts need to be made to make education more attractive without providing wheat.	8.33
f.	The responsibility of teachers to distribute wheat keeps them too busy to give much attention to teaching. This dual responsibility causes inefficiency in teaching on the one hand and mismanagement of food distribution on the other. Teachers should be given proper incentives, preferably financial in nature, for delivering optimum service.	8.33
g.	Wheat distribution gives rise to corruption, malpractice and internal conflicts among teachers and thus vitiates their professional sanctity. The responsibility should be given to some other authority.	7.29
h.	Locally influential people tend to reap undue benefits from the FFE programme.	4.17
i.	The current rule of selecting beneficiaries of food aid on the basis of their class attendance is inefficient, for mere attendance cannot ensure the quality of education. The eligibility criterion should be changed according to the performance of students in the examination which is the basis of the literacy movement.	4.17
j.	The FFE programme is responsible for creating various local hazards (eg factionalism) as well as adverse effects on the socio-economic condition. Therefore, it should be discontinued.	4.17
k.	The allocation of wheat is insufficient. Moreover, the amount supplied is often less than the amount allotted. This is why, teachers often get embarrassed in distributing wheat.	3.13
l.	Logistic support (number of schools, teachers, physical facilities, etc.) should be improved to accommodate the increasing flux of students.	2.08
m.	The awareness of parents is essential.	1.04

as many comments as he wished. It comes out from the summary table of comments that only 4.17% are on the side of discontinuing the FFE programme. Others have remarked on various weaknesses and problems associated with the programme, namely

i) small coverage;
ii) lack of material facilities others than wheat;
iii) discrimination in the wheat distribution among the eligible students;
iv) deterioration of the quality of education;
v) mismanagement in wheat distribution;
vi) inefficiencies of teachers;
vii) inappropriateness of the criterion of selecting potential beneficiaries;
viii) insufficient wheat supply and allocation;
ix) inadequate infrastructure;
x) several socio-political problems; and
xi) diversion of students from the non-FFE schools to the FFE ones.

Some of the respondents have provided useful suggestions for improving the effectiveness of the programme. The majority have, however, asked for the expansion of the FFE coverage and the provision of free extra facilities relevant to education.

It is, however, difficult to draw any definitive conclusion on FFE from the opinions gathered so far. For one thing, the FFE programme is not too old to be evaluated, and for the other, the sample size is too small to represent an approximate picture of the situation on a countrywide scale. But the insights accumulated from this survey can be used as considerations in the monitoring, evaluation and implementation of the FFE programme in order to arrive at some definitive policy decisions.

Education Policy

One of the basic objectives of the education policy in Bangladesh is Universal Free Primary Education. As of 1986-87, the government planned to set up one primary school for every 2000 people or for over 2 square kilometre area. In 1991, the targets set by the new government were:

i) achieving free primary education for all children by 1995; and
ii) increasing the density of primary schools from the current average of one primary school per 3.2 square kilometres to the level of one school per 2 square kilometres by 1995.

The enrolment ratio in primary education went up from 52% in 1985 to 78% in 1990, a substantial progress so far as the official statistics is concerned. The school participation rate for the 6-10 age group increased from 56% to 70% during 1990-95, the rate of increase being faster for girl children (Rahman 1996). It is, bowever, reported that there is a very high drop-out ratio (almost 80%). These data do not speak highly of the efficacy of the primary education programmes. Among several possible explanations of the poor performance of the sub-sector, lack of motivation of the poor households to continue their children's studies seems to be an important one. This is because there is a cost in sending children to school. If they stay at home they can help their parents in household chores or in some income generating activities.

The immediate monetary gain from income-generating activities is valued more by their parents than the 15 kg wheat offered per head for the school-going children. To state in economic terms, the opportunity cost of enrolling and keeping children in primary education exceeds the benefits. Another plausible explanation is that education is a 'merit good' (Musgrave 1959) and it pays off in the medium and long run, not immediately. Since people discount future gains and hence prefer present earning, they also discount the benefit of educating their children. But the social return on investment in education is far greater than the private return. It justifies the intervention of the government in the form of social investment. The launching of the FFE programme is in line with this view. This initiative has led to positive gains in terms of higher enrolment rates, lower drop-out rates both in primary and secondary education, and improvement in female enrolment during 1990-95. However, there are serious concerns about the misuse of resources in this programme and the quality of primary education imparted in the schools supported by this programme. The improvement in female education is also attributable to the countrywide drive of the government for girls' education with free studentship and several other incentives. The adult literacy rate has, however, disappointingly remained constant at 33% of the total population. This deficiency of the education movement needs to be given due attention in the budgetary allocations and decision-making.

The target of the government to achieve primary education for all children sounds over-ambitious as far as the evidence goes. In these circumstances, mobilizing the NGOs to complement the government efforts seems wise. In this context, the BRAC model of primary schools can be replicated because this model has proven successful in teaching basic literacy and numeracy in a cost effective manner. A number of other NGOs including Proshika are also contributing significantly towards educational development of children of the poor. In mobilizing NGO services, it should be remembered that there should be a clear division of coverage between government and non-government schools to prevent the wastage of resources.

One thing that is very clear from the poor performance in poverty alleviation is that merely increasing the allocation of public funds cannot ensure quality which needs to be prioritized in the reform agenda. Again, providing primary education to the children of poor families may not be sufficient for poverty alleviation. This level of education needs to be sustained and also further expanded in order to get the best mileage out of it.

To go one step further, the expansion of secondary education for children of the poor is equally important to make the poor conscious of their right to state resources and ensure gains in productivity. The government has set the target of universal secondary education by 2000. In June 1990, there was on an average one secondary school for every 4.36 primary schools. The target requires that this ratio be brought down to close to unity. During 1990-95, there has been a marginal improvement in the participation rate in secondary schools. The rate is currently 29% for the relevant age group and there was only a two percentage points increase over the 1990-95 period (Rahman 1996). One criticism that is often levelled at the expansion of higher education in the rural areas is that this may induce more people to migrate to the urban areas in expectation of higher-paid jobs. This trend in turn can exacerbate the already serious urban unemployment problem and the widening structural imbalances between the rural and urban areas. Indiscriminate investment in secondary education is, therefore, ambiguous in effect. However, investment in secondary education which will move towards technical education may in fact be more beneficial to the poor.

Programmes for Youth Development

For ensuring participation of the unemployed youth in the development process, the DYD has taken up several programmes among which the following are important:

i) skill development training programme for the youth;
ii) self-employment programme for the unemployed youth;
iii) poverty alleviation programme;
iv) youth leadership and human relations development programme;
v) involvement of the youth organizations in community development activities;

vi) involvement of the youth in population control and welfare activities; and

vii) participation of the youth in conservation.

Projects for Youth Development

To materialize the aforementioned programmes, the DYD has undertaken a number of projects which are described below. The respective cost and ADP allocations for 1994-95 have been shown in Annex II Table 6.24.

i) Under the Youth Training and Self-employment Project, a total number of 92,638 youths were targeted to be covered during 1990-96. After the completion of training it was expected that 60% of them would be self-employed.

ii) The Thana Resource Development and Employment Project (THARDEP) is aimed at the alleviation of poverty of the rural landless and poor, specially the poor youth through group initiatives. Five members comprise a group and the members of each group should have kinship or neighbourhood relations.

iii) The projects of the Technical Programme for the Unemployed Youth are designed to impart technical training to the unemployed educated youth on computer use, repair of radio, TV, VCP, VCR, wiring refrigeration, etc. These projects have ample scope for self-employment both at home and abroad.

iv) The main aim of the project of the Youth Training Centre is to impart training to the rural unemployed youth on livestock poultry and pisciculture. This project has enough scope for self-employment and is a successful one.

v) The main thrust of the National Youth Centre is to transform the unproductive youth into an organized, disciplined and productive pool of human resource by giving training on multifaced human development relations like youth leadership, communications, motivation, personnel management, problem-solving and decision-making, etc. This is the first human development centre of its kind in the country.

vi) Involvement of the youth in population and family welfare is designed to create awareness particularly among young women about the worst effects of overpopulation. It has also provided health care services, specially for the young women. Under this project, the youth are involved in the population control drive.

vii) Staff Development, Training Materials and Development Projects are intended to develop the skill of officers and staff through orientation training. New strategies are also being evolved for the smooth functioning of the project activities.

viii) The family-based employment programme is similar to THARDEP. Under this programme, a family is considered to be the vehicle of development and more emphasis is placed on the family for its all- round development.

ix) The Human Resources Development Project is designed to provide primary education to the illiterate youth and also impart skill development training to them so that they can involve themselves in self-employment activities.

x) The Entrepreneurship Development Project for the Educated Youth aims at imparting entrepreneurship development training to the educated youth including doctors and engineers and providing credit facilities to them for undertaking economic activities on self-employment basis.

ADP Allocation for Youth Development Projects

To turn the vast youth population of the country into manpower through self-employment and other assistance programmes the government allocates funds from the ADP for youth development projects. Project-wise ADP for 1990-91 to 1994-95 are shown in Annex II Table 6.25. It shows a substantial increase in the ADP allocation for youth development projects. It increased from Tk. 105.12 million in 1990-91 to Tk. 872.51 million in 1994-95 at 1989-90 constant prices, showing about 73% increase over the period. The simple explanation for this increase is that the number of projects has been greater in 1994-95 than in 1990-91. However, the ADP allocation on account of youth development was only 0.98% of the total ADP budget and 3.18% of the social sector budget of the ADP in 1994-95.

Coverage of the Programme

Since the inception of the DYD in 1981, a total number of 0.325 million unemployed youth have been trained under various programmes until June 1995. Of this, about 60% were self-employed. The number of youth trained up to June 1995 is only 1% of the total estimated youth in 1995, which signifies that the great bulk of the youth yet remains to be trained to take up self-employment activities and thereby rise above poverty. More specifically, 99% of the youth population is still outside the orbit of the programme of DYD.

Credit Programme

Under the project of youth training and self-employment a credit fund to the tune of Tk. 500 million has been allocated to facilitate credit to the trained unemployed youth. An amount of Tk. 223.6 million has been disbursed to the beneficiaries up to June 1995 under THARDEP. With the financial assistance of ADB, the activities of the project are spread over 32 *thanas* with a credit fund of Tk. 374 million.

Impact of the Programme

Though a comprehensive quantification of the impact of different youth development programmes and projects is still awaited, according to the available information these programmes do not seem to have had any substantial role in the eradication of poverty because of the sheer size of the problem. The official reports of the DYD indicate that about 3,25,000 unemployed young men and women have been trained for skill development in various trades under different projects up to June 1995. Out of the total trained youth, 60% are self-employed. The monthly income of successful self-employed youth ranges from Tk. 1,000 to Tk. 30,000. The DYD also reports that up to June 1995 a total of 21,189 youth have been economically self-reliant under the poverty alleviation programmes. In relation to the target population of 20 million unemployed youth this is a very insignificant coverage. Moreover, there is no evidence of the sustainability of these programmes intended for poverty alleviation and economic development. We, however, could not make an in-depth primary investigation to speak more decisively about the impact of these programmes on the ground. But the data available from secondary sources do not allow much room for complacency.

ANNEX II : TABLES

Table 3.1 Incumbent Government Agencies in the Budgetary Process

Components		Ministry/Department/Agencies
Receipt Components		
i) Major taxes (VAT, income tax, customs, excise, etc.)	:	National Board of Revenue (NBR) & Internal Resources Division (IRD), Ministry of Finance
ii) Land Revenue (land tax)	:	Ministry of Land Administration
iii) Minor taxes	:	Relevant administrative ministries and agencies
iv) Non-tax revenues/miscellaneous capital receipts (fees, user charges, etc.)	:	Relevant administrative ministries and agencies
v) Domestic borrowing	:	Finance Division
vi) External loans & grants (other than food aid)	:	Economic Relations Division (ERD)
vii) Food loans & grants from external resources	:	Ministry of Food (in consultation with ERD and Ministry of Finance)
viii) All transactions of the Public Account of the Republic	:	Finance Division in consultation with the Comptroller and Auditor General
Expenditure Components		
i) Expenditure in the Revenue Budget (current budget) and non-development capital budget	:	All Ministries/Agencies, including Ministry of Finance and its agencies
ii) Expenditure in the 'Food Budget' including procurement financed with foreign aid	:	Ministry of Food
iii) Expenditure on development projects included in the ADP	:	The Planning Commission on the basis of estimates prepared and proposed by the implementing ministries and agencies

Source: Various budget documents published by the Ministry of Finance (MOF) including *Budget Estimates, Bangladesh Economic Review*, Finance Division, Government of Bangladesh (GOB)

Table 4.1 Percentage Breakdown of Total Revenue into Tax and Non-Tax Revenue

Fiscal Year	Tax	Non-tax
1975-76	83.23	16.77
1976-77	84.13	15.87
1977-78	85.66	14.34
1978-79	85.14	14.86
1979-80	90.00	10.00
1980-81	81.12	18.92
1981-82	84.59	15.41
1982-83	82.90	17.10
1983-84	91.88	8.12
1984-85	89.20	10.80
1985-86	84.68	15.32
1986-87	82.11	17.89
1987-88	82.79	17.21
1988-89	81.23	18.77
1989-90	85.43	14.57
1990-91	82.78	17.22
1991-92	80.29	19.71
1992-93	81.27	18.73
1993-94	78.47	21.53
1994-95	78.18	21.82

Source: Budget Estimates; Ministry of Finance, Government of Bangladesh and various issues

Table 4.2 Percentage Breakdown of Total Tax Revenue into Direct and Indirect Taxes

Fiscal Year	Direct tax	Indirect tax
1975-76	18.50	81.50
1976-77	21.50	78.50
1977-78	20.00	80.00
1978-79	20.90	79.10
1979-80	19.00	81.00
1980-81	14.90	85.10
1981-82	17.57	82.43
1982-83	23.53	76.47
1983-84	10.12	89.88
1984-85	17.61	82.39
1985-86	21.95	78.05
1986-87	22.53	77.47
1987-88	20.91	79.09
1988-89	19.12	80.88
1989-90	19.84	80.16
1990-91	22.26	77.74
1991-92	21.34	78.66
1992-93	22.85	77.15
1993-94	30.98	69.02
1994-95	27.11	72.89

Source: ibid.

Table 4.3 Exemption Limits for Income Tax

Year	GDP Deflator (1989-90)	Exemption limit (Taka)	
		Nominal	Real
1975-76	25.33	6,000	23,687
1984-85	67.46	20,000	29,652
1994-95	126.06	50,000	39,664

Source: ibid.

Table 4.4 Tax Revenues from Three Broad Categories (Tk million)

Fiscal Year	Direct tax	Indirect tax	
		Taxes on International trade	Taxes on domestic goods & services
1975-76	1361	3924 (67.66)	1876 (32.34)
1976-77	1689	3841 (61.26)	2329 (38.74)
1977-78	2016	5554 (69.23)	2468 (30.77)
1978-79	2619	7161 (70.97)	2929 (29.03)
1979-80	2747	8669 (73.64)	3103 (26.36)
1980-81	3402	11134 (72.46)	4232 (27.54)
1981-82	4183	11134 (70.46)	4668 (29.54)
1982-83	5593	13084 (72.06)	5072 (27.94)
1983-84	2259	16641 (83.23)	3354 (16.77)
1984-85	5960	20929 (75.29)	6868 (24.71)
1985-86	7145	16800 (66.31)	8535 (33.69)
1986-87	8544	20463 (69.99)	8775 (30.01)
1987-88	8917	21670 (64.69)	11830 (35.31)
1988-89	9476	25529 (64.23)	14219 (35.77)
1989-90	11052	27040 (61.34)	17041 (38.66)
1990-91	15070	33769 (65.06)	18136 (34.94)
1991-92	16661	36762 (60.67)	23830 (39.33)
1992-93	21013	49586 (70.68)	20568 (29.32)
1993-94	30088	59351 (75.64)	19114 (24.36)
1994-95	30120	61150 (68.59)	28000 (31.41)

Source: ibid.

Note: Figures in parenthesis represent percentages of total indirect tax of the corresponding year.

Table 4.5 Estimated Parameter of Trend Equations for Tax Revenue

Dependent variable	a_1	a_2	b_1	b_2	Adjusted R^2	D.W. statistic
Analysis based on SA						
Direct Tax (DT)	8.0117*	-0.3568*	0.1104**	0.0677	0.9068	2.54
	(31.10)	(2.88)	(1.67)	(0.90)		
Taxes on International Trade (TIT)	9.1663*	-0.3756**	0.1197*	0.0309	0.9748	2.52
	(93.63)	(2.06)	(4.78)	(1.08)		
Taxes on Domestic Services (TDS)	8.1306*	0.2998	0.1215*	-0.0023	0.9284	2.18
	(40.01)	(79)	(2.33)	(0.04)		
Analysis based on VAT						
Direct Tax (DT)	9.9394*	-0.5245*	0.1384**	0.0592	0.9083	2.53
	(53.01)	(2.92)	(1.95)	(0.64)		
Taxes on International Trade (TIT)	9.2202*	-0.6341	0.1013*	0.0653**	0.9766	2.09
	(133.24)	(1.49)	(9.05)	(1.93)		
Taxes on Domestic Services (TDS)	7.9875*	1.1528**	0.1677*	-0.1028	0.9318	2.02
	(54.90)	(1.29)	(7.17)	(1.44)		

Source: ibid.

Notes: 1. The pre-SA period ranges from 1978-79 to 1985-86 and the post-SA period ranges from 1986-87 to 1994-95.
2. Figures in the parentheses represent corresponding t-values.
3. * Indicates significant at 1 per cent level.
4. ** Indicates significant at 5 per cent level.

Table 5.1 Pattern of Public Expenditure, 1990-91 to 1994-95

(Tk billion)

Year	Revenue Expenditure	Development Expenditure	Total Public Expenditure
1990-91	72.28 (8.7)	52.70 (6.3)	124.98 (15.0)
1991-92	77.92 (8.6)	60.24 (6.9)	138.16 (15.2)
1992-93	85.97 (9.1)	65.50 (6.9)	151.47 (16.0)
1993-94	91.69 (8.9)	89.83 (8.7)	181.52 (17.6)
1994-95	105.00 (9.4)	112.00 (10.0)	217.00 (19.4)

Source: *Bangladesh Economic Review*, Finance Division, Ministry of Finance, Government of Bangladesh, Dhaka, June 1995.

Note: Figures in parentheses represent per cent of GDP.

Table 5.2 Economic Classification of Revenue Expenditures (Revised Budget Estimates)

(Tk billion)

Classes	1990-91	1991-92	1992-93	1993-94	1994-95
1. Expenditure on goods and services	42.94 (59.00)	4.77 (60.40)	54.59 (64.20)	59.91 (65.50)	62.68 (63.00)
1.1 Pay and allowances	23.07	2.81	33.40	35.98	37.17
1.2 Operation and maintenance	3.19	4.35	5.48	6.64	7.21
1.3 Works (original)	2.51	2.36	2.52	1.83	1.84
1.4 Other contingencies	14.17	12.94	13.19	15.46	16.46
2. Interest payments:	8.56 (12.00)	11.08 (14.00)	10.25 (12.00)	10.68 (11.70)	11.48 (11.50)
2.1 Domestic	4.18	5.34	5.50	5.19	5.96
2.2 Foreign	4.38	4.73	4.70	5.49	5.52
3. Subsidies and other current transfers	23.92 (33.00)	22.48 (28.50)	22.31 (26.20)	23.31 (25.50)	23.29 (23.00)
3.1 Subsidies on foodgrains	3.73	3.44	1.53	1.49	1.45
3.2 Other subsidies	3.97	2.46	1.34	0.93	0.28
3.3 V.G.D. and Test Relief	3.87	2.78	2.95	2.62	2.30
3.4 Operational deficits of departmental enterprises	1.73	1.55	1.30	1.23	1.14
Railway	1.49	1.26	1.00	0.95	0.90
Post Office	0.24	0.29	0.30	0.28	0.24
3.5 Transfers to Local Governments	0.54	0.55	0.55	0.56	0.65
3.6 Grant-in-aid and other transfer payments	7.84	8.32	10.58	11.79	12.38
3.7 Pension & retirement benefits	2.24	3.40	4.05	4.70	5.10
4. Unallocated expenditure	0.63	0.23	0.22	0.57	3.98
Gross	76.04	81.54	87.37	94.47	101.42
Deduct: Recoveries	1.21	0.99	0.97	1.74	0.80
Deficit of departmental enterprises shown under receipt	1.83	1.55	1.30	12.27	1.14
Net	73.01	79.00	85.10	91.50	99.48

Source: ibid.

Note: Figures in the parentheses represent percentages of net revenue expenditures of the corresponding years.

Table 5.3 Revenue Expenditure on Social Sectors (Revised Estimate)

(Tk billion)

Items	1990-91	1991-92	1992-93	1993-94	1994-95
Education	11.82	13.82	16.74	17.56	18.76
Health and Population	3.87	4.31	5.17	6.07	6.65
Youth Sports and Cultural Affairs	0.18	0.23	0.38	0.43	0.31
Social Service Welfare and Women's Affairs	0.47	0.51	0.54	0.61	0.61
Total	16.34	18.87	22.83	24.67	26.33
As percentage of total revenue expenditure	23.00	24.00	27.00	27.00	25.00
Per capita revenue expenditure in social sector (in Tk)	146.60	165.70	201.41	207.54	216.80
Per capita revenue expenditure in social sector at 1989-90 constant prices	133.45	144.74	176.47	173.69	171.98
Total population	111.46	113.88	116.35	118.87	121.45

Source: ibid.

Note: Total population has been projected at a constant growth rate of 2.17%.

Table 5.4 Utilization of Development Expenditure

(Tk billion)

Year	Annual Development Programme				
	Actual expenditure	Revised target	Original target	Actual expenditure as % of revised target	Actual expenditure as % of original target
1990-91	52.70	61.21	56.68	86.10	92.98
1991-92	60.24	71.50	75.00	84.30	80.32
1992-93	65.50	81.21	86.50	80.70	75.72
1993-94	89.83	96.00	97.50	93.60	91.72
1994-95	112.00	111.50	110.00	100.45	101.81

Source: Implementation Monitoring and Evaluation Division, Planning Commission, Ministry of Planning, Government of Bangladesh, Dhaka

Table 5.5 ADP Expenditures on Social Sectors

(Tk billion)

Items of expenditure	1990-91	1991-92	1992-93	1993-94	1994-95 (Revised)
Education and Religious Affairs	1.73	2.99	5.28	9.20	15.43
Sports and Culture	0.28	00.16	0.26	0.rr	0.70
Family Welfare	3.10	2.71	2.83	4.08	5.36
Health	1.41	1.37	2.06	2.81	4.10
Social Welfare, Women's Affairs and Youth Development	0.31	0.29	0.31	0.43	1.34
Rural Development Institutions	2.22	3.19	3.66	4.80	6.34
Public Administration	0.05	0.03	0.30	0.08	1.15
Manpower and Labour	0.05	0.03	0.02	0.04	0.15
Sub-total	9.15	10.77	14.72	21.88	34.57
Total ADP	52.70	60.24	65.50	89.84	111.50
Social sectors as % of ADP	17.36	17.88	22.47	24.35	31.00
Per capita ADP Expenditure in social sector (in Tk)	82.00	94.57	126.51	184.06	284.64
Per capita ADP expenditure in social sector in 1989-90 constant prices	74.95	82.96	110.88	154.04	225.80

Source: ibid.

Table 5.6 Composition of ADP Allocation by Key Sectors (%)

Items	1990-91	1991-92	1992-93	1993-94	1994-95
Agriculture	5.8	7.0	5.7	5.8	5.7
Rural Development	4.2	5.3	5.6	5.3	7.0
Water Resources	1.3	8.9	9.4	6.3	7.6
Industry	1.8	2.0	1.1	1.7	1.6
Power	6.9	12.3	15.7	13.5	11.6
Oil, Gas and Natural Resources	7.2	5.4	7.3	3.6	1.9
Transport	12.0	13.9	15.1	17.2	21.7
Communications	2.2	2.7	2.2	6.0	4.5
Physical Planning, Housing and Water	4.4	5.2	3.6	3.5	5.0
Education	3.3	5.0	8.1	10.2	13.8
Population	5.9	4.5	4.3	4.5	4.8
Health	2.8	2.3	3.1	3.1	3.7
Total ADP	100	100	100	100	100

Source: ibid.

Table 5.7 Estimated Parameters of the Trend Model

Dependent variable	a_1	a_2	b_1	b_2	R_2	D.W. statistic (d)
Gross Domestic Product (GDP)	13.0695	-0.0443 (1.853)	0.0340 (17.298)	0.0060 (2.345)	0.9956	1.327
Revenue Expenditure (RE)	10.2662	0.0414 (0.276)	0.0490 (3.967)	0.01175 (0.730)	0.9484	1.993
Development Expenditure (DE)	10.8145	-0.6467 (2.853)	-0.0037 (0.197)	0.0645 (2.659)	0.5535	1.369

Source: *Bangladesh Economic Review*, Finance Division, Ministry of Finance, GOB, Dhaka, June 1995

Note: 1. Significant at 1 per cent level
2. Figures in parentheses below the coefficient are the corresponding t-values.

Table 5.8 Disaggregation of Development Expenditures by Functional Categories

(Tk billion)

Year	Social services	Economic services	Infrastructure	Others
1980-81	2.19	9.69	10.40	1.32
1981-82	2.16	9.53	11.07	1.06
1982-83	2.62	981.24	1289.99	128.47
1983-84	310.58	1094.37	1316.99	270.79
1984-85	348.17	820.97	1522.58	363.39
1985-86	304.36	1154.71	1747.35	210.64
1986-87	415.06	1348.38	1936.09	758.57
1987-88	483.09	1141.62	1899.20	619.40
1988-89	514.68	1395.53	2137.50	567.89
1989-90	584.92	1729.28	2426.94	967.18
1990-91	7.07	18.78	22.85	3.91
1991-92	765.42	1438.98	3321.95	478.70
1992-93	1098.44	1282.63	3489.38	631.71
1993-94	1694.91	1243.43	3878.62	1149.20
1994-95	26.92	16.61	57.90	8.79

Source: Implementation, Monitoring and Evaluation Department (IMED), Planning Commission, Government of Bangladesh

Table 5.9 Public Expenditure, 1972-73 to 1994-95

(Tk million)

Year	GDP Deflators		GDP		Rev. Expenditure		ADP	
	84-85 =100	89-90 =100	Current M.Price	89-90 Price	Current M.Price	89-90 Price	Current M.Price	89-90 Price
1978-79	51.41	34.68	174047	501866	10876	31363	14830	42765
1979-80	57.44	38.75	196050	505936	12359	31898	20820	53735
1980-81	65.58	44.24	231433	523131	14468	32706	23640	53441
1981-82	72.51	48.91	259015	529575	17894	36585	23910	48885
1982-83	78.51	52.96	294189	555499	19472	36769	26880	50757
1983-84	89.91	60.65	355185	585631	19712	32503	30060	49565
1984-85	100.00	67.45	406933	603311	25730	38145	31670	46951
1985-86	109.81	74.07	466227	629441	36870	49777	34290	46294
1986-87	121.90	82.23	539201	655723	39605	48166	44390	53985
1987-88	131.20	88.50	597136	674730	46958	53060	41500	46893
1988-89	141.36	95.35	659598	691765	61303	64291	46220	48473
1989-90	148.25	100.00	737571	737571	66358	66358	57170	57170
1990-91	162.19	109.40	834392	762698	72279	66067	52700	48171
1991-92	169.00	114.00	906502	795193	77915	68349	60240	52844
1992-93	169.20	114.13	947891	830536	85971	75326	65500	57390
1993-94	177.15	119.49	1034261	865563	91690	76732	89830	75175
1994-95	186.89	126.06	1118341 (P)	887150	105300 (E)	83291	111500 (E)	88447

Source: Bangladesh Bureau of Statistics, BBS, Finance Division and IMED

Note: P = Provisional; E = Estimate; M = Market

Table 5.10 Estimated Parameters of Trend Equation for Dis-aggregated Development Expenditure

Dependent variable	a_1	a_2	b_1	b_2	R_2	D.W. Statistic (d)
Economic Service(ES)	6.8436* (48.47)	0.2932 (1.12)	0.0154 (0.42)	-0.0031 (-0.08)	0.6527	1.85
Social Service(SS)	5.2816* (33.73)	-0.9637* (-3.3)	0.0929** (2.31)	0.1242* (2.72)	0.9558	1.06
Infrastructure Development. Sector(IDS)	6.8255* (73.71)	-0.3136** (1.82)	0.1020* (4.29)	0.0283 (1.04)	0.9651	1.90

Source: Implementation, Monitoring and Evaluation Development, Planning Commission, GOB

Note: 1. Figures in parentheses are the corresponding t-values
2. * Indicates significant at 1 per cent level
3. ** Indicates significant at 5 per cent level

Table 6.1 Trend in Distribution of Foodgrains from Public Stock by Channel

(Thousand tons)

Year	Channel		Total
	Monetized	Non-monetized	
1990-91	1,574 (66.36)	798 (33.64)	2,372 (100)
1991-92	1,421 (60.60)	924 (39.40)	2,345 (100)
1992-93	456 (42.50)	617 (57.50)	1,073 (100)
1993-94	531 (38.53)	845 (61.47)	1,378 (100)
1994-95	508 (32.29)	1,065 (67.71)	1,573 (100)

Source: *Database on Food Situation*, Bangladesh, June 1995, Food Planning and Monitoring Unit (FPMU), Ministry of Food, GOB

Note: Figures in parentheses show the percentage of total distribution of foodgrains.

Table 6.2 Economic Subsidies on Foodgrains, 1990-91 to 94-95

Year	Subsidies on foodgrains	
	(Tk million)	% of ADP
1990-91	3,727	7.08
1991-92	3,436	5.71
1992-93	1,534	2.34
1993-94	1,490	1.67
1994-95	1,950	1.75

Source: *Bangladesh Economic Review,* June 1995

Table 6.3 Volume of Public Foodgrain Distributed under TR Programme and Its Value

Year	Foodgrain (in '000' MT)			Value of foodgrain in Tk million (1989-90 constant prices)
	Rice	Wheat	Total	
1990-91	70	45	115	961.01
1991-92	52	145	197	1434.89
1992-93	104	12	116	897.50
1993-94	13	88	101	542.07
1994-95	9	118	127	822.92

Source: *Database on Food Situation Bangladesh,* Food Planning and Monitoring Unit (FPMU), Ministry of Food, Government of Bangladesh, June, 1995

Table 6.4 Volume of Public Foodgrain Distributed under FFW Programme and Its Value

Year	Foodgrain (in '000' MT)			Value of foodgrain in Tk million (1989-90 constant prices)
	Rice	Wheat	Total	
1990-91	38	420	458	3114.24
1991-92	12	485	497	3238.40
1992-93	205	163	368	2604.24
1993-94	1	424	425	4610.21
1994-95	7	493	500	3141.72

Source: ibid

Table 6.5 Distribution of Wheat under Union VGD Including WTC and IFDP

Year	Total beneficiaries (No.)	Total allocation of wheat (MT)	Total utilization of wheat (MT)	% of utilization
1990-91	5,25,124	1,91,936.726	1,72,742.400	89.99
1991-92	5,13,933	1,90,875.000	1,77,610.148	93.05
1992-93	4,66,272	1,71,641.489	1,59,977.198	93.20
1993-94	4,92,326	1,51,113.750	1,43,558.063	95.00
1994-95	3,86,951	1,49,659.125	1,30,203.330	86.99
Total	23,84,606	8,55,226.090	7,84,091.139	91.62

Source: A. Khatun, *A Handout Report on Vulnerable Group Development Programme*, Directorate of Relief and Rehabilitation, GOB, 1995

Table 6.6 Volume of Savings under Union VGD Programme

Year	Targeted no. of women	Actual no. of women covered	Total savings (Tk million)
1990-91	4,28,575	4,08,331	102.90
1991-92	4,17,384	3,86,488	103.73
1992-93	3,70,907	3,46,296	89.34
1993-94	3,96,961	3,66,703	100.11
1994-95	3,86,951	2,91,337	63.80
Total	20,00,778	17,99,155	459.88

Source: ibid

Table 6.7 Employment Generated under FFW and TR Programmes

(Million mandays)

Year	Volume of annual employment generated under		Total employment generated
	FFW	TR	
1990-91	90.57	28.57	119.14
1991-92	95.81	42.48	138.29(+16.67)
1992-93	89.62	32.00	121.62(-12.05)
1993-94	81.05	20.47	101.52(-16.53)
1994-95	95.90	25.05	120.95(+19.14)

Source: *Database on Food Situation in Bangladesh,* Food Planning and Monitoring Unit (FPMU), Ministry of Food, Government of Bangladesh, June 1995

Note: Figures in parentheses indicate percentage change over the previous year.

Table 6.8 Coverage of Main Poverty Alleviation Projects and Credit Operations of BRDB, June 1994

Name of the Project	No. of *thana* covered	No. of group members	No. of members having received credit	Total amount of credit disbursed (Tk million)
RD-5	32	66,415	22,220	86.41
RD-9	26	32,133	14,323	26.72
RD-12	139	46,857	81007	702.07
RPC	82	3,512	-	-
PFW	100	1,17,445	-	-
Total	379	2,66,362	1,17,550	8,15.20

Source: IRBD, CPD, 1995

Table 6.9 Public Expenditure on Rural Development

(Tk billion)

Year	Allocation in ADP	Share of total ADP (%)
1990-91	2.22	4.20
1991-92	3.19	5.30
1992-93	3.66	5.60
1993-94	4.80	5.30
1994-95	6.34	5.69

Source: *Bangladesh Economic Review,* June 1995, PP.32-33

Table 6.10 Population Below the Poverty Line by Male and Female Classification

Residence	Population (million) below										
	Total	Above 2,122 K.cal	Absolute poverty line (2,122 K. cal)			Hard core poverty line (1,805 K. cal)			Ultra poverty line (1,600 K. cal)		
		Consumption Level	Both	Male headed	Female headed	Both	Male headed	Female headed	Both	Male headed	Female headed
1991-92 National (% Pop.)	108.66	57.03	51.63 (47.52)	48.79 (47.31)	2.84 (51.35)	30.42 (28.00)	28.67 (27.80)	1.75 (31.62)	19.34 (17.80)	18.07 (17.52)	1.27 (22.92)
Rural (% Pop.)	94.05	49.24	44.81 (47.64)	42.26 (47.37)	2.55 (52.70)	26.59 (28.27)	25.01 (28.04)	1.58 (32.54)	17.18 (18.26)	16.04 (17.97)	1.14 (23.56)
Urban (% Pop.)	14.61	7.79	6.82 (46.70)	6.53 (46.93)	0.29 (42.07)	3.83 (26.25)	3.66 (26.31)	0.17 (25.02)	2.16 (14.81)	2.03 (14.62)	0.13 (18.50)
1988-89 National (% Pop.)	104.00	54.34	49.67 (47.75)	48.39 (47.89)	1.28 (43.14)	29.49 (28.36)	28.52 (28.23)	0.97 (32.88)	19.24 (18.50)	18.50 (18.31)	0.74 (24.89)
Rural (% Pop.)	90.79	53.23	43.37 (47.75)	42.28 (47.93)	1.09 (42.28)	26.01 (28.64)	25.16 (28.52)	0.85 (33.05)	17.23 (18.98)	16.58 (18.80)	0.65 (25.17)
Urban (% Pop.)	13.21	6.92	6.29 (47.63)	6.11 (47.59)	0.18 (49.00)	3.49 (26.38)	3.37 (26.23)	0.12 (31.67)	2.81 (15.16)	1.92 (14.93)	0.09 (23.00)

Source: *Report on the Household Expenditure Survey,* 1991-92, Bangladesh Bureau of Statistics, November 1995

Note: Figures estimated by direct caloric intake method

Table 6.11 Comparison of the Socio-Economic Status of Women in Bangladesh and Sweden

Heads	Sweden	Bangladesh
Female life expectancy	81.1 years	55.6 years
Adult literacy rate (%)	99.0	24.4
Professional & technical women (% of women)	63.3	23.1
Earned income share (% women)	41.6	22.8
Maternal mortality rate (live births per 1,00,000)	05.0	600.0
Female local council members (%)	34.0	-

Source: *Human Development Report*, 1995, UNDP

Table 6.12 ADP Allocation for Women Affairs, 1990-91 to 1994-95 (1989/90 Constant Prices)

(Tk million)

Year	ADP allocation	% of ADP	% of GDP
1990-91	138.98	0.29	0.02
1991-92	140.60	0.26	0.02
1992-93	116.77	0.20	0.01
1993-94	180.29	0.24	0.02
1994-95	275.38	0.31	0.03

Source: *Budget Estimates*, Ministry of Finance, various issues, Government of Bangladesh

Table 6.13 Coverage of Training Activities and Credit Operation up to June 1992

Sl. No.	Service area	Up to June 1992
1	No. of women trained in different vocational trades	88,889
2	No. of women given management and leadership training	1,044
3	No. of women given credit facilities	30,862
4	No. of women engaged in production unit	20,991
5	No. of children given day care facilities	6,873
6	No. of children and women immunized	30,136

Source: *Proceedings of National Seminar on Qoute Government of Bangladesh in Poverty Alleviation* Unqoute held in Dhaka, February 17-19, 1993, Edited by M. N. Amin

Table 6.14 Distribution of Foodgrains among Students under FFE, 1993-94 to 1995-96

Year	Quantity of foodgrain (MT) distributed		Cumulative no. beneficiaries (of students)	Cumulative no. of families benefited	Cumulative no. of schools	Cumulattative number of unions
	Rice	Wheat				
1993-94	216	79,337	706,519	549,881	4,914	460
1994-95	2,127	186,075	1,628,659	1,416,932	12,182	1,000
1995-96	N.A	345,564	1,904,505	1,759,980 (Dec. 05)	155,009 (Dec. '95)	1,193 (Dec. '95)
Target				1,729,556 (Target '96)	15,182 (Target '96)	12,500 (Target '96)

Source: *Database on Food Situation, Bangladesh*, FPMU, Ministry of Food, GOB, June 1995

Note: N.A. stands for 'not available'

Table 6.15 Quantity of Foodgrain Distributed under the FFE Programme

('000' MT)

Year	Quantity of foodgrain distributed			Value of foodgrain in million
	Rice	Wheat	Total	Tk (1989-90 constant prices)
1993-94	-	46,488	46,488	669.5
1994-95	6,105	132,048	138,153	1,189.9

Source: *Database on Food Situation, Bangladesh*, FPMU, Ministry of Food, GOB, June 1995; *Annual Development Programme 1993-94*, Planning Commission, Ministry of Planning, GOB

Table 6.16 Percentage of Girls among Total Enrolled Students Before and After the FFE Programme

Month and Year	Grade I	Grade II	Grade III	Grade IV	Grade V	All grades
			(per cent)			
			FFE schools			
April 1992 (before)	47.4	49.1	49.2	49.0	48.7	48.8
April 1993 (before)	47.6	45.7	48.7	50.7	48.4	48.7
April 1994 (after)	49.1	48.2	47.3	52.0	53.1	50.3
Among FFE beneficiaries	49.9	46.7	46.4	52.0	51.5	49.1
			Non-FFE schools			
April 1992	45.2	46.4	48.2	48.6	48.4	47.6
April 1993	46.4	45.7	47.4	49.9	47.9	47.9
April 1994	46.1	46.4	46.7	49.8	49.8	48.2

Source: Ahmed, U.A. and K. Billah, *FFE Early Assessment Survey, 1994*, IFPRI, Dhaka, 1994

Table 6.17 School Attendance Rates Before and After the FFE Programme

	Grade II	Grade V	All (Grades II and V)
(Attendance rates in per cent of total class-days) FFE schools			
April 1992 (before)			
All students	61.700	60.9000	61.3000
Boys	62.500	61.0000	61.8000
Girls	60.600	60.7000	60.3000
April 1993 (before)			
All students	62.800	64.2000	63.0000
Boys	63.600	64.1000	63.0000
Girls	60.400	64.0000	62.1000
April 1994 (after)			
All students	78.900	75.5000	77.2000
Boys	77.700	74.8000	76.8000
Girls	79.500	76.1000	78.4000
FFE beneficiaries	83.800	85.0000	84.1000
Non-beneficiaries	69.300	66.2000	68.1000
Levels at which means are significantly different			
between 1993 and 1994 (all students)	00.000	00.0000	00.0000
Boys versus girls (1994)	n.s.	n.s.	n.s.
Beneficiaries versus non-beneficiaries	00.000	00.0000	00.0000
Non-FFE Schools			
April 1992			
All students	59.800	62.8000	60.8000
Boys	59.200	63.8000	61.0000
Girls	60.100	62.2000	60.7000
April 1993			
All students	61.800	61.7000	61.8000
Boys	61.700	60.6000	61.7000
Girls	61.800	61.9000	61.6000
April 1994			
All students	61.400	61.0000	61.0000
Boys	61.500	62.0000	61.5000
Girls	61.600	60.4000	60.8000
Levels at which means are significantly different			
FFE versus non-FFE schools, 1994 (all students)	00.001	00.0001	00.0001
Non-beneficiaries in FFE schools versus non-FFE school students	00.001	00.0220	00.0001

Source: Ahmed, U.A. and K. Billah, IFPRI, *FFE Early Assessment Survey, 1994*, IFPRI, Dhaka, 1994

Note: Levels of significance are based on t-test; n.s. means not significant at the 0.10 level.

Table 6.18 Yearly Drop-Out Rates Before and After the Introduction of FFE

	Grade I	Grade II	Grade III	Grade IV	All grades
(Drop-out rates) FFE Schools					
Before (April 1992 to April 1993)					
All students	18.800	15.900	17.200	18.300	18.500
Boys	16.100	14.000	17.900	17.900	17.600
Girls	20.300	16.800	15.000	18.900	19.300
After (April 1993 to April 1994)					
All students	7.400	10.800	12.100	13.300	10.900
Boys	6.700	10.300	13.900	15.700	11.300
Girls	8.000	11.600	9.800	10.600	10.300
Levels at which means are significantly different					
Before versus after (all students)	0.000	0.014	0.035	0.019	0.000
Boys versus girls (after)	n.s.	n.s.	0.009	0.005	0.086
Non-FFE Schools					
Before (April 1992 to April 1993)					
All students	17.400	14.1	18.100	14.000	17.100
Boys	17.200	14.0	17.600	11.900	16.900
Girls	17.100	13.7	8.300	14.200	17.600
After (April 1993 to April 1994)					
All students	14.500	13.9	16.100	13.700	15.200
Boys	13.900	15.2	18.700	13.500	16.200
Girls	14.700	11.8	12.200	14.500	14.300
Levels at which means are significantly different					
Before versus after (all students)	0.080	n.s.	n.s.	n.s.	n.s.
FFE versus non-FFE schools (all students, April 1993 to April 1994)	0.001	n.s.	0.047	n.s.	0.008

Source: Based on data collected by IFPRI, *FFE Early Assessment Survey, 1994*, Bangladesh.
Note: Levels of significance are based on t-test; n.s. means not significant at the 0.10 level.

Table 6.19 Frequency Distribution of the Beneficiaries of FFE Programme in the Sample Schools by Gender and Grade

Grade	Total number of students			Number of beneficiaries		
	Male	Female	Total	Male	Female	Total
I	611	681	1292	206	210	416
II	656	691	1347	278	281	559
III	621	669	1290	248	292	540
IV	549	543	1092	233	258	491
V	337	381	718	137	180	317
Total	2,774	2,965	5,739	1,102	1,221	2,323

Source: Shamunnay Opinion Survey on FFE Programme

Table 6.20 Percentage Distribution of Total Number of Students and Beneficiaries of Sample Schools by Gender and Grade

Grade	% of total number of students			% of total number of beneficiaries		
	Male	Female	Total	Male	Female	Total
I	47.3	52.7	100.0	49.5	50.5	100.0
II	48.7	51.3	100.0	49.7	50.3	100.0
III	48.1	51.9	100.0	45.9	54.1	100.0
IV	50.3	49.7	100.0	47.5	52.5	100.0
V	46.9	53.1	100.0	43.2	56.8	100.0
Total	48.3	51.7	100.0	47.4	52.6	100.0

Source: *Shamunnay Opinion Survey on FFE Programme*

Table 6.21 Distribution of Students in Three FFE-funded and Three Non-FFE-funded Sample Schools of Khulna District by Gender and Grade

Grade	FFE School			Non-FFE School		
	Male	Female	Total	Male	Female	Total
I	364	443	807	62	47	109
II	382	450	832	62	61	123
III	349	389	738	61	46	107
IV	360	335	695	65	87	152
V	184	222	406	61	58	119
Total	1639	1839	3478	311	299	610

Source: *Shamunnay Opinion Survey on FFE Programme*

Table 6.22 Number and Percentage of Students Whose Parents Have Less Than 0.5 Acres of Land in 10 Sample Schools of Rajshahi District

Grade	Number of Students		
	Male	Female	Total
I	136.0	136.0	272.0
II	134.0	123.0	257.0
III	133.0	123.0	256.0
IV	93.0	91.0	184.0
V	76.0	73.0	149.0
Total	572.0	554.0	1126.0
% of Total	69.4	66.9	68.2

Source: *Shamunnay Opinion Survey on FFE Programme*

Table 6.23 Self-Assessment of the FFE Programme (No. of Respondents)

Types of school	FFE increases participation rate		FFE decreases dropout rate		FFE alleviates poverty		FFE diverts children from child labour	
	Yes	No	Yes	No	Yes	No	Yes	No
FFE School	71	0	69	2	69	2	67	4
Non FFE School	24	1	24	1	21	4	17	8
Total	95	1	93	3	90	6	84	12

Source: *Shamunnay Opinion Survey on FFE Programme*

Table 6.24 Project Cost and ADP Allocation by Project 1994-95

(Tk million)

Project	Total cost (Tk million)	ADP allocation for 1994/95
1. Youth Training and Self-Employment	782.20	246.01
2. Establishment Youth Training Center	192.00	80.18
3. Thana Resource Development and Employment Project	758.32	230.31
4. Technical Training for Unemployed Youth	21.50	5.75
5. National Youth Centre	100.00	300.00
6. Family Based Employment	500.00	500.00
7. Staff-Development, Training Material, Research Development	58.15	7.64

Source: Siddique, A. K. M. AB (1994), *Bangladesh Youth Development Activities: Past and Present*, Sharanika, Department of Youth Development, Ministry of Youth and Sports, November, 1994

Table 6.25 ADP Allocation for Youth Development: 1990-91 to 1994-95 (1989-90 Constant Prices)

Year	ADP allocation	% of ADP (Tk million)	% of GDP
1990-91	105.12	0.22	0.0138
1991-92	60.23	0.11	0.0076
1992-93	95.28	0.16	0.0011
1993-94	330.24	0.44	0.0038
1994-95	872.51	0.98	0.0098

Source: *Budget Estimation*, Ministry of Finance and various issues, GOB

Table 7.1 List of Poverty-related Projects and Their Budget Provisions

(Tk million)

SL	Name of Project and Agency	1991-92				1992-93				1993-94				1994-95			
		Budget allocation		Project aid		Budget allocation		Project aid		Budget allocation		Project aid		Budget allocation		Project aid	
		Original	Revised	Original	Revised	Original	Revised	Original	Revised	Original	Revised	Original	Revised	Original	Revised	Original	Revised
*	**Sub-Sector: Women Affairs**																
1.	Agriculture Training Centre for Women	0.870	-	-	-	-	-	-	-	-	-	-	-	-	-	-	-
2.	Agriculture based programme for rural women	1.640	6.770	-	-	2.500	-	-	-	-	-	-	-	-	-	-	-
3.	Community based programme for poor women and children through NGO's	5.425	5.425	4.500	4.500	5.000	-	4.000	-	21.500	20.95	20.400	20.000	25.247	21.200	24.009	20.000
4.	Advocacy awareness and strengthening of information base of WID	2.080	2.080	1.500	1.500	1.670	-	1.000	-	3.700	2.898	2.800	2.200	3.400	3.400	2.700	2.700
5.	Women support centre	4.600	4.600	4.600	4.600	5.300	4.800	4.800	4.800	3.000	3.000	3.000	3.000	2.500	2.600	2.51	2.600
6.	Day-care services for the children of working women	9.000	10.500	8.500	8.000	9.000	11.000	7.200	9.200	12.000	12.200	9.692	9.700	9.000	4.000	6.526	4.000

(contd.)

(Continued)

SL	Name of Project and Agency	1991-92				1992-93				1993-94				1994-95			
		Budget allocation		Project aid		Budget allocation		Project aid		Budget allocation		Project aid		Budget allocation		Project aid	
		Original	Revised	Original	Revised	Original	Revised	Original	Revised	Original	Revised	Original	Revised	Original	Revised	Original	Revised
7.	Integrated programme for participation of women in income generating activity and legal aid assistance	1.450	1.450	-	-	2.130	2.130	-	-	2.325	1.925	-	-	2.700	2.500	-	-
8.	Self-reliance project of rural women	7.500	7.500	5.000	5.000	13.600	6.000	10.000	10.000	18.800	0.200	12.500	0.100	0.200	0.100	0.100	-
9.	Rural women's employment creation project	-	-	20.826	-	20.000	12.000	12.000	10.000	10.000	92.727	26.100	89.360	28.600	138.400	93.000	138.300
10.	Urban women dev. project.	-	-	-	-	-	-	-	-	2.000	6.919	-	-	10.000	10.000	-	-
11.	Begum Rokaya Training Centre	-	-	-	-	-	-	-	-	-	-	-	-	10.800	2.000	-	-
12.	Landless women dev. programme	-	-	-	-	-	-	-	-	-	-	-	-	74.098	5.100	63.467	5.000
13.	Technologies for rural women's employment	9.300	9.300	9.300	9.300	11.700	6.000	10.700	6.000	6.370	4.946	5.370	3.948	14.300	10.000	14.300	10.000
14.	Legal training for district, upazilla level officers of the Women's Affairs Department	2.100	2.630	2.100	2.100	1.700	-	1.700	-	-	-	-	-	-	-	-	-
15.	Strengthening the National Women Training and Dev. Academy	4.200	5.000	4.200	4.400	2.910	-	2.510	-	-	-	-	-	-	-	-	-

(Contd.)

(Continued)

SL	Name of Project and Agency	1991-92				1992-93				1993-94				1994-95			
		Budget allocation		Project aid		Budget allocation		Project aid		Budget allocation		Project aid		Budget allocation		Project aid	
		Original	Revised	Original	Revised	Original	Revised	Original	Revised	Original	Revised	Original	Revised	Original	Revised	Original	Revised
*	**Sub-sector: Youth Development**																
16.	Skill dev. training for men and women and assistance for self-employment	33.776	37.000	-	-	43.800	-	-	-	60.000	70.000	-	-	246.000	300.000	-	-
17.	Upazila/Thana resource development and employment project (Phase-II)	10.659	10.657	-	-	25.000	-	-	-	195.000	238.368	150.000	190.268	230.300	212.300	187.500	172.300
18.	Rural training project (URDEP-III)	80.000	16.000	50.000	10.000	205.000	-	170.000	-	-	-	-	-	-	-	-	-
19.	Establishment of youth training centre	-	5.000	-	-	15.000	-	-	-	70.000	70.000	-	-	80.180	117.400	-	-
20.	Technical training project for the unemployed youth	-	-	-	-	5.000	7.696	-	-	12.000	14.000	-	-	5.700	5.800	-	-
21.	Establishment of national youth centre	-	-	-	-	-	-	-	-	13.000	2.500	-	-	30.000	30.000	-	-
22.	Family based employment programme	-	-	-	-	-	-	-	-	-	-	-	-	500.000	97.800	-	-
23.	Shrimp culture development project	328.000	343.300	295.000	305.100	187.300	211.500	158.000	180.400	78.000	61.200	64.600	56.500	-	-	-	-
24.	Second aquaculture dev. project	215.500	131.000	174.500	100.000	220.000	169.200	160.000	141.800	325.000	205.000	270.000	161.000	300.000	206.900	250.000	200.000

(Contd.)

(Continued)

SL	Name of Project and Agency	1991-92				1992-93				1993-94				1994-95			
		Budget allocation		Project aid		Budget allocation		Project aid		Budget allocation		Project aid		Budget allocation		Project aid	
		Original	Revised	Original	Revised	Original	Revised	Original	Revised	Original	Revised	Original	Revised	Original	Revised	Original	Revised
25.	Third fisheries dev. project	307.000	130.800	267.000	99.800	263.000	208.400	227.000	174.000	396.000	278.700	344.000	236.900	402.000	344.800	336.000	283.300
26.	Aquaculture extention proj. (Mymensing)	42.400	42.400	36.000	26.000	12.600	-	10.000	-	28.000	28.000	20.000	25.000	28.000	33.000	250.000	30.000
27.	*Beel* and *Baor* fisheries dev. project	90.000	70.000	82.700	62.700	40.000	55.500	35.000	50.000	95.600	110.000	90.000	105.000	101.000	81.000	96.000	76.000
28.	Integrated fisheries dev. project	65.000	50.000	-	-	63.500	33.500	-	-	38.800	41.000	-	-	27.000	3.700	-	-
29.	Improvement of fish seed farm	-	-	-	-	-	-	-	-	-	-	-	-	-	-	-	-
30.	Marine fisheries survey management and dev. project	-	-	-	-	-	10.000	-	-	15.000	14.500	-	-	-	-	-	-
31.	Coastal fisherfolk community development project	11.000	11.000	10.000	9.600	4.600	4.400	4.000	2.400	2.500	1.400	2.500	1.400	-	-	-	-
32.	Improved management of open water fisheries	1.500	2.500	1.500	2.500	4.300	2.000	4.300	2.000	3.500	2.500	3.500	2.500	2.000	2.000	2.000	2.000
*	**Sector: Agriculture Sub-sector: Fisheries Agencies, Department of Fisheries**																
33.	Effect of farming system on socio-economic development of fish farmer	3.000	3.000	3.000	3.000	3.000	6.000	3.000	3.000	3.000	1.800	3.000	1.800	-	-	-	-

(Contd.)

(Continued)

SL	Name of Project and Agency	1991-92				1992-93				1993-94				1994-95			
		Budget allocation		Project aid		Budget allocation		Project aid		Budget allocation		Project aid		Budget allocation		Project aid	
		Original	Revised	Original	Revised	Original	Revised	Original	Revised	Original	Revised	Original	Revised	Original	Revised	Original	Revised
34.	Technical and extention training for fish farmer and extention worker	-	12.000	-	11.000	10.000	7.300	5.000	3.800	17.400	11.500	16.000	10.000	17.000	17.000	17.000	15.000
*	**Agency: Department of Agri. Extention**																
35.	Marginal and small farm system crop intensification project	60.000	39.700	50.000	35.000	44.700	30.000	39.700	25.000	63.000	62.500	55.000	50.000	48.000	68.000	40.000	60.000
*	**Agency: Livestock Directorate**																
36.	Integrated livestock dev. proj.	80.000	-	-	-	-	-	-	-	-	-	-	-	-	-	-	-
37.	Small holder livestock dev. proj.	77.500	35.000	60.000	33.500	78.200	42.100	60.000	35.600	86.000	86.000	80.000	80.000	106.400	106.400	100.000	100.000
38.	Establishment of goat dev. proj.	30.000	25.400	-	-	53.900	25.000	-	-	51.500	17.500	-	-	28.000	18.400	-	-
*	**Sector: Rural Dev. and Institutions Agency: Bangladesh Rural Dev. Board (BRDB)**																
39.	North-west rural development project (NWRDP)	10.000	23.300	-	6.300	8.000	-	-	-	-	-	-	-	160.000	125.000	130.000	100.000

(Contd.)

(Continued)

SL	Name of Project and Agency	1991-92				1992-93				1993-94				1994-95			
		Budget allocation		Project aid		Budget allocation		Project aid		Budget allocation		Project aid		Budget allocation		Project aid	
		Original	Revised	Original	Revised	Original	Revised	Original	Revised	Original	Revised	Original	Revised	Original	Revised	Original	Revised
40.	Noakhali rural development project	111.600	-	110.000	-	-	-	-	-	-	-	-	-	-	-	-	-
41.	Integrated development of rural women and children through cooperation	32.800	27.800	30.000	25.000	27.800	-	25.000	-	-	-	-	-	-	-	-	-
42.	Rural development project-5	86.500	61.100	66.500	60.100	85.700	69.300	83.700	66.800	110.000	104.500	105.000	100.000	115.300	103.000	115.300	100.000
43.	Rural development project-9	91.000	101.600	86.500	101.100	120.000	79.800	119.500	79.300	72.000	50.000	70.000	46.300	60.000	63.500	59.500	61.000
44.	Rural development project-12	221.300	177.300	215.300	164.300	180.000	150.000	165.500	131.500	146.000	110.000	130.000	94.000	95.000	97.000	80.000	80.000
45.	Rural development project (Tangail)	85.000	-	80.000	-	-	-	-	-	-	-	-	-	-	-	-	-
46.	Model rural dev. project (BRDB) component	0.400	0.500	0.200	0.500	105.100	22.500	95.100	19.000	104.700	93.000	87.300	76.900	32.500	38.100	19.500	19.500
47.	Rural development project-15	0.300	-	0.200	-	-	-	-	-	-	-	-	-	-	-	-	-

(Contd.)

(Continued]

SL	Name of Project and Agency	1991-92				1992-93				1993-94				1994-95			
		Budget allocation		Project aid		Budget allocation		Project aid		Budget allocation		Project aid		Budget allocation		Project aid	
		Original	Revised	Original	Revised	Original	Revised	Original	Revised	Original	Revised	Original	Revised	Original	Revised	Original	Revised
*	**Agency: Local Government Division**																
48.	Rural development project-8	198.000	204.000	150.000	150.000	202.800	254.500	145.300	193.500	173.000	197.200	145.000	173.000	130.000	223.500	100.000	173.500
49.	Rural development project-4	298.100	367.000	280.000	348.000	289.000	320.301	252.700	252.700	300.000	307.800	280.000	280.000	246.300	363.400	233.800	324.800
50.	Rural development project-3	25.000	30.000	20.000	25.000	140.000	184.230	120.000	120.000	85.000	136.700	65.000	91.400	90.000	117.200	70.000	83.700
51.	Rural development project-6	79.000	62.500	63.000	50.000	103.700	115.500	83.700	83.700	123.000	108.700	98.000	85.000	80.000	80.000	60.000	60.000
52.	Rural development project-7	341.000	307.000	326.000	254.800	400.000	449.400	350.000	350.000	460.000	460.000	400.000	400.000	500.000	700.000	450.000	650.000
53.	Rural development project-10	16.000	1.500	15.000	1.000	1.700	5.200	1.000	-	0.600	-	0.500	-	-	-	-	-
54.	Rural development project-13	694.000	560.000	650.000	520.000	703.600	727.230	660.000	660.000	750.000	750.000	700.000	700.000	740.000	740.000	700.000	700.000
55.	Rural development project-14	53.800	48.800	38.800	38.800	110.000	130.500	90.000	95.000	128.800	114.800	101.800	88.700	60.000	69.000	50.000	55.000
56.	Rural development project-16	1.100	0.500	1.000	0.400	0.500	37.782	0.400	-	1.100	11.200	1.000	10.000	210.000	112.500	180.000	85.000

(Contd.)

(Continued)

SL	Name of Project and Agency	1991-92				1992-93				1993-94				1994-95			
		Budget allocation		Project aid		Budget allocation		Project aid		Budget allocation		Project aid		Budget allocation		Project aid	
		Original	Revised	Original	Revised	Original	Revised	Original	Revised	Original	Revised	Original	Revised	Original	Revised	Original	Revised
*	**Agency: Bangladesh Academy for Rural Dev. (BRDB)**																
57.	Small farmer and landless labourers development project	14.500	14.800	8.600	9.800	20.500	10.000	12.000	4.000	29.000	13.700	19.000	6.200	38.300	9.000	26.700	-
*	**Agency: Ministry of Land**																
58.	Operation thana - Establishment of cluster village	180.000	207.500	132.500	160.000	300.900	200.000	216.500	150.000	190.000	190.000	150.000	150.000	100.000	105.000	80.000	80.000
*	**Agency: Ministry of Relief**																
59.	Rural maintenance (RMP) institutionalization	4.000	4.200	4.000	4.200	1.700	-	1.700	-	-	-	-	-	-	-	-	-
60.	Vulnerable group development (VGD) programme	-	-	-	-	-	-	-	-	-	-	-	-	-	-	-	-

(Contd.)

(Continued)

SL	Name of Project and Agency	1991-92				1992-93				1993-94				1994-95			
		Budget allocation		Project aid		Budget allocation		Project aid		Budget allocation		Project aid		Budget allocation		Project aid	
		Original	Revised	Original	Revised	Original	Revised	Original	Revised	Original	Revised	Original	Revised	Original	Revised	Original	Revised
*	**Sector: Physical planning, water supply and housing Agency: Local Govt. and Engineering Bureau**																
61.	Slum improvement project	38.000	25.800	35.000	22.800	43.500	33.500	40.000	30.000	76.000	56.000	68.000	48.000	70.600	43.000	61.600	35.000
*	**Agency: Family Welfare Wing**																
62.	Family Planning Clinical Service	200.000	180.000	140.000	140.000	210.000	170.000	140.000	120.000	235.000	180.000	180.000	130.000	185.000	195.000	100.000	105.000
	Total (current prices)	4264.900	3446.038	3522.000	2839.700	4400.910	3814.269	3530.010	3013.500	4699.922	4279.214	3842.322	3467.416	5355.225	4982.600	4046.802	3787.900
	Total (1989/90 constant prices)	37411.40	3022.840	3089.474	2490.965	3856.050	3342.039	3092.973	2640.410	3933.318	3581.232	3215.601	2901.846	4248.156	3952.562	3210.219	3004.839

Source: *Annual Development Programme (ADP)*

Table 7.2 Budget Allocation in Different Poverty-related Projects

(Tk lakh)

Sector	1991-92				1992-93				1993-94				1994-95			
	Budget allocation		Project aid		Budget allocation		Project aid		Budget allocation		Project aid		Budget allocation		Project aid	
	Original	Revised	Original	Revised	Original	Revised	Original	Revised	Original	Revised	Original	Revised	Original	Revised	Original	Revised
Agriculture	13109.00	8961.00	9797.00	6982.00	9853.00	8049.00	7060.00	6180.00	12033.00	9216.00	9486.00	7301.00	10594.00	8812.00	8660.00	7663.00
Rural Development	25214.00	21949.00	22736.00	19151.00	27993.00	27562.40	24206.00	21884.00	26732.00	26476.00	23526.00	23015.00	26574.00	29462.00	23548.00	25725.00
Social Welfare, Women's Affairs & Youth Development	1726.05	1447.41	897.00	694.00	3613.10	496.26	2219.10	400.00	5124.20	4740.16	2931.20	2548.18	13828.30	9172.00	4394.02	3091.00
Physical Planning	380.00	1258.00	350.00	228.00	435.00	335.00	400.00	300.00	760.00	560.00	680.00	480.00	706.00	430.00	616.00	350.00
Public Administration	40.00	42.00	40.00	42.00	17.00	-	17.00									
Family Welfare	2000.00	1800.00	1400.00	1400.00	2100.00	1700.00	1400.00	1200.00	2350.00	1800.00	1800.00	1300.00	1850.00	1950.00	1000.00	1050.00
Total	42469.05	34457.41	35220.00	28497.00	44011.10	38142.66	35302.10	29964.00	46999.20	42792.20	38423.20	34644.78	53552.30	49826.00	38218.02	37879.00

Source: Annual Development Programme, 1991-92, 1992-93, 1993-94, 1994-95, Planning Commission, GOB

Table 7.3 Percentage of Sectoral ADP Allocation in Different Poverty-related Projects

(Tk lakh)

Sector	1991-92				1992-93				1993-94				1994-95			
	Budget allocation		Project aid		Budget allocation		Project aid		Budget allocation		Project aid		Budget allocation		Project aid	
	Original	Revised	Original	Revised	Original	Revised	Original	Revised	Original	Revised	Original	Revised	Original	Revised	Original	Revised
Agriculture	26.33	19.13	35.11	29.09	17.11	16.47	21.86	21.62	16.81	15.61	22.32	21.15	16.37	14.52	24.06	21.93
Rural Development	73.57	55.97	76.57	62.54	62.40	53.20	73.80	61.83	54.74	50.46	69.83	71.92	42.45	38.37	57.87	62.33
Social Welfare, Women's Affairs & Youth Development	41.53	39.76	62.86	64.25	57.64	9.41	82.19	25.0	66.14	66.03	89.75	94.48	77.08	70.61	88.93	99.74
Physical Planning	1.32	0.72	2.11	1.09	1.21	0.98	2.11	1.88	1.90	1.46	3.59	3.04	1.28	00.80	2.13	2.75
Public Administration	4.16	1.28	7.43	1.49	00.43	-	0.52	-	-	-	-	-	-	-	-	-
Family Welfare	n.a.	5.31	n.a.	6.04	5.75	4.91	5.49	5.62	5.57	4.03	6.29	4.28	3.7	3.8	3.005	3.09
Percentage of the total ADP, allocated in poverty related projects in different sectors	7.75	6.12	9.45	8.44	6.48	5.65	8.75	7.87	6.20	5.46	9.03	8.88	5.82	4.99	8.7	8.9

Source: Annual Development Programme 1991-92, 1992-93, 1993-94, 1994-95, Planning Commission, GOB

Table 7.4 Distribution of Respondents according to the Availability of Latrines

(per cent)

Areas	Kutcha latrines	Sanitary latrines	No latrines	Total
Urban	54.7	36.7	8.6	100.0 (n=139.0)
Rural	25.3	3.6	71.3	100.0 (n=150.0)
Total	39.4	19.4	41.2	100.0 (n=289.0)

Source: *A Survey on Evaluation of Budget from the Perspective of Poverty Alleviation*, Shamunnay (1996)
Note: x^2 value = 143.58, DF-2, significant level 0.001%

Table 7.5 Sources of Information through Which Knowledge of Family Planning Reached the Respondents

(per cent)

Areas	From govt. announcement (TV, radio, newspaper, posters)	From NGOs	Others	Total
Urban	88.8	9.0	2.2	100.0 (n=134.0)
Rural	92.9	6.4	0.7	100.0 (n=141.0)
Total	90.9	7.6	1.5	100.0 (n=275.0)

Source: ibid.

Table 7.6 Sources of Drinking Water

(per cent)

Areas	Tap water	Tubewell water	Well water	Other sources	Total
Urban	34.5	50.4	5.8	9.4	100.0 (n=139.0)
Rural	-	82.7	17.3	-	100.0 (n=150.0)
Total	16.6	67.1	11.8	4.5	100.0 (n=289.0)

Source: ibid.

Table 7.7 Providers of Drinking Water

(per cent)

Areas	Local Govt. or peoples representatives	NGO's	Illegal ways	Caretaker of the slum	The owner of the land	Others	Total
Urban	26.3	41.5	9.3	19.5	0.8	2.5	100.0 (n=118.0)
Rural	41.9	0.8	-	-	46.8	10.5	100.0 (n=124.0)
Total	34.3	20.7	4.5	9.5	24.4	6.6	100.0 (n=242.0)

Source: ibid.

Table 7.8 Opinion regarding Vaccination of Children

(per cent)

Areas	Opinions			Total
	Yes	No	Not applicable	
Urban	61.2	25.2	13.7	100.0
				n=139.0
Rural	74.7	7.3	18.0	100.0
				n=150.0
Total	68.2	15.9	15.9	100.0
				n=289.0

Source: *A Survey on Evaluation of Budget from the Perspective of Poverty Alleviation*, Shamunnay (1996)

Table 7.9 Distribution of Respondents according to Their Opinions regarding Completion of Full Vaccination Course

(per cent)

Areas	Opinions			Total
	Yes	No	Time period of course not over	
Urban	60.9	39.1	-	100.0
				n=87.0
Rural	61.6	20.5	17.9	100.0
				n=112.0
Total	61.3	28.6	10.1	100.0
				n=199.0

Source: ibid.

Table 7.10 Sources of Vaccination

(per cent)

Areas	Family planning welfare worker	Govt. health worker	NGO worker	Total
Urban	25.6	58.1	16.3	100.0
				n=86.0
Rural	25.2	73.9	0.9	100.0
				n=111.0
Total	25.4	67.0	7.6	100.0
				n=197.0

Source: ibid.

Table 7.11 Changes in Sources of Drinking Water and Types of Latrine of the Poorest Households in Urban Slums

(Number of households)

Areas/Groups	Year	Sources of drinking water				Types of latrine		
		Tubewell	Tap water	Pond	Others	Watersealed	Kutcha	Open field
Urban Slums (n=20)	1993	20.0	-	-	-	-	20.0	-
		(100.0)					(100.0)	-
	1996	20.0	-	-	-	10.0	10.0	
		(100.0)				(50.0)	(50.0)	-
Slum 1	1993	10.0	-	-	-	-	10.0	-
(Motahar)		(100.0)	-	-	-	-	(100.0)	
(N=10)	1996	10.0	-	-	-	-	10.0	-
		(100.0)					(100.0)	
Slum 2	1993	10.0	-	-	-	-	10.0	-
(Titipara)		(100.0)					(100.0)	
(n=10)	1996	10.0	-	-	-	10.0		-
		(100.0)				(100.0)		

Source: *Panel survey for Annual Budget Review*, 1996

Note: Figures in parentheses are percentage shares in total number of hhs.

Table 7.12 Changes in Sources of Drinking Water and Types of Latrine in Rural Areas

(Number of households)

Areas / Groups	Year	Sources of drinking water				Types of latrine		
		Tube-well	Tap water	Pond	Other	Water-sealed	Kutcha	Open field
OVERALL								
All villages	1993	60.0	-	-	-	-	5.0	55.0
(n=60)		(100.0)					(8.3)	(91.7)
	1996	60.0	-	-	-	-	8.0	52.0
		(100.0)					(13.3)	(86.7)
B. Programme	1993	20.0	-	-	-	-	5.0	15.0
villages		(100.0)					(25.0)	(75.0)
B.1. FFE hhs	1996	20.0	-	-	-	-	.5	15.0
(n=20)		(100.0)					(25.0)	(75.0)
B.2. Non-FFE hhs	1993	20.0	-	-	-	-	-	20.0
(n=20)		(100.0)						(100.0)
	1996	20.0	-	-	-	-	1.0	19.0
		(100.0)					(5.0)	(95.0)
C. Control villages	1993	20.0	-	-	-	-	-	20.0
(Non-FFE hhs)		(100.0)						(100.0)
(n-20)	1996	20.0	-	-	-	-	2.0	18.0
		(100.0)					(10.0)	(90.0)
CENTRAL PART								
A. All villages	1993	30.0	-	-	-	-	-	30.0
(n=30)		(100.0)						(100.0)
	1996	30.0	-	-	-	-	2.0	28.0
		(100.0)					(6.6)	(93.3)
B. Programme	1993	10.0	-	-	-	-	-	10.0
village		(100.0)						(100.0)
B.1. FFE hhs	1996	10.0	-	-	-	-	-	10.0
(n=10)		(100.0)						(100.0)
B.2. Non-FFE hhs	1993	10.0	-	-	-	-	-	(10)
(n=10)		(100.0)						(100.0
	1996	10.0	-	-	-	-	1.0	9.0
		(100.0)					(10.0)	(90.0)
C. Control village	1993	10.0	-	-	-	-	-	10.0
(Non-FFE hhs)		(100.0)						(100.0)
(n-10)	1996	10.0	-	-	-	-	1	9.0
		(100.0)					(10.0)	(90.0)
NORTHERN PART								
A. All villages	1993	30.0	-	-	-	-	5.0	25.0
(n=30)		(100.0)					(16.6)	(83.3)
	1996	30.0	-	-	-	-	6.0	24.0
		(100.0)					(20.0)	(80.0)
B. Programme	1993	10.0	-	-	-	-	5.0	5.0
village		(100.0)					(50.0)	(50.0)
B.1. FFE hhs	1996	10.0	-	-	-	-	5.0	5.0
(n=10)		(100.0)					(50.0)	(50.0)
B.2. Non-FFE hhs	1993	10.0	-	-	-	-	-	10.0
(n=10)		(100.0)						(100.0)
	1996	10.0	-	-	-	-	-	10.0
		(100.0)						(100.0)
C. Control village	1993	10.0	-	-	-	-	-	10.0
(Non-FFE hhs)		(100.0)						(100.0)
(n-10)	1996	10.0	-	-	-	-	1.0	9.0
		(100.0)					(10.0)	(90.0)

Source: ibid.

Note: ibid.

Table 7.13 Changes in the Incidence of Diseases Suffered by the Poorest Households (Urban and Rural Areas)

Diseases	Adults									Children			Overall		
	Men			Women			Total								
	1993	1996	Change (%)	1993	1996	Change (%)	1993	1996	Change (%)	1993	1996	Change (%)	1993	1996	Change (%)
Fever	6.0	13.0	116.7	3.0	11.0	266.7	9.0	24.0	166.6	18.0	34.0	88.9	27.0	58.0	114.8
Diarrhoea	-	-	-	-	2.0	0.0	-	2.0	0.0	3.0	13.0	333.3	3.0	15.0	400.0
Gastroenteritis	3.0	7.0	133.3	2.0	3.0	50.0	5.0	10.0	100.0	-	-	-	5.0	10.0	100.0
Intestinal pain	-	1.0	0.0	-	-	-	-	1.0	0.0	1.0	-	0.0	1.0	1.0	0.0
Asthma	5.0	6.0	20.0	1.0	1.0	0.0	6.0	7.0	16.7	-	-	-	6.0	7.0	16.7
Skin disease	-	-	0.0	1.0	2.0	100.0	1.0	2.0	100.0	-	1.0	0.0	1.0	3.0	200.0
Weakness	2.0	3.0	50.0	-	2.0	0.0	2.0	5.0	150.0	-	1.0	0.0	2.0	6.0	200.0
Sub-total	16.0	30.0	87.5	7.0	21.0	200.0	23.0	51.0	121.7	22.0	49.0	122.7	45.0	100.0	122.2
	(76.0)	(73.0)		(53.8)	(65.6)		(67.0)	(69.8)		(95.6)	(79.0)		(78.9)	(74.0)	
Others	5.0	11.0	120.0	6.0	11.0	83.3	11.0	22.0	100.0	1.0	13.0	1200.0	12(21.0)	5(25.0)	191.7
	(23.8)	(23.0)		(46.1)	(34.0)		(32.4)	(30.1)		(5.0)	(20.0)				
Total	21.0	41.0	95.2	13.0	32.0	146.1	34.0	73.0	114.7	23.0	62.0	169.6	57.0	135.0	136.8
	(100.0)	(100.0)		(100.0)	(100.0)		(100.0)	(100.0)		(100.0)	(100.0)		(100.0)	(100.0)	

Source: *Panel Survey for Annual Budget Review*, 1996

Note: Figures in parentheses show percentages of total.

Table 7.14 Changes in the Incidence of Diseases Suffered by the Poorest Households in Urban Slums

Diseases	Adults									Children			Overall		
	Men			Women			Total								
	1993	1996	Change (%)	1993	1996	Change (%)	1993	1996	Change (%)	1993	1996	Change (%)	1993	1996	Change (%)
Fever	1.0	1.0	0.0	1.0	2.0	100.0	2.0	3.0	50.0	4.0	6.0	50.0	6.0	9.0	50.0
Diarrhoea	-	-	-	-	-	-	-	-	-	2.0	3.0	50.0	2.0	3.0	50.0
Weakness	1.0	2.0	100.0	-	1.0	-	1.0	3.0	200.0	-	1.0	-	1.0	4.0	300.0
Intentional pain	-	-	-	-	-	-	-	-	-	-	-	-	-	-	-
Skin diseases	-	-	-	-	-	-	-	-	-	-	-	-	-	-	-
Asthma	-	-	-	1.0	1.0	0.0	1.0	1.0	0	-	-	-	1.0	1.0	0.0
Gastrointritis	-	-	-	1.0	1.0	0.0	1.0	1.0	0	-	-	-	1.0	1.0	0.0
Others	1.0	2.0	100.0	3.0	4.0	33.3	4.0	6.0	50.0	-	-	-	4.0	6.0	50.0
Total	3.0	5.0	66.7	6.0	9.0	50.0	9.0	14.0	55.6	6.0	10.0	66.7	15.0	24.0	60.0

Source: ibid.

Table 7.15 Changes in the Incidence of Diseases Suffered by the Poorest Households in Rural Areas

Diseases	Adults									Children			Overall		
	Men			Women			Total								
	1993	1996	Change (%)	1993	1996	Change (%)	1993	1996	Change (%)	1993	1996	Change (%)	1993	1996	Change (%)
Fever	5.0	12.0	140.0	2.0	9.0	350.0	7.0	21.0	200.0	14.0	28.0	78.6	21.0	49.0	109.5
Diarrhoea	-	-	-	-	2.0	0.0	-	2.0	0.0	1.0	10.0	1000.0	1.0	12.0	1200.0
Gastroenteritis	3.0	7.0	133.3	1.0	2.0	100.0	4.0	9.0	125.0	-	-	-	4.0	9.0	-
Intestinal pain	-	1.0	-	-	-	-	-	1.0	-	1.0	-	-	1.0	1.0	-
Asthma	5.0	6.0	20.0	-	-	-	5.0	6.0	20.0	-	-	-	5.0	6.0	20.0
Skin disease	-	-	-	1.0	2.0	100.0	1.0	2.0	100.0	-	1.0	-	1.0	3.0	-
Weakness	1.0	1.0	0.0	-	1.0	-	1.0	2.0	100.0	-	-	-	1.0	2.0	-
Others	4.0	9.0	125.0	3.0	7.0	133.3	7.0	16.0	128.5	1.0	13.0	300.0	8.0	29.0	168.7
Total	18.0	36.0	100.0	7.0	23.0	228.6	25.0	59.0	136.0	17.0	52.0	166.7	42.0	111.0	146.5

[contd.]

(Continued)

Diseases	Adults									Children			Overall		
	Men			Women			Total								
	1993	1996	Change (%)	1993	1996	Change (%)	1993	1996	Change (%)	1993	1996	Change (%)	1993	1996	Change (%)
Fever	2.0	6.0	200.0	2.0	6.0	200.0	4.0	12.0	200.0	9.0	22.0	144.4	13.0	34.0	161.5
Diarrhoea	-	-	-	-	2.0	0.0	-	2.0	0.0	1.0	9.0	800.0	1.0	11.0	1000.0
Gastroenteritis	3.0	6.0	100.0	1.0	2.0	100.0	4.0	8.0	100.0	-	-	-	4.0	8.0	100.0
Intestinal pain	-	-	-	-	-	-	-	-	-	1.0	-	0.0	1.0	-	-
Asthma	5.0	6.0	20.0	-	-	-	5.0	6.0	20.0	-	-	-	5.0	6.0	20.0
Skin disease	-	-	0.0	1.0	1.0	0.0	1.0	1.0	0.0	-	1.0	-	1.0	2.0	100.0
Weakness	-	-	-	-	1.0	0.0	-	1.0	0.0	-	-	-	-	1.0	-
Sub-total	10.0	18.0	80.0	4.0	12.0	200.0	14.0	30.0	114.3	11.0	32.0	190.9	25.0	62.0	148.0
Others	2.0	2.0	-	2.0	3.0	50.0	4.0	5.0	25.0	1.0	8.0	700.0	5.0	13.0	160.0
Total	12.0	20.0	66.7	6.0	15.0	150.0	18.0	35.0	94.4	12.0	40.0	233.3	30.0	75.0	150.0
NORTHERN PART															
Fever	3.0	6.0	100.0	-	3.0	0.0	3.0	9.0	200.0	5.0	6.0	20.0	8.0	15.0	87.5
Diarrhoea	-	-	-	-	-	-	-	-	-	-	1.0	-	-	1.0	-
Gastroenteritis	-	1.0	-	-	-	-	-	1.0	-	-	-	-	-	1.0	-
Intestinal pain	-	1.0	-	-	-	-	-	1.0	-	-	-	-	-	1.0	-
Asthma	-	-	-	-	-	-	-	-	-	-	-	-	-	-	-
Skin Disease	-	-	-	-	1.0	0.0	-	1.0	0.0	-	-	-	-	1.0	0.0
Weakness	1.0	1.0	0.0	-	-	-	1.0	1.0	0.0	-	-	-	1.0	1.0	0.0
Subtotal	4.0	9.0	125.0	-	3.0	0.0	4.0	13.0	225.0	5.0	7.0	80.0	9.0	20.0	122.2
Others	2.0	7.0	250.0	1.0	5.0	400.0	3.0	11.0	266.0	-	5.0	0.0	3.0	16.0	433.3
Total	6.0	16.0	166.7	1.0	8.0	700.0	7.0	24.0	257.1	5.0	12.0	140.0	12.0	36.0	200.0

Source: ibid.

Table 7.16 Changes in Expenditure on Health

(Taka/yearly)

Areas/Groups	Year	Total expenditure on health during the year					Total popu	Expenditure	Expenditure per capita				
		Men	Women	Boys	Girls	Total	lation	P. house	Men	Women	Boys	Girls	Total
Overall	1993	8290	3020	621	142	12073	321	150.9	138.1	33.1	6.2	2.0	37.6
(n=80)		(68.6)	(25.0)	(5.1)	(1.1)	(100.0)							
	1996	38265	2812	2548	378	44003	337	550.0	648.5	31.2	23.8	4.6	130.6
		(86.9)	(6.3)	(5.7)	(0.8)	(100.0)							
Urban slums	1993	2010	1800	46	42	3898	69	194.9	201.0	78.2	2.5	2.3	56.5
(n=20)		(51.5)	(46.1)	(1.1)	(1.0)	(100.0)							
	1996	1310	1425	43	73	2851	74	142.6	131.0	61.9	2.3	3.1	38.5
		(45.9)	(49.9)	(1.5)	(2.5)	(100.0)							
Rural areas	1993	6280	1220	575	100	8175	252	136.3	125.6	17.9	7.0	1.9	32.4
(n=60)		(76.8)	(14.9)	(7.0)	(1.2)	(100.0)							
	1996	36955	1387	2505	305	41152	263	685.9	754.1	20.7	28.1	5.2	156.5
		(89.8)	(3.3)	(6.1)	(0.7)	(100.0)							

Source: ibid.

Note: Figures in parentheses show percentages of total expenditure

Table 7.17 Changes in the Number and Percentage of Earning Members of the Poorest Households

Areas/Groups	Number		% of total	
	1993	1996	1993	1996
		OVERALL		
(n=80)				
Men	53.0	55.0	49.5	47.8
Women	28.0	30.0	26.1	26.1
Boys	25.0	27.0	23.3	23.5
Girls	1.0	3.0	0.9	2.6
Total	107.0	115.0	100.0	100.0
Family size	4.0	4.2	-	-
Dependency ratio	3.0	2.9	-	-
		URBAN SLUMS		
(n=20)				
Men	10.0	10.0	41.7	35.7
Women	10.0	10.0	41.7	35.7
Boys	4.0	6.0	16.7	21.4
Girls	-	2.0	-	7.1
Total	24.0	28.0	100.0	100.0
Family size	3.5	3.7	-	-
Dependency ratio	2.9	2.6	-	-
		RURAL AREA		
(n=60)				
Men	43.0	45.0	51.8	51.7
Women	18.0	20.0	22.0	22.9
Boys	21.0	21.0	25.3	24.1
Girls	1.0	1.0	1.2	1.1
Total	83.0	87.0	100.0	100.0
Family size	4.2	4.4	-	-
Dependency ratio	3.0	3.0	-	-

Source: ibid.

Note: Dependency ratio = (Number of family members) (number of earners)

Table 7.18 Changes in Expenditure on Health in Rural Areas

(Taka/yearly)

Areas/Groups	Year	Total expenditure on health during the year					Total Population	Expenditure per	Expenditure per capita				
		Men	Women	Boys	Girls	Total	(number)	household	Men	Women	Boys	Girls	Total
						OVERALL							
A. All villages	1993	6280	1220	575	100	8175	252	136.3	125.6	17.9	7.0	1.9	32.4
(n=60)		(76.8)	(14.9)	(7.0)	(1.2)	(100.0)							
	1996	8955	1387	2505	305	13152	262	149.2	754.1	20.7	28.1	5.2	50.2
		(68.1)	(10.5)	(19.0)	(2.3)	(100.0)							
B. Programme	1993	3770	120	130	10	4030	115	201.5	188.5	5.0	2.6	0.4	35.0
villages		(93.5)	(2.9)	(3.2)	(0.2)	(100.0)							
B.1 FFE hhs	1996	4085	652	1900	40	6677	120	333.9	204.2	27.1	35.8	1.7	55.6
(n=20)		(61.1)	(9.7)	(28.4)	(0.5)	(100.0)							
B.2 Non-FFE hhs	1993	1140	950	290	40	2420	69	121.0	71.2	41.3	16.1	3.3	35.1
(n=20)		(47.1)	(39.2)	(11.9)	(1.6)	(100.0)							
	1996	4555	625	260	205	5645	73	282.3	284.6	27.1	13.0	14.6	77.3
		(80.6)	(11.1)	(4.6)	(3.6)	(100.0)							
C. Control villages	1993	1370	150	155	50	1725	68	86.3	97.8	7.1	11.1	2.6	25.4
(Non - FFE hhs)		(79.4)	(8.6)	(8.9)	(2.8)	(100.0)							
(n=20)	1996	315	110	345	60	830	69	41.5	2178.0	5.5	21.5	2.8	12.0
		(37.9)	(13.2)	(41.6)	(7.2)	(100.0)							

(Taka/yearly)

Areas/Groups	Year	Total expenditure on health during the year					Total Population	Expenditure per household	Expenditure per capita				
		Men	Women	Boys	Girls	Total			Men	Women	Boys	Girls	Total
CENTRAL PART													
A. All villages	1993	3160	880	395	70	4505	128	150.2	121.5	25.8	9.6	2.5	35.2
(n=30)		(70.1)	(19.5)	(8.7)	(1.5)	(100.0)							
	1996	1895	567	2360	235	5057	131	168.6	1149.8	77.1	53.6	8.1	38.6
		(37.5)	(11.2)	(46.7)	(4.6)	(100.0)							
B. Programme	1993	1470	120	30	10	1630	53	163.0	147.0	9.2	1.4	1.1	30.7
villages		(90.1)	(7.3)	(1.8)	(0.6)	(100.0)							
B.1 FFE hhs	1996	1665	152	1800	40	3657	56	365.7	166.5	11.6	81.8	3.6	65.3
(n=10)		(45.5)	(4.1)	(49.2)	(1.1)	(100.0)							
B.2 NonFFE hhs	1993	400	650	210	10	1270	37	127.0	50.0	59.0	19.0	1.4	34.3
(n=10)		(31.4)	(51.1)	(16.5)	(0.7)	(100.0)							
	1996	155	335	240	145	875	39	87.5	19.3	30.4	18.4	20.7	22.4
		(17.7)	(38.2)	(27.4)	(16.5)	(100.0)							
C. Control villages	1993	1290	110	155	50	1605	38	160.5	1612.5	11.0	17.2	4.5	42.2
(Non FFE hhs)		(80.3)	(6.8)	(9.6)	(3.1)	(100.0)							
(n=10)	1996	75	80	320	50	525	36	52.5	3509.3	8.8	35.5	4.5	14.6
		(14.3)	(15.2)	(60.9)	(9.5)	(100.0)							

[Contd]

(Taka/yearly)

Areas/Groups	Year	Total expenditure on health during the year					Total Population	Expenditure per household	Expenditure per capita				
		Men	Women	Boys	Girls	Total			Men	Women	Boys	Girls	Total
						NORTHERN PART							
A. All villages (n=30)	1993	3120 (85.0)	340 (9.2)	180 (4.9)	30 (0.8)	3670 (100)	124	122.3	130.0	10.0	4.3	1.2	29.6
	1996	7060 (87.2)	820 (10.1)	145 (1.7)	70 (0.8)	8095 (100)	131	269.8	306.9	24.1	3.2	2.4	61.8
B. Programme villages	1993	2300 (95.8)	-	100 (3.3)	-	2400 (100)	62	240.0	230.0	-	3.4	-	38.7
B.1 FFE hhs	1996	2420	500	100	-	3020	64	302.0	2420.0	45.4	3.2	-	47.1
(n=10)		(80.1)	(16.5)	(4.1)		(100)							
B.2 Non FFE hhs	1993	740	300	80	30	1150	32	115.0	92.5	25.0	11.4	6.0	35.9
(n=10)		(63.3)	(26.0)	(6.9)	(2.6)	(100)							
	1996	4400 (92.2)	290 (6.1)	20 (0.4)	60 (1.2)	4770 (100)	34	477.0	550.0	24.1	2.8	8.5	140.2
C. Control villages (Non FFE hhs)	1993	80 (66.6)	40 (33.3)	-	-	120 (100)	30	12.0	13.3	3.6	-	-	4.0
(n=10)	1996	240 (78.6)	30 (9.8)	25 (8.1)	10 (3.2)	305 (100)	33	305.0	48.0	2.7	3.5	1.0	9.2

Source: ibid.

Note: Figures in parentheses indicate percentages of total expenditure

Table 7.19 Changes in the Frequency of Utilizing Medical Care

(Number of visits)

Areas/Groups	Year	Visit to health care providers by poorest households (during last one year)		Visit to poorest households by (during last one year)	
		Hospital	Drug Store	Family Welfare Assistants	Health Assistants
Overall n=80	1993	92 (1.2)	127 (1.6)	904 (11.3)	492 (6.2)
	1996	83 (1.0)	107 (1.3)	832 (10.4)	492 (6.2)
Urban slums n=20	1993	2 (0.1)	16 (0.8)	364 (18.2)	-
	1996	11 (0.6)	12 (0.6)	364 (18.2)	-
Rural areas n=60	1993	90 (1.5)	111 (1.9)	540 (9.0)	492 (8.2)
	1996	72 (1.2)	95 (1.6)	468 (7.8)	492 (8.2)

Source: ibid.

Note: Figure in parenthesis shows average number of visit per household

Table 7.20 Changes in the Frequency of Utilizing Medical Care in Urban Slums

(Number of visits)

Areas/Groups	Year	Visit to health care providers by poorest households (during last one year)		Visit to poorest households by (during last one year)	
		Hospital	Drug Store	Family Welfare Assistants	Health Assistants
Urban slums	1993	2 (0.1)	16 (0.8)	364 (18.2)	-
	1996	11 (0.6)	12 (0.6)	364 (18.2)	-
Slum-1 (Motahar) n=10	1993	-	16 (1.6)	364 (36.4)	-
	1996	-	12 (1.2)	364 (36.4)	-
Slum-2 (Titipara) n=10	1993	2 (0.2)	-	-	-
	1996	11 (1.1)	-	-	-

Source: ibid.

Note: ibid.

Table 7.21 Changes in the Frequency of Utilizing Medical Care in Rural Areas

(Number of visits)

Areas/Groups	Year	Visit to health care providers by poorest households (during last one year)		Visit to poorest households by (during last one year)	
		Hospital	Drug Store	Family Welfare Assistants	Health Assistants
		OVERALL			
A. All villages	1993	90 (1.5)	111 (1.9)	540 (9.0)	492(8.2)
(n=60)	1996	72 (1.2)	95 (1.6)	468(7.8)	492(8.2)
B. Programme	1993	35 (1.7)	44(2.2)	228 (11.4)	216 (10.8)
villages	1996	31 (1.6)	33 (1.7)	228 (11.4)	216 (10.8)
B.1. FFE hhs	1993	36 (1.8)	42(2.1)	168(8.4)	156(7.8)
(n=20)	1996	20 (1.0)	37 (1.9)	168(8.4)	156(7.8)
B.2. Non-FFE hhs					
(n=20)					
C. Control villages					
(Non-FFE hhs)	1993	19 (0.9)	25 (1.3)	144 (7.2)	120 (6.0)
(n-20)	1996	21 (1.1)	25 (1.3)	72 (3.6)	120(6.0)
		CENTRAL PART			
A. All villages	1993	63(2.1)	74(2.4)	288(9.6)	240(8.0)
(n=30)	1996	59(1.9)	55(1.9)	228(7.6)	240(8.0)
B. Programme villages	1993	25 (2.5)	34(3.4)	120 (12.0)	108 (10.8)
B.1. FFE hhs (n=10)	1996	22 (2.2)	25 (2.5)	120 (12.0)	108 (10.8)
B.2. Non-FFE hhs	1993	21 (2.1)	23(2.3)	72 (7.2)	60 (6.0)
(n=10)	1996	20 (2.0)	18 (1.8)	72 (7.2)	60 (6.0)
C. Control villages	1993	17 (1.7)	17 (1.7)	96 (9.6)	72 (7.2)
(Non-FFE hhs)	1996	17 (1.7)	12 (1.2)	36 (3.6)	72(7.2)
(n-10)					
		NORTHERN PART			
A. All villages	1993	27(0.9)	37(1.2)	252(8.4)	252(8.4)
(n=30)	1996	13(0.4)	40(1.3)	240(8.0)	252(8.4)
B. Programme villages	1993	10 (1.0)	10 (1.0)	108 (10.8)	108 (10.8)
B.1. FFE hhs (n=10)	1996	9 (0.9)	8 (0.8)	108 (10.8)	108 (10.8)
B.2. Non-FFE hhs	1993	15 (1.5)	19 (1.9)	96(9.6)	96(9.6)
(n=10)	1996	-	19 (1.9)	96(9.6)	96(9.6)
C. Control villages					
(Non-FFE hhs)	1993	2 (0.2)	8 (0.8)	48 (4.8)	48 (4.8)
(n-10)	1996	4 (0.4)	13 (1.3)	36 (3.6)	48 (4.8)

Source: ibid.
Note: ibid.

Table 7.22 Quality of Medical Services at Government Hospitals and Private Drugstores

Areas/Groups	Year	Hospital																									Private drugstore				
		Availlability of medicine					Service of doctors					Adequacy of doctors					Serviceabllity of Instruments					Availlability of beds					Availlability of medicine				
		VG	G	B	VB	NA	VG	G	B	VB	NA	VG	G	B	VB	NA	VG	G	B	VB	NA	VG	G	B	VB	NA	VG	G	B	VB	NA
Overall (n=80)	1993	2	5	5	19	49	1	1	16	12	50	-	3	12	15	50	-	-	3	24	53	-	2	1	23	54	43	8	1	1	27
		(2.5)	(6.3)	(6.3)	(23.8)	(61.3)	(1.2)	(1.2)	(20.0)	(15.0)	(62.5)	-	(3.8)	(15.0)	(18.8)	(62.5)	-	-	(3.8)	(30.0)	(66.3)	-	(2.5)	(1.3)	(28.8)	(67.5)	(53.8)	(10.0)	(1.3)	(1.3)	(33.8)
	1996	1	9	16	18	36	1	10	25	8	36	-	2	23	14	41	1	-	5	32	42	-	-	3	30	47	38	16	2	-	24
		(1.3)	(11.3)	(20.0)	(22.5)	(45.0)	(1.3)	(12.5)	(31.3)	(10.0)	(45.0)	-	(2.5)	(28.8)	(15.5)	(51.3)	(1.2)	-	(6.3)	(40.0)	(52.5)	-	-	(3.8)	(37.5)	(58.8)	(45.5)	(20.0)	(2.5)	-	(30.0)
Urban slums	1993	-	1	-	-	19	-	-	-	-	20	-	-	-	-	20	-	-	-	-	20	-	-	-	-	20	9	-	-		11
(n=20)		-	(5)	-	-	(95.0)	-	-	-	-	(100)	-	-	-	-	(100.0)	-	-	-	-	(100.0)	-	-	-	-	(100.0)	(45.0)	-	-		(55.0)
	1996	-	3	1	-	16	-	2	1	1	16	-	1	-	-	19	1	-	-	-	19	-	-	-	-	20	9	-	-	-	11
		-	(15.0)	(5.0)	-	(80.0)	-	(10.0)	(5.0)	(5.0)	(80.0)	-	(5.0)	-	-	(95.0)	(5.0)	-	-	-	(95.0)	-	-	-	-	(100.0)	(45.0)	-	-	-	(55.0)
Rural areas	1993	2	4	5	19	30	1	1	16	12	30	-	3	12	15	30	-	-	3	24	33	-	2	1	23	34	34	8	1	1	16
(n=60)		(3.3)	(6.8)	(8.3)	(31.8)	(50.0)	(1.7)	(1.7)	(26.7)	(20.0)	(50.0)	-	(5.0)	(20.0)	(25.0)	(50.0)	-	-	(5.0)	(40.0)	(55.0)	-	(3.3)	(1.7)	(38.3)	(56.7)	(56.7)	(13.3)	(1.7)	(1.7)	(26.7)
	1996	1	6	15	18	20	1	8	24	7	20	-	1	23	14	22	-	-	5	32	23	-	-	3	30	27	29	16	2	-	13
		(1.7)	(10.0)	(25.0)	(30.0)	(33.3)	(1.7)	(13.3)	(40.0)	(11.7)	(33.3)	-	(1.7)	(38.3)	(23.3)	(36.7)	-	-	(8.3)	(53.3)	(38.3)	-	-	(5.0)	(50.0)	(45.0)	(48.3)	(26.8)	(73.3)	-	(21.7)

Source: ibid.

Note: 1. VG=Very good, G=Good, B=Bad, VB=Very Bad, NA= Not Aware

2. Figures in parentheses show percentages of households

Table 7.23 Quality of Medical Services at Government Hospitals and Private Drugstores in Rural Areas

(Number of households)

Areas/Groups	Year	Hospital																									Private drugstore				
		Availlability of medicine					Service of doctors					Adequacy of doctors					Service ablilty of Instruments					Availlability of beds					Availlability of medicine				
		VG	G	B	VB	NA	VG	G	B	VB	NA	VG	G	B	VB	NA	VG	G	B	VB	NA	VG	G	B	VB	NA	VG	G	B	VB	NA
A. All villages	1993	2	4	5	19	30	1	1	16	12	30	-	3	12	15	30	-	-	3	24	33	-	2	1	23	34	34	8	1	1	16
(n=60)	1996	1	6	15	18	20	1	8	24	7	20	-	1	23	14	22	-	-	5	32	23	-	-	3	30	27	29	16	2	-	13
B. Experiemental																															
villages	1993	1	-	2	9	8	1	-	6	5	8	-	2	5	5	8	-	-	2	9	9	-	2	1	8	9	16	1	-	1	2
B.1 FFE hhs																															
(n=20)	1996	1	-	4	9	6	1	5	6	2	6	-	-	9	5	6	-	-	5	8	7	-	-	3	10	7	13	6	-	-	1
B.2 Non-FFE hhs	1993	-	1	1	6	12	-	1	4	3	12	-	1	2	5	12	-	-	-	8	12	-	-	-	8	12	11	3	-	-	6
(n=20)	1996	-	3	8	4	5	-	3	8	4	5	-	1	6	6	7	-	-	-	13	7	-	-	-	10	10	7	6	1	-	6
C. Control villages	1993	1	3	2	4	10	-	-	6	4	10	-	-	5	5	10	-	-	1	7	12	-	-	-	7	13	7	4	1	-	8
non-FFE hhs																															
(n=20)	1996	-	3	3	5	9	-	-	10	1	9	-	-	8	3	9	-	-	-	11	9	-	-	-	10	10	9	4	1	-	6
CENTRA L PART																															
A. All villages	1993	1	3	2	18	6	-	1	11	12	6	-	3	10	11	6	-	-	1	22	7	-	-	-	23	7	20	3	-	1	6
(n=30)	1996	-	4	9	17	-	-	6	18	6	-	-	1	19	10	-	-	-	3	27	-	-	-	-	30	-	15	12	1	-	2
B. Experiemental																															
villages	1993	-	-	-	8	2	-	-	3	5	2	-	2	3	3	2	-	-	-	8	2	-	-	-	8	2	8	-	-	1	1
B.1 FFEhhs (n=10)	1996	-	-	2	8	-	-	5	3	2	-	-	-	7	3	-	-	-	3	7	-	-	-	-	10	-	4	6	-	-	-
B.2 Non-FFEhhs	1993	-	1	1	6	2	-	1	4	3	2	-	1	2	5	2	-	-	-	8	2	-	-	-	8	2	6	2	-	-	2
(n=10)	1996	-	1	5	4	-	-	1	6	3	-	-	1	4	5	-	-	-	-	10	-	-	-	-	10	-	2	5	1	-	2

(Continued)

(Number of households)

Areas/Groups	Year	Hospital																									Private drugstore				
		Availlability of medicine					Service of doctors					Adequacy of doctors					Service ability of Instruments					Availlability of beds					Availlability of medicine				
		VG	G	B	VB	NA	VG	G	B	VB	NA	VG	G	B	VB	NA	VG	G	B	VB	NA	VG	G	B	VB	NA	VG	G	B	VB	NA
C. Control villages non-FFE hhs	1993	1	2	1	4	2	-	-	4	4	2	-	-	5	3	2	-	-	1	6	3	-	-	-	7	3	6	1	-	-	3
(n=10)	1996	-	3	2	5	-	-	-	9	1	-	-	-	8	2	-	-	-	-	10	-	-	-	-	10	-	9	1	-	-	-
NORTHERN PART																															
A. All villages	1993	1	1	3	1	24	1	-	5	-	24	-	-	2	4	24	-	-	2	2	26	-	2	1	-	27	14	5	1	-	10
(n=30)	1996	1	2	6	1	20	1	2	6	1	20	-	-	4	6	20	-	-	2	5	23	-	-	3	-	27	14	4	1	-	11
NORTHERN PART																															
B. Experiemental																															
villages	1993	1	-	2	1	6	1	-	3	-	6	-	-	2	2	6	-	-	2	1	7	-	2	1	-	7	8	1	-	-	
B.1 FFE hhs	1996	1	-	2	1	6	1	-	3	-	6	-	-	2	2	6	-	-	2	1	7	-	-	3	-	7	9	-	-	-	1
B.2 Non-FFE hhs	1993	-	-	-	-	10	-	-	-	-	10	-	-	-	-	10	-	-	-	-	10	-	-	-	-	10	5	1	-	-	4
(n=10)	1996	-	2	3	-	5	-	2	2	1	5	-	-	2	1	7	-	-	-	3	7	-	-	-	-	10	5	1	-	-	4
C. Control villages non-FFE hhs	1993	-	1	1	-	8	-	-	2	-	8	-	-	-	2	8	-	-	-	1	9	-	-	-	-	10	1	3	1	-	5
(n=10)	1996	-	-	1	-	9	-	-	1	-	9	-	-	-	1	9	-	-	-	1	9	-	-	-	-	10	-	3	1	-	6

Source: ibid.

Note: ibid.

Table 7.24 Quality of Medical Services at Government Hospitals and Private Drugstores in Urban Slums

Areas/ Groups	Year	Hospital																								Private drugstore				
		Availlability of medicine					Service of doctors					Adequacy of doctors					Serviceablity of Instruments					Availlability of beds					Availlability of medicine				
		VG	G	B	VB	NA	VG	G	B	VB	NA	VG	G	B	VB	NA	VG	G	B	VB	NA	VG	G	B	VB	NA	VG	G	B	VB	NA
Overall																															
(n=20)	1993	-	1	-	-	19	-	-	-	-	20	-	-	-	-	20	-	-	-	-	20	-	-	-	-	20	9	-	-	-	11
	1996	-	3	1	-	16	-	2	1	1	16	-	1	-	-	19	1	-	-	-	19	-	-	-	-	20	9	-	-	-	11
Slum-1	1993	-	-	-	-	10	-	-	-	-	10	-	-	-	-	10	-	-	-	-	10	-	-	-	-	10	9	-	-	-	1
(Motaher)																															
(n=10)	1996	-	1	-	-	9	-	-	1	-	9	-	-	-	-	10	-	-	-	-	10	-	-	-	-	10	9	-	-	-	1
Slum-2																															
(Titipara)	1993	-	1	-	-	9	-	-	-	-	10	-	-	-	-	10	-	-	-	-	10	-	-	-	-	10	9	-	-	-	10
n=10	1996	-	2	1	-	7	-	2	-	1	7	-	1	-	-	9	1	-	-	-	9	-	-	-	-	10	9	-	-	-	10

Source: ibid.

Note: ibid.

Table 7.25 Changes in the Quality of Services of Field Level Family Welfare and Health Assistants in Rural Areas

(Percentage of households)

Areas/groups	Year	Family Welfare Assistants					Health Assistants				
		Very good	Good	Bad	Very bad	Not aware	Very good	Good	Bad	Very bad	Not aware
						OVERALL					
All villages	1993	16	19	2	-	23	19	19	1	-	21
(n=60)		(26.7)	(31.7)	(3.3)		(38.3)	(31.7)	(31.7)	(1.7)		(35.0)
	1996	20	16	2	-	22	26	11	1	3(5.0)	19
		(33.3)	(26.6)	(3.3)		(36.7)	(43.3)	(18.3)	(1.7)		(31.7)
B. Programme	1993	5	12	-	-	3	10	8	-	-	2
villages		(25.0)	(60.0)			(15.0)	(50.0)	(40.0)			(10.0)
B.1. FFE hhs	1996	8	9	-	-	3	11	4	-	3	2
(n=20)		(40.0)	(45.0)			(15.0)	(55.0)	(20.0)		(15.0)	(10.0)
B.2. Non-	1993	7	4	-	-	9	8	5	-	-	7
FFE hhs		(35.0)	(20.0)			(45.0)	(40.0)	(25.0)			(35.0)
(n=20)	1996	8	2	1	-	9	11	2	-	-	7
		(40.0)	(10.0)	(5.0)		(45.0)	(55.0)	(10.0)			(35.0)
C. Control	1993	4	3	2	-	11	1	6	1	-	12
villages		(20.0)	(15.0)	(10.0)		(55.0)	(5.0)	(30.0)	(5.0)		(60.0)
(n=20)	1996	4	5	1	-	10	4	5	1	-	10
		(20.0)	(25.0)	(5.0)		(50.0)	(20.0)	(25.0)	(5.0)		(50.0)
						CENTRAL PART					
All villages	1993	5	12	-	-	13	6	12	-	-	12
(n=30)		(16.7)	(40.0)			(43.3)	(20.0)	(40.0)			(40.0)
	1996	9	9	1	-	11	13	7	-	-	10
		(30.0)	(30.0)	(3.3)		(36.7)	(43.3)	(23.3)			(33.3)
B. Programme	1993	1	8	-	-	1	4	5	-	-	1
village		(10.0)	(80.0)			(10.0)	(40.0)	(50.0)			(10.0)
B.1. FFE hhs	1996	4	5	-	-	1	5	4	-	-	1
(n=10)		(40.0)	(50.0)			(10.0)	(50.0)	(40.0)			(10.0)
B.2. Non- FFE hhs	1993	-	3	-	-	7	1	4	-	-	5
(n=10)				(30.0)			(70.0)	(10.0)	(40.0)		
(50.0)	1996	1	1	1	-	7	4	1	-	-	5
		(10.0)	(10.0)	(10.0)		(70.0)	(40.0)	(10.0)			(50.0)
C. Control village	1993	4(40.0)	1(10.0)	-	-	5	1	3	-	-	6
(n=10)						(50.0)	(10.0)	(30.0)			(60.0)
	1996	4	3	-	-	3	4	2	-	-	4
		(40.0)	(30.0)			(30.0)	(40.0)	(20.0)			(40.0)
						NORTHERN PART					
A. All villages	1993	11	7	2	-	10	13	7	1	-	9
		(36.7)	(23.3)	(6.7)		(33.3)	(43.3)	(23.3)	(3.3)		(30.0)
(n=30)	1996	11	7	1	-	11	13	4	1	3	9
		(36.7)	(23.3)	(3.3)		(36.7)	(43.3)	(13.3)	(3.3)	(10.0)	(30.0)

Table 7.26 Changes in the Quality of Services of Field Level Family Welfare and Health Assistants in Urban Slums

(Percentage of households)

Areas/Groups	Year	Family Welfare Assistants					Health Assistants				
		Very good	Good	Bad	Very Bad	Non-response	Very good	Good	Bad	Very Bad	Non-response
Urban Slums	1993	7	-	-	-	13	-	-	-	-	20
(n=20)		(35.0)				(65)					(100.0)
	1996	7	-	-	-	13	-	-	-	-	20
		(35.0)				(65)					(100.0)
Slum-1	1993	7	-	-	-	3	-	-	-	-	10
(Motahar)		(70.0)				(30.0)					(100.0)
(n=10)	1996	7	-	-	-	3)	-	-	-	-	10
		(70.0)				(30.0)					(100.0)
Slum-2	1993	-	-	-	-	10	-	-	-	-	10
(Titipara)						(100.0)					(100.0)
(n=10)	1996	-	-	-	-	10	-	-	-	-	10
						(100.0)					(100.0)

Source: ibid.

Note: ibid.

Table 7.27 Enrolment Rate of School-Age Children (Primary Level), 1996

(Percentage)

Social class	Villages under FFE Programme			Villages without FFE Programme			Overall		
	Boys	Girls	Total	Boys	Girls	Total	Boys	Girls	Total
Poorest	77	71	74	68	53	60	74	64	69
Poor*	71	100	83	86	90	89	77	94	86
Middle	88	83	86	100	93	96	93	89	91
Well-off	100	82	91	90	100	95	95	90	93
Poor	76	77	76	74	67	70	75	73	74
Non-poor	93	83	88	95	96	96	94	90	92
Overall	80	78	79	81	76	78	81	77	79

Source: *PRA for Annual Budget Review*, 1996

Note: 1. Poor* and poorest are comparable with moderate poor and hardcore poor respectively.

2. Poor = Poor* + poorest

3. Non-poor = Middle + well-off

Table 7.28 Drop-Out Rate of Primary Level Students, 1996

(Percentage)

Social class	Villages under FFE Programme			Villages without FFE Programme			Overall		
	Boys	Girls	Total	Boys	Girls	Total	Boys	Girls	Total
Poorest	2	-	1	11	6	8	5	2	3
Poor*	8	-	4	-	-	-	4	-	2
Middle	-	-	-	-	7	4	-	4	2
Well-off	-	-	-	-	-	-	-	-	-
Poor	4	-	2	6	3	4	5	1	3
Non-poor	-	-	-	-	4	2	-	2	1
Overall	3	-	1	4	3	4	3	2	2

Source: ibid.
Note: ibid.

Table 7.29 Prevalence of Child Labour among School-Age Children (Primary Level), 1996

(Percentage)

Social class	Villages under FFE Programme			Villages without FFE Programme			Overall		
	Boys	Girls	Total	Boys	Girls	Total	Boys	Girls	Total
Poorest	42	19	30	57	18	35	47	19	32
Poor*	12	15	13	29	5	14	19	9	14
Middle	19	-	11	42	13	26	29	7	18
Well-off	18	-	9	-	-	-	10	-	5
Poor	34	18	27	48	13	28	39	16	27
Non-poor	18	-	10	23	8	15	20	4	12
Overall	30	14	22	39	11	24	36	13	23

Source: ibid.
Note: ibid.

Table 7.30 The Coverage of FFE Programme among Children and Students in Programme Villages

Social class	Number of children in Programme villages			Number of students in Programme villages			Proportion of students under FFE Programme (%)			Proportion of children under FFE Programme (%)			Proportion of students under FFE Programme (%)		
	Boys	Girls	Total	Boys	Girls	Total	Boys	Girls	Total	Boys	Girls	Total	Boys	Girls	Total
Poorest	53	52	105	41	37	78	23	16	39	43	31	37	56	43	50
Poor*	17	13	30	12	13	25	4	3	7	24	23	23	33	23	28
Middle	16	12	28	14	10	24	1	4	5	6	33	18	7	40	21
Well-off	11	11	22	11	9	20	-	3	3	0	27	14	0	33	15
Poor	70	65	135	53	50	103	27	19	46	39	29	34	51	38	45
Non-poor	27	23	50	25	19	44	1	7	8	4	10	16	4	37	18
Overall	97	88	185	78	69	147	28	26	54	29	30	29	36	38	37
	Boys	Girls	Total	Boys	Girls	Total	Boys	Girls	Total	Boys	Girls	Total	Boys	Girls	Total

Source: ibid.

Note: ibid.

Table 7.31 Changes in Illiteracy among Adult Members and Participation of School-Age Children (Primary & Secondary Levels) in Schooling in Rural Areas

Areas/Groups		Year	Rate of illiteracy (%)		Rate of participation in schooling (%)	
			Men	Women	Boys	Girls
			OVERALL			
A.	All villages	1993	95.9	100.0	46.0	48.6
	(n=60)	1996	95.9	100.0	51.8	52.5
B.	Programme villages	1993	95.0	100.0	63.6	77.0
	B.1. FFE hhs (n=20)	1996	95.0	100.0	74.5	100.0
	B.2. Non-FFE hhs (n=20)	1993	93.8	100.0	11.8	9.1
		1996	93.8	100.0	10.0	7.1
C.	Control villages	1993	100.0	100.0	30.8	35.3
	(Non-FFE hhs) (n=20)	1996	100.0	100.0	28.6	36.8
			CENTRAL PART			
A.	All villages	1993	100.0	100.0	35.7	14.8
	(n=30)	1996	100.0	100.0	36.4	14.3
B.	Programme village	1993	100.0	100.0	61.9	27.3
	B.1. FFE hhs (n=10)	1996	100.0	100.0	63.6	27.3
	B.2. Non-FFE hhs (n=10)	1993	100.0	100.0	16.8	-
		1996	100.0	100.0	15.4	-
C.	Control village	1993	100.0	100.0	-	10.0
	(n=10)	1996	100.0	100.0	-	10.0
			NORTHERN PART			
A.	All villages	1993	91.3	100.0	59.4	61.9
	(n=30)	1996	91.3	100.0	68.3	80.9
B.	Programme village	1993	90.0	100.0	65.2	77.9
	B.1. FFE hhs (n=10)	1996	90.0	100.0	82.8	83.3
	B.2. Non-FFE hhs (n=10)	1993	87.5	100.0	-	20.0
		1996	87.5	100.0	-	14.3
C	Control village	1993	100.0	90.9	100.0	71.4
	(n=10)	1996	100.0	90.9	80.0	66.7

Source: *Panel Survey for Annual Budget Review*, 1996

Note: Rate of illiteracy and participation in schooling is measured according to the number of men, women, boys and girls available on education sheet.

Table 7.32 Changes in Illiteracy and Participation of School-Age Children (Primary and Secondary Levels) in Schooling in Urban Slums

Areas/Groups	Year	Rate of illiteracy (%)		Rate of participation in schooling (%)	
		Men	Women	Boys	Girls
Urban slums	1993	100.0	100.0	16.7	5.6
(n=20)	1996	100.0	100.0	11.1	-
Slum-1 (Motahar)	1993	100.0	100.0	11.1	-
(n=10)	1996	100.0	100.0	11.1	-
Slum-2 (Titipara)	1993	100.0	100.0	22.2	11.1
(n=10)	1996	100.0	100.0	11.1	-

Source: ibid.

Table 7.33 Changes in Expenditure on Education of the Poorest Households

Areas/Groups	Year	No. of students			Total annual expenditure on education (primary & secondary) (Tk)			Average annual expenditure per student (primary & secondary) (Tk)		
		Boys	Girls	Total	Boys	Girls	Total	Boys	Girls	Total
Overall	1993	37	18	55	5376	1860	7236	145.3	103.3	131.6
(n=80)	1996	46	21	67	13920	2700	16620	302.6	128.6	248.0
Urban slums	1993	3	1	4	2400	-	2400	800.0	-	600.0
(n=20)	1996	2	-	2	3600	-	3600	1800.0	-	1800.0
Rural areas	1993	34	17	51	2976	1860	4836	87.5	109.4	94.8
(n=60)	1996	44	21	65	10320	2700	13020	234.5	128.5	200.3

Source: ibid.

Table 7.34 Changes in Expenditure on Education (Primary & Secondary) in Rural Areas

Areas/Groups	Year	No. of students			Total annual expenditure on education (Tk)			Average annual expenditure per student (Tk)		
		Boys	Girls	Total	Boys	Girls	Total	Boys	Girls	Total
OVERALL										
A. All villages	1993	34	17	51	2976	1860	4836	87.5	109.4	94.8
(n=60)	1996	44	21	65	10320	2700	13020	234.5	128.5	200.3
B. Programme villages	1993	28	10	38	1236	1200	2436	44.1	120.0	64.1
B.1. FFE hhs (n=20)	1996	38	13	51	8040	2040	10080	211.5	156.9	197.6
B.2. Non-FFE	1993	2	1	3	1200	-	1200	600.0	-	400.0
hhs (n=20)	1996	2	1	3	1800	-	1800	900.0	-	600.0
C. Control villages	1993	4	6	10	540	660	1200	135.0	110.0	120.0
(Non-FFE hhs) (n=20)	1996	4	7	11	480	660	1140	120.0	94.3	103.6
CENTRAL PART										
A. All villages	1993	15	4	19	2100	-	2100	140.0	-	110.5
(n=30)	1996	16	4	20	4440	-	4440	277.5	-	222.0
B. Programme villages	1993	13	3	16	900	-	900	69.2	-	56.2
B.1. FFE hhs (n=10)	1996	14	3	17	2640	-	2640	188.6	-	155.3
B.2. Non-FFE hhs	1993	2	-	2	1200	-	1200	600.0	-	600.0
(n=10)	1996	2	-	2	1800	-	1800	900.0	-	900.0
C. Control villages	1993	-	1	1	-	-	-	-	-	-
(Non-FFE hhs) (n=10)	1996	-	1	1	-	-	-	-	-	-
NORTHERN PART										
A. All villages	1993	19	13	32	876	1860	2736	46.1	143.0	85.5
(n=30)	1996	28	17	45	5880	2700	8580	210.0	158.8	190.7
B. Programme villages	1993	15	7	22	336	1200	1536	22.4	171.1	69.8
B.1. FFE hhs (n=10)	1996	24	10	34	5400	2040	7440	225.0	204.0	218.8
B.2. Non-FFE	1993	-	1	1	-	-	-	-	-	-
hhs (n=10)	1996	-	1	1	-	-	-	-	-	-
C. Control villages	1993	4	5	9	540	660	1200	135.0	132.0	133.3
(Non-FFE hhs) (n=10)	1996	4	6	10	480	660	1140	120.0	110.0	114.0

Source: ibid.

Table 8.1 Distribution of Respondents according to Their Opinions regarding Knowledge about Budget

(per cent)

Areas	Opinions		Total
	Yes	No	
Urban	44.6	55.4	100.0 (n=139)
Rural	19.3	80.7	100.0 (n=150)
Total	31.5	68.5	100.0 (n=289)

Source: *A Survey on Evaluation of Budget from the Perspective of Poverty Alleviation,* Shamunnay (1996)
Note: χ^2 Value = 21.3570, DF-1, significant level 0.001

Table 8.2 Relationship between Respondents' Educational Level and Knowledge about Budget

(per cent)

Educational level	Opinions		Total
	Yes	No	
Illiterate	28.7	71.3	100.0 (n=223)
Literate	40.9	59.1	100.0 (n=66)
Total	31.5	68.5	100.0 (n=289)

Source: ibid.
Note: c^2 value=3.51916, DF-1, significant level 0.06066

Table 8.3 Relationship between Respondents' Level of Income and Knowledge about Budget

(per cent)

Household income group (Tk per month)	Opinions		Total
	Yes	No	
Upto 1000	8.3	91.7	100.0 (n=72)
1001-2500	33.1	66.9	100.0 (n=136)
2501+	49.4	50.6	100.0 (n=81)
Total	31.5	68.5	100.0 (n=289)

Source: ibid.
Note: c^2 value = 30.07837, DF-2, significant level .0000

Table 8.4 Distribution of Respondents Who Had Some Knowledge about Budget

(per cent)

Areas	Opinions about budget discussion		Total
	Yes	No	
Urban	95.2	4.8	100.0 (n=62)
Rural	75.9	24.1	100.0 (n=29)
Total	89.0	11.0	100.0 (n=91)

Source: ibid.

Note: c^2 value = 7.52360, DF-1, significant level 0.00609

Table 8.5 Distribution of Respondents Who Had Some Knowledge about Budget and Their Levels of Education

(per cent)

Educational level	Opinions		Total
	Yes	No	
Illiterate	90.6	9.4	100.0 (n=64)
Literate	85.2	14.8	100.0 (n=27)
Total	89.0	11.0	100.0 (n=91)

Source: ibid.

Note: c^2 value = 0.57447, DF-1, significant 0.44849

Table 8.6 Topics of Discussion on Budget

Educational level	High price of goods	Others	Total
Illiterate	91.4	8.6	1000 (n=58)
Literate	91.3	8.7	100.0 (n=23)
Total	91.4	8.6	100.0 (n=81)

Source: ibid.

Note: 1. c^2 value = .00012, DF-1, significant .99136

2. Others included supply of foodgrains, education, health and medical facilities, population and family planning, poverty, taxation, subsidy, fertiliser, etc.

Table 8.7 Distribution of Respondents according to Their Opinions about Solving Problems through Budget

(per cent)

Areas	Opinions regarding solution to problem through budget			Total
	Yes	No	Do not know	
Urban	41.7	2.9	55.4	100.0 (n=139)
Rural	16.0	3.3	80.7	100.0 (n=150)
Total	28.4	3.1	68.5	100.0 (n=289)

Source: ibid.
Note: c^2value = 23.60196, DF-2, significant level .00001

Table 8.8 Distribution of Respondents according to Their Opinions about Solving Problems

(per cent)

Areas	Opinions regarding solution to problem				Total
	Development of road in locality	Scope for employment	Environment and development/ building schools, colleges/supply of pure water	Development of drainage system/ increase in health facilities/improvement of law and order situation	
Urban	32.8	41.4	10.3	15.5	100.0 (n=58)
Rural	33.3	41.7	20.8	4.2	100.0 (n=24)
Total	32.9	41.5	13.4	12.2	100.0 (n=82)

Source: ibid.

Table 8.9 Distribution of Respondents according to Their Opinions about the Usefulness of Budget

(per cent)

Areas	Opinions about usefulness of budget			Total
	Yes	No	Do not know	
Urban	5.0	39.6	55.4	100.0 (n=139)
Rural	3.3	16.0	80.7	100.0 (n=150)
Total	4.2	27.3	68.5	100.0 (n=289)

Source: ibid.
Note: c^2 value = 21.88869, DF-2, significant level 0.00002

Table 8.10 Sources of Information on Budget

(per cent)

Areas	Opinions		Total
	From TV	From radio or other persons	
Urban	20.4	79.6	100.0 (n=54)
Rural	26.9	73.1	100.0 (n=26)
Total	22.5	77.5	100.0 (n=80)

Source: ibid.
Note: c^2 value = .43215, DF-1, significant 0.51094

Table 8.11 Percentage of Respondents Who Listened to the Budget Speech of the Finance Minister

(per cent)

Educational level	Opinions		Total
	Yes	No	
Illiterate	24.2	75.8	100.0 (n=223)
Literate	39.4	60.6	100.0 (n=66)
Total	27.7	72.3	100.0 (n=289)

Source: ibid.
Note: c^2 value = 5.86110, DF-1, significant level 0.01548

Table 8.12 Percentage of Respondents Who Listened to the Budget Speech (Distributed by level of Income)

(per cent)

Household income group (Tk per month)	Opinions		Total
	Yes	No	
Up to 1000	6.9	93.1	100.0 (n=72)
1001-2500	29.4	70.6	100.0 (n=136)
2501+	43.2	56.8	100.0 (n=81)
Total	27.7	72.3	100.0 (n=289)

Source: ibid.
Note: c^2 value = 25.42623, DF-2, significant level 0.00000

Table 8.13 Distribution of Respondents Understanding/Not Understanding the Budget Speech

(per cent)

Areas	Opinions		Total
	Budget understood	Not understood	
Urban	40.7	59.3	100.0 (n=54)
Rural	30.8	69.2	100.0 (n=26)
Total	37.5	62.5	100.0 (n=80)

Source: ibid.

Table 8. 14 Distribution of Respondents Stating the Reasons for Not Understanding the Budget Speech

(per cent)

Areas	Not easily understan-dable/complex sentence	Unable to understand due to lack of education	Total
Urban	50.0	50.0	100.0 (n=32)
Rural	11.1	88.9	100.0 (n=18)
Total	36.0	64.0	100.0 (n=50)

Source: ibid.

Table 8.15 Distribution of Respondents Stating the Reasons for Not Listening to the Budget Speech by the Place of Residence

(per cent)

Areas	Reasons for not listening to budget speech			Total
	No TV or radio/ no newspaper	No eagerness/ always busy with work	Do not understand	
Urban	9.5	32.9	61.2	100.0 (n=85)
Rural	8.1	18.5	73.4	100.0 (n=124)
Total	7.2	24.4	68.4	100 (n=209)

Source: ibid.

Note: χ^2 value = 5.71470, DF-2, significant level 0.05742

Ref: Data/ ICDAppendix File-2 pm5

Table 8.16 Distribution of Respondents Reacting to the Public Budget

(per cent)

Areas	Reaction on public budget		Total
	Yes	No	
Urban	35.3	64.7	100.0 (n=139)
Rural	9.3	90.7	100.0 (n=150)
Total	21.8	78.2	100.0 (n=289)

Source: ibid.
Note: χ^2 value = 28.42978, DF-1, significant level 0.00000

Table 8.17 Distribution of Respondents Who Did Not React to the Public Budget

(per cent)

Areas	Cause for not reacting		Total
	Ignorance of budget	Budget is not for the poor	
Urban	81.1	18.9	100.0 (n=90)
Rural	88.2	11.8	100.0 (n=136)
Total	85.4	14.6	100.0 (n=226)

Source: ibid.
Note: c^2 value = 2.20439, DF-1, significant level 0.13762

Table 8.18 Distribution of Respondents Responding to the Behavioural Impact After the Declaration of Budget

(per cent)

Areas	High price of commodities in market	Low price of commodities in market	Temporary crisis of commodities in market	No reaction observed	Total
Urban	33.8	-	1.4	64.7	100.0 (n=139)
Rural	5.3	0.7	3.3	90.7	100.0 (n=150)
Total	19.0	0.3	2.4	78.2	100.0 (n=289)

Source: ibid.

Table 9.1 Prevalence of Poverty in Bangladesh,1996

(Percentage of households)

Social class	Urban areas	Rural areas	Overall
Very poor	21	55	46
Moderate poor	51	20	27
Middle	19	14	16
Well-off	9	11	11
Poor	72	75	73
Non-poor	28	25	27
Overall	100	100	100

Source: PRA for Annual Budget Review, 1996

Note: 1. Moderate poor + Very poor

2. Non-poor = Middle + well-off

Table 9.2 Prevalence of Poverty in Urban Slums, 1996

(Percentage of households)

Social class	Slum 1 (Motaher)	Slum 2 (Titipara)	Overall
Very poor	19	23	21
Moderate poor	41	59	51
Middle	21	18	19
Well-off	19	-	9
Poor	60	82	72
Non-poor	40	18	28
Overall	100	100	100

Source: ibid.

Note: ibid.

Table 9.3 Prevalence of Poverty in Rural Areas, 1996

(Percentage of households)

Social class	Central part			Northern part			Overall		
	Prog. villages	Control villages	Total	Prog. villages	Control villages	Total	Prog. villages	Control villages	Total
Very poor	70	40	60	46	47	47	63	44	55
Moderate poor	10	29	17	29	22	25	15	25	20
Middle	13	17	15	7	20	14	12	18	14
Well-off	7	14	9	18	11	14	10	13	11
Poor	80	69	77	75	69	72	78	69	75
Non-poor	20	31	23	25	31	28	22	31	25
Overall	100	100	100	100	100	100	100	100	100

Source: ibid.

Note: ibid.

Table 9.4 Changes in the Population of the Poorest Households

Areas/Groups	Number		% of total		Change (%)
	1993	1996	1993	1996	1993-1996
OVERALL					
(n=80)					
Men	60.0	59.0	18.6	17.5	-1.6
Women	91.0	90.0	28.3	26.7	-1.0
Boys	100.0	107.0	31.1	31.7	7.0
Girls	70.0	81.0	21.8	24.0	15.7
Total	321.0	337.0	100.0	100.0	5.0
Family size	4.0	4.2	-	-	5.0
URBAN SLUMS					
(n=20)					
Men	10.0	10.0	14.5	13.5	0.0
Women	23.0	23.0	33.3	31.1	0.0
Boys	18.0	18.0	26.1	24.3	0.0
Girls	18.0	23.0	26.1	31.1	27.8
Total	69.0	74.0	100.0	100.0	7.2
Family size	3.5	3.7	-	-	5.7
RURAL AREAS					
(n=60)					
Men	50.0	49.0	19.8	18.6	-2.0
Women	68.0	67.0	26.9	25.4	-1.4
Boys	82.0	89.0	32.5	33.9	8.5
Girls	52.0	58.0	20.6	22.1	11.5
Total	252.0	263.0	100.0	100.0	4.4
Family size	4.2	4.4	-	-	4.8

Source: *Panel Survey for Annual Budget Review*, 1996

Table 9.5 Changes in the Population of the Poorest Households in Rural Areas

Areas/Groups	Central part				Northern part				Overall			
	Number		% of total		Number		% of total		Number		% of total	
	1993	1996	1993	1996	1993	1996	1993	1996	1993	1996	1993	1996
A. All villages			(n=30)				(n=30)				(n=60)	
Men	26.0	26.0	20.3	19.3	24	23	19.3	17.3	50	49	19.8	18.6
Women	34.0	33.0	26.5	25.0	34	34	27.4	25.9	68	67	26.9	25.4
Boys	41.0	44.0	32.0	33.3	41	45	33.1	34.3	82	89	32.5	33.8
Girls	27.0	29.0	21.1	21.9	25	29	20.1	22.1	52	58	20.6	22.1
Total	128.0	132.0	100.0	100.0	124	131	100.0	100.0	252	263	100.0	100.0
Family size	4.3	4.4	-	-	4.1	4.4	-	-	4.2	4.4	-	-
B. Programme villages												
B.I.FEE households			(n=10)				(n=10)				(n=20)	
Men	10.0	10.0	18.9	17.9	10	10	16.1	15.6	20	20	17.3	16.6
Women	13.0	13.0	24.5	23.2	11	11	17.7	17.1	24	24	20.9	20.0
Boys	21.0	22.0	39.7	39.2	29	31	46.7	48.4	50	53	43.4	44.1
Girls	9.0	11.0	16.9	19.6	12	12	19.3	18.8	21	23	18.2	16.1
Total	53.0	56.0	100.0	100.0	62	64	100.0	100.0	115	120	100.0	100.0
Family size	5.3	5.6	-	-	6.2	6.4	-	-	5.8	6.0	-	-
B.2.Non-FFF households			(n=10)				(n=10)				(n=20)	
Men	8.0	8.0	21.6	20.5	8	8	25.0	23.5	16	16	23.1	22.0
Women	11.0	11.0	29.8	28.2	12	12	37.5	35.2	23	23	33.3	31.5
Boys	11.0	13.0	29.8	33.3	7	7	21.9	20.5	18	20	26.0	27.3
Girls	7.0	7.0	18.9	17.9	5	7	15.6	20.5	12	14	17.3	19.1
Total	37.0	39.0	100.0	100.0	32	34	100.0	100.0	69	73	100.0	100.0
Family size	3.7	3.9	-	-	3.2	3.4	-	-	3.5	3.7	-	-
C. Control villages			(n=10)				(n=10)				(n=20)	
Men	8.0	8.0	21.0	21.6	6	5	20.0	15.1	14	13	20.5	18.5
Women	10.0	9.0	26.3	24.3	11	11	36.7	33.3	21	20	30.9	28.5
Boys	9.0	9.0	23.7	24.3	5	7	16.7	21.2	14	16	20.5	22.9
Girls	11.0	11.0	29.0	30.0	8	10	26.6	30.3	19	21	28.0	30.0
Total	38.0	37.0	100.0	100.0	30	33	100.0	100.0	68	70	100.0	100.0
Family size	3.8	3.7	-	-	3.0	3.3	-	-	3.4	3.5	-	-

Source: ibid.

Table 9.6 Changes in the Population of the Poorest Households in Urban Slums

Areas/Groups	Number		% of total	
	1993	1996	1993	1996
Urban slums (n=20)				
Men	10.0	10.0	14.5	13.5
Women	23.0	23.0	33.3	31.1
Boys	18.0	18.0	26.1	24.3
Girls	18.0	23.0	26.1	31.1
Total	69.0	74.0	100.0	100.0
Family size	3.5	3.7	-	-
Slum 1 (Motahar) (n=10)				
Men	8.0	8.0	21.6	19.0
Women	11.0	11.0	29.7	26.2
Boys	9.0	9.0	24.3	21.4
Girls	9.0	14.0	24.3	33.3
Total	37.0	42.0	-	-
Family size	3.7	4.2	-	-
Slum 2 (Titipara) (n=10)				
Men	2.0	2.0	6.2	6.2
Women	12.0	12.0	37.5	37.5
Boys	9.0	9.0	28.1	28.1
Girls	9.0	9.0	28.1	28.1
Total	32.0	32.0	-	-
Family size	3.2	3.2	-	-

Source: ibid.

Table 9.7 Changes in Earning Members of the Poorest Households in Urban Slums

Areas/Groups	Number		% of total	
	1993	1996	1993	1996
Urban Slums (n=20)				
Men	10.0	10.0	41.7	35.7
Women	10.0	10.0	41.7	35.7
Boys	4.0	6.0	16.7	21.4
Girls	-	2.0	-	7.1
Total	24.0	28.0	100.0	100.0
Family size	3.5	3.7	-	-
Dependency ratio	2.9	2.6	-	-
Slum 1 (Motahar) (n=10)				
Men	8.0	8.0	66.7	53.3
Women	2.0	1.0	16.7	6.7
Boys	2.0	4.0	16.7	26.7
Girls	-	2.0	-	13.3
Total	12.0	15.0	100.0	100.0
Family size	3.7	4.2	-	-
Dependency ratio	3.1	4.2	-	-
Slum 2 (Titipara) (n=10)				
Men	2.0	2.0	16.7	15.4
Women	8.0	9.0	66.7	69.2
Boys	3.0	2.0	16.7	15.4
Girls	-	-	-	-
Total	12.0	13.0	100.0	100.0
Family size	3.2	3.2	-	-
Dependency ratio	2.6	2.4	-	-

Source: ibid.

Table 9.8 Changes in Earning Members of the Poorest Households in Rural Areas

Areas/Groups	Central part				Northern part				Overall			
	Number		% of total		Number		% of total		Number		% of total	
	1993	1996	1993	1996	1993	1996	1993	1996	1993	1996	1993	1996
A. All villages												
Men	20.0	22.0	49.0	51.1	23.0	23.0	54.7	52.2	43.0	45.0	51.8	51.7
Women	9.0	9.0	22.0	21.0	9.0	11.0	21.4	25.0	18.0	20.0	22.0	22.9
Boys	11.0	11.0	27.0	25.6	10.0	10.0	24.0	22.7	21.0	21.0	25.3	24.1
Girls	1.0	1.0	2.4	2.3	-	-	-	-	1.0	1.0	1.2	1.1
Total	41.0	43.0	100.0	100.0	42.0	44.0	100.0	100.0	83.0	87.0	100.0	100.0
Earning members per Household	1.4	1.4	-	-	1.4	1.5	-	-	1.4	1.5	-	-
Dependency ratio	3.1	3.1	-	-	2.9	2.9	-	-	3.0	3.0	-	-
B. Programmes villages												
B.1.FEE households												
Men	8.0	8.0	53.3	53.3	10.0	10.0	58.8	58.8	18.0	18.0	56.2	56.2
Women	1.0	1.0	6.7	6.7	-	-	-	-	1.0	1.0	3.1	3.1
Boys	6.0	6.0	40.0	40.0	7.0	7.0	41.4	41.4	13.0	13.0	40.6	40.6
Girls	-	-	-	-	-	-	-	-	-	-	-	-
Total	15.0	15.0	100.0	100.0	17.0	17.0	100.0	100.0	32.0	32.0	100.0	100.0
Earning members per household	1.5	1.5	-	-	1.7	1.7	-	-	1.6	1.6	-	-
Dependency ratio	3.5	3.7	-	-	3.6	3.8	-	-	3.5	3.7	-	-
B.2.Non-FFF households												
Men	6.0	7.0	40.0	43.7	7.0	8.0	50.0	47.0	13.0	15.0	44.8	45.4
Women	4.0	4.0	26.7	25.0	5.0	7.0	35.7	41.1	9.0	11.0	31.0	33.4
Boys	4.0	4.0	26.7	25.0	2.0	2.0	14.2	11.7	6.0	6.0	20.6	18.1
Girls	1.0	1.0	6.7	6.2	-	-	-	-	1.0	1.0	3.4	3.0
Total	15.0	16.0	100.0	100.0	14.0	17.0	100.0	100.0	29.0	33.0	100.0	100.0
Earning members per household	1.5	1.6	-	-	1.4	1.7	-	-	1.5	1.7	-	-
Dependency ratio	2.4	2.7	-	-	2.3	2.0	-	-	2.3	2.2	-	-
C. Contorl villages												
Men	6.0	7.0	54.5	58.3	6.0	5.0	54.4	50.0	12.0	12.0	54.5	54.5
Women	4.0	4.0	36.3	33.3	4.0	4.0	36.3	40.0	8.0	8.0	36.3	36.3
Boys	1.0	1.0	9.0	8.3	1.0	1.0	9.0	10.0	2.0	2.0	9.0	9.0
Girls	-	-	-	-	-	-	-	-	-	-	-	-
Total	11.0	12.0	100.0	100.0	11.0	10.0	100.0	100.0	22.0	22.0	100.0	100.0
Earning members per household	1.1	1.2	-	-	1.1	1.0	-	-	1.1	1.1	-	-
Dependency ratio	3.4	3.0	-	-	2.7	3.3	-	-	3.0	3.1	-	-

Source: ibid.

Table 9.9 Changes in Average Nominal Wage Rate for Unskilled Wage Labourers

(Tk/day)

Sex/Age groups	Central part			Northern part			Rural areas			Urban areas		
	1993	1996	Change (%)	1993	1996	Change (%)	1993	1996	Change (%)	1993	1996	Change (%)
Men	26.0	27.3	5.0	22.3	25.6	14.8	24.0	26.4	10.0	66.1	73.9	11.8
Women	12.6	13.2	4.8	5.7	5.3	-7.0	9.1	8.8	-3.3	16.5	27.2	64.8
Boys	11.5	13.3	15.6	10.0	15.3	53.0	10.8	14.2	31.4	16.0	27.2	70.0
Girls	-	-	-	-	-	-	-	-	-	-	80.0	-
Average	18.5	20.1	8.6	15.8	18.2	15.2	17.1	19.1	11.7	35.8	46.1	28.7

Source: ibid.

Table 9.10 Contribution of the FFE Programme to the Income of FFE-Households, 1996

(Tk/day)

Types of income	Central part			Northern part			Rural areas		
	Contri-bution	Income	Share in income (%)	Contri-bution	Income	Share in income (%)	Contri-bution	Income	Share in income (%)
Per capita	0.97	7.4	13.1	0.67	7.4	9.1	0.81	7.4	10.9
Per household	5.42	32.7	16.6	4.28	32.3	32.3	4.85	32.5	14.9

Source: BBS and *Panel Survey for Annual Budget Review*, 1996

Note: 1. Instead of official allocation of 15 kgs of wheat per month/per student, an equivalent incom for 13 Kgs at the market price has been used because our field observation indicates that the beneficiaries actually receive on an average 13 kgs of wheat per month.

2. Tk. 9.88 and Tk. 12.51, the prices of wheat for the Central and Northern parts respectively, have been used to monetize the wheat actually received by the FFE households.

Source: BBS

Table 9.11 Changes in the Extent of Female-Headed Households

Areas/Groups	Year	No. of female-headed households
Overall	1993	25(31.2)
(n = 80)	1996	25(31.2)
Urban slums	1993	11 (55.0)
(n=20)	1996	11 (55.0)
Rural areas	1993	14(23.3)
(n= 60)	1996	14(23.3)

Source: *Panel Survey for Annual Budget Review*, 1996

Note: Figures in parentheses show percentage shares in total number of households.

Table 9.12A Changes in the Extent of Female-Headed Households in Rural Areas

Areas/Groups		Year	No. of female-headed households
		OVERALL	
A.	All villages	1993	14 (23.3)
	(n=60)	1996	14 (23.3)
B.	Programme villages		
	B.1 FFE hhs (n=20)	1993	1 (5.0)
		1996	1 (5.0)
	B.2 Non-FFE hhs (n=20)	1993	5 (25.0)
		1996	5 (25.0)
C.	Control villages	1993	8 (40.0)
	(Non-FFE hhs)(n=20)	1996	8 (40.0)
		CENTRAL PART	
A.	All villages	1993	7 (23.3)
	(n=30)	1996	7 (23.3)
B.	Programme villages		
	B.1 FFE hhs (n=10)	1993	1 (10.0)
		1996	1 (10.0)
	B.2 Non-FFE hhs (n=10)	1993	3 (30.0)
		1996	3 (30.0)
C.	Control villages	1993	3 (30.0)
	(Non-FFE hhs) (n=10)	1996	3 (30.0)
		NORTHERN PART	
A.	All villages	1993	7 (23.3)
	(n=30)	1996	7 (23.3)
B.	Programme villages		
	B.1 FFE hhs (n=10)	1993	-
		1996	-
	B.2 Non-FFE hhs (n=10)	1993	2 (20.0)
		1996	2 (20.0)
C.	Control villages	1993	5 (50.0)
	(Non-FFE hhs) (n=10)	1996	5 (50.0)

Source: ibid.

Note: ibid.

Table 9.12B Changes in the Extent of Female-Headed Households in Urban Slums

Areas/Groups	Year	No. of female-headed households
Urban slums	1993	11 (55.0)
(n =20)	1996	11 (55.0)
Slum 1 (Motahar)	1993	2 (20.0)
(n=10)	1996	2 (20.0)
Slum 2 (Titipara)	1993	9 (90.0)
(n=10)	1996	9 (90.0)

Source: ibid.

Note: ibid.

Table 9.13 Changes in the Number of Households Engaged in Begging

Areas/Groups	Year	No. of begging households	No. of family members				No. of earning members				Family size	Dependency ratio
			M	W	B	G	M	W	B	G		
A. Overall												
(n=80)	1993	5	4	6	2	5	4	3	-	-	3.4	2.4
	1996	5	4	6	3	6	4	3	-	-	3.8	2.7
B. Urban slums												
(n=20)	1993	-	-	-	-	-	-	-	-	-	-	-
	1996	-	-	-	-	-	-	-	-	-	-	-
C. Rural areas												
(n=60)	1993	5	4	6	2	5	4	3	-	-	3.4	2.4
	1996	5	4	6	3	6	4	3	-	-	3.8	2.7

Source: ibid.

Note: Dependency ratio = (all members) (all earning members). M= men, W= women, B= boy & G= girls

Table 9.14 Changes in the Number of Households Engaged in Begging in Rural Areas

Areas/Groups	Year	No. of begging households	No. of family members				No. of earning members				Family size	Dependency ratio
			M	W	B	G	M	W	B	G		
			OVER ALL									
A. All villages	1993	5	4	6	2	5	4	3	-	-	3.4	2.4
(n=60)	1996	5	4	6	3	6	4	3	-	-	3.8	2.7
B. Programme villages	1993	-	-	-	-	-	-	-	-	-	-	-
B.1 FFE hhs (n=20)	1996	-	-	-	-	-	-	-	-	-	-	-
B.2 Non-FFE hhs (n=20)	1993	1	2	2	2	1	2	-	-	-	7.0	3.5
1996	1	2	2	3	1	2	-	-	-	8.0	4.0	
C. Control villages	1993	4	2	4	-	4	2	3	-	-	2.5	2.0
(Non-FFE hhs) (n=20)	1996	4	2	4	-	5	2	3	-	-	2.8	2.2
			CENTRAL PART									
A. All villages												
(n=30)	1993	2	3	3	2	2	3	1	-	-	5.0	2.5
	1996	2	3	3	3	2	3	1	-	-	5.5	2.2
B. Programme village	1993	-	-	-	-	-	-	-	-	-	-	-
B.1 FFE hhs (n=10)	1996	-	-	-	-	-	-	-	-	-	-	-
B.2 Non-FFE hhs	1993	1	2	2	2	1	2	-	-	-	7.0	3.5
(n=10)	1996	1	2	2	3	1	2	-	-	-	8.0	4.0
C. Control villages	1993	1	1	1	-	1	1	1	-	-	3.0	2.0
(Non-FFE hhs) (n=10)	1996	1	1	1	-	1	1	1	-	-	3.0	1.5
			NORTHERN PART									
A. All villages	1993	3	1	3	-	3	1	2	-	-	2.3	2.3
(n=30)	1996	3	1	3	-	4	1	2	-	-	2.6	2.7
B. Programme village	1993	-	-	-	-	-	-	-	-	-	-	-
B.1 FFE hhs (n=10)	1996	-	-	-	-	-	-	-	-	-	-	-
B.2 Non-FFE hhs	1993	-	-	-	-	-	-	-	-	-	-	-
(n=10)	1996	-	-	-	-	-	-	-	-	-	-	-
C. Control villages	1993	3	1	3	-	3	1	2	-	-	2.3	2.3
(Non-FFE hhs) (n=10)	1996	3	1	3	-	4	1	2	-	-	2.6	2.7

Source: ibid.

Note: ibid.

Table 9.15 Changes in Sources of Income of the Poorest Households in Rural Areas

(Tk/day)

Areas/Groups		Labour sale	Agriculture	Livestock	Others	Total
			OVERALL			
All villages(n=60)	1993	1427.6	203.1	3.8	109.9	1744.4
		(81.8)	(11.6)	(0.2)	(6.2)	(100.0)
	1996	1632.1	194.4	17.3	109.9	1953.7
		(83.5)	(9.9)	(0.8)	(5.6)	(100.0)
Programme villages	1993	581.0	138.0	1.3	-	720.3
FFE households		(80.6)	(19.1)	(0.1)		(100.0)
(n=20)	1996	701.6	129.0	16.4	-	847.0
		(82.8)	(15.2)	(1.9)		(100.0)
Non-FFE	1993	480.0	35.0	2.4	37.0	554.4
households (n=20)		(86.5)	(6.3)	(0.4)	(6.6)	(100.0)
	1996	544.2	35.0	0.8	37.0	617.0
		(88.2)	(5.6)	(0.1)	(5.9)	(100.0)
Control villages	1993	366.3	30.1	-	73.3	470.0
(n=20)		(77.9)	(6.4)		(15.5)	(100.0)
	1996	387.0	30.6	-	73.3	441.0
		(87.7)	(6.9)		(16.6)	(100.0)
			CENTRAL PART			
All villages	1993	760.6	68.0	-	59.9	888.5
(n=30)		(85.6)	(7.6)		(6.7)	(100.0)
	1996	865.5	57.0	-	59.9	982.4
		(88.1)	(5.8)		(6.0)	(100.0)
Programme villages	1993	307.6	32.8	-	-	340.0
FFE households		(90.4)	(9.6)			(100.0)
(n=10)	1996	355.0	22.0	-	-	377.0
		(94.1)	(5.83)			(100.0)
Non-FFE	1993	240.0	35.0	-	36.6	312.0
households (n=10		(76.9)	(11.2)		(11.7)	(100.0)
	1996	267.5	35.0	-	36.6	340.0
		(78.6)	(10.2)		(10.7)	(100.0)
Control villages	1993	213.0	-	-	23.3	236.3
(n=10)		(90.1)			(9.8)	(100.0)
	1996	243.3	-	-	23.3	267.0
		(91.1)			(8.7)	(100.0)
			NORTHERN PART			
All villages	1993	667.0	135.1	3.8	50.0	855.9
(n=30)		(77.9)	(15.7)	(0.4)	(5.8)	(100.0)
	1996	766.6	137.4	17.3	50.0	971.3
		(78.9)	(14.1)	(1.7)	(5.8)	(100.0)
Programme villages	1993	273.3	105.2	1.3	-	379.8
FFE households		(71.9)	(27.6)	(0.3)		(100.0)
(n=10)	1996	346.6	106.8	16.4	-	469.8
		(73.7)	(22.7)	(0.3)		(100.0)
Non-FFE	1993	240.0	-	2.46	-	242.4
households (n=10)		(98.9)		(0.0)		(100.0)
	1996	276.7	-	0.8	-	277.5
		(99.7)		(0.2)		(100.0)
Control villages	1993	153.3	30.1	-	50.0	233.4
(n=10)		(65.6)	(12.9)		(21.4)	(100.0)
	1996	143.3	30.6	-	50.0	223.9
		(63.9)	(13.7)		(22.3)	(100.0)

Source: ibid.

Note: Figures in parentheses indicate percentage shares in total income.

Table 9.16 Changes in the Nominal Income of the Poorest Households in Rural Areas

(Tk/day)

Areas/Groups	Central part			Northern part			Overall		
	1993	1996	Change (%)	1993	1996	Change (%)	1993	1996	Change (%)
A. All villages		(n=30)			(n=30)			(n=60)	
1. Per capita	6.9	7.4	7.2	6.9	7.4	7.2	6.9	7.4	7.2
2. Per hh	29.6	32.7	10.5	28.5	32.3	13.4	29.0	32.5	12.0
3. Average family size	4.3	4.4	2.3	4.1	4.4	7.3	4.2	4.4	4.8
4. No. of earners per hh	1.4	1.4	0.0	1.4	1.5	7.1	1.4	1.5	7.1
B.1. Programme villages FFE hhs		(n=10)			(n=10)			(n=20)	
1. Per capita	6.4	6.7	4.7	6.1	7.3	19.7	6.2	7.1	14.5
2. Per household	34.0	37.7	10.8	37.9	47.0	24.0	36.0	42.3	17.5
3. Average family size	5.3	5.6	5.7	6.2	6.4	3.2	5.8	6.0	3.4
4. No. of earners per household	1.5	1.5	0.0	1.7	1.7	0.0	1.6	1.6	0.0
B.2. Non-FFE household		(n=10)			(n=10)			(n=20)	
1. Per capita	8.4	8.7	3.3	7.6	8.1	7.5	8.0	8.4	5.2
2. Per household	31.2	34.0	8.9	24.2	27.7	14.2	27.7	30.8	11.2
3. Average family size	3.7	3.9	5.4	3.2	3.4	6.2	3.5	3.7	5.7
4. No. of earners per household	1.5	1.6	6.7	1.4	1.7	21.4	1.5	1.7	13.3
C. Control villages		(n=10)			(n=10)			(n=20)	
1. Per capita	6.2	7.2	16.0	7.7	5.2	-32.2	6.9	6.3	-8.7
2. Per household	23.6	26.7	13.1	23.3	17.4	-25.4	23.5	22.0	-6.4
3. Average family size	3.8	3.7	-2.6	3.0	3.3	10.0	3.4	3.5	2.9
4. No. of earners per household	1.1	1.2	9.1	1.1	1.0	-9.0	3.0	3.1	3.3

Source: ibid.

Table 9.17 Changes in the Nominal Income of the Poorest Households in Urban Slums

(Tk/day)

Areas/Groups	Slum-1 (Motaher)			Slum-2 (Titipara)			Overall		
	1993	1996	Change (%)	1993	1996	Change (%)	1993	1996	Change (%)
1. Per capita	13.1	19.5	48.9	10.6	10.4	-1.9	11.9	18.6	30.5
2. Per household	48.4	81.8	69.0	34.0	33.5	-1.5	41.2	57.6	39.8
3. Average family size	3.7	4.2	13.5	3.2	3.2	0	3.5	3.7	5.7

Source: ibid.

Table 9.18 Changes in the Real Income of the Poorest Households in Rural Areas

(Rice in Kg/day)

Areas/Groups	Central part			Northern part			Overall		
	1993	1996	Change (%)	1993	1996	Change (%)	1993	1996	Change (%)
A. All villages									
i.Per Capita	0.8	0.7	-12.5	0.9	0.7	-22.2	0.9	0.7	-22.2
ii.Per household	3.5	3.1	-11.4	4.0	3.2	-20.0	3.7	3.1	-16.2
B. Prog. village									
B.I FFE hhs									
i. Per capita	0.7	0.6	-14.3	0.8	0.7	-12.5	0.8	0.7	-12.5
ii. Per hh	4.0	3.6	-10.0	5.4	4.7	-12.9	4.6	4.1	-10.9
B.2 Non-FFE hhs									
i. Per capita	1.0	0.8	-20.0	1.0	0.8	-20.0	1.0	0.8	-20.0
ii. Per hh	3.6	3.2	-11.1	3.4	2.7	-20.6	3.5	3.0	-14.3
C. Control village									
i. Per capita	0.7	0.6	-14.3	1.1	0.5	-54.5	0.8	0.6	-25.0
ii. Per hh	2.8	2.5	-10.7	3.3	1.7	-48.5	3.0	2.1	-30.0

Source: ibid.

Note: 1. Real income has been defined as the coarse rice equivalent wage.

2. For the prices of coarse rice, please refer to Table 11.20.

Table 9.19 Minimum Retail Price of Coarse Rice

(Tk/Kg)

Areas	1993 (30.6.93)	1996 (30.6.93)	Change (%)
Kishoregonj	8.5	10.5	24.2
Kurigram	7.0	10.0	43.0
Dhaka	8.62	11.50	33.4

Source: Directorate of Agriculture Marketing

Table 9.20 Changes in the Real Income of the Poorest Households in Urban Slums

(Rice in Kg/day)

Items	Slum-1 (Motaher)			Slum-2 (Titipara)			Overall		
	1993	1996	Change (%)	1993	1996	Change (%)	1993	1996	Change (%)
I. Per Capita	1.5	1.7	13.3	1.2	0.9	25.0	1.4	1.4	0.0
II. Per H.H	5.6	7.1	26.7	3.9	2.9	25.6	4.7	5.0	4.8

Source: *Panel Survey for Annual Budget Review,* 1996

Note: For definition of real wage, please see footnote in table 9.19

Table 9.21 Average Nominal Wage Rate for Unskilled Wage Labourers

(Tk/day)

Areas/Groups	Year	Total income from labour sale					Average nominal wage rate				
		Men	Women	Boys	Girls	Total	Men	Women	Boys	Girls	Total
A. Overall	1993	1630.3	329.9	290.9	-	2251.1	30.7	11.7	11.6	-	21.0
(n=80)	1996	1855.3	422.6	462.9	80.0	2820.8	33.7	14.1	17.1	26.6	24.5
B. Urban slums	1993	595.0	165.0	64.0	-	824.0	66.1	16.5	16.0	-	35.8
(n=20)	1996	665.0	245.0	163.0	80.0	1153.0	73.9	27.2	27.2	80.0	46.1
C. Rural areas	1993	1035.3	164.9	226.9	-	1427.2	24.0	9.1	10.8	-	17.2
(n=60)	1996	1190.3	177.6	299.9	-	1667.9	26.4	8.8	14.2	-	19.2

Source: ibid.

Note: Average nominal wage rate = Total wages earning members

Table 9.22 Average Nominal Wage Rate for Unskilled Wage Labourers in Urban Slums

(Tk/day)

Areas/Groups	Year	Total income from labour sale					Average nominal wage rate				
		Men	Women	Boys	Girls	Total	Men	Women	Boys	Girls	Total
A. Urban slums (n=20)	1993	595.0	165.0	64.0	-	824.0	66.1	16.5	16.0	-	35.8
	1996	665.0	245.0	163.0	80.0	1153.0	73.9	27.2	27.2	80.0	46.1
B. Slum 1 (Motahar) (n=10)	1993	445.0	30.0	9.0	-	484.0	55.6	15.0	4.5	-	40.3
	1996	625.0	50.0	63.0	80.0	818.0	78.1	50.0	15.7	80.0	58.4
C. Slum 2 (Titipara) (n=10)	1993	150.0	135.0	55.0	-	340.0	150.0	16.9	27.5	-	30.9
	1996	40.0	195.0	100.0	-	335.0	40.0	24.4	50.0	-	30.5

Source: ibid.

Note: ibid.

Table 9.23 Average Nominal Wage Rate in Rural Areas

(Tk/day)

Areas/Groups	Year	Total income from labour sale					Average nominal wage rate				
		Men	Women	Boys	Girls	Total	Men	Women	Boys	Girls	Total
OVERALL											
A. All villages	1993	1035.3	164.9	226.9	-	1427.2	24.0	9.1	10.8	-	17.2
	1996	1190.3	177.6	299.9	-	1667.9	26.4	8.8	14.2	-	19.2
B. Programme village B.1 FFE hhs	1993	430.0	13.3	136.6	-	579.9	23.8	13.3	10.5	-	18.1
	1996	503.0	15.0	183.3	-	701.3	27.9	15.0	14.1	-	21.9
B.2 Non-FFE hhs	1993	338.3	75.3	67.0	-	480.6	26.0	8.3	11.1	-	16.5
	1996	310.0	79.3	90.0	-	546.3	20.6	7.2	15.0	-	16.5
C. Programme village (Non-FFE hhs)	1993	267.0	76.3	23.3	-	366.6	22.2	9.5	11.6	-	16.6
	1996	310.3	83.3	26.6	-	420.2	25.8	10.4	13.3	-	19.1
CENTRAL PART											
A. All villages	1993	520.3	113.3	126.6	-	760.2	26.0	12.5	11.5	-	18.5
	1996	600.3	119.3	146.6	-	866.2	27.2	13.2	13.3	-	20.1
B. Programme village	1993	220.0	13.3	73.3	-	306.6	27.5	13.3	12.2	-	20.4
B.1. FFE hhs	1996	260.0	15.0	80.0	-	355.0	32.5	15.0	13.3	-	23.6
B.2 Non-FFE hhs	1993	153.3	47.0	40.0	-	240.3	25.5	11.7	10.0	-	17.1
	1996	170.0	48.0	50.0	-	268.0	24.2	12.0	12.5	-	17.7
C. Control village (Non-FFE hhs)	1993	147.0	53.0	13.3	-	213.3	24.5	13.2	13.3	-	19.3
	1996	170.3	56.6	16.6	-	243.2	24.3	14.0	16.6	-	20.2
NORTHERN PART											
A. All villages	1993	515.0	51.6	100.3	-	666.9	22.3	5.7	10.0	-	15.8
	1996	590.0	58.3	153.3	-	801.6	25.6	5.3	15.3	-	18.2
B. Programme village B.1 FFE hhs	1993	210.0	-	63.3	-	273.3	21.0	-	9.0	-	16.0
	1996	243.0	-	103.3	-	346.3	24.3	-	14.7	-	20.3
B.2 Non-FFE hhs	1993	185.0	28.3	27.0	-	240.3	26.4	5.6	13.5	-	17.1
	1996	203.0	31.3	40.0	-	278.3	25.8	4.4	20.0	-	18.5
C. Control village (Non FFE hhs)	1993	120.0	23.3	10.0	-	153.3	20.0	5.8	10.0	-	13.9
	1996	140.0	27.0	10.0	-	177.0	28.0	6.7	10.0	-	17.7

Source: ibid.

Note: ibid.

Table 9.24 Changes in the Average Real Wage Rate for Unskilled Wage Labourers

(Rice in Kg/day)

Sex/Age groups	Central part			Northern part			Rural areas			Urban areas		
	1993	1996	Change (%)	1993	1996	Change (%)	1993	1996	Change (%)	1993	1996	Change (%)
Men	3.1	2.6	-16.1	3.2	2.7	-15.6	3.1	2.6	-16.1	6.9	5.8	-15.9
Women	1.5	1.3	-13.3	0.8	0.5	-37.5	1.2	0.9	-25.0	1.9	2.1	10.5
Boys	1.4	1.3	-7.1	1.4	1.5	7.1	1.5	1.4	-6.7	1.9	2.4	26.3
Girls	-	-	-	-	-	-	-	-	-	-	3.5	-
Average	2.2	1.9	-13.6	2.3	1.8	-21.7	2.2	1.8	-18.2	3.9	3.6	-7.7

Source: ibid.

Note: For definition of real wage, please see footnote in Table 9.19

Table 9.25 Changes in Food (Rice and Wheat) Intake by the Poorest Households

(grams/day)

Items	Urban slums			Rural areas			Overall		
	1993	1996	Change (%)	1993	1996	Change (%)	1993	1996	Change (%)
1. Per capita	442.0	513.5	16.2	584.9	566.2	-3.2	554.2	554.6	-
2. Per adult equivalent units	598.0	703.7	17.7	796.8	785.8	-1.4	753.8	769.1	2.0
3. Per household	1525.0	1900.0	24.6	2456.7	2481.7	1.0	2223.8	2330.3	4.8
4. Average family size	3.5	3.7	5.7	4.2	4.4	4.7	4.0	4.2	5.0

Source: ibid.

Note: 1. Food = rice + wheat

2. Per adult equivalent unit: Two children = one adult

3. -=> Insignificant

Table 9.26 Changes in Food (Rice and Wheat) Intake by Members of the Poorest Households in Urban Slums

(grams/day)

Items	Slum 1 (Motaher)			Slum 2 (Titipara)			Overall		
	1993	1996	Change (%)	1993	1996	Change (%)	1993	1996	Change (%)
1. Per capita	452.7	547.6	20.9	429.7	468.7	9.1	442.0	513.5	16.2
2. Per adult equivalent units	598.2	741.9	24.0	597.8	652.1	9.1	598.0	703.7	17.7
3. Per household	1675.0	2300.0	37.3	1375.0	1500.0	9.1	1525.0	1900.0	24.6
4. Average family size	3.7	4.2	13.5	3.2	3.2	0	3.5	3.7	5.7

Source: ibid.

Note: ibid.

Table 9.27 Changes in Food (Rice and Wheat) Intake by Members of the Poorest Households in Rural Areas

(grams/day)

Items	Central part			Northern part			Overall		
	1993	1996	Change (%)	1993	1996	Change (%)	1993	1996	Change (%)
All villages		(n=30)			(n=30)			(n=60)	
1. Per capita	582.0	571.9	-1.7	587.9	560.3	-4.7	584.9	566.2	-3.2
2. Per adult equivalent unit	792.5	790.6	-0.2	801.1	780.9	-2.5	796.8	785.8	-1.4
3. Per household	2483.0	2516.7	1.4	2430.0	2446.7	0.7	2456.7	2481.7	1.0
4. Average family size	4.3	4.4	2.3	4.1	4.3	4.9	4.2	4.4	-4.7
B. Programme villages		(n=10)			(n=10)			(n=20)	
B.1. FFE hhs									
1. Per capita	603.7	589.3	-2.4	637.1	617.2	-3.1	621.7	604.2	-2.8
2. Per adult equivalent unit	842.1	835.4	-0.8	940.5	918.6	-2.3	899.4	884.1	-1.7
3. Per household	3200.0	3300.0	-3.1	3950.0	3950.0	-	3575.0	3625.0	1.4
4. Average family size	5.3	5.6	5.7	6.2	6.4	3.2	5.8	6.0	3.4
B.2 Non-FFE hhs		(n=30)			(n=30)			(n=60)	
1. Per capita	554.0	525.6	-5.1	578.1	544.1	-5.9	565.2	534.2	-5.5
2. Per adult equivalent unit	732.1	706.9	-3.4	711.5	685.2	-3.7	722.2	696.4	-3.6
3. Per household	2050.0	2050.0	-	1850.0	1850.0	0.0	1950.0	1950.0	0.0
4. Average family size	3.7	3.9	5.4	3.2	3.4	6.2	3.5	3.7	5.7
C. Control villages		(n=30)			(n=30)			(n=60)	
1. Per capita	578.9	594.6	2.7	497.6	466.5	6.2	542.9	557.1	2.6
2. Per adult equivalent unit	785.7	814.8	3.7	622.0	615.7	-1.0	710.0	750.0	5.6
3. Per household	2200.0	2200.0	0	1492.8	1539.4	3.1	1846.0	1870.0	1.3
4. Average family size	3.8	3.7	-2.6	3.0	3.3	10.0	3.4	3.5	2.9

Source: *Panel Survey for Annual Budget Review*, 1996

Note: 1. ibid.

2. '-' indicates insignificant.

Table 9.28 Percentage Distribution of Households of Food Availability Groups by Household Status

Food availability groups	Household status		
	Urban	Rural	Total
Chronic deficit	26.2	65.2	49.8
Occasional deficit	36.9	29.7	32.6
Break-even	27.2	3.8	13.0
Surplus	9.7	1.3	4.6
Total	100.0	100.0	100.0
	(n=103)	(n=158)	(n=261)

Source: *A Survey on Evaluation of Budget from the Perspective of Poverty*

Table 9.29 Shift in the Food Consumption Pattern of the Poorest Households in Rural Areas

(Kilogram)

Areas/Groups	Year	Central part			Northern part			Overall		
		Rice	Wheat	Total	Rice	Wheat	Total	Rice	Wheat	Total
			(n=30)			(n=30)			(n=60)	
A. All villages	1993	74.5	-	74.5	68.9	4.0	72.9	143.4	4.0	147.4
		(100.0)			(94.5)	(5.4)		(97.2)	(2.7)	
	1996	68.5	7.0	75.5	68.8	4.5	73.4	137.4	11.5	148.9
		(90.7)	(9.2)		(93.1)	(6.0)		(92.2)	(7.7)	
B. Programme villages			(n=10)			(n=10)			(n=20)	
B.1. FFE hhs										
	1993	32.0	-	32.0	36.5	3.0	39.5	68.5	3.0	71.5
		(100.0)			(92.4)	(7.5)		(95.8)	(4.1)	
	1996	27.0	6.0	33.0	36.5	3.0	39.5	63.5	9.0	72.5
		(81.8)	(18.1)		(92.4)	(7.5)		(87.5)	(12.4)	
B.2 Non-FFE hhs			(n=10)			(n=10)			(n=20)	
	1993	20.5	-	20.5	17.5	1.0	18.5	38.0	1.0	39.0
		(100.0)			(94.5)	(5.40)		(97.4)	(2.6)	
	1996	20.5	-	20.5	17.0	1.5	18.5	37.5	1.5	39.0
		(100.0)			(91.8)	(8.1)		(96.1)		
C. Control			(n=10)			(n=10)			(n=20)	
villages	1993	22.0	-	22.0	14.9	-	14.9	36.92	-	36.9
		(100.0)			(100.0)			(100.0)		
	1996	21.0	1.0	22.0	15.4	-	15.4	36.4	1.0	37.4
		(95.4)	(4.5)		(100.0)			(97.3)	(2.6)	

Source: *Panel Survey for Annual Budget Review*, 1996

Note: Figures in parentheses are percentage shares in total food consumed.

Table 9.30 Shift in the Food Consumption Pattern of the Poorest Households in Urban Slums

(Kilogram)

Slums	Year	Rice	Wheat	Total
Overall	1993	30.5	-	30.5
(n=20)		(100.0)		(100.0)
	1996	38.0	-	38.0
		(100.0)		(100.0)
Slum 1	1993	16.5	-	16.5
(Motahar)		(100.0)		(100.0)
(n=10)	1996	23.0	-	23.0
		(100.0)		(100.0)
Slum 2	1993	13.5	-	13.5
(Titipara)		(100.0)		(100.0)
(n=10)	1996	15.0	-	15.0
	-	(100.0)		(100.0)

Source: ibid.

Note: ibid.

Table 9.31 Changes in Average Food Intake by the Poorest Households in Rural Areas

(Frequency of food intake)

Areas/Groups	Year	Rice (daily)	Bread (daily)	Fish (monthly)	Meat (yearly)	Chicken (Yearly)	Egg (Monthly)	Milk (Monthly)	Veget. (daily)
				OVERALL					
A. All villages									
(n=60)	1993	2.6	0.1	5.9	2.4	1.1	1.0	0.7	2.1
	1996	2.4	0.3	5.6	2.2	0.8	1.0	0.6	2.0
B. Programme	1993	2.8	0.2	7.0	2.9	1.1	1.0	0.5	2.5
villages	1996	2.4	0.7	6.8	2.6	1.2	1.0	0.5	2.3
B.1 FFE hhs (n=20)									
B.2 Non-FFE	1993	2.4	0.1	6.3	2.4	0.8	1.1	1.5	2.3
hhs (n=20)	1996	2.4	0.1	6.2	2.3	0.8	1.0	1.4	2.1
C. Control villages	1993	2.6	-	4.3	2.1	1.6	1.0	-	1.7
(n=20)	1996	2.6	0.1	3.6	1.7	0.6	1.0	-	1.6
				CENTRAL PART					
A. All villages	1993	2.6	-	3.0	2.4	0.9	0.4	0.3	2.2
(n=30)	1996	2.2	0.4	2.6	2.0	0.4	0.3	0.2	2.0
B. Programme	1993	2.9	-	2.8	2.8	0.4	0.2	-	2.3
villages	1996	2.0	1.0	2.5	2.2	0.5	0.3	-	2.0
B.1 FFE hhs (n=10)	1993	2.4	-	2.4	2.0	0.4	0.8	0.8	2.3
B.2 Non-FFE1 hhs (n=10)	1996	2.3	-	2.2	1.7	0.4	0.6	0.6	2.0
C. Control villages									
(n=10) 1993	2.4	-	3.7	2.4	1.8	0.1	-	2.1	
	1996	2.3	0.1	3.2	2.1	0.2	0.1	-	2.0
				NORTHERN PART					
A All villages	1993	2.6	0.2	8.7	2.5	1.4	1.6	1.1	2.0
(n=30)	1996	2.6	0.2	8.4	2.3	1.3	1.6	1.1	2.0
B. Programme villages									
B. FFE hhs	1993	2.7	0.3	11.1	2.9	1.8	1.7	1.0	2.6
(n=10)	1996	2.7	0.3	11.1	2.9	1.8	1.7	1.0	2.6
B.2 Non-FFE	1993	2.4	0.2	10.3	2.8	1.1	1.4	2.2	2.2
hhs (n=10)	1996	2.4	0.2	10.3	2.8	1.1	1.4	2.2	2.2
C. Control villages									
(n=10)	1993	2.8	-	4.8	1.7	1.3	1.8	-	1.3
	1996	2.8	-	4.0	1.3	1.0	1.8	-	1.2

Source: ibid.

Table 9.32 Average Food Intake by the Poorest Households in Urban Slums

Areas/Groups	Year	Rice (daily)	Bread (daily)	Fish (monthly)	Meat (yearly)	Chicken (yearly)	Egg (monthly)	Milk (monthly)	Veget. (daily)
Urban slums	1993	2.6	-	4.6	1.3	-	0.4	0.2	2.5
(n=20)	1996	2.5	-	4.6	1.3	-	0.4	0.2	2.4
Slum-1(Motahar)	1993	3.0	-	8.1	1.5	-	0.9	0.4	2.7
(n=10)	1996	2.9	-	8.1	1.5	-	0.9	0.4	2.7
Slum-2 (Titipara)	1993	2.2	-	1.0	1.0	-	-	-	2.2
(n=10)	1996	2.1	-	1.0	1.0	-	-	-	2.0

Source: ibid.

Table 9.33 Average Food Intake by the Poorest Households

Areas/Groups	Year	Rice (daily)	Bread (daily)	Fish (monthly)	Meat (yearly)	Chicken (yearly)	Egg (monthly)	Milk (monthly)	Veget. (daily)
Overall	1993	2.6	0.1	5.6	2.1	0.4	0.8	0.5	2.2
(n=80)	1996	2.4	0.0	5.4	2.0	0.0	0.8	1.6	2.1
Urban slums	1993	2.6	-	4.6	1.3	-	0.4	0.2	2.5
(n=20)	1996	2.5	-	4.6	1.3	-	0.4	0.2	2.4
Rural areas	1993	2.6	0.1	5.9	2.4	1.1	1.0	0.7	2.1
(n=60)	1996	2.4	0.3	5.6	2.2	0.8	1.0	0.6	2.0

Source: ibid.

Table 9.34 Changes in Housing Conditions of the Poorest Households

(Number of households)

Areas/Groups	Year	Structure of houses						No. of rooms			
		A	B	C	D	E	F	One	Two	Three	Four
							OVERALL				
Overall (n=80)	1993	-	-	-	-	8	72	72	6	2	-
						(10.0)	(90.0)	(90.0)	(8.0)	(3.0)	
	1996	-	-	-	-	12	68	70	7	3	-
						(15.0)	(85.0)	(88.0)	(9.0)	(4.0)	
Urban slums (N=20)	1993	-	-	-	-	-	20	19	1	-	-
								(100.0)	(95.0)	(5.0)	
	1996	-	-	-	-	-	20	19	1	-	-
							(100.0)	(95.0)	(5.0)		
Rural areas (n=60)	1993	-	-	-	-	8	52	53	5	2	-
						(13.0)	(87.0)	(88.0)	(8.0)	(3.0)	
	1996	-	-	-	-	12	48	51	6	3	-
						(20.0)	(80.0)	(85.0)	(10.0)	(5.0)	

Source: ibid.

Note: 1. Figures in parentheses are percentage shares in total number of households

2. Types of houses and its construction materials

Type:	A	B	C	D	E	F
Wall:	Brick	Brick	Brick	C.I. Sheet	Straw/Muds	Straw/Muds
Roof:	Cement	C.I. Sheet/tile	Straw	C.I. Sheet	C.I. Sheet	Straw

Table 9.35 Changes in Housing Conditions of the Poorest Households in Rural Areas

(Number of households)

Areas/Groups	Year	Structure of houses						No. of rooms			
		A	B	C	D	E	F	One	Two	Three	Four
						OVERALL					
A. All villages (n=60)	1993	-	-	-	-	8(13.0)	52(87.0)	53(88.0)	5(8.0)	2(3.0)	-
	1996	-	-	-	-	12(20.0)	48(80.0)	51(85.0)	6(10.0)	3(5.0)	-
B. Programme villages	1993	-	-	-	-	4(20.0)	16(80.0)	15(75.0)	4(20.0)	1(5.0)	-
B.1. FFE hhs (n=20)	1996	-	-	-	-	7(35.0)	13(65.0)	13(65.0)	5(25.0)	2(10.0)	-
B.2. Non-FFE hhs	1993	-	-	-	-	-	20(100.0)	19(95.0)	1(5.0)	-	-
(n=20)	1996	-	-	-	-	1(5.0)	19(95.0)	19(95.0)	1(5.0)	-	-
Control villages	1993	-	-	-	-	4(20.0)	16(80.0)	19(95.0)	-	1(5.0)	-
(Non-FFE hhs) (n=20)	1996	-	-	-	-	4(20.0)	16(80.0)	19(95.0)	-	1(5.0)	-
						CENTRAL PART					
A. All villages	1993	-	-	-	-	8(27.0)	22(73.0)	30(100.0)	-	-	-
(n=30)	1996	-	-	-	-	9(30.0)	21(70.0)	30(100.0)	-	-	-
B. Programme villages	1993	-	-	-	-	4(40.0)	6(60.0)	10(100.0)	-	-	-
B.1. FFE hhs (n=10)	1996	-	-	-	-	5(50.0)	5(50.0)	10(100.0)	-	-	-
B.2. Non-FFE hhs	1993	-	-	-	-	-	10(100.0)	10(100.0)	-	-	-
(n=10)	1996	-	-	-	-	-	10(100.0)	10(100.0)	-	-	-
C. Control villages (Non-FFE hhs)	1993	-	-	-	-	4(40.0)	6(60.0)	10(100.0)	-	-	-
(n-10)	1996	-	-	-	-	4(40.0)	6(60.0)	10(100.0)	-	-	
						NORTHERN PART					
All villages (n=30)	1993	-	-	-	-	-	30(100.0)	23(77.0)	5(17.0)	2(7.0)	-
	1996	-	-	-	-	3(10.0)	27(90.0)	21(70.0)	6(21.0)	3(10.0)	-
B. Programme villages	1993	-	-	-	-	-	10(100.0)	5(50.0)	4(40.0)	1(10.0)	-
B.1. FFE hhs (n=10)	1996	-	-	-	-	2(20.0)	8(80.0)	3(30.0)	5(50.0)	2(20.0)	-
B.2. Non-FFE hhs	1993	-	-	-	-	-	10(100.0)	9(90.0)	1(10.0)	-	-
(n=10)	1996	-	-	-	-	1(10.0)	9(90.0)	9(90.0)	1(10.0)	-	-
C. Control villages (Non-FFE hhs)	1993	-	-	-	-	-	10(100.0)	9(90.0)	-	1(10.0)	-
(n-10)	1996	-	-	-	-	-	10(100.0)	9(90.0)	-	1(10.0)	-

Source: ibid.

Note: ibid.

Table 9.36 Changes in Housing Conditions of the Poorest Households in Urban Slums

(Number of households)

Areas/Groups	Year	Structure of houses						No. of rooms			
		A	B	C	D	E	F	One	Two	Three	Four
Overall (n=20)	1993	-	-	-	-	-	20	19	1	-	-
							(100.0)	(95.0)	(5.0)		
	1996	-	-	-	-	-	20	19	1	-	-
							(100.0)	(95.0)	(5.0)		
Slum=1	1993	-	-	-	-	-	10	9	1	-	-
(Motahar)							(100.0)	(90.0)	(10.0)		
(n=10)	1996	-	-	-	-	-	10	9	1	-	-
							(100.0)	(90.0)	(10.0)		
Slum-2	1993	-	-	-	-	-	10	10	-	-	-
(Titipara)							(100.0)	(100.0)			
(n=10)	1996	-	-	-	-	-	10	10	-	-	-
						(100.0)	(100.0)				

Source: ibid.
Note: ibid.

Table 9.37 Changes in Overcrowding in the Poorest Households in Rural Areas

(Number of inmates per room)

Areas/Groups		Central part (n=30)			Northern part (n=30)			Overall (n=60)		
		1993	1996	Change (%)	1993	1996	Change (%)	1993	1996	Change (%)
A.	All villages	4..3	4.4	2.3	3.2	3.1	-3.1	3.7	3.7	0.0
B.	Programme villages.									
	B.1 FFE hhs	5.3	5.6	5.7	3.9	3.4	-12.8	4.4	4.1	-6.8
	B.2 Non-FFE hhs	3.7	3.9	5.4	2.9	3.1	6.9	3.3	3.5	6.1
C.	Control villages									
	(Non -FFE hhs)	3.8	3.7	-2.6	2.5	2.8	12.0	3.1	3.2	3.2

Source: ibid.

Table 9.38 Changes in Overcrowding in the Poorest Households in Urban Slums

(Number of inmates per room)

Areas/Groups	1993	1996	Change (%)
Urban slums (n=20)	3.3	3.5	6.4
Slum 1 (Motahar)			
(n=10)	3.4	3.8	11.8
Slum 2 (Titipara)			
(n=10)	3.2	3.2	0.0

Source: ibid.

Table 9.39 Changes in Types of Fuel Used for Cooking and Lighting in Rural Areas

(Number of households)

Areas/Groups	Year	Types of fuel used for cooking: Electricity	Fire wood	Dry leaves	Cow-dung	Others	Types of lighting: Electricity	Kerosene lamp (covered)	Kerosene lamp (uncovered)
OVERALL									
A. All villages (n=60)	1993	-	6 (10.0)	59 (98.3)	20 (33.3)	-	-	-	60 (100.0)
	1996	-	7 (11.7)	59 (98.3)	20 (33.3)	-	-	-	60 (100.0)
B. Programme villages	1993	-	-	20 (100.0)	7 (35.0)	-	-	-	20 (100.0)
B.1. FFE hhs (n=20)	1996	-	1(5.0)	20 (100.0)	7 (35.0)	-	-	-	20 (100.0)
B.2. Non-FFE hhs (n=20)	1993	-	2(10.0)	20 (100.0)	8 (40.0)	-	-	-	20 (100.0)
	1996	-	2 (10.0)	20 (100.0)	8 (40.0)	-	-	-	20 (100.0)
C. Control villages (Non-FFE hhs) (n-20)	1993	-	4 (20.0)	19 (95.0)	5 (25.0)	-	-	-	20 (100.0)
	1996	-	4 (20.0)	19 (95.0)	5 (25.0)	-	-	-	20 (100.0)
CENTRAL PART									
A. All villages (n=30)	1993	-	2(6.7)	29 (96.7)	2 (6.7)	-	-	-	30 (100.0)
	1996	-	3(10.0)	29 (96.7)	2 (6.7)	-	-	-	30 (100.0)
B Programme villages	1993	-	-	10 (100.0)	1 (10.0)	-	-	-	10 (100.0)
B.1. FFE hhs (n=10)	1996	-	1 (10.0)	10 (100.0)	1 (10.0)	-	-	-	10 (100.0)
B.2.Non-FFE hhs (n=10)	1993	-	2 (20.0)	10 (100.0)	-	-	-	-	10 (100.0)
	1996	-	2 (20.0)	10 (100.0)	-	-	-	-	10 (100.0)
C. Control villages (Non-FFE hhs) (n-10)	1993	-	-	9 (90.0)	1 (10.0)	-	-	-	10 (100.0)
	1996	-	-	9 (90.0)	1 (10.0)	-	-	-	10 (100.0)
NORTHERN PART									
All villages (n=30)	1993	-	4 (13.3)	30 (100.0)	18 (60.0)	-	-	-	30 (100.0)
	1996	-	4 (13.3)	30 (100.0)	18 (60.0)	-	-	-	30 (100.0)
B. Programme villages	1993	-	-	10 (100.0)	6 (60.0)	-	-	-	10 (100.0)
B.1. FFE hhs (n=10)	1996	-	-	10 (100.0)	6 (60.0)	-	-	-	10 (100.0)
B.2.Non-FFE hhs (n=10)	1993	-	-	10 (100.0)	8 (80.0)	-	-	-	10 (100.0)
	1996	-	-	10 (100.0)	8 (80.0)	-	-	-	10 (100.0)
C Control villages (Non-FFE hhs) (n-10)	1993	-	4 (40.0)	10 (100.0)	4 (40.0)	-	-	-	10 (100.0)
	1996	-	4 (40.0)	10 (100.0)	4 (40.0)	-	-	-	10 (100.0)

Source: ibid.

Note: Figures in parentheses are percentages of total households.

Table 9.40 Changes in Types of Fuel Used for Cooking and Lighting in Urban Slums

(Number of households)

Area/Group	Year	Types of fuel used for cooking: Electricity	Fire wood	Dry leaves	Cow-dung	Others	Types of lighting: Electricity	Kerosene lamp (covered)	Kerosene lamp (uncovered)
Urban slums	1993	-	10	-	-	10	-	-	20
(n=20)		(50.0)			(50.0)			(100.0)	
	1996	-	10	-	-	10	-	-	20
			(50.0)			(50.0)			(100.0)
Slum-1 (Motahar)	1993	-	10	-	-	-	-	-	10
(n=10)		(100.0)						(100.0)	
	1996	-	10	-	-	-	-	-	10
			(100.0)						(100.0)
Slum-2 (Titipara)	1993	-	-	-	-	10	-	-	10
(n=10)					(100.0)			(100.0)	
	1996	-	-	-	-	10	-	-	10
						(100.0)			(100.0)

Source: ibid.

Note: ibid.

Table 9.41 Changes in the Asset (Land) Profile of the Poorest Households in Rural Areas

(Decimal)

Areas/Group samples	Year	No. of hhs owning land: Agri	HS	Total amount of land owned: Agri	HS	Total	Average size of landholding: Agri	HS	Size of land per household: Agri	HS	Total
OVERALL											
A. All villages (n=60)	1993	10	49	682	332.5	1014.5	68.2	6.8	11.4	5.5	16.9
	1996	10	49	637	332.5	969.5	63.7	6.8	10.6	5.5	16.2
B. Programme villages											
B.1 FFE hhs (n=20)	1993	5	16	471	214.5	685.5	94.2	13.4	23.6	10.7	34.3
	1996	5	16	471	214.5	685.5	94.2	13.4	23.6	10.7	34.3
B.2 Non-FFE hhs (n=20)	1993	2	16	105	82.0	187.0	52.5	5.1	5.3	4.1	9.4
	1996	2	16	105	82.0	187.0	52.5	5.1	5.3	4.1	9.4
C. Control villages (Non-FFE hhs) (n=20)	1993	3	17	106	36.0	142.0	35.3	2.1	5.3	1.8	7.1
	1996	3	17	61	36.0	97.0	20.3	2.1	3.1	1.8	4.9
CENTRAL PART											
A. All villages (n=30)	1993	3	22	280	76.0	356.0	93.3	3.4	9.3	2.5	11.8
	1996	3	22	280	76.0	356.0	93.3	3.4	9.3	2.5	11.8
B. Programme villages											
B.1 FFE hhs (n=10)	1993	1	7	175	41.5	216.5	175.0	5.9	17.5	4.2	21.6
	1996	1	7	175	41.5	216.5	175.0	5.9	17.5	4.2	21.6
B.2 Non-FFE hhs (n=10)	1993	2	8	105	22.0	127.0	52.5	2.7	10.5	2.2	12.7
	1996	2	8	105	22.0	127.0	52.5	2.7	10.5	2.2	12.7
C. Control villages (Non-FFE hhs) (n=10)	1993	-	7	-	12.5	12.5	-	1.7	-	1.3	1.2
	1996	-	7	-	12.5	12.5	-	1.7	-	1.3	1.2
NORTHERN PART											
A. All villages (n=30)	1993	7	27	402	256.5	658.5	57.4	9.5	13.4	8.6	21.9
	1996	7	27	357	256.5	613.5	51.0	9.5	11.9	8.6	20.4
B. Programme villages											
B.1 FFE hhs (n=10)	1993	4	9	296	173.0	469.0	74.0	19.2	29.5	17.3	46.9
	1996	4	9	296	173.0	469.0	74.0	19.2	29.5	17.3	46.9
B.2 Non FFE hhs (n=10)	1993	-	8	-	60.0	60.0	-	7.5	-	6.0	6.0
	1996	-	8	-	60.0	60.0	-	7.5	-	6.0	6.0
C. Control villages (Non FFE hhs) (n=10)	1993	3	10	106	23.5	129.5	35.3	2.4	10.6	2.3	12.9
	1996	3	10	61	23.5	84.5	20.3	2.4	10.6	2.3	8.4

Source: ibid.

Note: Agri = Agriculture; HS = Homestead

Table 9.42 Changes in the Asset (Livestock) Profile of the Poorest Households in Rural Areas

Areas/Groups	Year	Cow		Goat		Duck		Chicken	
		No. of cows	No. of hhs	No. of goats	No. of hhs	No. of ducks	No. of hhs	No. of chickens	No. of hhs
OVERALL									
All villages (n=60)	1993	8	4 (6.7)	10	6 (10.0)	11	3 (5.0)	21	5 (8.3)
	1996	9	5 (8.3)	7	4 (6.7)	11	5 (8.3)	24	13 (21.7)
B. Programme villages	1993	5	2 (10.0)	2	1 (5.0)	10	2 (10.0)	7	2 (10.0)
B.1. FFE hh (n=20)	1996	7	3 (15.0)	1	1 (5.0)	10	4 (20.0)	13	6 (30.0)
B.2. Non-FFE hh (n=20)	1993	1	1 (5.0)	3	3 (15.0)	1	1 (5.0)	6	1 (5.0)
	1996	1	1(5.0)	1	1 (5.0)	1	1 (5.0)	6	4 (20.0)
Control villages (Non-FFE hhs)	1993	2	1 (5.0)	5	2 (10.0)	-	-	8	2 (10.0)
(n-20)	1996	1	1 (5.0)	5	2 (10.0)	-	-	5	3 (15.0)
CENTRAL PART									
A. All villages (n=30)	1993	-	-	-	-	-	-	-	-
	1996	1	1 (3.3)	1	1 (3.3)	4	2 (6.7)	6	4 (13.3)
B. Programme villages	1993	-	-	-	-	-	-	-	-
B.1. FFE hhs (n=10)	1996	1	1 (10.0)	1	1 (10.0)	4	2 (20.0)	6	3 (30.0)
B.2. Non-FFE hhs	1993	-	-	-	-	-	-	-	-
(n=10)	1996	-	-	-	-	-	-	-	-
C. Control villages	1993	-	-	-	-	-	-	-	-
(Non-FFE hhs) (n-10)	1996	-	-	-	-	-	-	1	1 (10.0)
NORTHERN PART									
A. All villages (n=30)	1993	8	4 (13.3)	10	6 (20.0)	11	3 (10.0)	21	5 (16.7)
	1996	8	4 (13.3)	6	3 (10.0)	7	3 (10.0)	18	9 (30.0)
B. Programme villages	1993	5	2 (20.0)	2	1 (10.0)	10	2 (20.0)	7	2 (20.0)
B.1. FFE hhs (n=10)	1996	6	2 (20.0)	-	-	6	2 (20.0)	7	3 (30.0)
B.2. Non-FFE hhs (n=10)	1993	1	1 (10.0)	3	3 (30.0)	1	1 (10.0)	6	1 (10.0)
	1996	1	1 (10.0)	1	1 (10.0)	1	1 (10.0)	6	4 (40.0)
C. Control villages	1993	2	1 (10.0)	5	2 (20.0)	-	-	8	2 (20.0)
(Non-FFE hhs) (n-10)	1996	1	1 (10.0)	5	2 (20.0)	-	-	5	2 (20.0)

Source: ibid.

Note: Figures in parentheses show percentages of total hhs

Table 9.43 Changes in the Buying and Selling of Assets by the Poorest Households in Rural Areas

(Number of households)

Areas/Groups	Year	Utensils		Rickshaw		Rickshaw van		Bicycle		Cow		Radio		Plough		Consumer goods		Producer goods	
		B	S	B	S	B	S	B	S	B	S	B	S	B	S	B	S	B	S
(1)	(2)	(3)	(4)	(5)	(6)	(7)	(8)	(9)	(10)	(11)	(12)	(13)	(14)	(15)	(16)	(17)	(18)	(19)	(20)
OVER ALL																			
A. All villages (n=60)	1993	39 (65.0)	-	-	-	-	-	-	-	-	-	-	-	-	-	39 (65.0)	-	-	-
	1996	21 (35.0)	2 (3.3)	2 (3.3)	-	1 (1.7)	2 (3.3)	-	-	-	2 (3.3)	-	-	-	-	21 (35.0)	2 (3.3)	3 (5.0)	6 (10.0)
B. Programme villages	1993	9	-	-	-	-	-	-	-	-	-	-	-	-	-	9 (45.0)	(45.0)	-	
B.1 FFE hhs (n=20)	1996	9 (45.0)	1 (5.0)	1 (5.0)	-	-	-	-	-	-	1 (5.0)	-	-	-	-	9 (45.0)	-	1 (5.0)	2 (10.0)
B.2 Non FFE hhs (n=20)	1993	11																	
	1996	3 (15.0)	-	1 (5.0)	-	1 (5.0)	1 (5.0)	-	-	-	-	-	-	-	-	3 (15.0)	-	2 (10.0)	1 (5.0)
C. Control villages (Non FFE hhs)	1993	19 (9.50)	-	-	-	-	-	-	-	1 (5.0)	-	-	-	-	-	19 (9.50)	-	1 (5.0)	1 (5.0)
(n=20)	1996	9 (45.0)	1 (5.0)	-	-	-	1 (5)	-	-	-	1 (5.0)	-	-	-	-	9 (45.0)	1 (5)	1 (5.0)	1 (5.0)
CENTRAL PART																			
A. All villages (n=30)	1993	20 (66.7)	-	-	-	-	-	-	-	-	-	-	-	-	-	20 (66.7)	-	-	-
	1996	9 (30.0)	2 (6.7)	1 (3.3)	-	-	1 (3.3)	-	-	-	-	-	-	-	-	9 (30.0)	2 (6.7)	1 (3.3)	3 (10.0)
B. B. Programme villages	1993	5 (50.0)	-	-	-	-	-	-	-	-	-	-	-	-	-	5 (50.0)	-	-	-
B.1 FFE hhs (n=10)	1996	7 (70.0)	1 (10.0)	1 (10.0)	-	-	-	-	-	-	-	-	-	-	-	7 (70.0)	1 (10.0)	1 (10.0)	1 (10.0)
B.2 Non FFE hhs (n=10)	1993	6 (60.0)	-	-	-	-	-	-	-	-	-	-	-	-	-	6 (60.0)	-	-	-
	1996	1 (10.0)	-	-	-	-	-	-	-	-	-	-	-	-	-	1 (10.0)	-	-	-

(Contd.)

(Continued)

Areas/Groups	Year	Utensils B	Utensils S	Rickshaw B	Rickshaw S	Rickshaw van B	Rickshaw van S	Bicycle B	Bicycle S	Cow B	Cow S	Radio B	Radio S	Plough B	Plough S	Consumer goods B	Consumer goods S	Producer goods B	Producer goods S
(1)	(2)	(3)	(4)	(5)	(6)	(7)	(8)	(9)	(10)	(11)	(12)	(13)	(14)	(15)	(16)	(17)	(18)	(19)	(20)
C. Control villages (Non-FFE hhs)	1993	9 (90.0)	-	-	-	-	-	-	-	-	-	-	-	-	-	9 (90.0)	-	-	-
(n=10)	1996	1 (10.0)	1 (10.0)	-	-	-	1 (10.0)	-	-	-	-	-	-	-	-	1 (10.0)	1 (10.0)	1 (10.0)	-
NORTHERN PART																			
A. All villages (n=30)	1993	19 (63.3)	-	-	-	-	-	-	-	-	-	-	-	-	-	19 (63.3)	-	-	-
	1996	12 (40.0)	-	1 (3.3)		1 (3.3)	1 (3.3)		-	-	2 (6.7)	-	-	-	-	12 (40.0)	-	2 (6.7)	3 (10.0)
B. Programme villages	1993 (40.0)	4	-	-	-	-	-	-	-	-	-	-	-	-	- (40.0)	4	-	-	-
B.1 FFE hhs (n=10)	1996	2 (20.0)	-	-	-	-	-	-	-	-	1 (10.0)	-	-	-	:	2 (20.0)	-	-	1 (10.0)
B.2 Non FFE hhs (n=10)	1993	5 (50.0)	-	-	-	-	-	-	-	-	-	-	-	-	-	5 (50.0)	-	-	-
	1996	2 (20.0)	-	1 (10.0)	-	1 (10.0)	1 (10.0)	-	-	-	-	-	-	-	-	2 (20.0)	-	2 (20.0)	1 (10.0)
C. Control villages (Non FFE hhs) (n=10)	1993	10 (100.0)								1 (10.0)						10 (100.0)	-	1 (10.0)	-
		8 (80.0)									1 (8.0)					8 (80.0)	-	-	1 (10.0)

Source: ibid.

Note: 1. Figures in parentheses show percentages of total households

2. B= buying, S= selling

Table 9.44 Changes in the Buying and Selling of Assets by the Poorest Households in Urban Slums

(Number of households)

Areas/Groups	Year	Utensils		Rickshaw		Rickshaw Van		Bicycle		Cow		Radio		Plough		Consumer goods		Producer goods	
		B	S	B	S	B	S	B	S	B	S	B	S	B	S	B	S	B	S
Urban slums(n=20)	1993	15	-	-	-	-	-	-	-	-	-	-	-	-	-	15	-	-	-
		(75.0)														(75.0)			
	1996	8	-	4	-	-	-	-	-	-	-	-	-	-	-	8	-	4	-
		(40.0)		(20.0)												(40.0)		(20.0)	
Slum-1(Motahar)(n=10)	1993	10	-	-	-	-	-	-	-	-	-	-	-	-	-	10	-	-	-
		(100.0)														(100.0)			
	1996	8(80.0)	-	4	-	-	-	-	-	-	-	-	-	-	-	8	-	4	-
				(40.0)												(80.0)		(40.0)	
Slum-2 (Titipara)(n=10)	1993	5	-	-	-	-	-	-	-	-	-	-	-	-	-	5	-	-	-
		(50.0)														(50.0)			
	1996	-	-	-	-	-	-	-	-	-	-	-	-	-	-	-	-	-	-

Source: ibid.

Note: ibid.

Table 9.45 Changes in the Volume of Credit Classified by Purpose and Source for the Poorest Borrowers

(Taka)

Areas/Groups	Year	Purpose of credit								Source of credit				No of	Volume	Volume
		Business	Con-sumption	Agricul-ture	Repair-ing houses	Purchase of rickshaw/ rush cart	Repay-ment of loan	Health	Total	Money lender	Friend	NGO	Total	borrowers (gross)	of credit per bor-rower	of credit per hh
Overall (n=80)	1993	-	19000	4000	500	-	-	8500	32000	26700	5300	-	32000	19	1684.2	400.0
			(60.3)	(12.6)	(1.5)			(26.9)	(100.0)	(84.8)	(16.9)		(16.9)			
	1996	-	44050	25000	12100	22000	500	31100	134750	75800	22950	36000	134750	36	3743.1	1684.3
			(33.9)	(18.6)	(8.9)	(23.0)	(0.3)	(22.0)	(100.0)	(56.2)	(17.6)	(26.8)	(100.0)			
Urban slums	1993	-	5000	-	-	-	-	8500	13500	13500	-	-	13500	3	4500.0	675.0
(n=20)			(38.4)					(65.3)	(100.0)	(100.0)			(100.0)			
	1996	-	2400	-	5600	21000	-	2700	31700	13000	700	18000	31700	10	3170.0	1585.0
			(12.3)		(18.0)	(66.2)		(4.0)	(100.0)	(41.1)	(2.2)	(57.0)	(100.0)			
Rural areas	1993	-	14000	4000	500	-	-	-	18500	13200	5300	-	18500	16	1156.3	308.3
(n=60)			(75.6)	(21.6)	(2.7)				(100.0)	(71.3)	(28.6)		(100.0)			
	1996	-	41650	25000	6500	1000	500	28400	103050	62800	22250	18000	103050	26	3963.5	1717.5
			(40.4)	(24.2)	(6.3)	(0.9)	(27.6)	(27.6)	(100.0)	(60.9)	(21.6)	(17.5)	(100.0)			

Source: ibid.

Note: Figures in parentheses show percentage shares in total volume of credit.

Table 9.46 Changes in the Volume of Credit Classified by Purpose and Source for the Poorest Borrowers in Urban Slums

(Taka)

Areas/Groups	Year	Purpose of Credit								Source of credit				No of borrowers (gross)	Volume of credit per borrowers	Volume of credit per hh
		Business	Consumption	Agriculture	Repairing houses	Purchase of rickshaw/ push cart	Repayment of loan	Health	Total	Money lender	Friend	NGO	Total			
Urban slums (n=20)	1993	-	5,000 (37.0)	-	-	-	-	8,500 (62.9)	13,500 (100.0)	13,500 (100.0)	-	-	13,500 (100.0)	3	4,500.0	675.0
	1996	-	2400 (7.6)	-	5,600 (16.1)	21,000 (60.5)	-	2700 (8.5)	31,700 (100.0)	13,000 (41.0)	700 (2.2)	18,000 (56.7)				
Slum-1 (Motaher)	1993	-	5,000 (50.0)	-	-	-	-	5,000 (50.0)	10,000 (100.0)	10,000 (100.0)	-	-	10,000 (100.0)	2	5,000.0	1,000.0
(n=10)	1996	-	-	-	5,000 (19.0)	21,000 (80.0)	-	200 (1.0)	26,200 (100.0)	8,000 (30.5)	200 (0.7)	18,000 (68.7)	26,200 (100.0)	5	5,240.0	2,620.0
Slum-2 (Titipara)	1993	-	-	-	-	-	-	3,500 (100.0)	3,500 (100.0)	3,500) (100.0	-	-	3,500 (100.0)	1	3,500.0	350.0
(n=10)	1996	-	2400 (46.0)	-	600 (7.0)	-	-	2500 (45.5)	5,500 (100.0)	5,000 (90.9)	500 (9.9)	-	5,500 (100.0)	5	1,100.0	550.0

Source: ibid.

Note: Figures in parentheses show percentage sphares in total.

Table 9.47 Changes in the Volume of Credit Classified by Purpose and Source for the Poorest Borrowers in Rural Areas

(Taka)

Areas/Groups	Year	Purpose of credit: Con-sumption	Agricul-ture	Repair-ing houses	Purchase of rickshaw/ push cart	Repay-ment of loan	Health	Total	Source of credit: Money lender	Friend	NGO	Total	No. of borrow-rowers	Volume of credit per hh	Volume of credit per bor-rowers
OVERALL															
A. All villages (n=60)	1993	14000 (75.6)	4000 (21.6)	500 (2.7)	-	-	-	18500 (100.0)	13200 (71.3)	5300 (28.6)	-	18500 (100.0)	16	308.3	1156.3
	1996	41650 (40.5)	25000 (24.2)	6500 (6.4)	1000 (0.9)	500 (0.4)	28400 (27.5)	103050 (100.0)	62800 (60.9)	22250 (21.6)	18000 (17.4)	103050 (100.0)	26	1717.5	3963.5
B. Programme villages															
B.1 FFE hhs (n=20)	1993	6700 (5.7)	3000 (29.4)	500 (4.9)	-	-	-	10200 (100.0)	6700 (65.7)	3500 (34.3)	-	10200 (100.0)	7	510.0	1457.1
	1996	25600 (51.7)	16000 (32.3)	1500 (3.0)	-	-	6400 (12.9)	49500 (100.0)	40500 (81.8)	-	9000) (18.1	49500 (100.0)	11	2475.0	4500.0
B.2 Non-FFE hhs (n=20)	1993	2500 (71.4)	1000 (28.5)	-	-	-	-	3500 (100.0)	3500 (100.0)	-	-	3500 (100.0)	4	175.0	875.0
	1996	5100 (32.7)	9000 (57.7)	-	1000 (6.4)	500 (3.2)	-	15600 (100.0)	11600 (74.3)	-	4000 (25.6)	15600 (100.0)	6	780.0	2600.0
C. Control villages (n=20)	1993	4800 (100.0)	-	-	-	-	-	4800 (100.0)	3000 (6.2)	1800 (37.5)	-	4800 (100.0)	5	240.0	960.0
	1996	10950 (28.9)	-	5000 (13.1)	-	-	22000 (57.9)	37950 (100.0)	10700 (28.1)	22250 (58.6)	5000 (13.1)	37950 (100.0)	9	1897.5	4216.7
CENTRAL PART															
A. All villages	1993	14000 (75.7)	4000 (21.6)	500 (2.7)	-	-	-	18500 (100.0)	13200 (71.3)	5300 (28.6)	-	18500 (100.0)	16	616.7	1156.2
(n=30)	1996	29550 (36.9)	15000 (18.7)	6500 (8.1)	-	500 (0.6)	28400 (35.5)	79950 (100.0)	39700 (49.6)	22250 (27.8)	18000 (22.5)	79950 (100.0)	19	2665.0	4207.8

(Contd.)

(Continued) (Taka)

Areas/Groups	Year	Purpose of credit							Source of credit				Number of borrowers	Volume of credit per hh	Volume of credit per borrowers
		Consumption	Agriculture	Repairing houses	Purchase of rickshaw/ push cart	Repayment of loan	Health	Total	Money lender	Friend	NGO	Total			
B. Programme villages	1993	6700	3000	500	-	-	-	10200	6700	3500	-	10200	7	1020.0	1457.1
		(65.7)	(29.4)	(4.9)				(100.0)	(65.7)	(34.3)		(100.0)			
B.1 FFE hhs	1996	17100	6000	1500	-	-	6400	31000	22000	-	9000	31000	8	3100.0	3875.0
(n=10)			(55.1)	(19.3)	(4.8)			(20.6)	(100.0)	(70.9)		(29.0)	(100.0)		
B.2 Non-FFE hhs	1993	2500	1000	-	-	-	-	3500	3500	-	-	3500	4	350.0	875.0
		(71.4)	(28.6)					(100.0)	(100.0)			(100.0)			
(n=10)	1996	4000	9000	-	-	500	-	13500	9500	-	4000	13500	3	1350.0	4500.0
		(29.6)	(66.7)			(3.7)		(100.0)	(70.4)		(29.6)	(100.0)			
C. Control villages	1993	4800	-	-	-	-	-	4800	3000	1800	-	4800	5	480.0	960.0
		(100.0)						(100.0)	(62.5)	(37.5)		(100.0)			
(n=10)	1996	8450	-	5000	-	-	22000	35450	8200	22250	5000	35450	8	3545.0	4431.2
		(23.9)		(14.1)			(62.0)	(100.0)	(23.1)	(62.8)	(14.1)	(100.0)			
NORTHERN PART															
A. All villages	1993	-	-	-	-	-	-	-	-	-	-	-	-	-	-
(n=30)	1996	12100	10000	-	1000	-	-	23100	23100	-	-	23100	7	770.0	3300.0
		(52.3)	(43.2)		(4.3)			(100.0)	(100.0)			(100.0)			
Programme villages	1993	-	-	-	-	-	-	-	-	-	-	-	-	-	-
B.1 FFE hhs (n=10)	1996	8500	10000	-	-	-	-	18500	18500	-	-	18500	3	1850.0	6166.7
		(45.9)	(54.0)					(100.0)	(100.0)			(100.0)			
B.2 Non-FFE hhs (n=10)	1993	-	-	-	-	-	-	-	-	-	-	-	-	-	-
	1996	1100	-	-	1000	-	-	2100	2100	-	-	2100	3	210.0	700.0
		(52.3)			(47.7)			(100.0)	(100.0)			(100.0)			
C. Control villages	1993	-	-	-	-	-	-	-	-	-	-	-	-	-	-
(n=10)	1996	2500	-	-	-	-	-	2500	2500	-	-	2500	1	250.0	2500.0
		(100.0)						(100.0)	(100.0)			(100.0)			

Source: ibid.

Note: ibid.

Table 9.48 Whether You Have Taken Credit or Not

(per cent)

Household status groups	Opinions on credit taken		
	Yes	No	Total
Urban	59.7	40.3	100.0 (n=139)
Rural	82.7	17.3	100.0 (n=150)
Total	71.6	28.4	100.0 (n=289)

Source: *A Survey on Evaluation of Budget from the Perspective of Poverty Alleviation,* Shamunnay (1996)

Table 9.49 Amounts of Credit Received by Respondents from Different Sources

Sources	Average amount of money			Rate of interest (%)		
	Urban	Rural	Total	Urban	Rural	Total
BKB	-	6250.00	625.00	-	14.8	14.8
Commercial bank	-	7916.67	7916.67	-	14.2	14.2
NGO	4326.09	3662.16	3916.67	16.9	19.95	18.8
Usurer	3796.00	2796.55	3019.64	102.8	153.6	140.9
Relatives	3265.31	2929.41	3148.78	103.2	110	104.2
Others	3240.00	3111.43	3156.00	115.0	111.3	112.6

Source: ibid.

Table 9.50 Percentage Distribution of Respondents by Sources of Credit and by Social Groups in Respect of Food Availability

(per cent)

Sources	Urban					Rural					Grand Total
	Chroinic deficit	Occa-sional deficit	Break-even	Surplus	Total	Chronic deficit	Occa-sional deficit	Break-even	Surplus	Total	
Commercial bank	-	-	-	-	-	7.8	2.1	16.7	-	6.3	3.8
NGO	14.8	13.2	39.3	30.0	22.3	19.4	29.8	33.3	50.0	23.4	23.0
Money lender	29.7	28.9	17.9	10.0	24.3	58.3	48.9	50.0	50.0	55.1	42.9
Relatives	37.0	23.7	25.0	60.0	31.1	10.7	12.8	-	-	10.8	18.8
Shopkeeper	18.5	26.3	10.7	-	17.5	-	-	-	-	-	6.9
Others	-	7.9	7.1	-	4.9	3.9	6.4	-	-	4.4	4.6
Total	100.0	100.0	100.0	100.0	100.0	100.0	100.0	100.0	100.0	100.0	100.0
	n=27	n=38	n=28	n=10	n=103	n=103	n=47	n=6	n=2	n=158	n=261

Source: ibid.

Table 9.51 Changes in the Savings Profile of the Poorest Households

(Taka)

Areas/Groups	Year	No. of saving hhs (3)	Mode of savings: Society/ group (4)	Bank (5)	Cash (6)	Total (7)	Average savings (8)= [(7)/(3)]	Savings per hh
Overall	1993	-	-	-	-	-	-	-
(n=80)	1996	13 (16.3)	276	-	-	276	21.2	3.5
Urban slums	1993	-	-	-	-	-	-	-
(n=20)	1996	-	-	-	-	-	-	-
Rural areas	1993	-	-	-	-	-	-	-
(n=60)	1996	13 (21.6)	276	-	-	276	21.2	4.6

Source: *Panel Survey for Annual Budget Review*, 1996

Note: Figures in parentheses are percentages of respective total households.

Table 9.52 Changes in the Savings Profile of the Poorest Households in Rural Areas

(Taka)

Areas/Groups	Year (2)	No. of savings hhs (3)	Amount: Society/ group (4)	Bank (5)	Cash (6)	Total (7)	Average savings 8=(7/3)	Savings per hh 9=(7/n)
			OVERALL					
A. All villages	1993	-	-	-	-	-	-	-
(n=60)	1996	13(21.6)	276	-	-	276	21.2	4.6
B. Programme villages	1993	-	-	-	-	-	-	-
B.1 FFE hhs (n=20)	1996	6(30.0)	140	-	-	140	23.3	7.0
B.2 Non-FFE hhs	1993	-	-	-	-	-	-	-
(n=20)	1996	4(20.0)	80	-	-	80	20.0	4.0
C. Control villages	1993	-	-	-	-	-	-	-
(n=20)	1996	3(15.0)	56	-	-	56	19.0	3.0
			CENTRAL PART					
A. All villages	1993	-	-	-	-	-	-	-
(n=30)	1996	13(43.3)	276	-	-	276	21.2	9.2
B. Programme villages	1993	-	-	-	-	-	-	-
B.1 FFE hhs (n=10)	1996	6(60.0)	140	-	-	140	23.3	14.0
B.2 Non-FFE hhs	1993	-	-	-	-	-	-	-
(n=10)	1996	4(40.0)	80	-	-	80	20.0	8.0
C. Control villages	1993	-	-	-	-	-	-	-
(n=10)	1996	3(30.0)	56	-	-	56	19.0	6.0
			NORTHERN PART					
A. All villages	1993	-	-	-	-	-	-	-
(n=30)	1996	-	-	-	-	-	-	-
B. Programme villages	1993	-	-	-	-	-	-	-
B.1 FFE hhs (n=10)	1996	-	-	-	-	-	-	-
B.2 Non-FFE hhs	1993	-	-	-	-	-	-	-
(n=10)	1996	-	-	-	-	-	-	-
C. Control villages	1993	-	-	-	-	-	-	-
(n=10)	1996	-	-	-	-	-	-	-

Source: ibid.

Note: ibid.

Bibliography

Ahluwalia, Montek S. (1996), 'Rural Poverty, Agricultural Production and Prices: A Re-examination,' in Mellor W. John, and Desai Gunvant M. (eds.), *Agricultural Change and Rural Poverty: Variations on a Theme* by Dharm Nara, Oxford University Press, New Delhi.

Ahmed, U.A. and K. Billah (1994), *Food for Education Programme in Bangladesh: An Early Assessment*, Mimeo, Bangladesh Food Policy Project, International Food Policy Research Institute (IFPRI), Dhaka.

Amin, M.N. (ed.) (1993), 'Proceedings of National Seminar on Government of Bangladesh in Poverty Alleviation,' held in Dhaka, February 17-19, 1993.

Appadurai, Arjun (1985), 'Small-Scale Techniques and Large-Scale Objectives,' in Robert Chambers, 'Poverty in India: Concepts, Research and Reality,' *IDS Discussion Paper*, No. 241.

Baker, Judy L. and Margaret E. Grosh (1994), 'Measuring the Effects of Geographic Targeting on Poverty Reduction,' in *Measurement Study Working Paper, No.99*, World Bank, Washington D.C.

Bangladesh Rural Development Board (1994), *Annual Report, 1993-94*, Dhaka.

———, (1995), *Annual Report, 1994-95*, Dhaka.

Bardhan, Pranab (1995), 'Research on Poverty and Development after Redistribution with Growth,' in Michael Bruno and Boris Pleskovic (eds.), *Annual World Bank Conference on Development Economics 1995*, World Bank, Washington, D.C.

Baulch, Bob (1996), 'The New Poverty Agency: A Disputed Consensus,' *IDS Bulletin* 27(1).

Bangladesh Bureau of Statistics (1991), *Report of the Survey on Test Relief—1989*, Dhaka.

———, (993a), *Report on the Thana Development Monitoring Project*, Vol. IV, Dhaka.

———, (1993b), *Report of the Survey on VGD—1990*, Dhaka.

———, (1994a), *Statistical Pocketbook*, Dhaka.

———, (1994b), *Report of the Survey on FFW – 1991*, Dhaka.

———, (1995a), *Statistical Pocketbook*, Dhaka.

———, (1995b), *Report on the Household Expenditure Survey, 1991-92*, Dhaka.

———, (1995c), *Report on the Household Expenditure Survey 1991- 92*, Dhaka.

———, (1996), *Statistical Pocket Book*, Dhaka.

Cernea, Michael M. (1992), 'Re-tooling in Applied Social Investigation for Development Planning: Some Methodological Issues,' in Nevin S. Scrimshaw and Gray R. Gleason (eds.), *Rapid Assessment Procedure: Qualitative Methodologies for Planning and Evaluation of Health Related Programmes,* International Nutrition Foundation for Developing Countries (INFDC), Boston

Chambers, Robert (1983), *Rural Dèvelopment: Putting the Last First,* Longman, London.

———, (1988), 'Poverty in India: Concepts, Research and Reality,' *IDS. Discussion Paper*, No.241.

———, (1993), *Challenging the Professions: Frontiers for Rural Development,* Intermediate Technology Publications, London.

———, (1994a), 'Knowledge and Power: All Power Deceives,' *IDS Bulletin* 25(2).

———, (1994b), 'Poverty and Livelihoods: Whose Reality Counts?' *Overview Paper 11*, UNDP Stockholm Roundtable on 'Change: Social Conflict or Harmony.'

———, (1997), *Whose Reality Counts: Putting the First Last*, Intermediate Technology Publications, London.

Chowdhury, O.H. (1994), *Incidence of Indirect Taxation in Bangladesh: 1984/85*, Research Monograph: 16, BIDS, Dhaka.

———, (1995), 'Nutritional Dimensions of Poverty' in Rahman, H.Z. and Mahbub Hossain (eds.), *Rethinking Rural Poverty: Bangladesh as a Case Study*, University Press Limited (UPL), Dhaka.

Canadian International Development Agency (CIDA) (1992), 'Budget Review Study: Financial Years 1989-90, 190-91 & 1991-92,' Canadian High Commission, Dhaka.

———, (1993), 'Budget Review Study: Financial Years, 1989-90, 1990-91, 1991-92 & 1992-93,' Canadian High Commission, Dhaka.

Centre for Policy Dialogue (CPD) (1995), *Experiences with Economic Reform: A Review of Bangladesh's Development*, CPD/UPL Dhaka.

de Soto, Hernando (1989), *The Other Path: The Invisible Revolution in the Third World*, Harper and Row, New York.

Economic and Social Commission for Asia and the Pacific (ESCAP) (1993), 'Report of the Committee on Poverty Alleviation Through Economic Growth and Social Development,' E/ESCAP/CPA/2, ESCAP, Bangkok.

Gafur, A. Chowdhury, O.H. and D.K. Roy (1994), *Public Expenditure and Poverty Alleviation in Bangladesh*, Centre on Integrated Rural Development for Asia and the Pacific (CIRDAP), Dhaka.

Government of Bangladesh (1980), *Second Five-Year Plan 1980-85*, Planning Commission, Ministry of Planning, Dhaka.

———, (1985), *Third Five-Year Plan 1986-90*, Planning Commission, Ministry of Planning, Dhaka.

———, (1990), *Fourth Five-Year Plan 1991-95*, Planning Commission, Ministry of Planning, Dhaka.

———, *(1990) Memorandum for Bangladesh Aid Group 1990-91*, March, Dhaka.

———, (1991), *Report of the Task Forces on Bangladesh Development Strategies for the 1990s*, Vol.1, *Policies for Development*, UPL Dhaka.

———, (1994), *Five-Year Plans, Bangladesh Economic Survey 1993/94*, Ministry of Finance, Dhaka.

———, (1995a), *Five-Year Plans, Bangladesh Economic Review*, Finance Division, Ministry of Finance, Dhaka.

———, (1995b), *Five-Year Plans, Bangladesh Economic Survey*, Finance Division, Ministry of Finance, Dhaka.

———, (1995c), *Five-Year Plans, The Participatory Perspective Plan of Bangladesh 1995-2010*, Planning Commission, Ministry of Finance, Dhaka.

———, (1995d), *Five-Year Plans, Data base on Food Situation Bangladesh*, Food Planning and Monitoring (FFMU), Ministry of Food, Dhaka.

———, (1995e), *Five-Year Plans*, 'Guidelines for the Implementation and Monitoring of the Food For Education Programme,' Primary and Mass Education Department, Bangladesh Secretariat, Dhaka.

Grandin, Barbara E. (1994), 'Wealth Ranking,' in Hilary Sims Feldstein and Janice Jiggins, (eds.), *Tools for the Field*. Intermediate Technology Publications, London.

Greeley, Martin (1994), 'Measurement of Poverty and Poverty of Measurement,' in *IDS Bulletin* 25(2).

Guijt, Irene (1992), 'The Elusive Poor: A Wealth of Ways to Find Them,' *RRA Notes* No. 15, International Institute for Environment and Development, London.

Hamid, Shamim (1995), 'Gender Dimensions of Poverty,' in Rahman and Hossain, (eds.), *Rethinking Rural Poverty: Bangladesh As a Case Study*, UPL, Dhaka.

Hossain, M. and Binayak Sen (1995), 'Determinants of Poverty,' in Rahman and Hossain, (eds.), *Rethinking Rural Poverty: Bangladesh As a Case Study*, UPL, Dhaka.

Hussain, Motahar (1986), *The System of Government Budgeting in Bangladesh*, No. 85-910833, Vol. 6, No.1, January, Dhaka.

International Institute for Environment and Development (IIED), (1992), *RRA Notes* No. 15, IIED, London.

Jahan, Rounaq (1989), *Women and Development in Bangladesh: Challenges and Opportunities*, Ford Foundation, Dhaka.

Khandker, S.R., *et al.* (1995), Mimeo, *Sustainability of Grameen Bank: What Do You Know?* The World Bank, Washington D.C.

Khatun, A. (1995), 'A Handout Report on Vulnerable Group Development Programme,' Directorate of Relief and Rehabilitation, Ministry of Food, Government of Bangladesh, Dhaka.

Mellor, John W. and Gunvant M. Desai (eds.) (1986), *Agricultural Change and Rural Poverty: Variations on a Theme* by Dharm Narain, Oxford University Press, New Delhi.

Mukherjee, Neela (1995), *Participatory Rural Appraisal and Questionnaire Survey*, Concept Publishing Company, New Delhi.

Musgrave, Richard A. (1959), *The Theory of Public Finance: A Study in Pubic Economy*, International Student Edition, McGraw-Hill.

Oakley, Peter (1988), *The Monitoring and Evaluation of Participation in Rural Development*, FAO, Rome.

Patton, Michael Quinn (1990), *Qualitative Evaluation and Research Methods*, Sage Publications, California.

Pedersen, Duncan (1992), 'Qualitative and Quantitative: Two Styles of Viewing the World or Two Categories of Reality?' in Nevin S. Scrimshaw and Gray R. Gleason (eds.), *Rapid Assessment Procedures: Qualitative Methodologies for Planning and Evaluation of Health Related Programmes*, International Nutrition Foundation for Developing Countries (INFDC), Boston

Pradhan, Sanjay (1996), 'Evaluating Public Spending: A Framework for Public Expenditure Reviews,' *World Bank Discussion papers* No. 323, World Bank, Washington D.C.

Rahman, M.P.K. and A. Hossain (1993), Mimeo. *A Study on the Identification of Causes of Low Attendance and Estimation of Dropout from School with Special Reference to Class I and Girls Students*

Rahman, H.Z. and Mahbub Hossain (eds.) (1995), *Rethinking Rural Poverty: Bangladesh as a Case Study*, UPL, Dhaka.

Rahman, H.Z., *et al* (eds.) (1996), Mimeo. *Dynamics of Rural Poverty in Bangladesh*, BIDS, Dhaka.

Rahman, Md. Anisur (1997), 'Poverty Count, Poverty Alleviation and Growth with Social Justice,' *The Daily Star*, March 11.

Ravallion, M. (1992), 'Poverty Comparisons: A Guide to Concepts and Methods' in *Living Standards Measurement Study, Working Paper No. 88*, World Bank, Washington D.C.

Ravallion, M. and Binayak Sen (1994), 'Impacts on Rural Poverty of Land-Contingent Targeting: Some Further Results for Bangladesh,' *World Development* 22(6).

Sen, Amartya (1995), 'The Political Economy of Targeting,' in Walle and Nead, (eds.), *Public Spending and the Poor: Theory and Evidence*, World Bank, Washington D.C.

Shaffer, Paul (1996), 'Beneath the Poverty Debate: Some Issues,' *IDS Bulletin* 27(1).

——— , (1990), 'Poverty Concepts and Measurement,' *Bangladesh Development Studies* 18(3).

Task Force (1991), *Task Force Report*, Vol.1, UPL, Dhaka.

Taylor, C. (1985), 'Philosophy and the Human Sciences: Philosophical Papers,' Vol. II in Shaffer 1996. 'Beneath the Poverty Debate: Some Issues,' *IDS Bulletin* 27(1).

Townsley, Philip (1996), *Rapid Rural Appraisal, Participatory Rural Appraisal and Aquaculture*, FAO, Rome.

Toye, John and Carl Jackson 1996. 'Public Expenditure Policy and Poverty Reduction: Has the World Bank Got it Right?' *IDS Bulletin* 27(1).

United Nations Development Programme (UNDP) (1988), *Development Cooperation: Bangladesh: 1986 Report*, UNDP, Dhaka.

———, (1991), *Human Development Report 1991*, Oxford University Press, New York.

———, (1995a), *Human Development Report 1995*, Oxford University Press, New York.

———, (1995), *Poverty: Poverty Definitions and Indicators*, Vol. 1, Technical Support Document, UNDP, New York.

———, (1996), *Poverty: Poverty Definitions and indicators*, Module 1, Technical Support Document, UNDP, New York.

———, (1997), *Human Development Report 1997*, UNDP, New York.

United Nations Fund for Population (UNFP) (1992), *The State of World Population*, Nuffield Press, Oxford, U.K.

United Nations Fund for Children and Education (1987), *An Analysis of the Situation of Children in Bangladesh*, UNICEF, Dhaka.

Valadez, Joseph and Michael Bamberger (eds.) (1994), *Monitoring and Evaluating Social Programmes in Developing. Countries: A Handbook for Policy makers, Managers, and Researchers*, Economic Development Institute of the World Bank, Washington D.C.

Walle, Dominique Van de and Kimberly Nead (eds.) (1995), *Public Spending and the Poor: Theory and Evidence*, World Bank, Washington D.C.

World Bank (1989), *Bangladesh: Public Expenditure Review: Public Resource Management During the Fourth Five Year Plan 1991-95*, Report No. 7545-BD, Asian Country Department, World Bank, Washington D.C.

———, (1992), *Bangladesh: Selected Issues in External Competitiveness and Economic Efficiency*, World Bank, Washington D.C.

———, (1992), *Poverty Reduction Handbook and Operational Directive*, World Bank, Washington D.C.

———, (1995), *Bangladesh: Recent Economic Developments and Priority Reform Agenda for Rapid Growth*, Report No. 13875-BD, Country Operations Division, Country Department 1, South Asia Region, March 16.

About the Study Team

Atiur Rahman is Executive Chairman of Shamunnay and Senior Research Fellow at Bangladesh Institute of Development Studies (BIDS). He was awarded Ph.D. from the University of London. He has authored *Beel Dakatia: Environmental Consequences of a Development Disaster* (UPL) and *Peasants and Classes: A Study in Differentiation in Bangladesh* (Zed Books).

Pk. Md. Motiur Rahman is Professor of Econometrics at the Institute of Statistical Research and Training (ISRT), University of Dhaka. He was awarded Ph.D. from the University of Dhaka. Subsequently, he conducted a post-doctoral research at the Institute of Developing Economics, Tokyo. He has authored *Poverty Issues in Rural Development* (UPL) and contributed to *Experiences with Economic Reform : A Review of Bangladesh's Development* edited by Professor Rehman Sobhan (UPL).

Mirza Md. Shafiqur Rahman is Research Fellow at Shamunnay. He obtained his M.A. in Economics from the University of Rajshahi. He was subsequently trained at BIDS and completed an advanced course in Economics and Quantitative Techniques.

Nigar Nargis is Research Associate at Bangladesh Institute of Development Studies (BIDS). She is currently pursuing her Ph.D. at Cornel University, USA.